CHANGING FAMILIES, CHANGING FAMILY LAW IN EUROPE

European Family Law Series

Published by the Organising Committee of the
Commission on European Family Law

An open access version of this book is also available online, thanks to funding from the Max Planck Institute for Comparative and International Private Law.

CHANGING FAMILIES, CHANGING FAMILY LAW IN EUROPE

Edited by

Konrad DUDEN
Denise WIEDEMANN

INTERSENTIA

Cambridge – Antwerp – Chicago

Intersentia Ltd
8 Wellington Mews
Wellington Street | Cambridge
CB1 1HW | United Kingdom
Tel: +44 1223 736 170
Email: contact@larcier-intersentia.com
www.larcier-intersentia.com

Distribution for the UK and
Rest of the World (incl. Eastern Europe)
NBN International
1 Deltic Avenue, Rooksley
Milton Keynes MK13 8LD
United Kingdom
Tel: +44 1752 202 301 | Fax: +44 1752 202 331
Email: orders@nbninternational.com

Distribution for Europe
Lefebvre Sarrut Belgium NV
Hoogstraat 139/6
1000 Brussels
Belgium
Tel: +32 (0)2 548 07 13
Email: contact@larcier-intersentia.com

Distribution for the USA and Canada
Independent Publishers Group
Order Department
814 North Franklin Street
Chicago, IL 60610
USA
Tel: +1 800 888 4741 (toll free) | Fax: +1 312 337 5985
Email: orders@ipgbook.com

ISBN 978-1-83970-380-5
D/2024/7849/18
NUR 822

British Library Cataloguing in Publication Data. A catalogue record for this book is available from the British Library.

PREFACE

What constitutes a family in Europe? The answer to this question is constantly changing and increasingly varied. The lived realities of European families are becoming ever more diverse. This trend, which has a long history, seems to have intensified in the last decades. However, different Member States of the European Union have taken very different views on these changes. These divergent reactions raise the question we want to address with our book: how can law in Europe address changing family realities if the Member States of the Union disagree about the treatment of these realities?

This volume begins by discussing in its first chapters some of the rapid and substantial changes in family structures, concepts and values which have taken place in Europe in recent times – and the often divergent answers and approaches that different legal systems in Europe offer to the family law questions that go along with these changes. In this endeavour we understand family law in a broad sense, including in particular the law of gender identity.

Changes affect the concepts of marriage and partnership: ranging from the increasing recognition of same-sex marriage to the acceptance of private divorce, the changing treatment of early marriages and the increasing legal protection of partnerships outside of marriage. New patterns of childbearing and parenthood are also developing: assisted reproduction – particularly surrogate motherhood – is creating families that could not have existed before. In some places there is even discussion of granting legal parenthood to more than two persons. In the treatment of such new parenthood patterns, adoption often serves to establish a legal parent–child relationship where a social one already exists, but cannot be legally established under the law of filiation. Queer persons and families add another layer of complexity: this starts with the increasing recognition of different gender identities, for instance of transgender or non-binary persons, and continues with the question of how to legally address the parentage of trans persons. Finally, changing views of gender roles and a greater recognition of children's rights make it necessary to reconsider the balance between, on the one hand, the promotion of equality, self-reliance and autonomy of family members and, on the other, the need to protect financially and physically vulnerable family members.

On many of the above-mentioned issues there are disagreements within Europe. And to make matters worse, many of the views do not seem to be converging, but are instead diverging ever more. Most prominently, a rift seems to have opened up between Western and Eastern Europe on all matters relating to queer families and identities. These changes have gained a tremendous symbolic and political importance which can be seen as part and parcel of frictions within the European Union. Some Member States have embraced the diversity of families and grant legal protection. Other Member States are becoming more critical towards these rare family forms. For both factions, the treatment of these families is seen as a kind of litmus test for the fundamental values of the Member States: openness, inclusiveness and equality on the one side; tradition, national identity and religion on the other. For the families affected, this conflict threatens a core premise of the European Union: the freedom to move within the Union. The differences between family law systems in Europe can lead to 'limping' status relationships. Families affected are left to wonder whether they will still be families in the eyes of the law if they move between Member States.

This threat makes it increasingly important to foster a European exchange on these issues in order to envision a way forward that responds to the needs of international families. The final chapters of this volume address this perspective. Different approaches and ideas need to be explored to determine whether, and in what way, international family law in Europe – including conflict of laws, international civil procedure and even harmonized substantive family law – can and should respond to the different legal trends and developments in the individual Member States.

The issues described above can be approached only from a European and comparative perspective. This volume therefore brings together young European scholars in international and comparative family law from more than 15 European countries, whose contributions aim to not reflect only their respective national perspective but, rather, a comparative and European view. To prepare this book, a workshop was held at the Max Planck Institute for Comparative and International Private Law in Hamburg in March 2022. The workshop was conceptualized and organized by Jennifer Antomo, Konrad Duden and Denise Wiedemann. Since the workshop, Jennifer has been on family leave, which is why this book is edited by Konrad and Denise only.

Jennifer Antomo, Konrad Duden and Denise Wiedemann
Mainz, Frankfurt am Main and Hamburg, Spring 2023

CONTENTS

EUROPEAN COURT OF JUSTICE

INTERNATIONAL COURT OF JUSTICE

NATIONAL COURTS

AUSTRIA

CANADA

FRANCE

GERMANY

PART I

MARRIAGE AND PARTNERSHIP

HUMAN RIGHTS PROTECTION IN FAMILY REUNIFICATION LAW AND THE RECOGNITION OF CHILD MARRIAGES

Tone L. Wærstad

1. INTRODUCTION

This chapter focuses on the changes in family structures, concepts and values in Europe over the last decades, with a particular emphasis on children and marriage. Broadly speaking, people nowadays marry later. And the values tied to marriage and the legal regulation of marriage reflect this change.[1] One might say that the idea that children should not marry has gained clear support and that both the notion and concept of a child and the concept of marriage have evolved accordingly.[2]

These developments are part of a clear international trend. Worldwide, children enter into marriage less frequently. Concurrently, the fight against child marriages has gained momentum and international law now clearly acknowledges child marriage as a human rights violation.[3]

At the same time, there has been a shift in the type of marriages considered to be child marriage and the types of legal questions they give rise to in Europe. In national law, most countries have increased the minimum age for entering into marriage while decreasing the exceptions to this minimum age limit. The question of the status of a child marriage increasingly comes up in relation to marriages contracted abroad. Recognition of a marriage may be necessary, for example, in immigration cases based on family reunification with a spouse living in a European country. Thus, the question of the recognition of the marriage will often have consequences with regard to the couple's ability to live together in Europe. And again, this gives rise to new questions of a legal nature.

The aim of this chapter is to investigate these developments and give some advice on how to resolve the challenges they present from a European legal perspective.

2. LEGAL CONTEXT AND DELIMITATIONS

As noted, the shift regarding child marriage results mainly from a decrease in the number of domestic child marriages due to demographic and legal changes, and an increase in recognition cases because of increased migration and greater numbers of family reunification cases from countries that allow child marriages.

---

1 UNICEF, Global databases: Child marriages [data.unicef.org], last updated Feb 2021, accessed 09.03.2022.

2 As for instance expressed in the Council of Europe (CoE) Parliamentary Assembly Resolution 1468 (2005) on Forced marriages and child marriages, adopted 05.10.2005. For a review of the global scale and the negative impact of child marriage, as well as a discussion of research priorities on ending child marriage and supporting married girls, see J. Svanemyr et al., 'Research Priorities on Ending Child Marriage and Supporting Married Girls' (2015) 12 *Reproductive Health* 80.

3 UNICEF, 'Child marriage', <https://www.unicef.org/protection/child-marriage> accessed 09.06.2022; Y. Efevbera and J. Bhabha, 'Defining and Deconstructing Girl Child Marriage and Applications to Global Public Health' (2020) 20 *BMC Public Health* 1547.

This chapter will focus on the recognition of marriages contracted abroad with no connection to the recognizing State at the time the marriage was contracted. The focus will be on marriages where the recognition of the marriage is part of a family reunification application, in a situation where one of the parties has already migrated to the country of recognition and the other applies at a later date for a stay permit based on family reunification. However, the discussion also draws upon cases from the Norwegian legal system concerning the recognition of marriages where both parties have arrived together as part of a refugee situation, which illustrate more general discussions in the chapter. Both types of case exemplify the broader legal changes and the challenges that can arise in these situations.

It is quite clear that a marriage recognized in one EU Member State, but not another, may raise difficult questions for the principle of free movement within the EU. For reasons of space, the analysis in this chapter is limited to marriages that seek recognition in one European State, and not the issues that arise after the marriage has been recognized. This chapter will, however, include a presentation of the relevant EU regulations in order to give a more complete picture of the legislation at the European level regarding this issue.

Although there are few statistics at the European level on the recognition of early marriages, there is reason to believe that many of these cases involve persons who migrate due to situations of war and crisis.[4] This makes it important to specifically consider the risks and harmful practices that girls and women are exposed to in contexts of war and migration – early marriage being one such practice.

These changing family realities, which include marriages contracted outside of Europe and that seek recognition in Europe, have been met with different treatment. This is true not just at the level of the different EU Member States, but also as between the different international bodies that oversee the implementation of international norms in this field of law. Differential treatment can also be seen within different legal disciplines, such as human rights regulation and private international law, where tensions may arise when the two are applied, whether separately or in combination.

3. PRIVATE INTERNATIONAL LAW ON THE RECOGNITION OF MARRIAGES

The internationally acknowledged principle in private international law is that a marriage validly entered into will be recognized in another country.[5] There are

4 See, for instance, UNFPA, 'New Study Finds Child Marriage Rising Among Most Vulnerable Syrian Refugees' (31.01.2017), <https://www.unfpa.org/news/new-study-finds-child-marriage-rising-among-most-vulnerable-syrian-refugees> accessed 09.06.2022.

5 What is meant by 'recognition' here is that the marriage is considered valid according to the applicable law.

4.3. EUROPEAN CONVENTION ON HUMAN RIGHTS

From the perspective of the European Convention on Human Rights (ECHR), Article 8, setting out the right to family and private life, is the most relevant. The principles that the European Court of Human Rights (ECtHR) applies in deciding upon the obligations of Member States under Article 8 ECHR were summarized in *Gül v. Switzerland*:

> The Court reiterates that the essential object of Article 8 (art. 8) is to protect the individual against arbitrary action by the public authorities. There may in addition be positive obligations inherent in effective 'respect' for family life. However, the boundaries between the State's positive and negative obligations under this provision (art. 8) do not lend themselves to precise definition. The applicable principles are, nonetheless, similar. In both contexts regard must be had to the fair balance that has to be struck between the competing interests of the individual and of the community as a whole; and in both contexts the State enjoys a certain margin of appreciation.[14]

That the right to a family life may impose positive obligations upon State parties *to recognize a marriage* was later confirmed in *Dadouch v. Malta*.[15]

In *Z.H. and R.H. v. Switzerland*, the court summarized the content of Article 8 in recognition cases in this way:

> Factors to be taken into account in this context are the extent to which family life would effectively be ruptured, the extent of the ties in the Contracting State, whether there are insurmountable obstacles in the way of the family living in the country of origin of the alien concerned and whether there are factors of immigration control (for example, a history of breaches of immigration law) or considerations of public order weighing in favour of exclusion.

The case shows, however, that the ECtHR was very cautious in overturning the State's own evaluation of whether the recognition of a child marriage was in conflict with its public order.[16] *Z.H. and R.H. v. Switzerland* will be analysed later in this chapter in light of the private international law framework as well as children's human rights protection and the non-discrimination guarantee as set out in the CRC and CEDAW. The right to privacy and to family life under Article 8 ECHR may be protected even though the marriage was entered into while one or both parties were children, but only to a certain (unspecified) degree. It is reasonable, however, to suggest that the right will be interpreted in light of the duration of the marriage and the age of the parties. As will be shown,

---

14 *Gül v. Switzerland*, no. 23218/94, §38, ECHR 1996-I.

15 *Dadouch v. Malta*, no. 38816/07, [2010] ECHR 1140 (20.07.2010).

16 *Z.H. and R.H. v. Switzerland*, no. 60119/12, [2015] ECHR 386 (08.12.2015).

the child's right to be protected from marriage under the CEDAW and CRC will vary depending on the current age of the married child. The situation of a (now) adult, who entered into a marriage as a child, will in many ways be different from the situation faced while still a child.

4.4. THE COUNCIL OF EUROPE

In resolution 1468 (2005) on Forced Marriages and Child Marriages, the Council of Europe Parliamentary Assembly urged the national parliaments of the Council of Europe Member States to:

> refrain from recognizing forced marriages and child marriages contracted abroad except where recognition would be in the victims' best interests with regard to the effects of the marriage, particularly for the purpose of securing rights which they could not claim otherwise.

The resolution is not legally binding, but it is still a document of some standing in the development of legal development in Europe. The fact that few other legal sources on the international law arena discuss the situation of the marriage in a transnational context adds to its relevance. Still, what constitutes the victim's best interest as stated in the resolution must be further assessed.

4.5. EU/EEA LAW

Directive 2004/38/EC of the European Parliament and of the Council of 29 April 2004 on the right of citizens of the Union and their family members to move and reside freely within the territory of the Member States [2004] OJ L158/77, regulates the principle of free movement within the EU and guarantees the free movement of spouses and registered partners of Union citizens as specified in Article 2. The legal possibility for an EU Member State not to recognize a marriage due to the fact that at least one of the spouses was a child when the marriage was contracted is unclear. There are no exceptions to the right of a spouse to move freely within the EU/EEA area in the Directive itself. As most EU countries have an 18-year-old age limit for marriage and very few people marry before the age of 18 it may seem that the question is accessory. But given the different age limits involved in the recognition of marriages, it is possible that this issue will arise, even if, for the moment, the Court of Justice of the European Union has not heard any cases that concern limits on child marriages with respect to the Directive.

The focus of this chapter will be solely on marriages contracted outside Europe and which the spouses wish to have recognized by a European State.

It will not inquire further into the legal impact of the principle of free movement within the EU regarding these cases.

5. SUGGESTIONS FOR AN ANALYTICAL FRAMEWORK

5.1. INTRODUCTION

Against this backdrop of different legal sources informing the regulation of the recognition of child marriages in Europe, the analysis will focus on how arguments concerning human rights law and the best interests of the child have challenged the concept of marriage and the regulation of marriages in European law. International legal norms concerning children's rights may provide reasons for not recognizing a marriage, but these must be balanced with conflicting norms concerning the protection of family and private life and the best interests of the child in each individual case. Private international law and public international law provide two sets of law in this area that to some extent rest on a similar underlying reasoning while also coming into conflict. This chapter discusses how to harmonize the norms of private international law and international law in this area.

Following international human rights law, the principle of the child's best interest should be considered an overarching analytical framework when approaching the validity of the marriage in the forum State.[17] When the child becomes an adult, the rights and best interests of the now-grown up should still guide the recognition proceedings. After all, the rights of the child may still be of relevance in the case of the now-grown up, along with other human rights which may protect the person in the case at hand. These interests are well established in both human rights law and private international law, and as such should be protected.

This chapter also considers gender as an analytical concept. As stated above, the majority of children being married are girls and, in a transnational situation, girls and women are often at risk of being exposed to harmful practices because they are female. What bearing should this have for cases of marriage recognition in Europe today? The focus on girls and women, and the violations and vulnerabilities inherent to the transnational setting, are now on the international human rights agenda, but the need for further inquiry in this field is apparent.

Last, it is suggested that the transnational context should be investigated. The focus of the chapter on such transnational situations – namely the situation where one of the parties to a marriage has a permit to stay in a European country

---

[17] Art. 3 CRC. See the CRC committee General comment No. 14 (2013) on the right of the child to have his or her best interests taken as a primary consideration (art. 3, para. 1), CRC/C/GC/14, 29.05.2013.

and the other applies for a permit based on their marriage – is warranted given how prevalent this pattern is in cases of child marriage in European legal systems today. This suggests that issues traditionally considered in private international law of the family (such as parenthood and the economic consequences of the marriage) are not the most important. While it is important to acknowledge that these issues may also come up in cases of a more acute transnational character, here it is the couple's right to be together in itself that is at stake.

Sections 5.2 to 5.5 will discuss some ways forward to illuminate the concepts and standards in international law and so provide a better understanding of what is at issue in cases of recognition of a child marriage. Section 6 will sum up some of the broader issues in order to suggest how to better protect parties to such marriages in Europe today.

5.2. AN ILLUSTRATION FROM THE NORWEGIAN SUPREME COURT, HR-2021-1345-A

In June 2021, the Norwegian Supreme Court decided a case concerning the recognition of a child marriage.[18] The case involved the judicial review of a decision made by the Norwegian Immigration Appeals Board (UNE) refusing a residence permit on the basis of family reunification. The core question was whether it would be contradictory to the Norwegian public order to allow a marriage entered into by a minor to give a right to residence in Norway. The case is illustrative in several respects of the general discussions in this chapter.

The case concerned an application for family reunification by a Syrian woman who wished to be reunited with her husband, also a Syrian citizen, who had been granted asylum in Norway. The application included the couple's two children. The marriage was contracted when the woman was 12 years old, the day before she turned 13. At the time, the husband was 25 years old. The marriage was valid under Syrian law. Their children were born when the woman was 13 years old and 16 years old. The woman was 21 years old at the time of the application. The Norwegian Immigration Appeals Board (UNE) declined the application on the ground that the recognition of the marriage was in contradiction to Norwegian public order (*ordre public*). The Supreme Court overturned the decision, stating that recognizing the marriage would not be contradictory to Norwegian public order. In the assessment, the Supreme Court focused on the following arguments: a long time had passed between the marriage and the time of application; the woman was now a grown up; and she wanted to stay in the marriage. She wanted to come to Norway with her children and to live with her husband/their father. The court found it to be important that the parties could have married today

[18] HR-2021-1345-A.

without any arguments indicating that that would be contrary to public order and that therefore giving a permit to stay based on the marriage would not be in contradiction to Norwegian public order.

A second strand of arguments concerned the situation of the children and the principle of the child's best interests, coupled with the refugee situation the family found itself in. The court found that the husband could not return to Syria and that denying the application would therefore imply durable rupture for the family, which would not be in the best interests of the children. Furthermore, the court did not find that a denial of recognition of the marriage was likely to lead to fewer child marriages in Syria or elsewhere. It was also important that the couple had had no intention to evade Norwegian rules on marriage, as that court found that an application for a permit to stay in Norway could not have been 'in their thoughts' at the time of marriage.[19]

To sum up, the public order assessment of the court weighed up the interests of the family and the children (in the case of a successful application) against the child-spouse's best interests and the more general desire to combat early marriages (denial of the application). The court concluded that a residence permit was not contrary to Norwegian public order given the actual circumstances of the case.[20] The case will serve as an illustration for the more general discussions in the following subsections and will be returned to in more detail under the different headings below.

5.3. AGE AT MARRIAGE AND RECOGNITION

5.3.1. Introduction

As noted, the human rights conventions that concern child marriages most directly are the Convention of 20 November 1989 on the Rights of the Child (CRC) and the Convention of 18 December 1979 on the Elimination of All Forms of Discrimination against Women (CEDAW). In Joint general recommendation No. 31 (2014) on harmful practices (Gen. Rec. No. 31), the CRC Committee and the CEDAW Committee considered child marriage to be a human rights violation.[21] In the general recommendation, different categories based on age are considered and a general limit of 18 years of age is understood to be the minimum age limit to enter into marriage in both conventions:

> Child marriage, also referred to as early marriage, is any marriage where at least one of the parties is under 18 years of age ... A child marriage is considered to be a form

[19] ibid, para. 78.
[20] The assessment is summarized in the judgment, ibid, para. 80.
[21] Gen. Rec. No. 31, above n. 11.

> of forced marriage, given that one and/or both parties have not expressed full, free and informed consent.[22]

The general comment does not give any direct recommendations as to the recognition of such marriages, however. In this section, the age categories as outlined in the recommendation will be taken as a starting point before assessing what they mean for situations of recognition.

5.3.2. *Under 18 Years of Age*

The committees consider that below the age of 18 the child can not give a full, informed and free consent to the marriage. They consider any marriage entered into below this age to be a forced marriage.

In *Z.H. and R.H. v. Switzerland*, the ECtHR was cautious not to overturn the State's own notion of the age required in order for a marriage to be recognized under domestic law.[23] In the judgment, the ECtHR stated that 'Article 8 of the Convention cannot be interpreted as imposing on any State party to the Convention an obligation to recognize a marriage, religious or otherwise, contracted by a 14 year old child'.[24] Furthermore, the court made a general remark on the margin of appreciation to Article 12 regarding the notion of whether a marriage would be contrary to the public order of a Member State:

> Article 12 expressly provides for regulation of marriage by national law, and given the sensitive moral choices concerned and the importance to be attached to the protection of children and the fostering of secure family environments, this Court must not rush to substitute its own judgment in place of the authorities who are best placed to assess and respond to the needs of society.

The CRC and CEDAW apply a strict minimum age limit for when a child can enter into marriage (18 years old), based on the idea that any marriage under this age represents a grave violation of the child's human rights. To recognize a marriage contracted when the child is under this age would thereby directly violate the rights of the child. It thus appears to provide a minimum limit for how old a party to a marriage must be when applying for a residence permit based on family reunification. From the ECHR and ECtHR perspective, however, the relevant issue is not whether the marriage breaches an individual's human rights, but whether the decision would breach the rights to family and private life. Still, the case law shows that the State parties are under no obligation to

---

22 ibid, para. 20.
23 *Z.H. and R.H. v. Switzerland*, above n. 16.
24 ibid, para. 45.

recognize a marriage contracted by someone aged 14 and that the ECtHR is cautious to review the Member States' own regulations on the matter. From a right to family life perspective, it is possible to argue that the age limit stated in the two UN conventions could inform the understanding of the content of Article 8 ECHR, even though this has not been stated clearly in any legal sources within international law.

Moving back to the understanding of the public order regulation in Member States' internal law, it seems reasonable to conclude that the absolute main rule would be not to recognize a marriage as part of a family reunification application, when one or both of the parties were under the age of 18 at the time of the marriage and is still under the age of 18 when the application of family reunification is made. It is possible however to make a human rights argument that the child in question should be helped in other ways, without having to rely on the marriage as a basis for a residence permit. As regards the situation where recognition of the marriage is sought while the child-spouse is still under the age of 18, it could be argued that specific treatment is required. Courts should inquire into the individual situation of the child – in line with more general human rights norms and a more humane asylum system – and consider removing the child's reliance on the marriage to be able to seek a residence permit. This line of reasoning is not stated in any clear sense in the human rights obligations incumbent on European States. It will therefore raise difficult questions regarding the jurisdiction of State responsibility under immigration law and the understanding and content of protection against structural and indirect discrimination for women in refugee situations.

The Council of Europe resolution could support such a view. This would be in line with the overall arguments in the CEDAW committee's General recommendation No. 32 on the gender-related dimensions of refugee status, asylum, nationality and statelessness of women.[25] This chapter will return to this line of argument later, as it is supported by several of the elements that arise in the discussion of the status of early marriages.

The Norwegian Supreme Court case supports the view that the age at the time of marriage and at the time of recognition are central to a decision involving a public order reservation. First, the court reviewed the original marriage and its consequences for the child and concluded that the marriage was clearly a forced marriage that furthermore implied sexual abuse of the child.[26] The court found that the marriage contradicted Norwegian public order at the time it was contracted. Second, the court then proceeded to review whether

25 CEDAW Committee general recommendation No. 32 on the gender-related dimensions of refugee status, asylum, nationality and statelessness of women, CEDAW/C/GC/32, 14.11.2014.

26 HR-2021-1345-A, above n. 18, paras 64–66.

the developments since the marriage was contracted might provide a basis for another conclusion. In this sense, it appears that the court followed a similar logic to the two human rights committees.

5.3.3. Over the Age of 18

The CRC and CEDAW Committees have stated that a child marriage is any marriage entered into before the age of 18. As a result, anyone above this age is allowed to freely enter into marriage. However, in transnational settings, difficult questions may arise when someone contracts a marriage while under the age of 18, but has reached 18 years of age when the application for recognition of the marriage in a European country is submitted.

The Gen. Rec. No. 31 does not address this question directly, but some elements for consideration may still be drawn from the reasoning behind the recommendation. If adults are allowed to decide freely to enter into a marriage, one could argue that they should also be able to decide for themselves whether they wish to remain in a marriage that was contracted while they were underage. Whether the marriage is in the person's best interest is also of relevance. It would be paradoxical to deny someone the right to a residence permit on the basis that they need to be protected from a marriage entered into while they were underage when the marriage is clearly of benefit to the person.

This line of reasoning was used by the Norwegian Supreme Court in the case discussed above. The court found that the woman in question clearly wished to move to Norway with the children to reunite and live with her husband.[27] The court placed great weight on the fact that she was over the age of 18 when she applied for the permit and over 21 years old at the time of the court case. At the time the case was heard, eight years had passed since the marriage had been contracted and the parties had arranged their lives around the marriage. Furthermore, the couple would have been free to decide to marry under Norwegian law at the time of court case. The court therefore concluded that a residence permit would not amount to further abuse of the woman.[28]

The arguments in this case suggest that, with increasing age – and thus presumably the corresponding ability to make free and informed decisions, especially with regard to whether to stay in the marriage – there are fewer reasons to deny recognition of the marriage. There are, then, good reasons to analyse the marriage according to age at the time of marriage *and* at the time of recognition. This approach also has a certain basis in human rights law, and in

[27] ibid, para. 70.
[28] ibid, paras 71–72.

the CRC and CEDAW particularly. As noted in the introduction, the focus on age is in addition to other relevant considerations in the case at hand.

5.4. THE GIRL'S PERSPECTIVE IN THE REGULATION AND PRACTICE OF MARRIAGE RECOGNITION

Recognition of child marriages has a gendered pattern that may affect the legal reasoning of the process of recognition. First, child marriage is in general a practice that affects girls to a much greater extent than boys. According to UNICEF, child marriages are often a result of entrenched gender inequality, making girls disproportionately subject to the practice. UNICEF also notes that the prevalence of child marriage among boys is just one sixth of that among girls in the world today.[29]

The organization has documented the grave threats child marriage poses to girls' lives and health. Girls who marry before 18 are more likely to experience domestic violence and less likely to remain in school. They have worse economic and health outcomes than their unmarried peers, which are eventually passed down to their own children, further straining a country's capacity to provide quality health and education services.

The CRC and CEDAW monitoring bodies have built their recommendations concerning child marriages on similar information and consider child marriages to be a grave example of harmful practices that discriminate against women or children.[30]

There are reasons to believe that this pattern of gender inequality is often combined with other gendered patterns to the detriment of girls and women. For example, in refugee/migration situations, men tend to depart first, leaving their spouses and children behind. Left alone, in some cases with sole responsibility for children and in unsafe environments (e.g., if the family are refugees), women may find themselves in particularly vulnerable situations.[31]

Furthermore, wives left behind risk becoming more dependent on the husband for assistance and support in the process of seeking a residence permit based on the marriage and of travelling to the country of immigration. European statistics on migration permits show that women comprise the bulk of family migration applications (more than 60 per cent) whereas the majority of asylum and employment permits are applied for by men.[32] More specifically, statistics

29 UNICEF, 'Child marriage', above n. 3.

30 Gen. Rec. No. 31, above n. 11, paras 16, 20–24.

31 The underlying facts of the Norwegian Supreme Court case are an example of this, as well as the UNE case law mentioned in nn. 32 and 34 below.

32 See <https://ec.europa.eu/eurostat/statistics-explained/index.php?title=Residence_permits_-_statistics_on_first_permits_issued_during_the_year> (figure 4). Such a pattern is confirmed

from Norway, where marriage reunification per se can be identified, shows that women comprised more than 80 per cent of (adult) migrants coming to Norway on a family reunification permit for the period 1990 to 2020.[33] This pattern is further confirmed by the case law of the Norwegian Immigration Appeals Board (UNE) regarding applications for residence permits based on foreign marriages entered into while at least one of the parties was a child.[34] The most common pattern in these cases is an underage wife (at the time the marriage is contracted), who then seeks a residence permit on the basis of the marriage once the husband has secured a residence permit in Norway.

Child marriages have shifted from being an internal issue to a transnational issue. This shift has reinforced the gendered patterns underlying child marriages more generally. As the discussion above has shown, it is critical that courts pay attention to the girl's perspective and human rights in cases of foreign marriage recognition. These legal and demographic developments deserve attention in law.

5.5. LEGAL TECHNICAL SOLUTIONS

5.5.1. General Observations

Another way of analysing the question of recognition of child marriages is by assessing the legal technical solutions available when recognizing marriages. The main rule, as mentioned, is that a valid marriage contracted abroad should be recognized. The exceptions to this main rule vary across the European States. There are two main types of legal solutions for regulating the recognition of marriages in European States today. The first relies on the general public order reservation and the second applies positive regulation of recognition combined with an exception clause for certain specific circumstances. The choice of approach may impact the ability of the parties to predict their legal position, to grasp the whole range of considerations that arise in the case and thereby

more specifically in the case law of the Norwegian Immigration Appeals Board (UNE) regarding applications for residence permits based on early marriages entered into while at least one of the parties was underage. UNE gave me access to their case law from 2018–2019, a total of 13 cases, confirming a clear pattern of the wife, a child when married, seeking a residence permit on the basis of the marriage after the husband had first secured a residence permit in Norway.

33 C.S. Molstad et al., *Familieinnvandring og ekteskapsmønster 1990–2020 [Family immigration and marriage patterns 1990–2020]*, Statistics Norway, 28.01.2022: <https://www.ssb.no/befolkning/innvandrere/artikler/familieinnvandring-og-ekteskapsmonster-1990-2020/_/attachment/inline/d14d2547-8ec5-4952-86e6-d26ac2189abe:1c95d401c430a8b421f5ceb230a43a4a655b2320/RAPP2022-03.pdf> accessed 09.06.2022.

34 UNE gave me access to relevant case law from 2018–2019, a total of 13 cases. The cases are not made public, but they are anonymized and can be accessed by contacting the author.

also the outcome in a given case. Since the technical approach may impact the outcome in recognition cases, it is worth analysing further.

5.5.2. *The Public Order Regulation vs Specific Mandatory Regulation*

The problems with the construction of exceptions to the main rule of recognition of marriages through the *ordre public* reservation relates to the general character of assessing public order in the *lex fori* State. When public order regulation is not given attention by legal scholarship and the authorities, a situation may arise where law and the general values of society have shifted significantly and the formal legal sources that inform the content and understanding of the rule become outdated.

An illustration of how the *ordre public* reservation has been understood in Norwegian law as regards child marriages, from 2015 until today, may serve as an example. There was an increase in the number of refugees arriving in Europe in 2015 due to the war in Syria. Several married girls (the youngest just 11 years old) sought refuge in Norway. The question of whether these marriages should be recognized in Norway became of immediate importance. In Norway, it is a crime to engage in sexual acts with a child under the age of 16.[35] At the time, the age limit for entering into marriage was 18, but with a narrow exception for those between the ages of 16 and 18.[36] No one had written on the topic of the recognition of child marriages in Norwegian law for quite some time. The legal sources informing the subject were dated, reflecting a view of children's rights that no longer aligned with contemporary practice. There was great attention given to the situation of these children in the Norwegian media and several authorities expressed the need to clarify the regulation on recognition of child marriages in Norwegian law. The internal legal situation, along with the public understanding of and opinion on children's needs and their rights to protection against marriage, had changed dramatically. The legal sources informing the understanding of the *ordre public* reservation with regard to the recognition of child marriages had not, however, kept up. This highlighted some weaknesses in the regulation of child marriage recognition through the *ordre public* reservation, especially in cases where at least one of the parties to the marriage was still a child. In turn, the parties to these marriages were exposed to a difficult situation, for it was unclear what their personal legal status in Norway was. Finally, the

---

35 Lov om straff (straffeloven) av 20. mai 2005 nr 28 [The Penal Code], section 304.

36 Lov om ekteskap (ekteskapsloven) av 4. juli 1991 nr 47 [The Marriage Act], section 1 a. The exception was later removed from the Act in 2018, making 18 years of age an absolute limit for entering into marriage in Norway.

weaknesses also caused problems for the authorities involved, which did not have appropriate legal sources to rely on in support of their decision-making.

This author has argued elsewhere that the *ordre public* reservation does not function adequately when the legal recognition in question relates to persons who are vulnerable and often invisible to society and the legal system,[37] and that parliamentary regulation of the recognition of child marriages would ensure that basic legal guarantees are given sufficient attention.[38] The Norwegian government recently acted on this situation, proposing a new regulation on the recognition of child marriages, which resulted in a decision by the Norwegian parliament in 2021.[39] The new Act is a specific regulation which sets out the main rule: any marriage contracted when one or both parties were under the age of 18 years will not be recognized. However, there are two exceptions to the main rule included in the new regulation. First, an exception may be made when the parties seeking recognition of the marriage are now over 18 years old, they were both over 16 at the time the marriage was contracted, and the spouse who was underage at the time of marriage wants the marriage to be recognized. Second, an exception may be made if there are strong reasons to recognize the marriage. The two exceptions are independent, meaning that a marriage entered into before the age of 16 may still be recognized in exceptional circumstances in Norway.

On the other hand, such specific mandatory regulation comes with its own drawbacks. The flexible and open character of an *ordre public* reservation means that relevant elements of the case in question may be given weight, which a specific regulation often does not allow for. In this sense, it is a valuable trait of the *ordre public* assessment that a case may have a result that is not contradictory to the basic values of the *lex fori*, even though the underlying facts of the child marriage are contradictory to these basic values.[40] This is exemplified in the Norwegian Supreme Court case discussed above, as the marriage itself was clearly at odds with the basic values of Norwegian society, but the consequences

37 T.L. Wærstad, 'Den norske reguleringen av anerkjennelse av barneekteskap inngått i utlandet. Menneskerettslige og rettstekniske vurderinger' [Recognition of child marriages contracted abroad in Norwegian law. Human rights and legal techical assessments] (2018) 3&4 *Retfærd. Nordisk Juridisk Tidsskrift*, pp. 49–61.

38 ibid.

39 Lov om endringer i ekteskapsloven (ekteskap inngått med mindreårig, etter utenlandsk rett mv.) av 11. juni 2021 nr 63 [Act on amendments to the Marriage Act (marriage entered into with a minor, according to foreign law, etc.)], section 18 c. At the time of publication, the Act has not yet entered into force.

40 G. Cordero-Moss, 'Den norske rettsorden (ordre public), familiegjenforening og barneekteskap – Høyesteretts kjennelse HR-2021-1345-A' [Norwegian public order (ordre public), family reunification and child marriage – The Supreme Court judgment HR-2021-1345-A], (2021) 23(3) *Nytt i privatretten* 12.

of recognizing the marriage in the actual case were considered not to be in contradiction with these values.[41] This fine-toothed assessment of the actual consequences of recognition may be hard to accomplish in the context of a mandatory regulation with specific requirements listed in the wording itself.[42]

6. CONCLUDING REMARKS ON A WAY FORWARD

This chapter has considered both demographic and legal developments that require attention in the process of recognition of early marriages in European countries today.

First, there is a need for nuance regarding age at marriage and age at the time of recognition. From the legal sources on the rights of the child and protection against discrimination for women, a limit of 18 years of age at the time of recognition can be drawn, based on a clear notion that children under this age should be protected from marriage. In addition to this age limit, the need to consider the interests of the child (and later as an adult) is apparent.

Second, there is further a need for increased acknowledgement of child marriages as a gendered problem. The legal ramifications of this acknowledgement are not clear. However, both, at the individual and the structural level, it is important to acknowledge the risks and harm girls and women are exposed to because of their sex. One proposed line of reasoning may be to substitute rights based on the marriage with other solutions based on the individual situation of the girl/woman. Furthermore, in situations where a permit is granted as a result of the marriage, the authorities should provide support services (including medical, psychological and legal services), as recommended by the CRC and CEDAW Committees, in order to fulfil the obligations of the two conventions.[43]

Finally, as regards the situation of recognition of early marriages, there is a need for increased focus on transnational settings, both at the national level as well as by key actors in international law, including the examination of harmonization of private international law and international (human rights) law.

In sum, the analysis in this chapter highlights grave concerns with regard to child marriages, both in terms of protecting children's (and especially girls')

---

41 HR-2021-1345-A, above n. 18, para. 46.

42 For such a critique of new regulations in Norwegian law on the recognition of marriages, see G. Cordero-Moss, 'Nytt fra norsk rett om anerkjennelse av barneekteskap: Høyesterett og lovendring' [New regulation in Norwegian law on the recognition of child marriages: The Supreme Court and new legislation], in *Festskrift till Maarit Jänterä-Jareborg*, Iustus forlag, Uppsala 2022.

43 Gen. Rec. No. 31, above n. 11, paras 82, 87.

human rights, and in terms of the legitimate need for migrants to be united with their families in their new home country after seeking refuge there. This backdrop makes it increasingly important to foster legal developments in Europe to try to envision a way forward that responds to the needs of international families, as well as the individual child, in cases of recognition of child marriages in cross-border situations.

THE RECOGNITION OF NON-JUDICIAL DIVORCES IN EUROPE

Pablo Quinzá Redondo

1. INTRODUCTION

Marriage has been and still is a key institution in (every) society. It is, in fact, the most common way of living as a couple, including within the EU.[1] However, in the last few years (or rather, in the last decades), an updating of the understanding of the institution, including its dissolution, has been subject to intense political, social and legal debates. In this regard, the possibility to dissolve a marriage without the involvement of a court (in strict sense) has recently been particularly relevant, at least in continental law systems. This is a phenomenon that, no doubt, is not new under various religion-based laws (in general terms),[2] but is certainly leading to (r)evolution in the field of family law of other legal systems.

---

[1] R. Arenas García, 'Concepto y tratamiento del matrimonio en el Derecho internacional privado europeo' (2020) 26 *La ley Derecho de familia* 1, 2.

[2] Throughout the world, there are different arrangements of religion-based legal pluralism. For example, some States incorporate religious laws in their state laws; others (simply) recognize their binding force. At the same time, the application of religious laws in some States is made

Known in the literature in various ways – such as non-judicial divorces, out-of-court divorces or non-contentious divorces – the truth is that many countries in the world no longer limit marriage dissolution to judicial decisions. This 'fall of the empire of the judicial divorce monopoly'[3] can be encompassed in a more global phenomenon of finding alternative or even complementary ways for resolution of family disputes. With these non-judicial pathways for resolution, the parties avoid the long duration of court proceedings and have a more amicable method for resolving their dispute, especially in simple cases where there is no real need for intervention by a court.[4]

Having said that, to distinguish the different kinds of non-judicial divorces can be challenging: an analysis of comparative law evidences that, in this area, diversity is the dominant feature.[5] However, in short, they can be purely private, with no intervention of any public authority, or count on the intervention of a public authority with an heterogenous role.[6]

The situation in the EU Member States is not alien to this phenomenon and this opens the door to new problems in the field of family law. On the one hand, it should be recalled that the EU has no competence to unify the substantive family law of the Member States[7] which, in the end, means that every Member State is, in principle, free to regulate how to dissolve a marriage, including those authorities with competence to render it.[8] However, on the other hand, the increasing number of cross-border marriages within the EU, and, consequently, of cross-border divorces, requires a recognition of the personal status of the former spouses in the other Member States.[9] There is a conflict of interest

under their state tribunals while in others it is applied only by the religious tribunals. What is more, in some cases state tribunals coexist with religious tribunals (I. Gallala-Arndt, 'Interreligious law' in J. Basedow, G. Rühl, F. Ferrari and P. De Miguel Asensio (eds), *Encyclopedia of private international law*, vol. II, Edward Elgar, Cheltenham 2017, pp. 1020–6, at p. 1020).

3 This expression has been used by several authors, and is difficult to attribute to a particular one.

4 S. Moracchini-Zeidenberg, 'La contractualisation de la séparation et de ses conséquences en droit français' (2018) 59(4) *Les cahiers de droit* 1119–27.

5 See N. Marchal Escalona, 'La eficia en España de los divorcios extrajudiciales otorgados en el extranjero' (2021) 13(21) *Cuadernos de Derecho transnacional* 462–74, where non-judicial divorces are classified from a geographical point of view (Latin America, Northern Europe, Oriental-Central Europe, Occidental Europe, Asia and Africa).

6 Of course, there are other ways for classifying them, where different names can be found with their own hints. However, for the purposes of this chapter, this overall classification will be used.

7 The adoption of measures concerning family law provided in Article 81(3) of the Treaty on the Functioning of the European Union clearly refers to private international law rules and not substantive (family) law.

8 A.-L. Calvo Caravaca and J. Carrascosa González, 'Crisis matrimoniales' in A.-L. Calvo Caravaca and J. Carrascosa González (eds), *Tratado de Derecho internacional privado. Tomo II*, Tirant Lo Blanch, Valencia 2020, pp. 1606–806, at p. 1792.

9 S. Bernasconi, 'The application of Brussels IIa to the circulation of out-of-court and private divorces within the European Area of Justice: current difficulties and future perspectives' in

between national autonomy in substantive family law and the need to coordinate cross-border divorces.

This situation leads, in practical terms, to the problem of circulation of non-judicial divorces among Member States according to the applicable private international law rules. Particularly, this chapter will mainly focus on the applicability of the Brussels II instruments to non-judicial divorces. Thus, the chapter will first discuss the 'old' Brussels II bis Regulation[10] but also, secondly, the 'new' Brussels II ter Regulation,[11] which both apply to marriage dissolution (alongside with parental responsibility and child abduction). To this end, a distinction will be made between private divorces and non-judicial divorces with intervention of a public authority.

2. PRIVATE DIVORCES

What is a private divorce? As explained before, there is not a homogenous expression for referring to this reality. However, for the purposes of this chapter, it will be referred, on the one hand, to mere agreements of the spouses themselves, without any intervention of a public authority and, on the other hand, to proceedings which are religious, that is to say, divorces pronounced by religious authorities not empowered by the State and according to religious rules only.[12] In this latter case, it is important to clarify that a reference is made only to situations where a State does not give civil effect to religious proceedings taking place within its jurisdiction.

2.1. BRUSSELS II BIS

Can private divorces be included in the scope of application of the Brussels II bis Regulation? In contrast to the Borrás Report,[13] the Explanatory Memorandum

C. Esplugues Mota, P. Diago Diago and P. Jiménez Blanco (eds), *50 años de Derecho internacional privado de la Unión Europea en el diván*, Tirant Lo Blanch, Valencia 2019, pp. 339–52, at pp. 340–41.

10 Council Regulation (EC) No 2201/2003 of 27 November 2003 concerning jurisdiction and the recognition and enforcement of judgments in matrimonial matters and the matters of parental responsibility, repealing Regulation (EC) No 1347/2000 [2003] OJ L338/1.

11 Council Regulation (EU) 2019/1111 of 25 June 2019 on jurisdiction, the recognition and enforcement of decisions in matrimonial matters and the matters of parental responsibility, and on international child abduction [2019] OJ L178/1.

12 S. Bernasconi, above n. 9, p. 342.

13 Explanatory Report on the Convention, drawn up on the basis of Article K.3 of the Treaty on European Union, on Jurisdiction and the Recognition and Enforcement of Judgments in Matrimonial Matters (approved by the Council on 28 May 1998) prepared by Dr Alegría Borrás Professor of Private International Law University of Barcelona [1998] OJ C221/27.

of the Proposal for the Brussels II Regulation[14] and the Brussels II Regulation[15] itself, the Brussels II bis Regulation does not expressly exclude private divorces. Does the absence of an express exclusion mean a change in position?[16] We think not. The autonomous concepts of *court* and *judgment* provided by the Brussels II bis Regulation follow the basic lines of its predecessors,[17] which means that the Brussels II bis Regulation also seems to require a certain level of formality and intervention of State authorities, in the way that proceedings become official. 'Civil effectiveness' is the touchstone of eligibility[18] and thus, for example, the *get*-procedure before a Jewish rabbinic court in a Member State or repudiation in a consulate in the territory of a Member State[19] stay outside this Regulation as long as they are not approved or converted by a civil court. The same holds true for mere agreements between the spouses themselves when they remain in their personal sphere and do not involve any public authority.

The exclusion of private divorces from the Brussels II bis Regulation was supported by the Court of Justice of the European Union (CJEU) in the case *Sahyouni II*,[20]

---

14 Proposal for a Council Regulation on jurisdiction and the recognition and enforcement of judgments in matrimonial matters and in matters of parental responsibility for joint children COM(1999) 220 final, 4 May.

15 Council Regulation (EC) No 1347/2000 of 29 May 2000 on jurisdiction and the recognition and enforcement of judgments in matrimonial matters and in matters of parental responsibility for children of both spouses [2000] OJ L160/19.

16 Literally, the exclusion was referred to 'religious proceedings', which in fact can potentially be considered a kind of private divorce as defined in this chapter. However, at the same time, there might be 'religious proceedings' which might not be private (i.e., if a public authority approves/converts it into a civil act). See below n. 18.

17 The former is defined in Article 2.1 as '*all the authorities* in the Member States with jurisdiction in the matters falling within the scope of the regulation', while the latter is defined in Article 2.4 as 'a divorce, legal separation or marriage annulment, as well as a judgment relating to parental responsibility, pronounced by a court of a Member State, *whatever the judgment may be called*, including a decree, order or decision'.

18 M. Ní Shúilleabháin, *Cross-border divorce law*, Oxford University Press, Oxford 2010, p. 126 and P. Hammje, 'Article 2' in S. Corneloup (ed.), *Droit européen du divorce*, LexisNexis, Paris 2013, paras 1–47, at paras 7–9. According to these authors, these means that religious proceedings producing civil effects in a particular Member State would also be covered by the Brussels II bis Regulation.

19 W. Pintens, 'Article 1' in U. Magnus and P. Mankowski (eds), *Brussels IIbis Regulation*, Sellier European Law Publishers, Munich 2012, paras 1–73, at para. 12.

20 Case C-372/16, *Soha Sahyouni v. Raja Mamisch*, ECLI:EU:C:2017:988. This case was referred twice to the CJEU. In the first referral (Case C-281/15, *Soha Sahyouni v. Raja Mamisch*, ECLI:EU:C:2016:343), the Court declared that it had no jurisdiction to answer the questions. It seems that in *Sahyouni I* the Court confused the concepts of 'recognition of foreign divorce decision' and (German) 'recognition of a foreign divorce by private international law' to consider its lack of jurisdiction (S.L. Gössl and J. Verhellen, 'Article 1' in S. Corneloup (ed.), *The Rome III Regulation. A commentary on the law applicable to divorce and legal separation*, Edward Elgar, Cheltenham 2020, paras 1.01–1.29, at para. 1.12). According to A. Gandía Sellens and C. Zimmer, 'Reconocimiento y divorcios privados – Reflexiones a la luz del Auto del TJUE de 12 de mayo de 2016, asunto C-281/15, *Sahyouni c. Mamisch*' (2016) 4 *Bitácora Millenium DIPr* 12, the Court did not try to make even a minimum effort to understand the functioning of the legal order of the Member State to which the referring court belonged. See below n. 22.

extensively analysed by legal doctrine. To sum up, this case concerned a divorce by unilateral declaration of the husband before a religious court in Syria and its recognition in Germany by virtue of the Rome III Regulation.[21] Attention will not be paid to the reason why this Regulation could have been, or not, applied to a non-EU case and the problem of the German national conflict-of-law rules.[22] What is important from the *Sahyouni II* case, for the specific purposes of the current research matter, is that the CJEU stated that both the Brussels II bis and Rome III Regulations only cover 'divorces pronounced either by a national court or by, or under the supervision of, a public authority'.[23] Consequently, private divorces fall outside the scope of the Brussels II bis Regulation and the Rome III Regulation. They are treated in accordance with the domestic private international law rules of each Member State.

2.2. BRUSSELS II TER

The main update incorporated by the Brussels II ter Regulation in the treatment of private divorces across Member States is that the Regulation states that they will remain outside its scope of application. This is clarified by recital 14, that expressly impedes the circulation of mere private agreements, at least those which have not been registered by a public authority competent to do so. In brief, the main conclusion of the *Sahyouni II* case seems to be incorporated in the 'new' Brussels II instrument, at least in a recital.

---

21 Council Regulation (EU) No 1259/2010 of 20 December 2010 implementing enhanced cooperation in the area of the law applicable to divorce and legal separation [2010] OJ L343/10.

22 In Germany, a private divorce is recognized if the divorce is valid under the law applicable to the case, once the German national conflict-of-laws rules have been applied. In other words, there is a substantive control of the private divorce through the so-called 'method of acceptance by conflict-of-laws' (S.L. Gössl, 'Open issues in European International Family Law: Sahyouni, "Private divorces" and Islamic Law under Rome III Regulation' (2017) 3–4 *The European Legal Forum* 69). At that time, following the amendments introduced by a law of 23 January 2013, Regulation Rome III was applicable by reference of Article 17 Einführungsgesetz zum Bürgerlichen Gesetzbuche (EGBGB). Germany trusted, as did other Member States such as Hungary, that Regulation Rome III covered divorce comprehensively, so it used a catch-all technique (A. Dutta, 'Private divorces outside Rome III and Brussels II bis? The *Sahyouni* gap' (2019) 56 *Common Market Law Review* 1662). However, at the same time, it has to be said that it was the German national legislator who 'tied' himself and (unconsciously?) decided to depend upon the CJEU reasonings of Regulation Rome III, including, in this particular case, the exclusion of private divorces (S. Álvarez González, '*Sahyouni* mas allá del espejo. Un comentario posible a la STJ de 20 de diciembre de 2017 (C-372-16)' (2018) 35 *Revista electrónica de estudios internacionales* 19). As a result of this maze, in 2019 the German legislator updated the content of Article 17 EGBGB to allow the application of some specific provisions of Regulation Rome III to cases which primarily do not fall inside their scope of application.

23 Paragraphs 39, 45 and 48 of the decision.

3. NON-JUDICIAL DIVORCES, BUT INTERVENTION OF A PUBLIC AUTHORITY

As mentioned before, there is a second type of non-judicial divorces: divorces not rendered by a court (again, in strict sense) but where a public authority intervenes. For the purpose of this chapter, this group includes a variety of national models. In these models, a public authority, such as a notary, a civil registrar or a public prosecutor, among others, intervenes in the dissolution of the marriage. The level of intervention and the kind of judgment these public authorities render is the key point.

Apart from that, differences can also be found as to the requirements to access this kind of divorce (e.g., in some cases it is also possible for marriages with minor children) as well as to procedural or formal aspects (e.g., in some cases there is a need for a lawyer or lawyers, representing and assisting the parties), among others. There is, indeed, a huge diversity in the different aspects that define this legal institution.

3.1. COMPARATIVE OVERVIEW IN THE EUROPEAN UNION: SOME EXAMPLES

What is the situation in the EU? Non-judicial divorces with intervention of a public authority are allowed in some Member States (e.g., Estonia, France, Greece, Italy, Latvia, Lithuania, Portugal, Romania, Slovenia and Spain) while not in others (e.g., Germany or Austria). Particularly, attention will be paid to the cases of Spain, Italy and France. For each of them, sections 3.1.1 to 3.1.3 will present two different aspects: first, the substantive institution as such (the non-judicial divorce with intervention of a public authority); second, their main problems or difficulties as well as the national positions regarding their inclusion (or not) in the Brussels II bis Regulation, which is actually the most controversial issue.[24]

3.1.1. Spain

In Spain, it is possible to get divorced by mutual consent. The divorce agreement requires the drawing-up of a public deed before a notary, which includes not only the wish of the spouses to get divorced, but also a regulatory settlement

24 It is important to clarify that one thing is the national position regarding the potential application of Brussels II instruments to this type of divorce and, a different one, what in the end the CJEU states about their application, which must (or, at least, should) prevail. This will be analysed in section 3.2.

on their personal and/or patrimonial effects.[25] The spouses must attend in person and must be assisted by a lawyer. The regulatory settlement should contain, particularly in the case of this type of divorce, the following aspects: the destination of the family home; the attribution of care of domestic pets; liquidation of the matrimonial property regime; and the content of maintenance payment.

The *Spanish notarial divorce* is not allowed where there are minor children, and even when there are children over 18 years or emancipated, it will be necessary that they consent before the notary regarding those measures that will affect them. And even more importantly, the notary might refuse this method of dissolution of the marriage, if the notary considers that it could be harmful for one of the spouses, or any children over 18 years or emancipated children. Such a refusal means that approval of the regulatory agreement by a judge will be necessary. It follows from this that the role of the notary is not merely receptive, since it is up to the notary to carry out a (real) control of legality and even fairness or equity.[26] In addition, the regulatory settlement's performance is subject to supervision: first, by the Dirección General de Seguridad Jurídica y Fe Pública and, second, by courts.

There is a rule of domestic territorial jurisdiction with regard to the notary: that of the last common domicile of the spouses or that of the habitual residence or domicile of either of the spouses.[27] Besides, according to a Resolution of the Dirección General de Seguridad Jurídica y Fe Pública of 7 June 2016,[28] the notaries are bound by the international jurisdiction rules of the Brussels II bis Regulation.[29] What is more important, according to this Resolution, notaries

25 Articles 82, 83, 87, 89 and 90 of the Spanish Civil Code (introduced by Law 15/2015 of non-judicial affairs of 2 July 2015).

26 M. Pereña Vicente, 'El divorcio sin juez en el Derecho español y francés: entre el divorcio por notario y el divorcio por abogado. Dificultades teóricas y prácticas' (2019) LXXII (I) *Anuario de Derecho civil* 16–17.

27 Article 54.1 of Notarial Law of 28 May 1862 (introduced by Law 15/2015 of non-judicial affairs of 2 July 2015).

28 See *Resolución-Consulta de la Dirección General de los Registros y del Notriado de 07.06.16 formulada por el notario de Bilbao don Javier Vinader Carracedo, a través del Iltre. Colegio Notarial del País Vasco, en relación a ciertos efectos internacionales del divorcio ante notario.*

29 However, taking into account that the Spanish notarial divorce fulfils a regulatory settlement dealing with related questions such as the liquidation of the matrimonial property regime and the content of maintenance payments, it will be up to their respective international jurisdiction rules to 'check' if the Spanish notary has international jurisdiction to deal with them, since these are questions excluded from the Brussels II instruments. Note that the Spanish Government has declared that 'there are no authorities with the characteristics and scope listed in Article 3(2) falling under the Regulation 2016/1103', which would mean that the Spanish notaries are not bound by the international jurisdiction rules of this regulation <https://e-justice.europa.eu/559/EN/matters_of_matrimonial_property_regimes?SPAIN&init=true&member=1> accessed 10.05.2021. More doubts arise in the case of maintenance obligations, since the authorities included in the term 'court' for the purposes of applying the Regulation 4/2009 have not been notified (N. Marchal Escalona, 'El tratamiento de la

can issue a certificate by virtue of Article 39 of the Brussels II bis Regulation for the public deed's recognition and enforcement in the other Member States. It also seems that the public deeds of divorce should be recognized in other Member States as *judgments* (Articles 21 et seq.) and not as *authentic instruments* (Article 46).[30]

3.1.2. Italy

In Italy, two non-judicial divorces were introduced in 2014. First, it is possible to enter into a legal separation or divorce agreement before the official of the Civil Register Office[31] of the habitual residence of either of the spouses or where the marriage was registered. The parties can be assisted by a lawyer (optionally). The official of the Civil Register Office is in charge of receiving the consensual statements of the parties. The spouses must return to the Civil Register Office no earlier than 30 days (the so-called 'period of reflection') and confirm their statements and their wish to conclude the agreement (not in case of amendment of the conditions of separation or divorce). The agreement is then collected in an (administrative) act. Although not explicitly stated in the particular Italian law introducing this kind of divorce, it seems that the control of the official of the Civil Register Office is essentially formal.[32] It is only possible to conclude this agreement if there are no children under 18 nor adult children with severe disabilities in need of care or economically dependent. The agreement cannot include any patrimonial transfer clause, but it might be referred to maintenance obligations.

---

plurinacionalidad en el divorcio no judicial' in M. Moya Escudero (ed.), *Plurinacionalidad y Derecho internacional privado de familia y sucesiones*, Tirant Lo Blanch, Valencia 2021, pp. 450–513, at pp. 462–8).

30 C. González Beilfuss, 'El divorcio notarial: cuestiones de Derecho internacional privado' in E. Pérez Vera, J.C. Fernández Rozas, M. Guzmán Zapater, A. Fernández Pérez and M. Guzmán Peces (eds), *El Derecho internacional privado entre la tradición y la innovación. Libro homenaje al profesor doctor José María Espinar Vicente*, Iprolex, Madrid 2020, pp. 347–64, at p. 363. However, the recognition of those parts of the regulatory settlement referred not to the divorce as such but to their effects, would not be covered by the rules of recognition and enforcement of Regulation Brussels II bis, since they are excluded from its scope of application. See above n. 29.

31 Article 12 Decree-Law nº 132 of 2014 (amended by Law nº 162 of 2014). Specifically, this provision provides for different scenarios: (i) consensual separation; (ii) termination of the civil effects of marriage; (iii) dissolution of the marriage/amendment of the conditions of separation or divorce agreement.

32 C. Honorati and S. Bernasconi, 'L'efficacia cross-border degli accordi stragiudiziali in materia familiare tra i regolamenti Bruxelles II-bis e Bruxelles II-ter' (2020) 2 *Rivista quadrimestrale online sullo Spazio europeo di libertà, sicurezza e giustizia* 25, 26. These authors state that the official of the Civil Register office must check the personal data of the spouses, their capacity to act, the absence of children as provided by law and the absence of any patrimonial transfer clause. They also address the importance of verifying that the agreement does not infringe the public policy of Italy as well as public morals.

Second, the spouses are able to go through a negotiation agreement assisted by lawyers regarding their legal separation or divorce.[33] It is open both for marriages with children (or adult children with severe disabilities in need of care or economically dependent) or marriages without children. In this latter case, the agreement must be forwarded to the public prosecutor serving at the competent court, who is in charge of checking the absence of any irregularity. Provided that is done, the agreement will be authorized for compliance. In the former case, the agreement is also sent to the public prosecutor serving at the competent court, who will authorize the agreement provided that it safeguards the interests of the children. Otherwise, the public prosecutor will forward it to the president of the competent court, who will summon the spouses for a hearing; it will then be the decision of the president of the competent court to authorize the agreement or not. The agreement has to state that the lawyers informed the former spouses about the possibility of a mediation and, in its case, the importance that children spend the appropriate time with both parents.

Particularly relevant for intra-European cases is the Resolution of the Ministero della Giustizia of 22 May 2018,[34] where it is stated that in the case of an agreement before the Civil Register Office, the official of the Civil Register Office can issue a certificate according to Article 39 of the Brussels II bis Regulation for its recognition and enforcement in the rest of the Member States. Otherwise, in the case of a negotiation agreement on divorce assisted by lawyers, it depends. If there are no children, it will be issued by the public prosecutor serving at the competent court; if there are children and the case has arrived before the president of the court, he/she will issue the certificate.

3.1.3. France

In 2016, France introduced a divorce by mutual consent,[35] which consists of an agreement in the form of a document signed privately by the spouses and countersigned by their respective lawyers. The agreement, drafted by the lawyers in representation of the spouses, must include the following aspects: the personal information of the parties and lawyers; the consent of the spouses regarding the dissolution of the marriage and its effects; information regarding possible maintenance payments and liquidation of the matrimonial property regime; and

---

33 Article 6 Decree-Law n° 132 of 2014 (amended by Law n° 162 of 2014 and n° 206 of 2021). Specifically, this provision provides for different scenarios: (i) consensual separation; (ii) termination of the civil effects of marriage; (iii) dissolution of the marriage; (iv) amendment of the conditions of separation or divorce; (v) custody and support of children born outside marriage plus determination of the maintenance obligations.

34 See *Circolare del Ministero della Giustizia di 22.05.18 – Misure di degiurisdizionalizzazione in materia di famiglia ed emissione del certificato previsto dall'art. 39 del Regolamento CE n. 2201 del 2003.*

35 Article 229 Civil Code, introduced by Law 2016-1547 of modernization of justice.

evidence on the opportunity offered to the children to be heard by a judge. This agreement is then filed in the minutes of a notary. With this filing, the agreement takes effect and becomes enforceable. According to the Civil Code, the notary verifies the compliance of the formal requirements of the agreement (i.e., that it includes the above-mentioned aspects) and verifies that the reflection period (15 days) has been respected. The intervention of a judge only takes place if the children of the marriage, when possible, require to be heard.

In order to complete the regulation of the divorce by mutual consent and to deal with its circulation among Member States, the Ministère de la Justice issued a Resolution on 26 January 2017,[36] which according to the doctrine seems to bring more problems than solutions. First, it states that notaries are not bound by domestic and even international jurisdiction rules, since they cannot be considered as a *court* in the sense of the Brussels II bis Regulation.[37] Second, it stipulates that notaries can issue a certificate according to Article 39 of the Brussels II bis Regulation[38] and that the recognition of the divorce by mutual consent in the rest of the Member States would then depend on the application of Article 46 of the Brussels II bis Regulation.[39] Third, taking into account that the agreement on divorce shall include the regulation of their effects, it reveals how the recognition in other Member States of these parts of the agreement should be carried out.[40]

---

36 See *Circulaire du 26 janvier 2017 de présentation des dispositions en matière de divorce par consentement mutuel et de succession issues de la loi n°2016-1547 du 18 novembre 2016 de modernisation de la justice du XXIe siècle et du décret n°2016-1907 du 28 décembre 2016 relatif au divorce prévu à l'article 229-1 du code civil et à diverses dispositions en matière successorale.*

37 Something which has been catalogued by some authors such a 'legal tourism', since the French legislation does not seem to require personal or territorial links with France in order to be involved in this kind of divorce. In other words, they consider the French divorce by mutual consent as 'divorce without forum' (P. Hammje, 'Le divorce par consentement mutuel extrajudiciaire et le droit international privé. Les aléas d'un divorce sans for' (2017) 2 *Revue critique de Droit international privé* 146).

38 Article 509-3 Procedural Civil Code, modified by Decree 2016-1907 dealing with divorce regulated in article 229-1 of the Civil Code and different provisions on succession.

39 One of the main critiques to consider the application of this provision is that it explicitly deals with *authentic instruments* or *agreements* which *are enforceable* in the Member State of origin and the truth is that the agreement dealing with the mere dissolution of the marriage aims to be recognized, not enforced (S. Francq, 'Réforme avortée et réforme surprise: compétence et reconnaissance en matière de dissolution du mariage après la refonte du règlement Bruxelles IIbis, en particulier à propos des divorces non judiciaires' in S. Francq and S. Sarolea (coords), *Actualités européens en droit international privé familial*, Anthemis, Wavre 2019, pp. 53–86, at p. 72).

40 In some cases, parts of the agreement that, apparently, could be covered by a European Union Regulation (since, potentially, they cover the substantive institution as such included in the agreement) would finally depend on the application of the domestic private international rules of the recipient State. For example, since the French resolution itself declares that the divorce by mutual consent cannot be considered an *authentic instrument* (and, obviously, it is neither a decision nor a court settlement), those parts of the agreement dealing with

3.2. BRUSSELS II BIS

As mentioned before, private divorces – as defined above – remain outside the Brussels II bis Regulation. What is, however, the situation of non-judicial divorces where a public authority intervenes? The point of departure should be (again) the Borrás Report, the Explanatory Memorandum of the Proposal for the Brussels II Regulation and the Brussels II Regulation itself, according to which non-judicial proceedings occurring in matrimonial matters in certain Member States (i.e., proceedings officially recognized in a Member State) shall be regarded as equivalent to judicial proceedings (e.g., administrative divorces). In contrast to them, the Brussels II bis Regulation avoided the specific treatment of this problem. However, as already mentioned, it apparently follows the basic lines of its predecessors, which it would mean it also includes divorces pronounced by national courts or anyway obtained by virtue of other proceedings recognized as having equivalent effects. This goes in line with the conclusions of the *Sahyouni II* case, referring to the need for the intervention of a public authority. Nevertheless, the truth is that neither the Regulation nor the decision of the CJEU specify the intensity and legal quality of the intervention of this authority. As a result, it is not clear whether non-judicial divorces such as the Spanish, Italian or French ones, among others, can be included in Regulation's scope of application.[41]

It is in this context that a great deal of expectation was generated around the CJEU's preliminary ruling in the *Senatsverwaltung* case.[42] This preliminary ruling concerns specifically the divorce agreement before the official of the Civil Register Office in Italy, but it should be conclusive or, at least, offer valuable guidelines, for the non-judicial divorces included in the domestic legislation of other Member States.

To sum up, the CJEU was asked whether a divorce decree drawn up by the official of the Civil Register Office of Italy could be recognized in Germany by virtue of the Brussels II bis Regulation or by applying the procedural internal law. In the former case, it was asked whether Article 21, which referred to *judgments* or, if not, Article 46, dealing with *authentic instruments* and *agreements* would be applicable. Some authors, the most optimistic, predicted that this type

maintenance obligations will fall outside the scope of application of Regulation 4/2009 (G. Khairallah, 'Aspects européens et internationaux du nouveau divorce par consentement mutuel' in M-E. Ancel, L. d'Avout, J.C. Fernández Rozas, M. Goré and J-M. Jude (eds), *Le droit à l'épreuve des siècles et des frontières. Mélanges en l'honneur du professeur Bertrand Ancel*, Iprolex, Madrid 2018, pp. 965–78, at p. 969).

41 However, this does not mean – far from it – that they resemble each other. On the contrary, each one presents its own characteristics that could well justify a different result regarding its inclusion in the Regulation Brussels II bis.

42 Case C-646/20 *Senatsverwaltung für Inneres und Sport v. TB*, ECLI:EU:C:2022:879.

of divorce would be included in the Regulation,[43] while others expected that the answer would be negative.[44] The CJEU confirmed the former prediction on 15 November 2022: the Italian divorce decree constitutes a *judgment* for the purposes of the Brussels II bis Regulation.

The point of departure of the CJEU's decision deals with the degree of control which must be exercised by the authority with jurisdiction in relation to the divorce. In this regard, what it seems to be relevant is that the public authority 'must retain the control over the grant of the divorce', i.e., the public authority must examine that the divorce has been obtained in accordance with the requirements laid down in the law of the Member State of origin and with a valid consent of the parties involved.[45] On the basis of this circumstance, the CJEU analyses the requirements laid down in the Italian legislation and their effective fulfilment, which in this case doesn't seem to pose any problems.[46] However, the control of their valid, free and informed' consent is treated in a very simplistic and reductionist way, assimilating it with the receipt of the spouses' declarations concerning their wish to divorce,[47] which is certainly far from an examination of the substance.

Apart from that, there are arguments used in the decision, which might be questionable or not entirely convincing. Three in particular will be mentioned.

First, it is striking that there is what might be called an 'unequal invocation' of the vertical influence of domestic law of the Member States with respect to European regulations if the case *Senatsverwaltung* is compared with the case *Sahyouni II*. In the latter case, the CJEU relied on a very specific argument such as the influence of the substantive law existing in the Member States at the time of the adoption of a Regulation for the purposes of interpreting it.[48] However, in the former case, the CJEU seems to imply that the existence or non-existence of substantive law institutions in the Member States at the time of the development

---

43 For example, K. Bogdzevič, N. Kaminskienė and L. Vaigė, 'Non-judicial divorces and the Brussels II bis Regulation: to apply or not apply' (2021) 7(1) *International Comparative Jurisprudence* 35, pointed out that there was 'hope', since the truth is that the *Sahyouni II* case did not differentiate, in the end, between all kinds of divorces and it was clear that the Italian non-judicial divorce was not the same as a religious divorce.

44 For example, M. Kramme, 'Private divorce in Light of the Recast of the Brussels II bis Regulation' (2021) 3 *European Union private law review*, 102–03, considered that the CJEU was going to reject the application of Brussels II bis taking into account the reasonings of the *Sahyouni II* case, specially that referring to the fact that, at the time Regulation Rome III was adopted – and consequently also Brussels II bis – non-judicial divorces were, broadly, not yet introduced in the Member States. Nevertheless, he was in favour of the recognition of this divorce according to the Brussels II bis Regulation.

45 Paragraph 54 of the decision.

46 Paragraph 65 of the decision.

47 Paragraphs 64 and 66 of the decision.

48 Paragraphs 45 and 46 of the decision.

and adoption of a Regulation should not be taken as a basis for justifying the scope of the rule.[49] In other words, and despite the fact that both decisions are referred to different non-judicial divorces, it seems that the arguments of both are opposite.

Second, it is important to remember that it is not possible to interpret provisions of EU law in the light of amendments contained in legislation enacted subsequently.[50] The Advocate General of the case, Mr Collins, warned of this in his legal opinion.[51] In the case *Senatsverwaltung*, the CJEU interpreted the Brussels II bis Regulation on the basis of the Brussels II ter Regulation, by assuming that the purpose of the latter instrument, at least as far as recognition and enforcement provisions were concerned, was not to 'innovate and introduce new rules, but only to clarify'.[52] This argument is particularly striking, since one of the most unique and genuine aspects of the Brussels II bis Regulation is the introduction of a detailed and exhaustive regulation of *authentic instruments* and *agreements* (Articles 64 to 68) compared to its predecessor, which referred to them in a very basic way in a single provision (Article 46).

The last idea deals with one of the gaps of the decision. It is more related with what the CJEU does not mention than what is treated as such in the decision. The idea is the following: it is clear that the CJEU must answer what is strictly asked, but given the outcome of its decision (the qualification of the Italian divorce decree as a *judgment*), it would have been interesting to put this type of non-judicial divorce in context with the overall system of private international law. As a result, several questions arise. First, if a *judgment* is, in short, a divorce pronounced by the courts of a Member State, is the Civil Registrar of Italy a *court* for the purposes of the Brussels II Regulation? If so, did that Civil Registrar check whether he had international jurisdiction? On the other hand, was there any control of the law applicable to the divorce? These questions, among others, are not explicitly addressed in the decision, but would be clearly connected with the case.

To sum up, the case *Senatsverwaltung* confirms the inclusion of a certain type of non-judicial divorce with intervention of a public authority in the Brussels II bis Regulation, but its reasoning is debatable at times. This is not welcomed. What does seem to be clear is the future consequences of the decision in relation to other non-judicial divorces provided for in other Member States. Thus, if the divorce concluded before the Italian civil registrar passes the 'filter' of the Brussels II bis Regulation, and even the divorce decree is considered a *judgment*,

---

49 Paragraph 50 of the decision.

50 Case C-224/16 *Aebtri v. Nachalnik na Mitnitsa Burgas*, ECLI:EU:C:2017:880, paras 18, 19 and 64.

51 ECLI:EU:C:2022:357, para. 54.

52 Paragraph 61 of the decision.

all those in which the public authority carries out a greater or at least similar control should receive the same response.[53]

3.3. BRUSSELS II TER

Given the above-mentioned uncertainties, it is not surprising that the 'new' Brussels II instrument deals more specifically with the issue of non-judicial divorces. The basic idea is that the Brussels II ter Regulation departs from the difficulties of classification and distinction between *decisions*, *authentic instruments* and *agreements* to offer a more accurate approach of all of them in comparison to the Brussels II bis Regulation. The distinction, it is true, will be essentially terminological, since *authentic instruments* and *agreements* should be treated as equivalent to *decisions* for the purpose of the application of the rules on recognition and enforcement (Recital 70), unless otherwise provided in their specific rules (Article 65.1).

Having said that, according to Recital 14 and Article 2 of the Brussels II ter Regulation, the application of the provisions on *decisions* or *authentic instruments* and *agreements* would depend, among other things, on the level of intervention provided by the authority of the Member State where the divorce agreement is issued. On the one hand, if this authority offers an 'examination of the substance' in accordance with national law, then the divorce in question could be treated as a *decision* for its recognition in the other Member States. On the other hand, if this authority only manages a 'formal intervention' of the agreement, the application of the rules on *authentic instruments* and *agreements* is expected. More importantly, the Recital 14 itself mentions the case of 'notaries registering agreements', which could actually be the 'French case'.[54] They would be treated, specifically, as *agreements* for the purposes of its circulation in other Member States according to the rules of the Regulation.

In general terms, *authentic instruments* and *agreements* regarding divorce shall be recognized in other Member States without any special procedure being required (Article 65.1). Only when they violate one of the grounds for refusal

---

[53] This should have probably been the case of the Spanish notarial divorce if the preliminary ruling (Case C-304/22 (2022/C 318/36) had not been withdrawn <https://curia.europa.eu/juris/document/document.jsf?mode=DOC&pageIndex=0&docid=269486&part=1&doclang=FR&text=&dir=&occ=first&cid=10062587> accessed 10.05.2023. The referring court seems to have considered that after the *Senatsverwaltung* case there was no point in keeping its request.

[54] It appears that the initiative of the French and Italian delegations was decisive for the inclusion of this new set of rules, which tend to provide for an explicit answer to all the questions derived from its antecessor (E. D'Alessandro, 'The impact of private divorces on EU private international law' in J. Scherpe and E. Bargelli (eds), *The Interaction between Family Law, Succession Law and Private International Law. Adapting to Change*, Intersentia, Cambridge 2021 pp. 59–75, at pp. 73–75).

(Article 68),[55] its recognition would be rejected. There are two main updates in this specific regard in the Brussels II ter Regulation. The first is that it does not require that *authentic instruments* and *agreements* concerning divorce are enforceable in the Member State of origin, but only that they have binding legal effect (Article 65.1). The second is that it requires international jurisdiction of the authorities of the Member State issuing the divorce (Article 64).

In the light of the foregoing, it can be inferred that mostly all non-judicial divorces with the intervention of a public authority carried out in a Member State should be included in the scope of application of the Brussels II ter Regulation for its recognition in the rest of the Member States by including them in any of these three autonomous concepts, which would ultimately depend on the level of intervention of the public authority. The new scheme is very convincing and marks a step forward in clarifying most of the issues which have arisen under the 'old' Brussels II.[56]

4. CONCLUSIONS

The dissolution of the marriage by divorce without a court's intervention is becoming more and more popular in the legislation of EU Member States. Yet again, the development of new substantive family law institutions is not only a matter of 'national level' but a broader one: it presents clear implications with regard to EU law instruments, at least, in two ways.[57]

It is possible that a legal institution 'arises' years after a particular EU regulation is adopted. Then it will be necessary to decide whether the new institution is covered by their scope of application. It is a true task of 'legal

55 Grounds for refusal which are not 'new'. There are specifically three for legal separation and divorce contained in *authentic instruments* or *agreements*: public policy and the two 'classical' ones for irreconcilability.

56 Solutions for the 'old' problems but, however, 'new' points for discussion, as addressed by J. Antomo, 'Der Umgang mit Privatscheidungen aus EU-Mitgliedstaaten – vor und nach der Reform der Brüssel IIa-VO' in C. Budzikiewicz, B. Heiderhoff, F. Klinkhammer and K. Niethammer-Jürgens (eds), *Neue impulse in europäischen Familienkollisionsrecht*, Nomos, Baden-Baden 2021, pp. 81–144, at p. 124. The author mentions, for example, the following issues: a possible misunderstanding among the definitions or guidelines provided in Article 2 and Recital 14 as to what a *decision*, an *authentic instrument* or *agreement* is; a lack of specification of the law applicable to the binding legal effect of the *authentic instrument* or *agreement* dealing with the divorce; an absence of the question of the legal authorities in charge of applying and verifying the application of the international jurisdiction rules of the regulation or the dogmatic question of what the recognition of the *authentic instrument* or *agreement* entails: only the evidentiary effects or the substantive ones as well?

57 As suggested by J. Scherpe and E. Bargelli, 'The interaction between Family Law, Succession Law and Private International Law' in J. Scherpe and E. Bargelli (eds), *The Interaction between Family Law, Succession Law and Private International Law: Adapting to Change*, Intersentia, Cambridge 2021, pp. 1–9, at pp. 1–5.

engineering', where not only the text of the rules but also the legal precedents or explanatory documents must be considered, at least until the CJEU clarifies an issue. This is, for example, the case of the Brussels II bis Regulation and the potential inclusion of non-judicial divorces with intervention of a public authority, as analysed above.

Perhaps a less obvious issue is how 'new' EU regulations are affected by surfacing national substantive law. Its 'upward impact' means that they influence the 'update' of the EU regulations in the sense that the regulations tend to embrace emerging national legal institutions within their autonomous concepts. More comprehensive legal definitions and, more importantly, a growing tendency of providing for more recitals in EU regulations are proof of this effect. This is, in fact, the situation of the Brussels II ter Regulation and the divorces analysed alongside.

In conclusion, while the field of research of this chapter – the inclusion, or not, of non-judicial divorces in the Brussels II instruments – is still developing, the truth is that the procedure to detect the problem and the legal technique to settle it should not be regarded as unusual for private international law researchers. It has happened before with other legal institutions and other EU regulations and will continue to be repeated. It demonstrates that 'where there is a will, there is a way'.

EMANCIPATORY POTENTIAL OF MAINTENANCE AND MATRIMONIAL PROPERTY AFTER DIVORCE

Reflections Based on the Concept of Relational Autonomy

Caroline VOITHOFER*

* For useful comments on an earlier draft, I want to thank Malte KRAMME, Heidi U. SILLER, Denise WIEDEMANN and John A. FOULKS.

1. INTRODUCTION

This chapter compares selected regulations on post-divorce spousal maintenance, the dissolution of the marital home, post-divorce pension splitting, and certain spousal divorce agreements within the German-speaking legal family. The regulations are examined for convergence with the emancipatory law approach, aiming at reflecting on the interconnections of family law and individual and relational autonomy and solidarity.

2. THEORETICAL BACKGROUND: EMANCIPATORY LAW APPROACH AND RELATIONAL AUTONOMY

The emancipatory law approach[1] focuses on changes within the scope and degree[2] of autonomous action and agency as well as on various interconnections between legal and other social norms impacting the autonomy of individuals. This approach focuses on relational aspects of autonomy, switching from the concept of individual autonomy – which is dominant within 'legal dogmatics', legal philosophy and legal theory and which has a strong focus on self-determination – to the concept of relational autonomy.

The concept of relational autonomy[3] implies that the individual's scope of action is limited by, and depends on, the scopes of action of others within society. The individual's autonomy expresses itself through interactions with

1 See E. Holzleithner, 'Emanzipation durch Recht?' (2008) *Kritische Justiz* 250–57; E. Holzleithner, 'Emanzipatorisches Recht: Über Chancen und Grenzen rechtlicher Geschlechtergleichstellung' (2010) 1 *juridikum* 6–13.

2 See M. Friedman, 'Autonomy, Social Disruption, and Women' in C. Mackenzie and N. Stoljar (eds), *Relational Autonomy: Feminist Perspectives on Autonomy, Agency, and the Social Self*, Oxford University Press, New York / Oxford 2000, pp. 35–51, at p. 41.

3 See J. Herring, *Relational Autonomy and Family Law*, Springer, Cham 2014, pp. 11–33; S. Thompson, 'Feminist Relational Contract Theory: A New Model for Family Property Agreements' (2018) 45(4) *Journal of Law and Society* 626–27; for an insightful overview on the debates on relational autonomy see, e.g., the contributions in C. Mackenzie and N. Stoljar Natalie (eds), *Relational Autonomy. Feminist Perspectives on Autonomy, Agency, and the Social Self*, Oxford University Press, New York and Oxford 2000.

others. The 'other' not only limits the scope and degree of one's own autonomy but is also a precondition for its expression. This assumption remains constant as long as people are living interdependently within societies and are not atomized. Relational obligations need to be considered, as should be interpersonal power relations and the spheres of individual autonomy. Herring, for example, proposes focusing on the spheres of autonomy that remain after having considered all relational obligations.[4]

Of special interest are analyses of party agreements, which the legal discourse has discussed under Relational Contract Theory (RCT) – an umbrella term that emphasizes the context of an agreement 'by looking first to the relationship between the parties before looking at the transaction'.[5] Feminist Relational Contract Theory (FRCT)[6] furthermore addresses the potential for gendered power relations[7] and often understands family itself as 'a stabilizing force for structural inequality'.[8] As a result, power relations are thought to reproduce or reinforce themselves within contracts between (former) spouses, presumably affecting the degree of autonomous decision-making.[9] Therefore, the context of an agreement – for example, the reasons why a contract was entered into – once more bears consideration in order to ascertain the extent of autonomous decision-making by the contracting parties.[10] Here, what is known as a 'dilemma of choice' gains in relevance: how can anyone be protected 'from oppressive consequences of harmful, constrained choices ... without divesting [this person] of agency'?[11]

> FRCT does not view choice simply as saying 'yes' or 'no' to a bad agreement and argues instead that it is possible to follow a third route: negotiating an agreement that is beneficial for both parties. And so, whilst an orthodox approach might view signing a bad agreement as an irrational choice, FRCT can see that *for that individual*, signing might have been the most rational thing to do in the circumstances.[12]

This chapter focuses on selected statutes on spousal divorce agreements (section 3.4.). An analysis of concrete agreements would have to be conducted on an empirical level, which would go beyond the confines of this chapter.

---

4 J. Herring, above n. 3, p. 16.
5 S. Thompson, above n. 3, p. 628.
6 S. Thompson, above n. 3, pp. 617–45.
7 S. Thompson, above n. 3, p. 630.
8 S. Thompson, above n. 3, p. 622.
9 E.g., S. Thompson, above n. 3, pp. 623 and 642.
10 E.g., S. Thompson, above n. 3, p. 623.
11 G.K. Hadfield, 'An Expressive Theory of Contract: From Feminist Dilemmas to a Reconceptualization of Rational Choice in Contract Law' (1998) 146 *University of Pennsylvania Law Review* 1236 f.
12 S. Thompson, above n. 3, p. 633.

3. COMPARISON OF SELECTED REGULATIONS WITHIN THE GERMAN-SPEAKING LEGAL FAMILIY

This chapter will focus on the German-speaking legal family, i.e., on the jurisdictions of Austria, Germany, Liechtenstein and Switzerland, as well as on the CEFL Principles, as the CEFL (Commission on European Family Law) started its principles series with the 'Principles of European Family Law regarding Divorce and Maintenance between Former Spouses' in November 2004.[13]

3.1. POST-DIVORCE SPOUSAL MAINTENANCE

3.1.1. Regulations on Post-Divorce Spousal Maintenance

According to principle 2:2 CEFL, 'each spouse should provide for his or her own support after divorce'. The self-sufficiency principle is one of the core principles of the CEFL. It is also found right at the beginning of the regulations on post-divorce spousal maintenance in Austrian, German, Liechtenstein and Swiss law (§66 Austrian Marriage Act = AMA; §§1569, 1577 German Civil Code = GCC; Art. 68 Lichtenstein Marriage Act = LMA; Art. 125 para. 1 Swiss Civil Code = SCC). The German Matrimonial Law Reform of 2008 explicitly added, in §1574 para. 1 GCC, the obligation to earn one's own living.[14] Furthermore, in §1578b GCC the reform introduced potential reductions in the amount of maintenance and time limits to the entitlement to maintenance on grounds of equity.[15] In general, a tendency to reduce post-divorce maintenance obligations with respect to amount and duration can be observed in Germany.[16] The Liechtenstein regulations on post-divorce spousal maintenance were based on the Swiss regulations.[17] In German, Swiss and Liechtenstein law, a lack of capacity for self-sufficiency is a strict prerequisite for any post-divorce maintenance. In Austrian law (§§66–69b AMA), various grounds for post-divorce maintenance exist.

In German law, marital responsibility and solidarity (§1353 para. 2 GCC) may apply beyond divorce[18] if a former spouse is not able to provide for

---

13 See <https://www.larcier-intersentia.com/en/principles-european-family-law-regarding-divorce-maintenance-former-spouses-9789050954266.html> accessed 16.05.2023.

14 See M. Ivo, 'Deutschland' in R. Süß and G. Ring (eds), *Eherecht in Europa mit Eingetragene Lebenspartnerschaft und Adoption*, zerb verlag, Bonn 2021, pp. 479–515 n. 84; N. Dethloff, D. Martiny and M. Maurer, 'Update Germany. February 2021', <https://ceflonline.net/wp-content/uploads/Germany-Dethloff-Martiny.pdf> accessed 15.05.2023, p. 2.

15 E.g., N. Dethloff, D. Martiny and M. Maurer, above n. 14, p. 2.

16 See M. Ivo, above n. 14, pp. 479–515 n. 84.

17 Art. 68 para. 1 LCL requires the spouse demanding post-divorce maintenance to realize his or her assets. There is also an additional paragraph in the LCL (para. 3 leg. cit.) compared to the Swiss regulation.

18 See M. Ivo, above n. 14, pp. 479–515 n. 83.

him- or herself and one of the maintenance grounds is fulfilled. This requires the impossibility or unreasonableness of self-sufficiency (§1570 GCC due to child care; §1571 GCC due to age; §1572 GCC due to illness or afflictions; §§1573, 1576 GCC due to unemployment or underemployment, §1575 GCC due to occupational training) and the other spouse's ability to afford post-divorce maintenance (§1581 GCC).

The Austrian regulations differentiate degrees of fault and grounds for divorce and are therefore hard to compare with the other jurisdictions' regulations. In Swiss, Liechtenstein and German law, maintenance is determined irrespective of fault,[19] the reasons for divorce, or the type of divorce.[20]

In all four jurisdictions, courts may completely deny, limit or reduce maintenance (§§73 f. AMA; §§1578b, 1579 GCC, Art. 68, 71, 72 para. 4 LMA; Art. 125 para. 3 SCC). All the jurisdictions consider cases of obvious inequity (e.g., §68, §68a para. 3, 69 para. 2 AMA; §1579 GCC; Art. 68 para. 4 LMA; Art. 125 para. 3 SCC).

Monthly in-advance maintenance payments are the model solution in all jurisdictions analysed (§70 para. 1 AMA; §1585 para. 1 GCC; Art. 69 para. 1 LMA; Art. 126 SCC). The beneficiary may demand a lump-sum settlement if there is good cause and the other spouse is not unreasonably burdened thereby (§70 para. 3 AMA; §1585 para. 2 GCC; Art. 69 para. 2 LMA; Art. 126 para. 2 SCC). Under Austrian jurisdiction, a lump-sum settlement may stand in the way of payment of a public widow's or widower's pension after a divorce.[21]

3.1.2. *Some Reflections on the Emancipatory Potential of the Regulations*

A good starting point of analysis is the self-sufficiency principle. Outside the broader context of a society's other social norms (e.g., gendered division of the labour market, social welfare system and distribution of income and wealth), self-sufficiency appears to be the perfect expression of individual autonomy as each individual is responsible for providing for him- or herself. Relational aspects or solidarity among the members of a society, especially with care workers, is ignored.[22] From an abstract perspective, the principle of self-sufficiency after divorce seems likely to discourage people from entering marriages primarily for the purpose of being economically well-provided for during the marriage.

---

19 For Switzerland H. Hausheer and S. Wolf, 'Grounds for divorce and maintenance between former spouses – Switzerland. September 2002', <https://ceflonline.net/wp-content/uploads/Switzerland-Divorce.pdf> accessed 15.05.2023, pp. 24, 26.

20 For Switzerland H. Hausheer and S. Wolf, above n. 19, p. 24.

21 E.g., S. Ferrari and M. Koch-Hipp, 'Österreich' in R. Süß and G. Ring (eds), *Eherecht in Europa mit Eingetragene Lebenspartnerschaft und Adoption*, zerb verlag, Bonn 2021, pp. 935–1006, at pp. 990 f n. 204.

22 See the fundamental critique on the self-sufficiency assumption M. Fineman, *The Autonomy Myth. A Theory of Dependency*, The New Press, New York and London 2004, p. 21.

Self-sufficiency might have a positive effect on the gendered division of labour and might help achieve equal pay. This will take time, and many couples will opt out via post-maintenance agreements (see sections 3.4.1. and 3.4.2.). In the short term, if the self-sufficiency principle were to be fully realized, a partner who primarily conducted care work[23] in the partnership and did not earn an income on the labour market would have to bear the cost. Due to the gendered division of labour, in a marriage between a male and female partner this would (still) very likely be the female partner.

Rules that soften the principle will support the autonomy of the partner who receives post-marital maintenance in the short term, but in the long term such rules undermine the advantages of the self-sufficiency principle. They reinforce the other spouse's responsibility for providing maintenance to the former family and thus take responsibility away from the community.

All four jurisdictions provide regulations on post-spousal maintenance to secure the needs of the dependent spouse. An unconditional basic income for all would enhance everyone's spheres of autonomy in a society and would do a better and faster job overcoming the gendered division of labour. Or, as Fineman has put it:

> Autonomy is only possible when one is in a position to be able to share in society's benefits and burdens. And sharing in benefits and burdens can only occur when individuals have the basic resources that enable them to act in ways that are consistent with the tasks and expectations imposed upon them by the society in which they live.[24]

Compared to a lump sum settlement, the model solution of monthly maintenance payments in these legal provisions hinders a clean break of the relationship as the former spouses remain in a legal relationship with each other. A clean break would enhance both former spouses' chances of getting a fresh start and of overcoming the psychological effects of the breakdown of the marriage. De Vaus et al. for example found that women's labour market earnings after divorce differed according to the extent to which re-partnering occurred.[25] Against this background, it is not only the model solution of monthly maintenance payments that has to be viewed critically. Especially the Austrian regulations, according to which a lump-sum settlement may negate the public widow's and widower's pension entitlement, also appear to be an obstacle to autonomy and emancipation. Once more, solidarity and the other spouse's responsibility for providing maintenance is placed within the private sphere of the family rather

---

[23] 'Care work' includes taking care of children, elderly and those who need support as well as taking care of the household. See, e.g., J. Herring, *Caring and the Law*, Bloomsbury Publishing, Oxford 2013.

[24] M. Fineman, above n. 22, p. 29.

[25] D. de Vaus, M. Gray, L. Qu and D. Stanton, 'The economic consequences of divorce in six OECD countries' (2017) 52(2) *Australian Journal of Social Issues* 180.

than in the public or shared sphere. Only in the aforementioned cases, of denied or restricted maintenance obligations, does the responsibility to provide for a former spouse cease and the former spouse depend on maintenance provided by the welfare state according to the rules of social security law.

3.2. REGULATIONS ON MATRIMONIAL PROPERTY: THE MARITAL HOME

In all four jurisdictions, the division of matrimonial property depends on the matrimonial property regime and on any contractual modifications made during marriage or in a divorce agreement. Once again, in Austria the determination of fault for divorce also plays a minor role when it comes to the division of marital property (§83 para. 1 AMA). Due to the limits on space, this chapter focuses on a topic of utmost day-to-day relevance for former spouses: the provisions regarding the marital home. As the partition of pension rights is also of great importance for elderly spouses, and since the legal categorization of such rights varies – whether as part of maintenance or as part of matrimonial property or as something in between – some brief remarks are made on this topic in section 3.3.

3.2.1. Regulations on the Marital Home

All four of the analysed jurisdictions have special provisions dealing with the marital home (e.g., §§82 para. 2, 87, 88 AMA; adopted by Art. 75 para. 2, 81, 82 LMA; §1568a GCC; Art. 121 SCC), and all have provisions to protect a spouse who is dependent on the marital home irrespective of the legal status or ownership of the marital home.

The provisions in Liechtenstein law were based on the Austrian Marriage Act. In Austrian and Liechtenstein law, the marital home is in general considered to be part of the marital property (§81 para. 2 AMA; Art. 73, 75 para. 2, 81 f. LMA). A marital home that one spouse has brought into the marriage or acquired by inheritance or that has been gifted to him or her by a third party is only included in the division of marital property if this has been explicitly agreed upon; if the other spouse is dependent on its continued use to secure the necessities of life; or if a joint child has a need for its continued use (§82 para. 2 AMA; Art. 75 para. 2 LMA). In a case where the marital home is part of the division of marital property, the court may assign rights and obligations to one spouse under a tenancy agreement or even reallocate ownership of it or grant a temporary right of residence under present conditions and in return for appropriate compensation (§87 AMA; Art. 81 LMA). If the marital home is used on the basis of an employment relationship or a spouse's legal relationship to the marital home is established in connection with an employment relationship, the court may only make an order regarding the use of such a home with the consent of the employer or the legal entity responsible under the provisions of §88 AMA, Art. 82 LMA.

In Swiss law, there are different regulations on the marital home according to the particular matrimonial property regime in question. A spouse who depends on the marital home is always protected: if a former spouse is dependent on the family home because of children or for other important reasons, the Swiss court may assign rights and obligations under a tenancy agreement to that person alone provided this can reasonably be imposed on the other spouse (Art. 121 para. 1 SCC). The court has broad discretion in this respect.[26] If the family home belongs to one spouse, the court may grant the other spouse a temporary right of residence under existing conditions in return for appropriate compensation or by charging it against maintenance contributions. Again, the court here has broad discretion. A spouse's right to the use of the residence can be restricted or revoked by the court (Art. 121 para. 3 SCC). If the family home belongs to both spouses, the court can assign the property to the spouse more in need of it (Art. 205 para. 2, 245, 251 SCC). If the spouses did not share the matrimonial property during the marriage, a former spouse who did not own the home they lived in during the marriage may also request that ownership thereof to be allocated to him or her, and a usufruct or right of residence may also be granted by the court instead. In any case, the spouse seeking such a determination needs to prove an overriding interest in the reallocation, usufruct or right of residence (see Art. 244 SCC) and has to compensate the other as well.

In German law, too, §1568a GCC protects the spouse who is more dependent on the marital home; he or she may even demand that the other spouse surrender the matrimonial home. Among the equitable factors to be considered is the welfare of any children living in the household and the spouses' living conditions.[27] A spouse may only demand a transfer of rights (irrespective of the nature of such rights or their connection with an employment relationship) if it is necessary to avoid undue hardship. The (new) landlord may demand an appropriate rent as well as a reasonable fixed term for the tenancy. German courts only decide on an allocation of the marital home upon the request of one spouse (§203 para. 1 Act on Proceedings in Family Matters and in Matters of Non-contentious Jurisdiction = FamFG).

3.2.2. *Some Reflections on the Emancipatory Potential of the Regulations*

The regulations on the marital home address a few aspects of the relational autonomy concept by considering the needs and welfare of joint children.

---

[26] E.g., S. Wolf and Y. Minning, *Familienrecht*, Helbing Lichtenhahn Verlag, Basel 2021, pp. 84–85.

[27] E.g., M. Wellenhofer, '§1568a BGB' in MüKoBGB, 9th Edition, C.H. Beck, München 2022, m. 21.

However, the immense power of the courts to reallocate ownership and other rights in the marital home interferes with the autonomous individual property rights of the formerly entitled spouse. While this might be understood as an expression of post-marital solidarity, the public sphere is nevertheless relieved of the burden of providing affordable housing, and the burden is again consigned to the private sphere. If there is a tenancy agreement or a usufruct, a clean break between the spouses is postponed, and the former spouses remain in a legal relationship with each other. This might create emotional costs on both sides. On one hand, the spouse who depends on the marital home is protected with respect to his or her basic need for housing. But on the other hand, that person is (re)construed as needy, which might come at an emotional cost and pose a barrier to emancipation.[28] Affordable housing provided by the public hand would enhance everyone's sphere of autonomy within a society.

3.3. BRIEF REMARKS ON POST-DIVORCE PENSION RIGHTS

3.3.1. *Regulations on Post-Divorce Pension Rights*

The division of pension benefits is of immense importance for the former spouses' future spheres of autonomy, especially when one bears in mind the high level of poverty among the elderly, particularly among elderly women.[29] The four jurisdictions' national pension systems differ significantly, although Austria, Germany and Switzerland in theory all have the same kind of three-pillar pension system – 1. a public insurance pension; 2. a professional pension; and 3. a voluntary pension.

In Swiss law, provision for an adequate pension is considered to be an aspect of maintenance. The provisions under Liechtenstein law were based on Swiss law.

In the event of divorce under the Swiss pension system,[30] a public insurance pension is divided between the spouses according to binding provisions of insurance law (see Art. 29bis, 29quinquines para. 3 lit. c, 29sexies para. 3, 29septies para. 6 Federal law on old-age and survivors' insurance = AHVG). A professional pension is divided by the court according to the rules set out in Art. 122–124e SCC in what is known as 'pension equalization' (= Vorsorgeausgleich).

---

[28] See discussion of the 'dilemma of difference', e.g., M. Sagmeister, *Der arbeitsrechtliche Schutz von Eltern zwischen Gleichheit und Autonomie. Wie das Recht zu einer gerechteren Verteilung unbezahlter Sorgearbeit zwischen Männern und Frauen beitragen kann*, Verlag Österreich, Wien 2021, pp. 153–58.

[29] See, e.g., L. Richter, 'Altersarmut in Zahlen', <https://www.altarmweiblich.at/unit/aaw/altersarmutinzahlen> accessed 15.05.2023.

[30] E.g., S. Wolf and Y. Minning, above n. 26, pp. 86–92.

The spouses may themselves determine the division of the professional pension within a divorce agreement as long as an adequate pension remains guaranteed for both (Art. 124b para. 1 SCC) and their determination wins court approval according to Art. 280 para. 1 Swiss Civil Procedure = SCP. The court examines whether the agreement is contrary to law. A voluntary pension is divided according to the same rules as other marital property.

Since 1977, German law has provided for the equalization of pension rights under a separate statute, the Versorgungsausgleichsgesetz (Pension Equalization Act = GPEA).[31] The equalization of pension rights is not linked to the matrimonial property regime, post-divorce maintenance or the need or capacity of the former spouses.[32] Irrespective of their nature, all forms of pension rights acquired during marriage are to be divided, in principle 50:50, according to the provisions of the GPEA.[33] Only if the marriage lasted less than three years is a request by one spouse needed to initiate an equalization of pension rights, and the spouses can grant partial or complete waivers in the form of explicit spousal or divorce agreements subject to the court's review (§8 GPEA; see further sections 3.4.3. and 3.4.4.).[34]

In Austria, matrimonial property and matrimonial savings are subject to division upon the request of either spouse within one year of divorce (§§82, 95 AMA). Matrimonial property is everything that was used by both spouses during their ongoing marital partnership. Matrimonial savings are all kinds of assets, including savings, that were accumulated during their ongoing marital partnership and which, by their nature, are normally intended for usage by the spouses. A very important consequence of that definition is that pension rights – whatever their nature – are not divided between the spouses in Austria even if they are guaranteed by foreign law in another country.[35]

Instead of pension splitting, Austrian public insurance law grants a widow's or widower's pension to a former spouse under certain circumstances even after divorce:[36] if the marriage lasted at least 10 years and maintenance was in fact paid; or, if the divorce was granted without the fault of, and against the will of, the surviving former spouse, the marriage lasted more than 15 years, and the surviving former spouse was older than 40 at the time of the divorce, was incapable of work, or had to take care of a child on the child's orphan's pension

31 See M. Ivo, above n. 14, pp. 504 f. n. 90–95.

32 See M. Ivo, above n. 14, p. 504 n. 90.

33 The details of calculation are highly debated and the 50/50 principle sounds easier than the handling in fact is. See, e.g., W. Schwamb, '3.Teil. A.' in H. Göppinger and I. Rakete-Dombek (eds), *Vereinbarungen anlässlich der Ehescheidung*, 11th Edition, C.H. Beck, München 2018, <http://beck-online.de>, accessed on 31.07.2023; BGH 22.07.2015, IV ZR 437/14, NJW 205, 3306.

34 See M. Ivo, above n. 14, p. 506 n. 100.

35 E.g., OGH 14.12.2021, 1 Ob 190/21d.

36 See S. Ferrari and M. Koch-Hipp, above n. 21, pp. 989 f. n. 200 ff.

(§264 para. 10, 258 para. 4 Austrian General Social Security Act = ASVG). Only Germany lacks a comparable public widow's or widower's pension after divorce, though it does provide one for public servants;[37] Switzerland, too, provides one.[38] The public widow's or widower's pension in Austria cannot be regarded as adequate compensation for the lack of pension-splitting provisions.

3.3.2. *Some Reflections on the Emancipatory Potential of the Regulations*

Let us revisit the emancipatory potential of pension splitting. Because it considers more than just the needs of the person who made the pension insurance contributions, the splitting of pension rights might be understood as respectful of certain aspects of relational autonomy. And in any case, instead of an individual approach that considers individual needs and capacities, a 50:50 division is suited to a formal equality and equity approach. A provision like Art. 124b para. 2 SCC, which takes into account the economic situation of the spouses after divorce as well as their needs specifically in regard to their potential future capacity for self-sufficiency, seems preferable.

The effect of pension splitting on the spouses' reasons for entering a marriage needs further empirical investigation, as do the restricted options within the three jurisdictions for opting in or out (see section 3.4. for details on spousal divorce agreements).

Furthermore, a comparison of the gendered poverty rates among the elderly in the analysed jurisdictions (and beyond) might help to understand the impact of family law. Pension splitting might have a long-term effect on the gendered division of labour and equal pay, because once the spouses have retired, splitting pensions 50:50 leads to an equal distribution of income in this respect. But on the other hand pension splitting might be accompanied by the risk of not achieving equal pay before retirement and reinforcing the gendered division of labour reflected in the gender pay gap.

3.4. SPOUSAL DIVORCE AGREEMENTS

This chapter focuses on selected divorce agreement options in the four jurisdictions. Due to the limited space available in this chapter, the sample is based on the everyday relevance of these options for the (former) spouses, and thus this chapter covers agreements on post-divorce maintenance, pension equalization and the consensual divorce agreement.

---

37 See M. Ivo, above n. 14, p. 516 n. 100.

38 See S. Wolf and B. Spichinger, 'Schweiz' in G. Süß and G. Ring (eds), *Eherecht in Europa mit Eingetragene Lebenspartnerschaft und Adoption*, zerb verlag, Bonn 2021, pp. 1217–73, at p. 1258 n. 122.

3.4.1. *Spousal Agreements on Post-Divorce Maintenance*

The spouses may settle an agreement on post-divorce maintenance, including partial or complete maintenance waivers, in all four jurisdictions (§55a AMA, §80 AMA; Art. 282 SCP; Art. 67 para. 1 LMA; §1585c GCC).

In Austria, the requirements for post-divorce maintenance agreements differ according to the grounds for divorce (see also section 3.4.5. on consensual divorce). For non-consensual divorce, there are no formal requirements and no restrictions on when the agreement can be settled, and this also applies to (complete) waivers.[39] Agreements may be scrutinized by the court ex-post under the same conditions as other contracts under Austrian law (e.g., lack of free consent, contractual incapacity, fraud, simulated transaction, immorality). An agreement concluded before the divorce decree became final is not null and void merely because it facilitated or enabled the divorce; however, it is null and void if the spouses asserted a ground for divorce that did not exist or no longer existed, or if it otherwise appears from the content of the agreement or from other circumstances of the case that the agreement is contrary to morality (§80 AMA). Cases dealing with post-divorce agreements before the Austrian Civil High Court are very rare unless they deal with post-divorce agreements necessary for the joint divorce (see section 3.4.5.). In general, it is considered a violation of good morals if the obligor's income is grossly disproportionate to the agreed amount of maintenance; the obligor's subsistence is endangered by the maintenance payment; the agreement was concluded only with the intention of passing on the maintenance obligation to third parties; or, irrespective of cases of severe need, if a waiver includes a rebus sic stantibus clause.[40]

Under German jurisdiction, a waiver requires that the parties be completely informed about its legal consequences; and all agreements on post-divorce maintenance require either certification by a public notary (§1585c GCC) or recording of the declarations in a court protocol (§1585c, §127a GCC).[41] The agreements may be reviewed by the court for conformity with the general requirements for contracts, including compliance with good morals (§138 GCC).[42]

The Swiss procedural provision, Art. 282 SCP, prescribes a specific minimum content for the agreement. The spouses have to state 1. the assumed income and

39 E.g., S. Ferrari and M. Koch-Hipp, above n. 21, p. 985 n. 186.

40 E.g., S. Ferrari and M. Koch-Hipp, above n. 21, pp. 985f. n. 187 f. B. A. Koch, '§80 EheG' in KBB, 6th Edition, Verlag Österreich, Wien 2020, p. 2126 m. 4; OGH 24.11.1999, 3 Ob 229/98t, JBl 2000, 512 (F. Bydlinski); OGH 29.08.2001, 3 Ob 39/01h; OGH 18.10.2016, 3 Ob 136/16w.

41 E.g., N. Dethloff and D. Martiny and M. Maurer, above n. 14, p. 2.

42 See M. Ivo, above n. 14, pp. 507–509 n. 115, 107–11.

assets of each spouse; 2. the amount of maintenance for the spouse and for each child; 3. if the right to seek subsequent maintenance increases has been reserved, the amount necessary to assure proper maintenance of the entitled spouse; 4. whether and to what extent the payment rate is to be adjusted to changes in the cost of living.

The spouses may further agree to not, or to only partly, modify the regular payments or to restrict the circumstances for their modification (Art. 127 SCC; Art. 70 para. 4 LMA). This agreement falls under the rebus sic stantibus clause of Art. 2 SCC and the excessive binding restrictions of Art. 27 para. 2 SCC.[43] Under both Swiss and Liechtenstein jurisdiction, post-divorce maintenance agreements need court approval to be effective (Art. 67 para. 1 LMA; Art. 279 SCP).

3.4.2. *Some Reflections on the Emancipatory Potential of Agreements on Post-Divorce Maintenance*

The above-mentioned considerations (section 3.1.2.) on the emancipatory potential of the post-maintenance regulations, as well as the critique of the division of responsibilities between the private and public spheres, also apply to the kinds of agreements analysed in this chapter. The following considerations complement those discussed above.

The regulations on formal and substantive review that aim at securing the informed consent of both spouses may be considered to be supportive of relational autonomy. But conversely the Austrian regulation, which does not impose any formal requirements, is a realization of the concept of individual autonomy. According to §80 AMA, the fact that an agreement facilitated or enabled a divorce would violate the concept of relational autonomy unless the courts consider the specific circumstances, including any imbalance of power between the spouses. Such considerations may be part of the court's review of the agreement for immorality.

In general, ex-ante review and (legal) advice mechanisms (e.g., via mandatory court approval) are preferable to ex-post substantial control mechanisms alone because ex-post review can nullify agreements *ex tunc*, which means legal uncertainty for both parties.

When review of agreements by the courts corresponds with the general standards for contract review, it means that the statutes do not take the special situation of the spouses into account. Provisions aiming at the power relationship between the (former) spouses would better fit the concept of relational autonomy

43 See S. Wolf and B. Spichinger, above n. 38, p. 1262 n. 134.

and would support the courts in considering potential consent-influencing factors. The following four statements by German high courts may stand as models for how relational autonomy can be taken into account when reviewing spousal agreements ex post:

> The more directly the contractual waiver of statutory provisions interferes with the core area of the law governing the consequences of divorce, the heavier the burden on one spouse will be and the more closely the interests of the other spouse will need to be examined.[44]
>
> [W]hen it is evident that in a contractual relationship one partner has such weight that it can de facto unilaterally determine the content of the contract, it is the task of the law to work towards the preservation of the fundamental rights positions of both contracting parties in order to prevent self-determination from turning into external determination for one party to the contract ... The state must therefore set limits to the freedom of the spouses to shape marital relations and mutual rights and obligations by means of contracts where the contract is not an expression and result of equal partnership, but reflects a one-sided dominance of one spouse based on unequal bargaining positions.[45]
>
> A situation of inferiority is regularly to be assumed if an unmarried pregnant woman is faced with the alternative of either bearing responsibility and care for the expected child alone in the future or involving the child's father in this responsibility through marriage, albeit at the price of a matrimonial agreement to be concluded with him, which, however, places a heavy burden on her.[46]
>
> Whether the contractual agreements place a significantly greater burden on the woman than on the man also depends to a large extent on the family constellation the contracting partners are striving for and on which their contract is based. ... The more legal rights are waived or additional obligations are assumed in the marriage contract, the more this effect of unilateral disadvantage can increase.[47]

When we focus on the spouses, Art. 282 SCP, which lays down requirements for the content of agreements, may increase the spouses' awareness of and readiness to reflect on the aspects named in the statute. Such a provision may be interpreted as showing awareness of aspects of relational autonomy and could function as a role model for other statutes that would respect the special situation of spouses who plan to get a divorce.

---

44 BGH, 29.01.12014, XII ZB 303/13, m. 16; BGH 17.01.2018, XII ZB 20/17, m. 12; BGH 27.05.2020, XII ZB 447/19, m. 18.

45 BVerfG, 06.02.2001, 1 BvR 12/92, NJW 2001, p. 958. In this spirit also BVerfG, 29.03.2001, 1 BvR 1766/92, NJW 2001, p. 2248.

46 BVerfG, 06.02.2001, 1 BvR 12/92, NJW 2001, p. 958.

47 BVerfG, 06.02.2001, 1 BvR 12/92, NJW 2001, p. 959. In this spirit also BVerfG, 29.03.2001, 1 BvR 1766/92, NJW 2001, p. 2248.

3.4.3. *Spousal Agreements on Pension Equalization*

Spousal agreements on pension equalization can only be entered into in those jurisdictions where pension equalization exists; thus, considerations on this matter are out of the question in Austria.

In the Swiss and the Liechtenstein pension systems, only a professional pension may be subject to such an agreement, as the other statutes on pension equalization are of a binding nature.[48] According to Art. 124b para. 1 SCC, Art. 89c LMA, in a divorce agreement as part of the divorce proceedings the spouses my deviate from the 50:50 division of a professional pension or waive its equalization as long as adequate old-age and invalidity coverage remains guaranteed.[49] Such an agreement requires court approval according to Art. 280 para. 1 SCP, Art. 89e LMA, whereby the court examines whether the agreement is contrary to law.

As pension equalizations fall within the core legal consequences of divorce in Germany, they are only partially under the spouses' disposition.[50] Within strict boundaries (§§6-8 GPEA, §1408 para. 2 GCC; §§6, 8 GPEA)[51] the spouses may settle an agreement on a pension equalization; but they may not do so at the expense of third parties without their consent.[52] The agreement requires either certification by a public notary or recording of the settlement in a court protocol (§7 para. 1 GPEA; §§7 para. 3 GPEA, §1410 GCC). The formal requirements are strict, and their violation leads to the nullity of the agreement, as the formalities are to protect the spouses' free and informed consent.[53] According to §6 GPEA the spouses may agree, for example, to include or exclude pension equalization in their settlement of matrimonial property or to reserve compensation claims after divorce in accordance with §§20–24 GPEA. The binding force of the agreement on the family court is dealt with in §6 para. 2 GPEA. The court is bound by the agreement if there are no impediments to validity and enforcement.[54] This is an expression of the general principle that the court, on its own motion, must examine objections that could impede or destroy a right.[55] If the agreement is considered binding, the court must order that no equalization of pension rights

---

48 E.g., S. Wolf, 'Der Ehevertrag und insbesondere sein Inhalt in Deutschland, Österreich und der Schweiz – eine rechtsvergleichende Übersicht' in S. Laimer and C. Kronthaler and B. A. Koch (eds), *Europäische und internationale Dimensionen des Privatrechts. Festschrift für Andreas Schwartze*, Jan Sramek, Wien 2021, pp. 511–64, at p. 562.

49 See S. Wolf and B. Spichinger, above n. 38, p. 1262 n. 134.

50 E.g., BGH 27.05.2020, XII ZB 447/19, m. 22; W. Schwamb, above n. 33, 3.Teil B.2. b), m. 25.

51 Act on the structural reform of the pension equalization ('Gesetz zur Strukturreform des Versorgungsausgleichs'), German BGBl. 2009 I 700.

52 E.g., W. Schwamb, above n. 33, 3.Teil A., m. 11.

53 E.g., W. Schwamb, above n. 33, 3.Teil B.2., m. 19 f.

54 E.g., W. Schwamb, above n. 33, 3.Teil A., m. 1.

55 E.g., W. Schwamb, above n. 33, 3.Teil B.2., m. 16.

according to the provisions of the statutes will be conducted (§224 para. 3 FamFG).

The substance (Inhaltskontrolle) as well as the execution (Ausübungskontrolle) of pension equalization agreements is subject to court review (§8 para. 2, §6 para. 2 GPEA). The substantive review is the starting point for the court, and it leads to an analysis of whether the agreement adhered to the provisions of §138 GCC at the time it was entered into.[56] A complete waiver of pension equalization violates good morals (§138 GCC) if it leads to one spouse not having a sufficient old-age pension due to the division of care work versus paid work the parties had contemplated at the time the agreement was entered into. This also violates the requirements of marital solidarity.[57] Providing for compensation to secure the self-sufficiency of the spouse could remedy a violation of §138 GCC.[58] Review of the execution of an equalization agreement includes a comparison of the planned marital reality with the enacted one; the rebus sic stantibus clause may be considered inherent to an agreement on pension equalization.[59] The court may modify the agreement according to §242 GCC. The court may also consider whether there has been a cessation of the basis of the agreement (§313 GCC).[60]

And finally, under German jurisdiction the general principles established in the case law on divorce agreements apply to agreements on pension equalization as well.[61]

3.4.4. *Some Reflections on the Emancipatory Potential of Agreements on Pension Equalization*

The above-mentioned considerations (section 3.3.2.) on the emancipatory potential of regulations on post-divorce pension splitting, as well as the critique of the division of responsibility between the private and public sphere, also apply to agreements of the kind dealt within this chapter. The following thoughts should be seen complementary to those.

The availability of agreements of the type that this chapter introduces softens the critique that a regulation may respect neither individual needs nor the arrangements of family life, with its allocation of the burdens of care work versus paid work on the labour market. Regulations intended to secure a minimum old-age or invalidity pension pay due respect to the economic autonomy of the spouse but might have the above-described gendered effects.

---

56 E.g., W. Schwamb, above n. 33, 3.Teil.

57 E.g., BGH 27.05.2020, XII ZB 447/19, m. 23; BGH 18.03.2009, XII ZB 94/06; BGH 09.07.2008, XII ZR 6/07, BeckRS 2008, 20657.

58 E.g., BGH 29.01.2014, XII ZB 303/13, NJW 2014, 1101.

59 E.g., W. Schwamb, above n. 33, 3.Teil.

60 E.g., BGH, 27.02.2013, XII ZB 90/11, NJW 2013, 1359, m. 19.

61 See W. Schwamb, above n. 33, 3. Teil B.2. b), m. 26 ff.

The formal requirements secure the informed consent of the spouses. The ex-post review of an agreement could be seen as little conducive to legal certainty for the spouses. But considering the judicial standards for substantive review and monitoring of the agreement, one has to conclude that ex-post review secures to a certain extent the relational autonomy of the spouse who was in the less powerful position (see section 3.4.2.).

3.4.5. *Brief Remarks on Consensual Divorce or Divorce on Joint Request of the Spouses*

Under Austrian, Liechtenstein and Swiss jurisdiction as well as within the CEFL, a consensual divorce requires the parties to agree on certain legal consequences of the divorce (§55a para. 2 AMA;[62] Art. 111 SCC; Art. 50 LMA; Principle 1:6 (1)). Under German jurisdiction, the spouses have to declare in their joint petition for divorce whether they have agreed on the concerns of their minor children, post-divorce spousal maintenance, marital home and marital household goods (§133 para. 1 2. FamFG). Divorce agreements in the other jurisdictions have comparable requirements as to the concerns of any minor children (§55a para. 2 AMA; Art. 133 SCC; Art. 50 para. 2 LMA), post-divorce spousal maintenance (§55a para. 2 AMA; Art. 125 ff. SCC, Art. 282 SCP; Art. 50 para. 2 LMA) and the division of matrimonial property (§55a para. 2 AMA; Art. 204 ff. SCC, Art. 236 ff. SCC; Art. 50 para. 2 LMA) – including, under Swiss and Liechtenstein law, the marital home (Art. 121 SCC; Art. 50 para. 2 LMA) – as well as to the equalization of professional pension rights (Art. 111, 123 ff. SCC; Art. 50 para. 2 LMA). Under Austrian jurisdiction, no agreement is necessary on matters a court has already decided (§55a para. 3 AMA). If the spouses cannot reach an agreement or can reach only a partial agreement, the court may determine any unresolved matters (Principle 1:7 (3) CEFL; Art. 112 SCC,[63] Art. 286 SCP; Art. 51 para. 1 LMA) or lead the spouses to an agreement (§/Art. 95 para. 2 Austrian and Liechtenstein Non-Contentious Proceedings Act = AußerStrG).

In Switzerland and Liechtenstein, the court hears the spouses both separately and together (Art. 111 para. 1 SCC; Art. 50 para. 1 LMA) in order to ascertain that the agreement is based on the free will and mature considerations of both spouses (Art. 287 SCP, Art. 111 para. 2 SCC; Art. 50 para. 1, para 2. LMA, Art. 96 para. 1 Liechstenstein AußerStrG) and that the agreement is likely to be approved.[64] It will be approved if the court is convinced that the spouses have come to it of their own free will and after careful consideration, and that the

[62] See for details, e.g., M. Roth, 'Update – AUSTRIA. February 2021' <https://ceflonline.net/wp-content/uploads/Austria-Roth-.pdf> accessed 15.05.2023, p. 1.

[63] E.g., H. Hausheer and S. Wolf, above n. 19, pp. 8–9.

[64] See S. Wolf and B. Spichinger, above n. 38, p. 1247 n. 87.

agreement is clear, complete and not manifestly unreasonable (Art. 279 para. 1 SCP; Art. 50 para. 1, 2 LMA). 'In practice, because of the limited scope of control (sic), the court seldom interferes.'[65]

In Austria and Liechtenstein, both spouses have to appear in person before the court; otherwise, their joint petition for divorce is deemed withdrawn (§/Art 94 Austrian and Liechtenstein AußerStrG). If one of the spouses is not represented by an attorney in the divorce proceedings and has not been advised on all the consequences of divorce, including in social security law and as they pertain to the prerequisites of a decree of liability for loans, the court is to instruct said spouse on appropriate counselling and, in general, on the disadvantages that may result from insufficient knowledge of these consequences (§95 para. 1 Austrian AußerStrG; §/Art 95 para. 1 Liechtenstein AußerStrG).

In Austria, the court's review of the substance of the agreement is limited; only obvious violations of statutes or good morals lead to the court's rejection of the agreement.[66] Germany is comparable to Austria in that the court may review agreements for conformity with the general standards for contracts, especially for their observance of good morals.[67]

3.4.6. *Some Reflections on the Emancipatory Potential of Agreements for Consensual Divorce*

The general possibility of obtaining a divorce on the mere consent of the spouses respects their individual as well as their relational autonomy. Although German divorce law only recognizes divorce due to breakdown of the marriage, an irrefutable presumption of breakdown combined with a joint petition for divorce or a petition on consent of the other spouse (§§1565 f. GCC) leads to the same result. None of the four jurisdictions forces the spouses to stay married or fulfil any other ground for divorce, as was common in the past.[68]

That all four jurisdictions permit courts to determine any unresolved matters may also be seen as reducing barriers to obtaining a divorce and as respecting the spouses' individual and relational autonomy under the precondition that they do not want to stay married.

Similarly, provisions providing for divorce petitions to be deemed withdrawn can be interpreted as furthering relational autonomy, as under Austrian and

65 I. Schwenzer and A.-F. Bock, 'Property Relations – National Report: Switzerland. August 2008' <https://ceflonline.net/wp-content/uploads/Switzerland-Property.pdf> accessed 15.05.2023, p. 41.

66 See S. Ferrari and M. Koch-Hipp, above n. 21, p. 966 n. 113.

67 See M. Ivo, above n. 14, pp. 507–09 n. 115, 107–11.

68 For an overview dealing with the Austrian legal history see, e.g., U. Floßmann and H. Kalb and K. Neuwirth, *Österreichische Privatrechtsgeschichte*, 8th Edition, Verlag Österreich, Wien 2019, pp. 89 ff.

Liechtenstein jurisdiction it is very easy to withdraw the petition simply by not appearing before the court. An in-depth analysis of the individual reasons why parties do not show up would go a step further toward securing relational autonomy, as such reasons might lie in power inequalities within the relationship or in fear of the (legal) consequences of divorce. That the court has no duty to investigate the reasons is consistent with the approach of non-interference and of respecting the private sphere as protected under Art. 8 European Charter of Fundamental Rights.

Regulations that deal with a spouse who is not represented by an attorney might be interpreted as a means of guaranteeing that a minimum of legal advice is provided and of securing informed consent (and thereby also that spouse's individual autonomy).

The considerations on ex-ante and ex-post control of the agreements as well as on the formal requirements also apply to the agreements described within this chapter.

4. CONCLUSION

It is crucial to consider how family law should position itself on the question of solidarity: is solidarity internalized and consigned to the private sphere, or is there a focus on solidarity in relation to all of society, one aimed at avoiding 'losses due to marriage' that in reality are due not to marriage but to the gendered division of labour and the devaluation of care work both in and out of families? If family support obligations prevail over welfare state social benefits, the state reduces its own responsibility for providing sufficient care for its citizens. Post-divorce maintenance obligations not only support the entitled spouse but also conform with state austerity interests and might have a negative effect on both spouses' individual and relational spheres of autonomy. These thoughts apply also to the supply of affordable housing. A clean, complete dissolution of the former spouses' relationship is hindered as long as monthly payments are due. Lump-sum settlements would most easily facilitate a clean break between the former spouses.

Playing devil's advocate, one might suggest replacing all maintenance and pension-splitting regulations with an unconditional basic income financed though transfer payments (such as tax and social security). This might reduce conflicts within families as well as costs to the welfare system, and could also support a clean separation of the former spouses.

NEW MODELS FOR FAMILY SOLIDARITY BETWEEN UNMARRIED PARTNERS

Elise GOOSSENS

1. INTRODUCTION: COHABITATION SCHEMES AS APPROXIMATIONS OF MARRIAGE

Today, many Western jurisdictions have a specific legal scheme for unmarried cohabitation.[1] Such cohabitation schemes offer a framework for financial solidarity between people in an extramarital relationship. Cohabitation schemes can take various shapes. Some jurisdictions give unmarried cohabitants the option to formally register their relationship, hence transforming it into a

1 For an overview of the existing unmarried cohabitation schemes in the Western jurisdictions, see E. GOOSSENS, 'One Trend, a Patchwork of Laws. An Exploration of Why Cohabitation Law is so Different throughout the Western World' (2021) 35 *International Journal of Law, Policy and the Family* 1, doi: 10.1093/lawfam/ebaa017 and the references there.

'registered partnership'.[2] Other jurisdictions do not require a registration and simply apply a specific set of rules to all cohabiting couples that meet certain requirements ('default regimes').[3]

Interestingly, most of these cohabitation schemes are modelled after marriage. Both registered partnership schemes and default regimes primarily focus on 'marriage-like' relationships: stable, affectionate, committed relationships between two people. The legal effects of cohabitation schemes generally take marriage as a benchmark, too. When outlining the legal consequences that (should) ensue from unmarried cohabitation, legislators and judges often consider the similarities and differences between cohabitants and married couples, and then decide to what extent the legal consequences of marriage also apply to cohabitants.

This approximations-of-marriage-approach[4] to unmarried cohabitation has its merits. In particular, it treads on familiar legal ground, so that policy choices on cohabitation can relatively easily be transposed into law using the known rules of marriage. Furthermore, mirroring the rules on marriage might prove a good solution for those cohabitants whose relationship closely resembles traditional marriage (e.g., cohabitants in a long-term relationship with children).

At the same time, this approach lacks creativity. It is remarkable that legal schemes intended for people outside the marriage category still mimic marriage. In particular, the mould of marriage is too rigid to fit the needs of unconventional family formations (e.g., polyamorous families, multiple parent families, queer families etc.). Moreover, the approximations-of-marriage-approach sometimes also stands in the way of legal reforms advancing the status of cohabitations. It can lead legislators to conduct ideological discussions on the similarities between marriage and cohabitation, instead of focusing on the real-life needs of cohabitants.

In this chapter, two new models for family solidarity between partners that do not take marriage schemes as a benchmark will be explored. The focus is on private solidarity, i.e., solidarity between partners. Public solidarity (i.e., on behalf of the state) falls outside the scope of this chapter. The first model – the three-step solidarity ladder – deconstructs family solidarity into three rationales: needs, compensation and sharing. This model allows for a modulation of family solidarity according to the nature of the relationship and the partners' degree of commitment. The second model – a care-centred relationships law – completely

---

2 Hereto J.M. Scherpe and A. Hayward (eds), *The Future of Registered Partnerships*, Intersentia, Cambridge 2018.

3 Also called 'informal cohabitation' or 'de facto cohabitation'. Hereto J. Miles, 'Unmarried Cohabitation in a European Perspective' in J.M. Scherpe (ed.), *European Family Law volume III*, Edward Elgar, Cheltenham 2016, pp. 82–115 and J.M. Scherpe and A. Hayward (eds), *The Legal Status of De Facto Relationships*, Intersentia, Cambridge, forthcoming.

4 *Cf.* F. Swennen (ed.), *Contractualisation of Family Law – Global Perspectives*, Springer, Cham 2015, p. 26.

separates the financial solidarity between partners from their relationship and links it to an external element: childcare. The chapter draws from comparative law to demonstrate that these models are less detached from current law than one would think at first sight.

2. FIRST ALTERNATIVE MODEL: THE THREE-STEP SOLIDARITY LADDER

2.1. THE RATIONALES OF FAMILY SOLIDARITY: NEEDS, COMPENSATION AND SHARING

2.1.1. Conceptual Groundwork in the Case Law of the UK House of Lords

In order to envision an alternative model of family solidarity between partners, it is useful to first question the underlying assumption of solidarity itself. Why should (ex-) partners be expected to demonstrate financial solidarity towards each other at all? And if there is a case for financial solidarity between (ex-) partners, what are its contours?

The case law of the House of Lords in the UK offers guidance in this regard. In its landmark case of *Miller v. Miller, McFarlane v. McFarlane*, the House of Lords identified three rationales that guide a fair division of assets after divorce: 'needs', 'compensation' and '(equal) sharing'.[5]

According to the House of Lords, the most common rationale for financial redistribution is the obligation to meet the other partner's financial needs. Every marriage gives rise to a relationship of interdependence, especially with regard to the division of labour and household roles. Mutual dependence begets mutual obligations of support. When the marriage ends, fairness requires that the assets of the parties should be divided primarily so as to make provision for the parties' housing and financial needs. Usually, these needs are the consequence of the parties' relationship (e.g., related to care for children or other dependent relatives), but that is not always the case (e.g., needs arising from age or disability). In determining the parties' needs, one must take into account a wide range of matters such as their ages, their future earning capacities, the family's standard of living, and any disabilities.[6]

A second rationale is compensation for relationship-generated disadvantage. This is aimed at redressing any significant prospective economic disparity

5 *Miller v. Miller; McFarlane v. McFarlane* [2006] UKHL 24. For an analysis, see, e.g., E. Cooke, 'Miller/McFarlane: Law in Search of Discrimination' (2007) 19 *Child and Family Law Quarterly* 98 and M. Welstead, 'Miller v Miller; McFarlane v McFarlane [2004] UKHL 24' (2006) 18 *Denning Law Journal* 209.

6 *Miller v. Miller; McFarlane v. McFarlane* [2006] UKHL 24, paras [11] and [138].

between the parties arising from the way they conducted their marriage. For instance, the parties may have arranged their affairs in a way which has greatly advantaged the husband in terms of his earning capacity but left the wife severely handicapped so far as her own earning capacity is concerned.[7]

A third rationale is the equal sharing of the fruits of the matrimonial partnership. Marriage is now widely perceived as a partnership of equals. The parties commit themselves to sharing their lives. They live and work together. When their partnership ends, each spouse is entitled to an equal share of the assets of the partnership, unless there is a good reason to the contrary. The equal sharing of assets hence derives from the basic concept of equality permeating a marriage as understood today.[8]

These rationales for a fair distribution of assets were developed in the context of financial relief after divorce. So far, no similar reasoning has been applied to unmarried cohabitation. Nevertheless, this chapter argues that these rationales can be used more broadly to underpin financial solidarity between all partners. Many of the arguments advanced by the House of Lords transcend the specific context of marriage. Moreover, we find the same underlying rationales in the unmarried cohabitation schemes of other Western jurisdictions, as demonstrated in the next section.

2.1.2. Needs, Compensation and Sharing as the Common Core for Family Solidarity

The concepts of needs, compensation and sharing are not particular to the context of marriage in England and Wales. They also underlie marriage and unmarried cohabitation schemes in many other Western jurisdictions. It could even be argued that they reflect *common core* mechanisms by which Western jurisdictions deal with the adverse consequences of relationships.[9]

This does not mean that all three rationales – needs, compensation and sharing – are equally present in all Western cohabitation schemes. Most jurisdictions base their cohabitation scheme on one or two rationales. Which rationale features most prominently in cohabitation law differs from jurisdiction to jurisdiction.

The essence of the Swedish cohabitation law, for instance, lies in an equal division of the value of the so-called 'cohabitation property', i.e. the family home and joint household goods. This is a clear expression of the 'sharing' rationale. After the breakdown of the relationship, unmarried cohabitants in principle

---

7 ibid., paras 13 and 140.

8 ibid., paras 16 and 141.

9 W.M. Schrama, 'General lessons for Europe based on a comparison of the legal status of non-marital cohabitants in the Netherlands and Germany' in K. Boele-Woelki (ed.), *Common core and better law in European family law*, Intersentia, Cambridge 2005, pp. 257–81, at p. 270.

share equally in the value of the family home and household goods, in so far as these were intended for common use.[10] The shares can be adjusted if an equal division is deemed unreasonable considering the circumstances.[11]

Scottish cohabitation law, on the other hand, aims at redressing economic disadvantage suffered by a cohabitant due to unequal contributions during the relationship.[12] Upon separation, the partner that has suffered an economic disadvantage may petition the court to oblige the other partner to pay a compensation.[13] In evaluating both partners' contributions during the relationship, the court also takes indirect and non-financial contributions into account, including childcare or looking after the family home.[14] The Scottish emphasis on restoring economic disadvantage resulting from the relationship embodies the 'compensation' rationale.

Finally, Irish cohabitation law gives certain cohabitants[15] the possibility to apply for a property adjustment order, a compensatory maintenance order or a pension adjustment order, given that they are financially dependent on the other cohabitant as a result of the relationship.[16] The criterion of financial dependency has been criticized for being unclear.[17] The legislator's intention seems to be that the claimant must be in need of financial support for his or her maintenance as a result of the relationship or its termination.[18] This interpretation is in line with the Irish Law Reform Commission's report, which formed the basis for Ireland's cohabitation scheme. Indeed, the Law Reform Commission points out that the reform intended to provide a protective scheme for relationships 'in respect of which economic dependency existed and have resulted in some

---

10 Sambolag 2003:376. Hereto M. Jänterä-Jareborg, M. Brattström and L. Eriksson, 'National report: England and Wales' in Commission on European Family Law (ed.), *Informal Relationships*, 2015, pp. 1–49, at pp. 8–9 <http://ceflonline.net/wp-content/uploads/Sweden-IR.pdf> and G. Lind, 'The Development of Cohabitation and Cohabitation Law in the Nordic Countries' in J. Asland, M. Brattström, G. Lind, I. Lund-Andersen, A. Singer and T. Sverdrup, *Nordic Cohabitation Law*, Intersentia, Cambridge 2015, pp. 1–56, at p. 15.

11 G. Lind, above n 10, p. 15.

12 A. Barlow, 'Legislating for Cohabitation in Common Law Jurisdictions in Europe. Two Steps Forward and One Step Back?' in K. Boele-Woelki, N. Dethloff and W. Gebhart, *Family Law and Culture in Europe: Developments, Challenges and Opportunities*, Intersentia, Cambridge 2014, pp. 73–93, at p. 83.

13 Family Law (Scotland) Act 2006, s. 28.

14 Family Law (Scotland) Act 2006, s. 28(9).

15 The described court orders are only open to so-called 'qualified cohabitants'. These are cohabitants that were living together as a couple for a period of two years or more, in the case where they are the parents of one or more dependent children, and of five years or more, in any other case (section 172(5) Civil Partnership and Certain Rights and Obligations of Cohabitants Act 2010).

16 Sections 173, 174, 175 and 187 Civil Partnership and Certain Rights and Obligations of Cohabitants Act 2010 and A. Barlow, above n. 12, pp. 86–87.

17 J. Mee, 'Cohabitation law reform in Ireland' (2011) 23 *Child & Family Law Quarterly* 323, 333.

18 ibid., 334.

form of vulnerability on termination of the relationship'.[19] The use of financial dependency as a requirement for financial redress hence seems to reflect an underlying attachment to the rationale of 'needs'.

2.2. STRUCTURING FAMILY SOLIDARITY: FROM RATIONALES TO STEPS

The deconstruction of solidarity into three rationales offers a conceptual framework for modulating financial solidarity in relationships. The nature of the relationship and the partners' degree of commitment would then determine the extent of their financial solidarity. The more serious the relationship, the more solidarity should be provided for. Instead of being presented with a 'package deal', as is usually the case in existing cohabitation schemes, partners could tailor financial solidarity to their specific relationship. This also offers a solution for unconventional and/or more casual relationships.

By way of structuring these three rationales, a solidarity ladder with three steps, as shown in Figure 4.1, is proposed.[20] As a minimum, partners can be expected to contribute to the relationship. If the partners' contributions are out of balance and one partner has suffered an economic disadvantage as a result, this partner should be entitled to compensation at the end of the relationship. The rationale of 'compensation' is therefore at the bottom of the solidarity ladder and applies as a *minimum minimorum* for all relationships. 'Needs' is ranged one step higher in the solidarity ladder. If a partner has needs as a result of a relationship breakdown, that person should be entitled to a financial claim. At the top of the solidarity ladder is the most far-reaching rationale for solidarity: 'sharing', or a participation in the other partner's wealth creation.

Figure 1. The three-step solidarity ladder

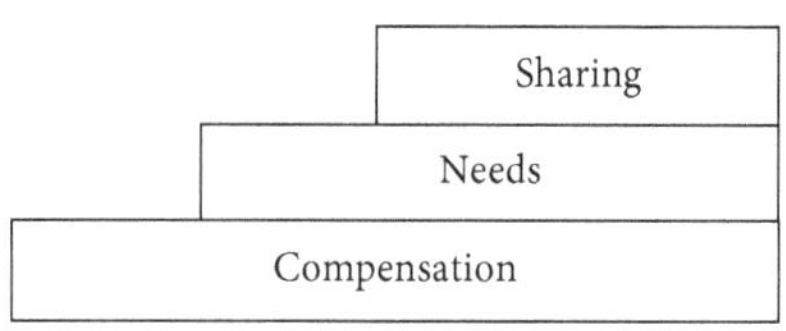

Source: Produced by the author.

---

19 The Law Reform Commission, *Report: Rights and Duties of Cohabitants*, 2006, p. 3 <https://www.lawreform.ie/_fileupload/Reports/R822006cohabitants.pdf> and B. Tobin, 'The Regulation of Cohabitation in Ireland: Achieving Equilibrium between Protection and Paternalism?' (2013) 35 *Journal of Social Welfare and Family Law* 279, 284ff, doi: 10.1080/09649069.2013.801681.

20 See also E. Goossens, 'Kompas voor een nieuw samenwoningsrecht: neutraal, coherent en compensatie- en behoeftegericht' (2019) *Tijdschrift voor Belgisch Burgerlijk Recht* 537, 555 and E. Goossens, 'Outside the box. Twee pistes voor een fundamentele herijking van het relatierecht' (2021) *Tijdschrift voor Familie- en Jeugdrecht* 86, 88.

The exact order of the steps is open to debate. In particular, one could question whether compensation or needs should be at the bottom of the solidarity ladder. The latter view seems to be more in line with the House of Lords' reasoning in *Miller v. Miller, McFarlane v. McFarlane*. Indeed, the House of Lords referred to needs as 'the most common rationale'[21] and pointed out that:

> In most cases the search for fairness largely begins and ends at this stage [needs]. In most cases the available assets are insufficient to provide adequately for the needs of two homes. The court seeks to stretch modest finite resources so far as possible to meet the parties' needs.[22]

Accordingly, UK courts will only consider the second (compensation) and third (sharing) rationale of fairness once needs have been met, namely when there is any excess income or capital.[23]

While these are convincing arguments, one should bear in mind that the *Miller v. Miller, McFarlane v. McFarlane* case dealt with financial relief after divorce. It is widely accepted that married partners are supposed to care for each other and look after each other's needs. Consequently, it is rather uncontroversial to envisage a temporary extension of this marital commitment vis-à-vis a former spouse as a basis for financial relief after divorce. By contrast, a similar duty of care is not so readily acknowledged for extramarital relationships, especially for unconventional or more casual family formations. Compensation might constitute a less controversial rationale here, because it is a more transactional concept that is less tied to a family context. Indeed, the idea that unequal contributions disadvantaging one of the parties must be compensated is also present in general law. Think for instance about the general legal concept of unjustified enrichment. Although its precise contours differ, the key idea is the same in nearly all Western jurisdictions: nobody should be unjustly enriched at another's expense.[24] The same key idea also underlies the 'compensation' rationale. 'Needs', on the other hand, implies a deeper commitment, specific to a more intimate personal relationship. Therefore, in this author's opinion compensation should be at the bottom of the family solidarity ladder.

---

21 *Miller v. Miller; McFarlane v. McFarlane* [2006] UKHL 24, para. [138].

22 ibid., para. [12].

23 M. Welstead, above n. 5, p. 214.

24 See extensively D. Johnston and R. Zimmermann (eds), *Unjustified Enrichment: Key Issues in Comparative Perspective*, Cambridge University Press, Cambridge 2002, 3ff. Unjustified enrichment also constitutes a separate book in the Draft Common Frame of Reference, an academic set of principles for European private law drafted by a group of legal scholars from different European Union Member States. See Book VII in C. von Bar, E. Clive and H. Schulte-Nölke (eds), *Principles, Definitions and Model Rules of European Private Law Draft Common Frame of Reference (DCFR)*, Sellier European Law Publishers, Munich 2009.

This view also seems to be in line with the position of the Commission on European Family Law (CEFL). In their recent Principles Regarding Property, Maintenance and Succession Rights of Couples in *de facto* Unions, the CEFL proposes a model for the harmonization of unmarried cohabitation in Europe.[25] The three rationales of family solidarity are also present in their model. Firstly, the Principles provide for financial compensation after a relationship breakdown for unequal contributions to the household or professional activities of the other partner.[26] Secondly, the Principles also stipulate a maintenance claim on behalf of the partner who has insufficient resources to meet his or her needs, but only in case of a cohabitation of at least five years or in case the partners have a common child.[27] Finally and by contrast, the Principles maintain a separation of assets when it comes to the division of the partners' property. There is no participation in the assets accumulated by the ex-partner.[28]

The CEFL Principles thus show the same hierarchy between the three rationales of financial solidarity. In the CEFL model, the rationale of compensation underpins financial solidarity for all cohabitants. Needs only create obligations for cohabitants who meet additional conditions. Conversely, a sharing of assets is not part of the default model and must be arranged conventionally.[29]

3. SECOND ALTERNATIVE MODEL: A CARE-CENTRED RELATIONSHIP LAW

3.1. INTRODUCING A CARE-CENTRED RELATIONSHIP LAW

A more radical approach would be to completely separate financial solidarity between partners from their relationship and to link it to an external element: childcare. This approach puts forward a care-centred relationship law,[30] in

---

25 K. Boele-Woelki, F. Ferrand, C. González-Beilfuss, M. Jänterä-Jareborg, N. Lowe, D. Martiny and V. Todorova, *Principles of European Family Law Regarding Property, Maintenance and Succession Rights of Couples in* de facto *Unions*, Intersentia, Cambridge 2019.

26 Principles 5:17 and 5:16.

27 Principle 5:20.

28 Principle 5:15. The competent authority may, however, grant one of the partners the continued use of the family home and household goods if the partners have been in an enduring relationship for at least five years or have a common child, who is either minor or is dependent upon them, and if this serves the interests of the family. See Principle 5:18(2).

29 *Cf.* principle 5:7.

30 Many authors have previously explored refocusing (family) law around the notion of care. See in particular J. Herring, *Caring and the Law*, Hart Publishing, Oxford 2013, p. 187ff and the literature on a feminist ethic of care, rooted in the work of C. Gilligan, *In a Different Voice*, Harvard University Press, Cambridge 1982. Specifically for a care-centred relationship law, see also W.M. Schrama, 'Een redelijk en billijk relatierecht' (2010) *Tijdschrift voor Privaatrecht* 1703, 1733.

which horizontal financial claims between partners stem from a vertical caring relationship between a parent and a child.[31]

The idea of a care-centred relationship law is inspired by Martha Fineman's work on dependency.[32] Fineman distinguishes two dimensions of dependency.[33] Inevitable dependency refers to persons who are intrinsically in need of care. This primarily concerns children, but vulnerable older persons and persons with a disability also belong to this category. Derivative dependency alludes to the dependency of the caretaker, who needs financial support to be able to care for children and other vulnerable persons. These two dimensions of dependency make it clear that care duties create a financial need not only on the part of those in need of care, but also on the part of those providing care. This insight provides the conceptual underpinning for a financial claim on behalf of the person providing care vis-à-vis the other partner.[34]

A care-centred relationship law takes a clear position on who is entitled to financial solidarity and why. By focusing on the financial implications of providing care, it offers a solution for those cases with perhaps the most pressing need for financial solidarity. Think of the hypothesis in which one partner cuts back on their own professional activities in order to take care of the children, allowing the other partner to invest more time in their career.[35] This risks putting the partner who provides care in a precarious economic position. Not only will they earn less money and accumulate fewer pension rights, but they

---

31 In a similar vein, M.H. Weiner proposes a parent-partner status for American family law, in which parenthood would trigger a (much larger) set of legal obligations between the parents. See M.H. Weiner, 'Family Law for the Future: An Introduction to Merle H. Weiner's *A Parent-Partner Status for American Family Law*' (2016) 50 *Family Law Quarterly* 327 and M.H. Weiner, *A Parent-Partner Status for American Family Law*, Cambridge University Press, Cambridge 2015.

32 Fineman theorized the notion of dependency in some of her earlier work (see in particular M.A. Fineman, *The Neutered Mother, the Sexual Family and Other Twentieth Century Tragedies*, Routledge, New York 1995). In her recent work, she has shifted the focus to vulnerability (following her seminal article M.A. Fineman, 'The Vulnerable Subject: Anchoring Equality in the Human Condition' (2008) 20 *Yale J.L. & Feminism* 1).

33 M.A. Fineman, *The Neutered Mother*, above n. 32, p. 8.

34 Although Fineman herself sees the financial support for care as a task for the state, not for family members (e.g., M.A. Fineman, 'Vulnerability and Inevitable Inequality' (2017) 4 *Oslo Law Review* 133, 138ff). For a European reflection on the responsibilities of the state and of family members in this regard, see H. Willekens, 'Ein Plädoyer für eine neue Ehe als kindbezogene Institution der sozialen Sicherung' in K. Scheiwe (ed.), *Soziale Sicherungsmodelle revisited. Existenzsicherung durch Sozial- und Familienrecht und ihre Geslechterdimensionen*, Nomos, Baden-Baden 2007, pp. 143–56.

35 This issue has a strong gender dimension. In practice, it is often the woman who starts working part-time if there are children. The gender dimension of caregiving has been amply recorded: see, e.g., for Belgium, A.L. Verbeke, E. Alofs, C. Defever and D. Mortelmans, 'Gender Inequalities and Family Solidarity in Times of Crisis' in L. Cornelis (ed.), *Finance and Law: Twins in Trouble*, Intersentia, Cambridge 2015, pp. 57–88, at pp. 59–66; for the United Kingdom J. Herring, above n. 30, p. 6; and for the United States <https://www.caregiver.org/resource/caregiver-statistics-demographics>.

will also have a flatter or interrupted career path, which will in turn affect future career prospects.[36] On the other hand, the other partner can have both children and a flourishing career thanks to their partner's efforts. Granting the caretaker a financial claim vis-à-vis the other partner would thus restore the balance, especially in the event of the relationship ending. Moreover, children also benefit from stable economic home situations with both parents after a break up of the relationship.[37]

3.2. CHILDCARE VS A BROADER NOTION OF CARE

As mentioned before, the model suggested in this chapter focuses on childcare as a prerequisite for financial solidarity. There are good reasons for a *primary* focus on the care for children as a basis for financial relief (as opposed to care in general). First, it is indisputable that having and raising children is the shared responsibility of both parents. Consequently, the financial burden of childcare must be shared equally among the parents. By contrast, it is less clear-cut that caring for an elder or disabled relative or friend of one partner is also the responsibility of the other partner to such an extent that it should give rise to a financial claim. Here one enters a grey zone, whereas with children the responsibilities are clearer. Secondly, taking care of children generally implies a substantial, time-consuming and long-lasting commitment, while other types of care come in many variations. Therefore, caring for children is a more obvious starting point for a financial claim than caring in general. Thirdly, having and raising children is an essential function of any society, necessary for its very existence.[38] Again, the societal relevance of childcare and the obvious role of families in this regard (as opposed to institutional care) justify a primary focus on the care for children.

However, an *exclusive* focus on the care for children is also problematic, especially from the perspective of unconventional families. The above-mentioned model works best for traditional families: partners who have and raise children together. In this case, a financial claim by the caregiver against the other partner can easily be justified, as they are both the parents of the children being cared for. Yet the situation of blended families, where one or both partners (also) have children from previous relationships, is very different. Against whom should the caregiver in such families make a financial claim: against the new partner or against the child's other parent? Moreover, a care-centred relationship

[36] See also A.L. Verbeke et al., above n. 35, p. 63.

[37] W.M. Schrama, 'Een redelijk en billijk relatierecht', above n. 30, p. 1734.

[38] H. Willekens, 'De liefde, het kind en de institutionalisering van persoonlijke relaties' in K. Raes (ed.), *Liefde's onrecht: het onmogelijke huwelijk tussen liefde en recht*, Mys and Breesch, Ghent 1998, pp. 1–37, at pp. 23–24.

law model geared towards childcare could be viewed as repronormative[39] and heteronormative.[40] Indeed, the model clearly privileges families with children and legitimizes childcare as the dominant (and only valid?) type of care. In that way, it inscribes itself in a societal model aimed at heterosexual families. This disadvantages queer families and other unconventional families, which can also take on major caregiving responsibilities outside a parental context.

3.3. INSPIRATION FROM QUEBEC: THE '*RÉGIME PARENTAL IMPÉRATIF*'

The idea of a care-centred relationship law model geared towards childcare has been further developed in Quebec. In 2015, the *Comité consultatif sur le droit de la famille* – a government-appointed committee composed of experts and representatives of the Ministry of Justice – presented its report on the reform of Quebec family law.[41] The current Quebec law on relationships is based on the formal status of the relationship. Married couples are subject to an extensive regime of rights and duties. In contrast, there is no special legal regime for unmarried cohabitants, whose rights and obligations are governed by general law. The *Comité consultatif sur le droit de la famille* proposed a radical reversal of the starting point. As soon as two people have a child together, the law would impose a number of obligations on them, regardless of the formal status of their relationship. Concretely, this '*régime parental impératif*' consists of three key components:[42]

- contribution to the family expenses, either in cash or in kind;
- protection of the family home;
- introduction of a new compensation mechanism in favour of the partner who has suffered an economic disadvantage due to the care of the common child.

---

39 The expression of a normative societal preference for reproduction, externalized in cultural and financial benefits that encourage procreation. The term repronormativity was first introduced by K. Franke, 'Theorizing Yes: An Essay on Feminism, Law, and Desire' (2001) 101 *Columbia Law Review* 181.

40 A hegemonic system of norms, discourses, and practices that constructs heterosexuality as natural and superior to all other expressions of sexuality (B.A. Robinson, 'Heteronormativity and Homonormativity' in *The Wiley Blackwell Encyclopedia of Gender and Sexuality Studies*, John Wiley & Sons, Hoboken 2016, pp. 1–3, DOI: 10.1002/9781118663219.wbegss013). The term 'heteronormativity' was coined by L. Berlant and M. Warner, 'Sex in Public' in S. During (ed.), *The Cultural Studies Reader*, Routledge, London 1999, pp. 547–66, at p. 548.

41 Comité consultatif sur le droit de la famille (chaired by A. Roy), *Pour un droit de la famille adapté aux nouvelles réalités conjugales et familiales*, Ministère de la Justice du Québec, Quebec 2015, <https://www.justice.gouv.qc.ca/fileadmin/user_upload/contenu/documents/Fr__francais_/centredoc/rapports/couple-famille/droit_fam7juin2015.pdf>.

42 ibid., p. 72ff.

While some applauded the proposed focus on the common child, others criticized it for being 'severely underinclusive in the light of other situations that can engender asymmetrical familial investment and consequent vulnerability, such as blended families … and eldercare'.[43] This critique is in keeping with the arguments developed above against a care-centred relationship law focused exclusively on the care for children.

4. OPPORTUNITIES AND CHALLENGES FOR THE NEW MODELS

Both the three-step solidarity ladder and the care-centred relationship law model show that there are alternatives for the marriage centrism that still dominates Western relationship law. These alternative models have clear advantages compared to the current approximations-of-marriage approach to non-marital relationships (*supra*).

The three-step solidarity ladder allows for a modulation of financial solidarity in relationships, so that nature of the relationship and the partners' degree of commitment can determine the extent of their financial solidarity. This model would especially be beneficial for unconventional and/or more casual families, where financial solidarity could be limited to the first or the second step of the ladder. At the same time, nothing would change for the most committed relationships (such as marriage): they would be entitled to the most extensive financial solidarity.

The care-centred relationship law model, on the other hand, offers a solution for partners who cut back on their own professional activities in order to take care of the children, allowing the other partner to invest more time in their career. By focusing on childcare as the basis for a financial claim, this model restores the derivative dependency of the partner who cares for the children.

At the same time, both models need further elaboration before they can be implemented. The aim of this contribution was to give an impetus to move away from marriage centrism. Follow-up research is needed to further think through these models and to operationalize them.

For the three-step solidarity ladder, the main challenge is the definition and interrelation of the three rationales. What is considered 'compensation' and

---

43 R. Leckey, 'Cohabitation Law in Quebec: Confusing, Incoherent, and Unjust' (forthcoming) *Houston Journal of International Law*. See also S. Zaccour, 'All Families Are Equal, but Do Some Matter More than Others: How Gender, Poverty, and Domestic Violence Put Quebec's Family Law Reform to the Test' (2019) 32 *Canadian Journal of Family Law* 425.

what constitutes 'needs'? Where does one rationale end and the other begin?[44] Furthermore, one has to determine the threshold for the different steps. What criteria must be met in order to be entitled either to compensation, to the satisfaction of needs or to the sharing of assets? What types of relationships give rise to what degree of financial solidarity? Finally, it should be established whether the steps of financial solidarity apply either imperatively, or by default with the possibility to opt out, or whether they require an opt in.[45]

The care-centred relationship law model comes with a number of fundamental open questions. The first key question was already pointed out above: should a care-centred relationship law be geared exclusively towards childcare, or be opened to other types of care? In order to include unconventional families, a broader notion of care seems appropriate. However, that approach could also call the whole model into question. Indeed, one may well question whether caring for an elder or disabled relative or friend is a shared responsibility of both partners, to such an extent that this care should give rise to a financial claim by the carer against the other partner. Secondly, it is not always easy to operationalize childcare (let alone other types of care). When are the care duties performed by the partners out of balance, so that the main carer is entitled to a financial claim? How can childcare be qualified and quantified in order to give rise to a financial claim?

Finally, the two models also face some common challenges. Since both models rely on open norms (compensation, needs, sharing, care), a careful definition of these norms is needed to avoid overburdening the court system. Moreover, there is the question as to how these models relate to marriage. For the sake of feasibility, one might consider implementing these models alongside marriage, and not instead of. In the three-step solidarity ladder model, marriage would then automatically give rise to the highest level of financial solidarity. In a care-centred relationship law, marriage could lead to an additional financial claim, next to the one resulting from childcare. The models would then form a safety net for non-marital relationships, rather than aiming for a radical overhaul of family law. An additional challenge are the cross-border implications of the new models. As a rule, private international law is centred around marriage, so these new models would also require a new framework in that regard.[46]

---

44 The UK House of Lords also outlined this difficulty in its *Miller v. Miller; McFarlane v. McFarlane* judgment. See *Miller v. Miller; McFarlane v. McFarlane* [2006] UKHL 24, e.g. para. [15].

45 Comp. F. Swennen, 'Un-Coupling Family Law: The Legal Recognition and Protection of Adult Unions Outside of Conjugal Coupledom' (2020) 28 *Feminist Legal Studies* 39, 54.

46 For an overview of the current private international law framework regarding marriage and extramarital relationships in the European Union, see W. Schrama, 'Empowering Private Autonomy as a Means to Navigate the Patchwork of EU Regulations on Family Law' in J.M. Scherpe and E. Bargelli (eds), *The Interaction between Family Law, Succession Law and Private International Law: Adapting to Change*, Intersentia, Cambridge 2021, pp. 35–57, at pp. 35–58.

5. CONCLUSION

Today, most cohabitation schemes in the Western jurisdictions are modelled after marriage. Discussions on a legal scheme for unmarried cohabitation are often limited to variations of greater or lesser equality with marriage. In this chapter, two models beside the beaten track were explored.

The first alternative model distinguishes three rationales of financial solidarity between partners and structures them into a three-step solidarity ladder, with compensation at the bottom, needs in the middle, and sharing at the top. The second alternative model – a care-centred relationship law – links the horizontal obligations between partners to the vertical caring relationship between a parent and a child.

These models offer the outlines of a new relationship law that moves away from marriage centrism. Examples from comparative law show that both models are less far-fetched than they may appear at first sight. Nevertheless, they certainly need to be developed further in order to be applied in current law. Some key questions for follow-up research have been identified in this chapter.

Finally, it should be pointed out that the models are not mutually exclusive. For example, the presence of children can be a factor in moving up the solidarity ladder. Likewise, the three rationales for financial solidarity can give substance to a care-centred relationship law, as was the case with the compensation rationale in the proposed reform in Quebec. Future reform projects may thus find inspiration in these models for a new approach to relationship law in general, and to unmarried cohabitation in particular.

PART II

CHILDBEARING AND PARENTHOOD

SURROGACY AND ASSISTED REPRODUCTION

A Challenge for Family Law and for Private International Law Methodology

Konstantinos A. Rokas

1. INTRODUCTION

Assisted reproductive techniques (ARTs[1]) have radically changed people's potential to form families, thus affecting the traditional family model. Infertile heterosexual couples, single women and female couples have obtained access to parenthood. Surrogacy has made parenthood possible for women unable to bear a child and given access to parenthood to single men and male couples. Post-mortem fertilization has enabled the creation of offspring genetically linked with an individual who had died before the birth. Children have been born and new family realities and family ties created. National legislators have taken highly differing approaches to these realities. Even within the EU, countries sharing common principles have adopted diametrically opposed positions.

---

1 This term is used in this chapter as an all-encompassing term which includes surrogacy.

The divergence of national rules and the ease of information exchange and travel have led to cross-border access to ARTs. This cross-border dimension has necessarily involved the intervening private international law rules, mostly at the phase of recognition of the new parentage links.

The study of judicial proceedings could lead to the impression that surrogacy and ARTs in general constitute a major challenge to the concept of family. Countries prohibiting surrogacy, such as France, Germany, Austria, Italy, Switzerland, Denmark, Iceland and others, have faced the problem of recognizing parentage in this situation. Bulgaria, Poland and Greece have had to deal with the recognition of parentage in female same-sex couples following in vitro fertilization (IVF). Despite their liberal solutions, the UK and Greece have both faced problems of recognizing parentage following a commercial surrogacy and post-mortem fertilization. An examination of the solutions adopted in these cases reveals that the problems of recognizing parentage do pose a challenge to the concept of family, at least as regards its creation and official recognition by the law. Nonetheless, it should be noted that in most cases the new family ties created are able to develop and function within different societies. These solutions reveal deficiencies in the way private international law has functioned: direct confrontation and collisions of opposing views and solutions have prevailed over smooth coordination and coexistence. This finding invites us to rethink the terms of the public policy mechanism.

First, this chapter will explain why, despite the emerging challenge as to the creation and recognition of family bonds, the overall challenge to the concept of 'family' and to the function of new family realities has not been as significant as one might think. Second, this chapter will explain that a serious challenge has also appeared for private international law, which must reconsider the terms of the intervening public policy mechanism. This chapter argues that the existing challenges for family law would have been more efficiently dealt with by means of certain improvements in the function of private international law.

2. PARENTAGE THROUGH SURROGACY AND ARTs: AN OVERSTATED CHALLENGE FOR FAMILY

National courts have had to deal with hundreds of cases involving problems of recognizing parentage following surrogacy or the use of ARTs in general. Problems have arisen regardless of whether the relevant national legislation has adopted a prohibitive or liberal stance towards these techniques. These techniques have created a challenge for the way the institution of 'family' is perceived by the law and for its functioning. The model of a family composed by a husband and wife who have children through natural or assisted procreation remains dominant. But ARTs have led to the emergence of same-sex couples who either assume a de facto parent role or are recognized as parents under the law of some countries.

Nevertheless, a careful evaluation of how these problems have been dealt with shows that this challenge has been overstated. Although the individuals concerned have faced thorny issues, the judiciary has often managed to guarantee, at domestic level, the symbiosis of the new parentage bonds created through ARTs with existing forms of parentage. The creation and construction of parentage has been challenged numerous times and yet, for a significant number of countries, enabling the final acceptance of parentage links has not required the creation of new categories. Regulation of surrogacy allows for the active involvement of a third woman in the birth of a child who, however, then enters a two-parent family, as most children do. Certainly, an important number of EU countries have not accepted same-sex family realities.[2] However, even then, the function of family life has only marginally been altered. Crossing borders has neither disrupted the reality of the ensuing family ties nor reversed the dominant parentage paradigm. Individuals who have resorted to ARTs have frequently become involved in arduous judicial battles to have their parentage recognized. The nature of these difficulties, the reasons for the initial denials of parentage and how continuity of parentage has subsequently been safeguarded will be presented in this chapter, starting with the parentage of children born through surrogacy (section 2.1) and continuing with IVF in same-sex couples (section 2.2) and post-mortem fertilization (section 2.3).

2.1. CHILDREN BORN THROUGH SURROGACY

Surrogacy has attracted the attention of legal doctrine and public opinion even though surrogate children represent a tiny fraction of the total number of children born through ARTs. This interest is explained by the intricacies of a

2 In a recent case (ECtHR, 22.11.2022, *D.B and others v. Switzerland*, appl. n° 58817/15 and 58252/15; for a different outcome in a different context see ECtHR, 18.05.2021, *Valdís Fjölnisdóttir and others v. Iceland*, appl. n° 71552/17) involving the establishment of parentage of same-sex intended parents following surrogacy, the ECtHR condemned Switzerland on grounds of violation of Article 8. The Court held that the absence for a significant period of time of any means for the recognition or establishment of the parentage bond between the child and an intended parent in a same-sex couple and with no genetic link with the child constituted a violation of the child's right to respect for their private life. This bold judgment constitutes a step towards recognition of same-sex parentage. However, the contours of an obligation for CoE Member States to recognize a same-sex parentage following cross-border recourse to assisted reproductive technologies (ARTs) remain uncertain; N. Koumoutzis, 'D.B. and others v. Switzerland: Tracing the Origins of the Right to Recognition of Same-Sex Parentage in International Surrogacy', *Strasbourg Observers*, 23 December 2022 <https://strasbourgobservers.com/2022/12/23/d-b-and-others-v-switzerland-tracing-the-origins-of-the-right-to-recognition-of-same-sex-parentage-in-international-surrogacy/?subscribe=many_pending_subs> accessed 25.12.2022.

process whereby a third person (woman) contributes, often for a fee, to another family's parental project. This section will successively present the problems that intended parents have faced in prohibitive countries, namely France and Italy, and in a liberal country, i.e., the UK.

French courts, which had already dealt with surrogacy cases in mid-1980s,[3] considered surrogacy contracts to be void.[4] Later, Articles 16-7 and 16-9 of the French Civil Code explicitly prohibited them. Any route for the recognition of the intended mother as a legal parent[5] was gradually excluded despite some determinations by lower courts, which allowed the transcription[6] of birth certificates mentioning both intended parents.[7] The refusal to recognize the intended mother's parentage links was based on public policy; surrogacy was thought to violate two fundamental principles of French law, i.e., that civil status and the human body are inalienable. Subsequently, French courts refused to allow recognition of parentage for a genetic father who had resorted to surrogacy, on grounds of evasion of law (*fraude à la loi*).[8]

The *Mennesson* litigation, in one of the most famous cross-border surrogacy cases, lasted almost 15 years and shaped French law. It concerned two children born in California through a gestational surrogacy arrangement and their parents' efforts to obtain recognition in France of their parent-child relationship established in the US, which had initially been refused completely. After bringing their case to the European Court of Human Rights (ECtHR), as in other cases, the intended father (i.e., the biological father) was recognized, although the intended mother was not. The judgment of ECtHR in *Mennesson* has been crucial

---

3 TGI, Aix-en-Provence, 05.12.1984, 2ème esp., *JCP* 1986 II.20561, 2e esp., F. Boulanger.

4 CC, Plenary, 31.05.1991, n° 90-20.105; H. Capitant, F. Terré, Y. Lequette, *Les grands arrêts de la jurisprudence civile*, Paris, Dalloz, vol. I, 13th Ed., 2015, n° 51; CC,13.12.1989, *JCP* 1990, II, 21526, A. Sériaux; J.L. Aubert, *D.* 1991, 318; Jur., 273, J. Massip; *RTD civ.* 1990, 254, J. Rubelin-Devichi.

5 CC, Plenary, 31.05.1991, n° 90–20.105; H. Capitant, F. Terré, Y. Lequette, *Les grands arrêts de la jurisprudence civile*, Paris, Dalloz, vol. I, 13th Ed., 2015, n° 51; *Rev.crit. DIP* 1991, 711–31, C. Labrusse-Riou; CC, 1st Civil Chamber, 29.06.1994, *D.* 1994, 581–582, Y. Chartier; CA Rennes, 04.07.2002, 01/02471 *D.* 2002, 2902–2904, F. Granet; *Dr. fam.* 2002. comm. 142, P. M; TGI Lille, 22 mars 2007, *D.* 2007, 1251, X. Labbée; CC., 1st Civil Chamber, 06.04.2011, n° 09-17.130; D. Berthiau, L. Brunet, 'L'ordre public au préjudice de l'enfant', (2011) *D*, 1522–1529; *Rev.crit. DIP* 2011, 722, P. Hammje.

6 The term 'transcription' and 'transcribe' here literally reflect the French term for a procedure by which the civil status authorities of several countries register a personal status situation recorded for the first time in a foreign document in an official document of the registering authority. The terms 'registration' and 'register' respectively are closer to the meaning of this practice, followed by a number of civil law countries. Nonetheless, the term transcription is preferred because it was used in the bibliography by S. Fulli-Lemaire, 'International Surrogate Motherhood before the French Cour de cassation – The Door is now Ajar' (2017) *Zeitschrift für Europäisches Privatrecht (ZEuP)*, 471.

7 CA Paris (1re Ch.), 25.10.2007, (27–29.01.2008), *gaz. pal.*, nos 27–29, 128ème année, 20–28.

8 CC, 1st Civil Chamber, 13.09.2013, n° 12–18.315 and n° 12–30.138.

for the recognition of the father's parentage, and a turning point in the treatment of parentage following surrogacy. The Court held that a total prohibition of establishing the children's legal relationship with the biological father violated the children's right to respect for their private life.[9]

Following that decision, courts have systematically accepted partial transcription of birth certificates issued following a surrogacy.[10] The issue of the full registration of birth certificates then came back before French courts in the *Mennesson* case. The French Supreme Court sent a request for an opinion to the ECtHR,[11] which made clear that States have discretion to choose how to establish a parentage link with the intended mother. Despite this margin, French courts have followed the most liberal approach, proceeding to full transcription of birth certificates naming both intended parents. This solution, initially thought to correspond to the specificities of *Mennesson*, has since been generalized to all intended parents.[12] However, in a 2021 reform of French bioethics law, the civil code was amended with the objective of reversing that case-law. Article 47 of the civil code provides that:

> Faith must be given to records of civil status of French nationals and aliens made in a foreign country and drawn up in the forms in use in that country, unless other records or documents possessed, external data or elements drawn from the record itself establish that the record is irregular, forged or that the facts declared therein do not square with truth. This is assessed in the light of French law.

This amended provision aimed at forcing an intended parent with no genetic link to the child to reconstruct their bond through adoption;[13] it can be criticized on multiple levels, but suffice it to say that it will remain largely ineffective as regards its goals. Under Article 509 of the General Instruction on Civil Status, transcription is a non-compulsory measure of publicity. Foreign birth certificates are valid in France, and families can use them before French authorities. Intended mothers or intended fathers in same-sex relationships are not required to proceed to adoption solely for the purpose of parentage; despite numerous judicial battles in France since the early 1990s, people who resorted to surrogacy have managed to have their parentage recognized.

---

9 CEDH, 26.06.2014, *Mennesson v. France*, appl. n° 65192/11.

10 CC, Plenary, 03.07.2015, n°14-21323 & n°15-50002; see S. Fulli-Lemaire, above n. 6, pp. 471–84.

11 Advisory Opinion concerning the recognition in domestic law of a legal parent-child relationship between a child born through a gestational surrogacy arrangement abroad and the intended mother, req. No P16-2018-001 ECHR, 10.04.2019.

12 CC, 18.12.2019, n° 18-11815 & n° 18-12337 and CC, 13.01.2021, n° 19-17929.

13 C. Bidaud, 'La force probante des actes de l'état civil étrangers modifiée par la loi bioéthique : du sens à donner à l'exigence de conformité des faits à la réalité « appréciée au regard de la loi française » …' (2022) *Rev.crit. DIP*, 35.

The most radical treatment of intended parents who have resorted to surrogacy abroad was adopted by the Italian authorities in the *Paradiso and Campanelli* case,[14] where a couple, both Italian citizens, resorted to surrogacy in Russia. A child was born, and the intended parents claimed that it was conceived with the intended father's genetic material. After its birth, on 30 April 2011, the child returned to Italy with one of the intended parents. Later, DNA testing performed upon request of the authorities showed that the child had no genetic link with either of the intended parents. On 20 October 2011 the child was removed from their care and placed in the care of social services pending adoption. Every effort by the intended parents to get the child back failed. In an action the family brought against Italy before the ECtHR, the Court condemned Italy for violating Article 8 of the European Convention on Human Rights (ECHR). Italy appealed to the Grand Chamber, which reversed the judgment, finding that there had been no violation of the ECHR as regards the rights of the parents. *Paradiso and Campanelli* is one of the very exceptional cases in which the intended parents have been deprived of parental care and custody of a surrogate child of theirs.

Similar cases dealing with the recognition of parentage in intended parents have been brought before German,[15] Austrian[16] and Swiss courts, among others.[17] These courts have recognized or reconstructed the parentage links at issue with less hesitancy. Countries like the UK and Greece, which have legalized surrogacy, have also faced problems as to the recognition of parentage.[18]

The UK has faced parentage recognition issues concerning couples who resorted to surrogacy abroad. Surrogacy in the UK is altruistic, which makes it more difficult to find a surrogate. Consequently, a significant number of people travel abroad for surrogacy. Upon return to their country of domicile, there is no registration system regarding the birth certificate nor any other recognition system such as those in other EU countries. Section 54 of the UK Human Fertilisation and Embryology Act (HFEA) provides that intended parents have to apply for a parental order to have their parentage 'normalized' so as to be able to invoke it. This is a solution of unilateral character, in that UK law specifies the conditions under which a relationship created abroad can become effective.

---

14 ECtHR, 27.01.2015, *Paradiso and Campanelli v. Italie*, appl. n° 25358/12; ECtHR (gr.ch.), 24.01.2017, *Paradiso and Campanelli v. Italie*, appl. n° 25358/12.

15 BGH, 10.12.2014, XII ZB 463/13.

16 Österr. VfGH, 11.10.2012, B99/12, p. 271, no. 20 and österr. VfGH, 14.12.2011, B13/11-10, p. 275, no. 21.

17 ATF 141 III 312, 21.05.2015; ATF 141 III 328, 14.09.2015; ECtHR, 22.11.2022, *D.B and others v. Switzerland*, appl. n° 58817/15 and 58252/15; A. Bucher, *SRIEL* (2021), 475.

18 For problems in Greece as regards the recognition of parentage following surrogacy, see: K. Rokas, *L'assistance médicale à la procréation en droit international privé comparé*, Title of doctoral dissertation, University Paris 1 Panthéon-Sorbonne, 2016, pp. 366–67, 373–79 <https://tel.archives-ouvertes.fr/tel-01677943/document> accessed 10.08.2022.

A parental order is granted upon strict conditions, such as the surrogate and her spouse consenting, one of the intended parents being domiciled in the UK, the Channel Islands or the Isle of Man, and the judge verifying that there has been no exchange of money (HFEA, s. 54(8)).

These conditions have often posed serious obstacles for English judges.[19] In principle, the clear wording of those provisions ought to make it impossible for judges to grant a parental order if any of these conditions have been broken, especially in commercial surrogacies. However, courts have worked their way out of this conundrum. Couples have managed to obtain a parental order even where several conditions were not met.[20] Similar outcomes have been reached in Greece.

2.2. CHILDREN BORN TO FEMALE SAME-SEX COUPLES THROUGH RECOURSE TO ARTs

Over time, ARTs have become more readily available to female same-sex couples. Several pieces of legislation in Europe and elsewhere allow for recourse to ARTs and the establishment of parentage in favour of two female partners from the child's birth. However, there are significant divergences in the relevant legislation, entailing problems with a cross-border dimension.

In 2019 a couple, a Bulgarian and an English woman, who had been living in Spain since 2015, succeeded in having a child through IVF (*Pancharevo* case).[21] The Bulgarian woman tried to register the Spanish birth certificate, which named both women as parents, in Bulgaria. Given that Bulgaria does not recognize same-sex marriage, local authorities refused transcription, on grounds of public policy. The couple appealed to the administrative courts, which stayed proceedings in order to refer questions to the Court of Justice of the European Union (CJEU). Because the other parent only had UK citizenship, the child could only obtain EU citizenship if the Bulgarian woman were recognized as a parent in Bulgaria.

The CJEU had to evaluate the impact of Articles 7, 21 and 45 of the Charter of the Fundamental Rights of the EU (Charter) and secondary EU law on the authorities' obligation to recognize the birth certificate issued by the Spanish

---

19 *Re G (Surrogacy: Foreign Domicile)* [2007], EWHC 2814 (Fam); D. Howe, 'International Surrogacy – A Cautionary Tale' (2008) *Fam. Law* 60; *X & Y (Foreign Surrogacy)* [2008] EWHC 3030 (Fam), [2009] 1 FLR 733; C. Bridge, *Fam. Law*, February 2009, 115–16; L. Theis, N. Gamble and L. Ghevaert, '*Re X and Y (Foreign surrogacy)*: "A trek through a thorn forest"' (2009) *Fam. Law* 239.

20 K. Parizer-Krief, 'Gestation pour autrui et intérêt de l'enfant en Grande-Bretagne, De l'indemnisation raisonnable de la gestatrice prévue par la loi à la reconnaissance judiciaire des contrats internationaux à but lucratif' (2011) *RIDC* 645.

21 C-490/20, *V.M.A. v. Stolichna obshtina, rayon 'Pancharevo'*, ECLI:EU:C:2021:1008.

authorities. The referring court also raised the question whether protecting the constitutional identity of EU Member States (Article 4(2) of the Treaty on European Union (TEU)) could be interpreted as leaving broader discretion to Member States as regards the rules for establishing parentage in a way that would allow for a reconciliation of the best interests of the child with the position of those Member States that do not recognize such new types of parentage.

The CJEU provided a bold but carefully circumscribed decision – in its wording clarifying that Bulgarian authorities had no obligation to issue a Bulgarian birth certificate or introduce such an institution into their internal law. They did however have an obligation to allow these families to invoke their documents before state authorities exclusively for the needs of the exercise of their right to move and reside freely within the EU. Despite that the Supreme Administrative Court of Bulgaria in a recent decision contradicts the position adopted by the CJEU and its EU law interpretation.[22] The Court ruled that there are no ties between the child and the Bulgarian mother and therefore the Bulgarian authorities are not obliged to issue a birth certificate.

Similar problems have appeared in Poland and Greece. In the case *Rzecznik Praw Obywatelskich*, the CJEU answered the preliminary question referred by Polish courts (C-2/21) in the same way as in *Pancharevo*. Greek authorities have had to deal with several cases. Contrary to the French practice, Greek nationals who are habitually resident in a foreign country have an obligation to declare events related to their civil status in Greece. The competent authority is the Special Registry in Athens as well as the Greek consular authorities.

Several female couples living outside Greece have had children through IVF and simultaneously established their parentage. In one such case, a couple, a Greek and a British woman who had two children through IVF, wanted to have the children's birth certificates transcribed. The birth mother in this case was the British woman. In January 2021, the Greek authorities denied transcription without seeking information as to the biological mother. The reason advanced was that it was impossible to transcribe civil status acts from countries where same-sex marriage is legal and same-sex couples can legally have children, given that no similar provisions exist in Greek law.[23]

Then, in spring 2022, after the CJEU judgment in *Pancharevo*, a female same-sex couple of two Greek–British dual nationals also tried to have their

---

22 H. Luku, 'The Supreme Administrative Court of Bulgaria's final decision in the Pancharevo case: Bulgaria is not obliged to issue identity documents for baby S.D.K.A. as she is not Bulgarian (but presumably Spanish)', *ConflictofLaw.net*, 22 May 2023, <https://conflictoflaws.net/2023/the-supreme-administrative-court-of-bulgarias-final-decision-in-the-pancharevo-case-bulgaria-is-not-obliged-to-issue-identity-documents-for-baby-s-d-k-a-as-she-is-not-bulgarian-but-presuma> accessed 25.05.2023.

23 Reply no. 47567/47568/47569/11.01.2021 (files accessible to author on account of his professional activities as a lawyer).

child's birth certificate, naming them as the parents, transcribed in Greece.[24] In their answer, the Greek authorities chose a wording which marked a shift in their previous practice, but the application for transcription was nonetheless rejected, on grounds of public policy (Article 33 Civil Code). In particular, it was held that:

> The Special Registry does not question the parentage link created and recognized in the UK between A and the child's parents, B and C. The Special Registry does not contest that A has acquired Greek citizenship at birth, given that the child was born to a mother duly registered in the public records in force … The Special Registry, in its capacity as the competent authority for registration of civil status acts of Greek citizens that have taken place abroad, is not authorized to register an act which contains elements contrary to our legal order pursuant to Article 33 [Greek] Civil Code. The acts of civil status kept in the public records make no reference to 'Parent 1' and 'Parent 2', but to 'Mother' and 'Father' instead.

This answer affords to female same-sex couples an indirect recognition of bonds created abroad. However, there is no guidance as to how the two parents could effectively invoke their parentage before Greek authorities; moreover, this approach shows serious inconsistencies that will be discussed hereafter.

2.3. CHILDREN BORN FOLLOWING POST-MORTEM FERTILIZATION

Post-mortem fertilization is a very exceptional means of having children – even more so when combined with surrogacy, as happened in a case brought before the Court of First instance of Thessaloniki in 2013.[25] In this case, a woman habitually resident in Greece (a doctor by profession) resorted to two surrogacy procedures in Russia with her son's genetic material, the eggs of donors and with the help of two gestational surrogates. Her son had died of leukaemia at the age of 26 but had previously provided his sperm to be cryopreserved. Four children were born of surrogacies that took place in Ukraine. The intended (grand-)mother managed to adopt the children in Russia and sought

---

24 Reply no. 12695/13.04.2022 (files accessible to author on account of his professional activities as a lawyer).

25 CFI Thessaloniki 7013/2013, *Efarmoges Astikou Dikaiou*, 340, K. Pantelidou [in Greek]; A. Anthimos [in Greek] (2013) *Armenopoulos*, 1291; D. Papadopoulou, 'Post mortem artificial fertilisation and surrogacy in practice' in E. Symeonidou-Kastanidou, *Assisted Reproduction in Europe: Social, Ethical and Legal Issues*, Sakkoulas, Thessaloniki 2015, pp. 113–20; K. Rokas, 'Difficulties of recognition in Greece of parentage links created in foreign legal orders following recourse to techniques of medically assisted reproduction' in E. Symeonidou-Kastanidou, *Assisted Reproduction in Europe: Social, Ethical and Legal Issues*, Sakkoulas, Thessaloniki 2015, pp. 463–70, at pp. 464–65.

recognition of the adoptions in Greece. The Greek court did not recognize the foreign determinations on grounds of their incompatibility with public policy and referred to fraud and to an effort to circumvent Greek law.

At first sight, recourse to public policy in this case seems reasonable. In support of the decision, the judge underlined that the post-mortem fertilization and surrogacy, which took place abroad, were conducted pursuant to Russian law but that the procedure was contrary to the Greek rules. The intended mother had no medical condition preventing her from bearing a child and was over the age at which Greek law would have afforded her a right to access ARTs. Nor did the intended mother have a judicial authorization for post-mortem insemination. The court held that:

> The solution given by foreign decision entails, in the Greek territory, legal consequences running contrary to fundamental principles which are dominant in Greece and reflect social, religious, moral and other generally accepted principles, which govern and regulate social relations in Greece in a consistent manner and which constitute a barrier to the application in the forum of the rules of a foreign law which may create a distortion of the prevailing rhythm of life in the country … in this case there is no doubt that what is at stake is the coherence of family law, and of private law in general as a system of values, … since we are led to the paradox of the biological grandmother being recognized as the children's mother although neither the conditions of adoption nor those relating to medically assisted procreation of Greek law are met …[26]

The family situation was nevertheless safeguarded through other means. The surrogate children had never lived with anyone other than the biological grandmother, their de facto parent, who sought judicial redress once again after recognition of the Russian adoptions was refused. The Peace Court of Thessaloniki 229E/24.02.2014 removed the parental rights of the surrogates and granted the applicant parental responsibility. Consequently, the intended (grand-)mother finally managed to obtain recognition of parental responsibility. Although the children will never obtain a legal parent, rights of succession or other rights stemming from parentage, their intended mother succeeded in her ultimate goal, i.e., to preserve the continuity of the family situation.

At first glance, all these cases show a clash between the solutions adopted in foreign countries and the fundamental principles of the country of recognition. Thus, one would expect that stricter rules would be enforced to prevent individuals from seeking ART services in more liberal countries. This has not been the case; instead, judicial practice and legislation have gradually permitted recognition of these links.

---

[26] CFI Thessaloniki 7013/2013, (2013) *Efarmoges Astikou Dikaiou* 340 [in Greek].

In addition, the evolution of several countries' substantive law shows that the challenge to family law although existent has been moderate. More and more countries are allowing recourse to ARTs for female same-sex couples, thus limiting the need to travel abroad to access ARTs and the ensuing parentage recognition problems. On 2 August 2021, the new French bioethics law opened ARTs up to female couples and single women.

As for legislation on surrogacy, there are no significant changes in Europe. Only a few countries have legalized surrogacy; however, in almost all countries that prohibit surrogacy, parentage following surrogacy has been systematically recognized or reconstructed through adoption.[27] In addition, several proposals to adopt stricter rules and sanctions against people resorting to surrogacy abroad have failed. Therefore, it could be argued that resorting to ARTs in a foreign country has indirectly become acceptable. Even after the extremely harsh result of the ECtHR *Paradiso and Campanelli* judgment (Grand Chamber), no amendment was adopted, in any national legislation, to limit the recognition of intended parents to specific cases or impose stricter controls on surrogate children born abroad.[28] And couples habitually resident in Italy are still having recourse to surrogacy and managing to have their parentage recognized.[29]

Moreover, it is becoming more and more clear that the exercise of parental duties is affected neither by how a child is conceived nor by the sexual orientation of the prospective parents.[30] The new reproduction methods do not alter the concept of parenthood. The parent of a surrogate child does not care, feed or educate their child any differently than a parent in a case of 'normal' procreation. The equality of rights and duties between parents, recognized in most countries around Europe, means that parentage of children born through ARTs corresponds to the traditional mould of parentage regulated, as ever,

27 See in that sense L. Brunet, *A Comparative Study on the Regime of Surrogacy in EU Member States*, European Union, May 2013: 'As the national case law analysis in Section 2, Part B of this Report has indicated, all European countries accept to formally recognise (with more or less enthusiasm) the relationship between the surrogate child and the intended parent(s)', p. 154, and in the national reports, pp. 206 et seq.; <http://www.europarl.europa.eu/RegData/etudes/STUD/2013/474403/IPOL-JURI_ET(2013)474403_EN.pdf> accessed 10.08.2022; For Germany see: K. Duden, 'International Surrogate Motherhood – Shifting the Focus to the Child' (2015) *Zeitschrift für Europäisches Privatrecht (ZEuP)* 637, 657; see for further case law: K. Rokas, above n. 18, p. 431, note 1015.

28 However, the government of Prime Minister Giorgia Meloni recently ordered municipalities in Italy to stop certifying foreign birth certificates for same-sex couples who had recourse to surrogacy: J. Horowitz, 'Surrogacy Emerges as the Wedge Issue for Italy's Hard Right' *NY Times*, 4 April 2023, <https://www.nytimes.com/2023/04/04/world/europe/italy-surrogacy-same-sex-couples.html> accessed 25.05.2023.

29 Information provided to the author by the Italian attorney Alexander Schuster on account of his professional activities as a lawyer.

30 See for instance the conclusions reached by 79 scholarly studies in 'What does the scholarly research say about the well-being of children with gay or lesbian parents?' <https://whatweknow.inequality.cornell.edu/topics/lgbt-equality/what-does-the-scholarly-research-say-about-the-wellbeing-of-children-with-gay-or-lesbian-parents> accessed 20.12.2022.

in family law. Furthermore, children born and raised in same-sex families or born through surrogacy are a reality recognized, both directly and indirectly, in Council of Europe (CoE) countries, and protected under Article 8 ECHR. It would be inconceivable for CoE countries to remove parental responsibility because of the parents' sexual orientation or solely because of how the children were conceived. One could claim that where same-sex families do exist there was often no need to remove parental responsibility because the persons exercising a de facto parent role were never granted parentage or parental responsibility. Even if this view is considered to be accurate, it should be recalled that in those legal orders the main reason against recognizing parentage is precisely the fact that children grow up with two parents of the same sex. Therefore, by indirectly accepting the development of de facto same-sex families, the authorities of those countries actually undermine their most important arguments against recognition or establishment of these new parentage bonds.

That said, in this author's opinion the overall outcome of the confrontation of national legal orders with new forms of parentage at the recognition phase, on the one hand, and the reaction of national legislators at the level of substantive law, on the other, show that the challenge to the concept of family, although existent, should not be overstated. This challenge would be less palpable if private international law mechanisms functioned more efficiently. In what ways private international law could be more efficient will be explained below.

3. PARENTAGE THROUGH SURROGACY AND ARTs: THE CHALLENGE FOR PRIVATE INTERNATIONAL LAW

The evolution of substantive law in one country and the resulting divergence in the substantive rules of different countries have always caused problems for people potentially affected by the different sets of rules. This explains why in the aftermath of substantive law reforms in one country questions arise as to the adaptability of private international law rules.[31]

Over time, and on a global level, surrogacy, ARTs and parentage have generated the most extensive case-law in private international law. This case-law has posed a major challenge for private international law, occasioning specific issues of its general theory such as whether the method of recognition is to be preferred over the bilateral conflict of law rules. Elsewhere, in the UK for instance, unilateralist solutions have been applied without further analysis.

---

31 G. Kessler, *Les partenariats enregistrés en droit international privé*, préf. de P. Lagarde, L.G.D.J., Paris 2004; G.P. Romano, 'La bilatéralité éclipsée par l'autorité' (2006), *Rev.crit. DIP*, 457–519, esp. 464–68.

Given the abundant judicial procedures and case-law, some thoughts can be advanced as to how private international law mechanisms have worked. In its mediation mission, private international law has not always produced the most satisfying results and this not only in countries that have adopted restrictive solutions as to new ARTs but also in more liberal ones. Courts have managed neither to satisfactorily coordinate solutions given by different legal orders (where compatible) nor to protect the values invoked in support of mechanisms such as public policy or *fraude à la loi*. The role of public policy in international family law cases has not been sufficiently examined, at least in certain jurisdictions.

The method of recognition and unilateralist approaches are in no way able to address, any better than the conflict of law rules, the specific difficulties that have arisen from parentage created following recourse to ARTs; this will be explained in the following section (section 3.1.). Why the way the public policy mechanism has been used is not satisfactory in the context of international family law will be demonstrated (section 3.2.). Therefore, this chapter suggests that the functioning of this mechanism ought to be reconsidered even when dealing with sensitive family law cases.

3.1. A NEED FOR RECONSIDERATION OF THE CONFLICT OF LAW RULE?

In Europe, bilateral conflict of law rules are given preference over unilateral conflict of law rules as the solution for determining the law applicable to parentage.[32] It should be noted that, at least when cross-border cases of recourse to ART first emerged, no additional analysis had been devoted to whether the conflict of law rules then in force were appropriate in face of new modes of creation of parentage. More recently, in German as well as in French[33] and EU law there have been different proposals suggesting the adoption of new conflict of law rules. Nonetheless, in EU countries which have legalized surrogacy there has been no in-depth discussion of the eventual need to reform the existing conflict of law rules. In the past, when dealing with private international law problems, such analyses have been conducted every time an institution of a foreign legal

32 A bilateral conflict of law rule can designate as applicable both the substantive law of the forum as well as the law of another legal order. On the contrary, a unilateral conflict of law rule determines exclusively the conditions of application of the substantive law of the forum.

33 See for instance Articles 62 and 63 of the French Project for a Private International Law Code and Articles 17 and 18 of the Proposal for a Council Regulation on jurisdiction, applicable law, recognition of decisions and acceptance of authentic instruments in matters of parenthood and on the creation of a European Certificate of Parenthood, Brussels, 07.12.2022, COM(2022) 695 final 2022/0402 (NLE) <https://commission.europa.eu/document/928ae98d-d85f-4c3d-ac50-ba13ed981897_en> accessed 29.07.2023.

order has appeared to be structurally different from the known institutions. Polygamy is one such example; in this context, judges and scholars did not question the appropriateness of the conflict of law rules in force, especially not as regards their conformity with the basic principles that private international law serves. While a re-evaluation of the existing conflict of law rules would not necessarily mean that new such rules should be adopted, regarding methods such as surrogacy it nonetheless seems that the existing conflict of law rules fail to consider the interests of specific stakeholders. They are therefore in violation of the proximity principle, which is a guiding principle of private international law.

Moreover, in France and Greece, both central to the surrogacy debate,[34] even the role of the existing conflict of law rules has often been neglected in the context of transcription of foreign birth certificates. In France, it was advanced that the institution of civil status reflects the reality as envisaged by French law.[35] Consequently, a foreign birth certificate can be transcribed only if it reflects the reality of the father and the mother as perceived under French law. But in that case, a French agency asked to transcribe a foreign birth certificate need not examine whether the parentage indications conform with the applicable law pursuant to French conflict of law rules; the examination is rendered superfluous, and those rules are bypassed. The acceptance of this idea introduces inconsistencies in the way a given jurisdiction deals with parentage: parentage indicated on a birth certificate whose transcription has been refused could be recognized in another context such as judicial proceedings.

Unlike in civil law countries, parentage in the UK and Australia is dependent on the additional judicial procedure of seeking a parental order, a solution of unilateralist character.[36] These jurisdictions do not recognize the legal links created abroad but instead require parentage to be reconstructed provided that specific conditions are met. This approach is no better; the reconstruction of parentage according to the *lex fori*, which will not always be possible, is compulsory. This leads to a burdensome, costly procedure that still does not impede individuals from choosing destinations that have accepted commercial surrogacy. Nor does it better protect the rights of vulnerable people involved in a surrogacy.

But irrespective of the existing analysis of the bilateral conflict of law methodology, and despite the lack of in-depth discussion of whether the

---

34 France for its prohibitive stance towards surrogacy and the case-law produced both at national level and at the level of the European Court of Human Rights and Greece for being the first civil law country in the EU having legalized surrogacy.

35 B. Ancel, 'L'épreuve de vérité – Propos de surface sur la transcription des actes de naissance des enfants issus d'une gestation pour autrui délocalisée' in *Le droit entre tradition et modernité – Mélanges à la mémoire de Patrick Courbe*, 2012, pp. 1–9, at pp. 1, 4, 6–7.

36 L. Theis, N. Gamble, L. Ghevaert, above n. 19, esp. pp. 241–42; M. Keyes, 'Cross-border surrogacy arrangements' (2011) *Australian Journal of Family Law* 28, esp. at 33.

unilateralist-inspired solutions are well-founded, those methods were not the main culprits of the serious complications that surfaced.

In none of the cases before national courts were bilateral conflict of law rules an obstacle to the acceptance of parentage created through ARTs. The refusal to recognize parentage was not the outcome of the designation of applicable law by means of a conflict of law rule. On the contrary, those rules were in some cases advanced as an argument in favour of recognition. This was the case in *Mennesson*, and it could have been so in numerous other ones, too. Article 311-14 of the French Civil Code points to the law of the mother's nationality on the day the child was born. Sticking to the way that French substantive law defines 'mother' means that the birth mother should be taken into consideration. Consequently, application of this rule leads to the personal law of the surrogate, who in most cases has the nationality of the country where the process has taken place. Therefore, this rule will often lead to substantive legislation that considers surrogacy to be legal and provides for the establishment of the child's link with the intended parents.

The same can be observed for the first case of a same-sex couple's parentage brought before Greek authorities.[37] The potentially applicable conflict of law rule is Article 19 of the Greek Civil Code, which provides that:

> The relationship between mother and child born outside marriage of the child's parents shall be governed in the following order of decreasing priority: 1. by the last common national law of the mother and child 2. by the law of their last common habitual residence 3. by the national law of the mother

In this case, the mother had Greek–British citizenship and the child only had British citizenship. Therefore, the applicable law would be that of the habitual residence, which in this case was England. In these two examples the conflict of law rule indicates in a more transparent way the connection that a person or situation might have with a foreign legal order. Finally, the recognition-of-parentage cases do not prove that promoting the method of recognition over the conflict of law rule – as it has been proposed especially in France[38] – would lead to different outcomes, neither as to the parentage of intended parents

[37] See above, section 2.2.

[38] P. Lagarde, 'Introduction au thème de la reconnaissance des situations : rappel des points les plus discutés' in P. Lagarde (sous la dir. de), *La reconnaissance des situations en droit international privé*, Éditions A. Pédone, Paris 2013, pp. 19–25; CH. Pamboukis, 'Les actes publics et la méthode de reconnaissance' in P. Lagarde (sous la dir. de), *La reconnaissance des situations en droit international privé*, Éditions A. Pédone, Paris 2013, pp. 133–46; P. Lagarde, civ. 1re, 17.12.2008, *Rev. Crit DIP* 2009, 320; CH. Pamboukis, 'La renaissance-métamorphose de la méthode de reconnaissance' *Rev. Crit DIP* 2008, 513–60; G. Salamé, *Le devenir de la famille en droit international privé. Une perspective postmoderne* (préf. Horatia Muir Watt), PUAM, 2006, p. 241, n° 369, p. 254, n° 392, p. 260, n° 402.

in surrogacy nor for same-sex couples. The recognition method would not lead to substantially different results because the public policy mechanism is an indispensable precondition of both the conflict of law rules as well as the recognition method and most difficulties in the treatment of these cases resulted from the recourse to public policy.[39]

3.2. THE NEED FOR RECONSIDERATION OF THE PUBLIC POLICY MECHANISM

The terms under which public policy has been invoked and used in ART cases are not substantially different than those of the past. Keeping in mind international family law practices, it is therefore reasonable to be highly sceptical of any criticism formulated. However, the function of public policy observed in ART-related case-law over the last 30 years shows it manages neither to protect the values in the name of which national courts have used it nor to guarantee the desired coordination where substantive law differences are less radical than they appear.

Various elements reveal deficiencies in the use of this mechanism and explain why national courts should adhere to a more stringent motivational threshold before invoking public policy. The reasons for this may be found both in the ECtHR and CJEU case-law and in Dworkin's theory of 'law as integrity'.

Case-law in France, Greece, Italy, Switzerland and elsewhere suggests that recourse to public policy has been unsatisfactory, first and foremost because of the frequently changing solutions arrived at in cases of recognition of parentage following ART. This has been especially true in France and Switzerland,[40] Italy and elsewhere as regards children born of surrogacy abroad. The way national courts have vacillated within such a short time frame between different, often contradictory solutions, towards these new types of family bonds is a first sign of failure. Furthermore, it has been demonstrated that even in jurisdictions with the strictest policies regarding ARTs, courts have eventually either recognized parentage links created abroad or allowed reconstruction. Both approaches have guaranteed the continuity of family status, an ultimate outcome and another important sign of the inadequacies in the operation of public policy. This is so because the shift towards more liberal solutions by courts in countries with

---

[39] S. Corneloup, 'Les questions préalables de statut personnel dans le fonctionnement des règlements européens de droit international privé', *Trav. com. fr. dip* 2011–2012, pp. 189, 223–28.

[40] V. Boillet and E. de Luze, 'Les effets de la gestation pour autrui à caractère international en Suisse: analyse de la jurisprudence du Tribunal fédéral' in E. de Luze, M. Roca i Escoda and V. Boillet (eds), *La Gestation pour autrui, Approches juridiques internationales*, Anthémis / Helbing Lichtenhahn Verlag, 2018, pp. 143–82.

restrictive legal frameworks has not been the outcome of a liberalization of national substantive law. Nor is this shift explained by changes in the way these methods have been perceived in legal and societal terms so as to neutralize the intervening public policy considerations.

Moreover, various elements in the case-law reveal a lack of consistency resulting from recourse to the public policy mechanism. Thus, in the French, Swiss and other domestic case-law regarding surrogacy, recourse to public policy results in a sanction aimed at only one of the participants in the whole process. In heterosexual couples, the intended father having a genetic link with the child has in principle been able to have his parentage recognized based on his supposed genetic connection with the child; therefore, the intended mother has been treated differently, although she and the intended father jointly formulated their parental project and both bypassed a prohibition of internal law. She alone faces most difficulties in having her bond recognized.

Yet another problem of unequal treatment can be observed in the French case-law on surrogacy: as already noted, French citizens are generally under no obligation to request the transcription of their children's birth certificates. But intended parents have been forced to do so whenever they have resorted to surrogacy in countries where their children cannot obtain citizenship and travel documents because the respective jurisdiction applies the *ius sanguinis* principle. Single men and couples who have resorted to surrogacy in countries that have adopted the *ius soli* principle as to the attribution of nationality have, by contrast, been able to return to France with their children without having to seek transcription of their birth certificates.[41]

Inconsistencies can also be identified in Greek case-law as regards the recognition of parentage in female same-sex couples. Contrary to other EU countries' law, access to ARTs in Greece was open to single women very early on. It was conditioned on the existence of a medical problem and available even in the absence of a male partner. Thus, Greek law allowed women to overcome not only a medical problem but also a social impediment to reproduction, i.e., the lack of a male companion. Consequently, the women in a female couple were able to create their own de facto family relations. Further observations can be made as regards the Greek decisions on children born through a combination of surrogacy and post-mortem fertilization: first of all, Greek law allows for post-mortem fertilization and surrogacy. And although Greek courts refused to recognize the adoptions decreed by Russian courts, they did grant parental responsibility to the biological grandmother. It should be added that in Greece it is common for children to grow up under the care of their grandparents, and it is

41 According to the *ius soli* principle a person's citizenship is determined by the place where they were born. In contrast, according to the *ius sanguinis* principle a person's citizenship is acquired through one or both of their parents' citizenships.

not unheard of for childless relatives to adopt children of close family members, out of gratitude for the care received from those family members – a situation often motivated by an expectation of giving the children a benefit, such as the right to inherit. The Greek courts' refusal to recognize the foreign adoptions deprived the children of certain important rights and created risks to their well-being because of the need for lengthier and costly judicial procedures. If Greek courts deemed the petitioner worthy of bearing parental responsibility for the children despite the parental project violating Greek rules on ARTs, their refusal to recognize the Russian adoptions on grounds of public policy does not seem convincing. The situation in question is so exceptional in nature that it is far-fetched to suppose that it could jeopardize fundamental principles of the Greek legal order. The recognition of a parental status created in a foreign jurisdiction, which would have been the optimal way to guarantee the best interests of the child under such exceptional circumstances, cannot sensibly be thought of as generating a conflict capable of triggering the public policy mechanism.

The above show that there is a need for a more stringent threshold for invoking the public policy mechanism. In a considerable number of countries, it is traditionally taught that public policy is an exceptional mechanism.[42] And at the same time, we are more accustomed to the use of the public policy mechanism in international family law cases. So, recourse to public policy in the

---

42 P. Lagarde, 'Public Policy', Chapter 11 in International Encyclopedia of Comp. Law, vol. III, chap. 11, J.C.B. Mohr (Paul Siebeck), Tübingen, Martinus Nijhoff Publishers, Dordrecht/Boston/Lancaster, 1994, p. 4, n°2, 5, n°3; A. Bonomi in A. Bonomi and P. Wautelet (sous la dir. de), *Le droit européen des successions, Commentaire du Règlement (UE) n° 650/2012 du 4 juillet 2012*, 2e édition, 2016, p. 576, n° 2; In France: B. Ancel and Y. Lequette, *Les grands arrêts de la jurisprudence française de droit international privé*, préf. H. Batiffol, 5ème éd., Dalloz, Paris 2006, pp. 174–75, §19, nos 10–11; B. Audit and L. D'Avout, *Droit international privé*, 8ème éd., Economica, Paris, 2018, pp. 331–32, nos 384–386; V. Heuzé, P. Mayer and B. Rémy, *Droit international privé*, 12ème éd., L.G.D.J/Lextenso, Paris, 2019, pp. 152–61, nos 204–220; Y. Loussouarn, P. Bourel and P. (de) Vareilles-Sommières, *Droit international privé*, 10ème éd., Dalloz, Paris 2013, p. 331; M.-L. Niboyet and G. (de) Geouffre de la Pradelle, *Droit international privé*, L.G.D.J., Paris 2007, p. 222, n° 305; D. Bureau and H. Muir Watt, *Droit international privé/1, Partie générale*, 4ème éd., Thémis droit, PUF, 2017, pp. 548–49, n° 464; F. Rigaux and M. Fallon, *Droit international privé*, 3ème éd., Larcier, Bruxelles 2005, p. 306, n° 7.34; A. Bucher, 'L'ordre public et le but social des lois en droit international privé', *RCADI*, t. 239, 1993, pp. 19–20, 22; F. Knoepfler, P. Schweizer and S. Othénin-Girard, *Droit international privé suisse*, 3ème éd., Staempfli Éd. SA, Berne 2005, p. 173, n° 352; C.H. Pamboukis, *Droit international privé, t. I, Partie générale*, Nomiki Vivliothiki, Athènes 2018, p. 243 [in Greek]; S. Vrellis, *Private international law*, Athens 2008, p. 125 [in Greek]; for UK see: Lord Collins, A. Briggs, A. Dickinson, J. Harris and J.D. McClean (eds), *Dicey, Morris & Collins' The Conflict of Laws*, 15ème éd., Sweet & Maxwell, London 2012, pp. 99–101; A. Briggs, *Private International Law in English Courts*, Oxford University Press, Oxford 2014, pp. 163–167 nos 3.202–3.211; P. Torremans and J.J. Fawcett (eds), *Cheshire and North's Private International Law*, 15ème éd., Oxford University Press, Oxford 2017, pp. 132–33; G. Goldstein and E. Groffier, *Droit international privé, t. I, théorie générale*, Les éditions Yvon Blais, Québec 1998, pp. 266, 269.

field of family law has enjoyed a certain immunity from criticism. Perhaps this is one of the reasons why courts have often failed to provide sufficient reasons for recourse to this mechanism in parentage recognition cases.

The decisions of the ECtHR and more recently the CJEU have exercised a welcome influence in the way these problems have been dealt with. In particular, the case-law of the ECtHR has been crucial to the recognition of intended parents in heterosexual[43] as well as same-sex couples who have resorted to surrogacy.[44] In reality, national courts could – or better yet, should – have reached the same outcome without the intervention of European courts, following the example of German[45] and Austrian[46] courts in cases of recognition of parentage following surrogacy. ECtHR and CJEU case-law highlights contradicting positions in law and practice adopted by national authorities and the judiciary in a single legal order; such case-law thus appears to point to a possible need for more consistency in the way national legal orders invoke public policy. That public policy requires consistency becomes particularly clear in the ECtHR *Wagner & Negrepontis* judgment.[47] More recently, the CJEU has reminded us that although public policy is a national mechanism, it has been interpreted strictly every time its use poses an obstacle to the fundamental freedoms enjoyed under the Treaty on the Functioning of the European Union (TFEU) and the Charter, and it remains under the control of the Court.[48]

Consistency on the part of national courts in the way they justify recourse to public policy would benefit not only the liberal legal systems but also those that consider it contrary to their values to recognize such situations legally established abroad. Such a consistency requirement would force restrictive national legal orders to strengthen their controls on the circulation of statuses they deem contrary to the values they invoke in support of public policy.

The need for more consistency in the relevant reasoning can also be inspired by the work of Ronald Dworkin in *The Law's Empire*.[49] According to Dworkin's vision, 'law as integrity' requires that 'propositions of law are true if they figure in or follow from the principles of justice, fairness and procedural due process that

---

43 ECtHR, 26.06.2014, *Mennesson v. France*, n° 65192/11 and *Labassee v. France*, n° 65941/11; ECtHR, 19.01.2017, *Laborie v. France*, n° 44024/13.

44 ECtHR, 21.07. 2016, *Foulon and Bouvet v. France*, n° 10410/14.

45 See above n. 15.

46 See above n. 16; B. Lurger, 'Das österreichische IPR bei Leihmutterschaft im Ausland- das Kindeswohl zwischen Anerkennung, europäischen Grundrechten und inländischem Leimutterschaftsverbot' (2013) *IPrax* 282; J. Basedow, 'The law of open societies – private ordering and public regulation of international relations', *RCADI* 2012, t. 360, 426, n° 534.

47 ECtHR, 28.06.2007, *Wagner v. Luxembourg*, n° 76240/01, §130; ECtHR, 03.05.2011, *Negrepontis-Giannissis v. Greece*, n° 56759/08, §§72–73.

48 C-490/20, above n. 21, para. 55.

49 R. Dworkin, *Law's Empire*, Harvard University Press, Cambridge, Massachusetts, London, 1986.

provide the best constructive interpretation of the community's legal practice'.[50] 'Judges who accept the interpretative ideal of integrity decide hard cases by trying to find, in some coherent set of principles about people's rights and duties, the best constructive interpretation of the political structure and legal doctrine of their community. They try to make that complex structure and record the best these can be.'[51] To do so, a judge must examine the legal system, the applicable rules, and the way these rules are applied in practice. In other words, a legal order or government 'must speak with one voice'. Such a divergence in the way several actors within the same legal order act may be observed in certain decisions of the French administrative courts[52] or the ministerial circular named after Justice Minister Taubira,[53] which permitted children born of surrogacy to obtain travel documents and a certificate of French nationality. Similarly, the disparate treatment of intended parents has been an important sign of inconsistency.

The fact that national judicial decisions are subject to review by the ECtHR and the CJEU shows that public policy, as grounds for opposing recognition, should only withstand such scrutiny where the legal order as a whole is opposed to an institution or to the solutions of foreign law; or at the very least, where there are no significant inconsistencies in the way a particular situation is perceived and treated in that legal order by its authorities and the judiciary.

In summary, the case-law on recognition of parentage following the use of ARTs shows a certain degree of evolution – gradual and not so radical – in the concept and functioning of family. A better-functioning private international law would have found a smoother, prompter solution to the problem of recognizing parentage. Such an improvement may potentially result from raising the standard required for the use of public policy. The need for tightening the terms under which public policy may intervene is all the more crucial given that significant divergences exist in how fundamental issues such as parentage are regulated, even among countries in the same region that share common values and principles.

---

50 ibid., p. 225.

51 ibid., p. 255.

52 Ordinance Conseil d'État: CE, 03.08.2016, n° 401924; TA Paris, réf., 15.11.2011, n° 1120046/9; CE 04.05.2011, n° 348778.

53 Ministerial Circular on the 'Délivrance des certificats de nationalité française – convention de mère porteuse – état civil étranger' circular n° CIV/02/13 – NOR JUSC 1301528C of 25.01.2013.

THREE MODELS FOR REGULATING MULTIPLE PARENTHOOD

A Comparative Perspective

Dafni Lima*

1. INTRODUCTION

How many parents can a child have? This timeless family law question demands new answers in light of the rapid changes that family law has undergone in western jurisdictions over the years.[1] The current rules regulating parenthood across many European jurisdictions can be traced back to the same archetype: a married opposite-sex couple that raises their biological child under the same

* The author can be reached at dafni.lima@durham.ac.uk.

1 Especially as it became increasingly child-centred, see J.M. Scherpe, 'Breaking the existing paradigms of parent-child relationships' in G. Douglas et al. (eds), *International and National Perspectives on Child and Family Law*, Intersentia, 2018, pp. 343–59, at p. 345. For an overview of these developments, see inter alia M. Antokolskaia, *Harmonisation of Family Law in Europe: A Historical Perspective*, Intersentia, 2006; J.M. Scherpe, *The Present and Future of European Family Law*, EE, 2016; P. Servais, 'Historical Insights – The historic evolution of the place of the child in his or her family' in J. Sosson et al. (eds), *Adults and Children in Postmodern Societies*, Intersentia, 2019, pp. 625–40, at pp. 625, 634ff.

roof. Traditionally, maternity is assigned to the person who gives birth,[2] relying on the Roman maxim 'mater semper certa est'. On the other hand, ascribing paternity has been mediated by the father's relationship to the mother, with the most prominent example being the marital presumption of paternity.[3] However, that archetype is increasingly outdated, not only in the practices and realities of parenting on the ground, but also within the spectrum of family formats now recognized in the law.

In recent years, family law across Europe has undergone rapid developments that have challenged these traditional grounds for ascribing parenthood and contributed towards unpicking the constituent elements of this archetype. The introduction of divorce, which did not occur in certain jurisdictions until the late 20th and even early 21st century,[4] and the ensuing gradual liberalization of divorce laws[5] meant that an increasing number of children were now raised by separated parents or by a parent and their new partner. Coupled with rising social acceptance of divorce and a change in legal recognition and societal attitudes towards children born out of wedlock, marriage is no longer viewed as the bedrock of the family[6] – and thus, its central position in the framework of determining paternity is reconsidered.

At the same time, the advent of accurate DNA testing has led to a recalibration of the importance of the genetic connection between father and child and introduced a separate basis both for claiming and for denying paternity.[7] Working in the opposite direction, rapid medical advances in assisted reproduction have challenged the significance of a genetic or gestational connection for establishing parenthood. Gamete donation and surrogacy, both of which remain controversial and indeed not allowed in several European jurisdictions,[8] have nonetheless made it possible for someone to be the legal parent from birth to a biologically unrelated child. It is now possible for a person to carry a pregnancy

---

2 See e,g. in Germany – Bürgerliches Gesetzbuch (BGB) §1591: '*Mutterschaft. Mutter eines Kindes ist die Frau, die es geboren hat*'; in England – The Ampthill Peerage Case [1977] AC 547; in France – Code Civil Article 310-3: '*La filiation se prouve par l'acte de naissance de l'enfant, par l'acte de reconnaissance ou par l'acte de notoriété constatant la possession d'état*'; in Greece – Article 1463 Civil Code.

3 This again dates back to Roman law and the maxim 'pater is est quem nuptiae demonstrant' – the father is he whom the marriage demonstrates. See Dig. 2.4.5.

4 Divorce in Italy was introduced in the 1970s, in Spain in the 1980s, in Ireland in the 1990s, and in Malta only in 2011.

5 See M. Antokolskaia, 'Divorce law in a European perspective' in J.M. Scherpe (ed.), *European Family Law Volume III – Family Law in a European Perspective*, EE, 2016, pp. 41–81.

6 S. Day Sclater et al., 'Introduction' in A. Bainham et al. (eds), *What Is a Parent? A Socio-Legal Analysis*, Hart, 1999, pp. 1–22, at pp. 1, 15.

7 R. Mykitiuk, 'Beyond Conception: Legal Determinations of Filiation in the Context of Assisted Reproductive Technologies' (2001) 39 *Osgoode Hall Law Journal* 771, 783.

8 See, e.g., C. Fenton-Glynn and J.M. Scherpe, 'Surrogacy in a Globalised World' in J.M. Scherpe et al. (eds), *Eastern and Western Perspectives on Surrogacy*, Intersentia, 2019, pp. 515–92.

and give birth using someone else's egg, challenging the unavoidability of the genetic connection between mother and child that arguably underlies the 'mater semper certa est' rule. It is also possible for a child to be born with a genetic connection to more than two persons, via mitochondrial donation,[9] which brings fresh challenges to the centrality of the genetic link for establishing parenthood.

Finally, increasing legal recognition of new family formats has diversified our conceptions of what a parent can look like in the eyes of the law. Same-sex relationships and parenthood have steadily gained recognition across Europe,[10] and along with recent legal debates on trans parenthood[11] and intersex[12] and non-binary individuals, they have challenged the importance of gender in determining parenthood. Emerging attention to other pathways to parenthood, such as co-parenting,[13] living apart together and polyamorous relationships, are bound to present their own unique challenges.

Within this context, our conceptions of parenthood keep evolving in order to accommodate these new realities, albeit in a patchwork fashion. However, one key aspect of this traditional parenthood paradigm remains largely unquestioned: that of the maximum number of two parents. Yet in light of our evolving conceptions of who can be a parent, it is important to open up this pivotal question: can a child have more than two parents? And if so, how should this be regulated? This chapter aims to explain the topicality of recognizing

---

9 See J. Miles et al., *Family Law: Text, Cases, and Materials*, OUP, 2019, p. 659; P-L. Chau and J. Herring, 'Three parents and a baby' (2015) *Family Law* 912. It is also possible to have three genetic parents via ooplasm transfer: see H. Abraham, 'A Family Is What You Make It? Legal Recognition and Regulation of Multiple Parents' (2017) 25(4) *Journal of Gender, Social Policy & the Law* 405, 417.

10 This has led to the expansion of current rules in order to accommodate same-sex couples, including the marital presumption of 'paternity' – or, in the case of same-sex couples, of second male or female parenthood. Two years after Obergefell, the US Supreme Court issued its judgment in *Pavan v. Smith* [137 S. Ct. 2075 (2017)], which held that same-sex spouses had the same right to be listed as parents on a child's birth certificate as opposite-sex spouses did, which means that states should either allow same-sex spouses to be listed on the child's birth certificate, or deprive opposite-sex couples of that right.

11 See A. Margaria, 'Trans Men Giving Birth and Reflections on Fatherhood: What to Expect?' (2020) 43(3) *International Journal of Law, Policy and the Family* 225. In the context of England and Wales, see *Re TT and YY* [2019] EWHC 1823 (Fam) and the subsequent Court of Appeal judgment *R (McConnell and YY) v. Registrar General* [2020] EWCA Civ 559. For a critique of the controversial decision, see C. Fenton-Glynn, 'Deconstructing Parenthood: What Makes a "Mother"?' (2020) 79 *Cambridge Law Journal* 34. By contrast, see *X, Y and Z v. the United Kingdom* – 21830/93 [1997] ECHR 20 [GC], 17, where the European Court of Human Rights found that the UK's refusal to register a trans man as the father of the child born to his partner through artificial insemination by a donor, reasoning that 'only a biological man could be regarded as a father for the purposes of registration', did not violate the applicants' rights under Article 8 of the European Convention on Human Rights.

12 For an overview, see J.M. Scherpe et al. (eds.), *The Legal Status of Intersex Persons*, Intersentia, 2018.

13 As Abraham puts it, 'co-parenting does not only illustrate how "it takes a village to raise a child", but also that it sometimes creates the village': H. Abraham, above n. 9, p. 418.

multiple parenthood and explore the ways in which it can be regulated, identifying three models currently applied in law: the functional approach, the 'best interests' approach and the 'private autonomy' approach.

2. THE IMPORTANCE OF REGULATING MULTIPLE PARENTHOOD

2.1. PARENTAGE, PARENTHOOD AND PARENTAL RESPONSIBILITY

Before turning to cases where multiple claims to *parenthood* can arise, it is important to distinguish between three different concepts: parentage, parental responsibility and parenthood.[14] Parentage denotes a genetic or biological link to a child.[15] This usually means contributing the genetic material, which until recently included the egg and sperm, but can now include some genetic material passed on through mitochondrial donation. Importantly, the biological contribution of gestation can also be included in the scope of parentage, so that the surrogate birth parent in cases of full surrogacy can claim biological parentage.

Parental responsibility is usually defined as the bundle of rights and duties included in the day-to-day parenting of a child, although its exact scope and modes of exercising it (jointly or independently)[16] may differ across jurisdictions.[17] Parental responsibility typically includes daily acts of taking care and providing support for the child, both materially and emotionally, as well as making important decisions that can range from schooling or relocating the child to providing consent for medical treatment. It is important to note that parental responsibility has evolved over the years from the adult-centric parental (or, rather, paternal) *authority*, which reflected the Roman 'patria potestas' and focused on the rights of the parent over the child, to the child-centric notion of

14 A. Bainham, 'Parentage, Parenthood and Parental Responsibility: Subtle, Elusive Yet Important Distinctions' in A. Bainham et al. (eds), *What is a Parent? A Socio-Legal Analysis*, Hart, 1999, pp. 25–46; J.M. Scherpe, 'Breaking the existing paradigms of parent-child relationships', above n. 1.

15 Note that in the US and Canadian jurisdictions examined in this chapter, the term 'parentage' is used rather than 'parenthood'. See, e.g., Connecticut, Sec. 46b-451. Definitions. (15) '"Parentage" or "parent-child relationship" means the legal relationship between a child and a parent of the child'; '"Parentage" means the legal relationship between a child and a parent as established in this chapter' Me. Stat. tit. 19-A §1832.

16 J.M. Scherpe, 'Parental Responsibility – To Consult or Consent, is that the Question?' in J.M. Scherpe and S. Gilmore (eds), *Family Matters – Essays in Honour of John Eekelaar*, 2022, pp. 637–53.

17 See Commission on European Family Law, *Principles of European Family Law Regarding Parental Responsibilities*, 'Chapter V: Content of Parental Responsibilities', Intersentia, 2007, pp. 119–63.

parental *responsibility*, which places emphasis on the best interests of the child at the core of the respective duties and rights of the parent.

Finally, legal parenthood is the overarching legal position of being a parent to a child. This may or may not include parental responsibility, but it will routinely provide a pathway to it. Parenthood is an important and lifelong legal status which provides the highest degree of legally binding commitment for both parent and child. It determines lineage and can have significant consequences in other areas of law, which may include citizenship, immigration, succession, healthcare, tax, consent to adoption, participating in major decisions in a child's life such as relocating abroad etc. As such, it is hard to strip a parent of it – as a rule, a parent must lose parenthood before someone else can acquire it, as in the case of adoption. Therefore, making the leap to break the two-parent paradigm and recognize parenthood across more than two persons without requiring a determination of unfitness of an existing legal parent is a pivotal milestone for any jurisdiction, with an impact not only in family law but also in other areas of law.

2.2. MULTIPLICATION OF POTENTIAL PARENTAL TIES

The recent medical, social, and legal developments that have challenged the traditional grounds for assigning legal parenthood have given rise to competing claims to parenthood. These claims can rest on various sources across the currently recognized potential bases for ascribing parenthood, and can include one or more of them: a genetic or gestational/biological link, legal presumptions, social/psychological parenthood and intention. Intention has routinely been recognized as a potential basis for parenthood in the context of adoption, which dates back to Roman law,[18] but its scope was significantly expanded within the context of assisted reproduction, as it claims priority over a genetic or gestational contribution. As will be shown below, social parenthood and intention are particularly important in the context of multiple parenthood.

In contemporary realities of parenthood, it is not difficult to imagine case studies where more than two people can claim a parental status in a child's life.[19] Diverse pathways to parenthood have been practiced for a long time within the LGBTQ+ community, with same-sex couples often turning to a friend or same-sex couple of the opposite sex to produce a child, with or without a mutual understanding that everyone will be involved – sometimes to varying degrees – in raising the child. Yet multiple parenthood is hardly an issue that is exclusive

18 T. Parkin, 'The Ancient Family and the Law' in L. Kassell et al. (eds), *Reproduction: Antiquity to the Present Day*, CUP, 2018, pp. 81–94, at p. 88.

19 See also G. Motte, 'Multiplication of Potential Social and Emotional Ties' in J. Sosson et al. (eds), *Adults and Children in Postmodern Societies*, Intersentia, 2019, pp. 793–823.

to queer parents.[20] Both assisted reproduction and family reshuffling makes multiple parenthood particularly pertinent for both queer and 'traditional' families.

In assisted reproduction, claims to parenthood can rest on genetic contributions, gestation, legal presumptions and the intention to be a parent. Taking the example of surrogacy, any two of the following people can claim parenthood at birth, depending on the rules governing surrogacy in a specific jurisdiction: the surrogate and their spouse/partner, if they have one (based on gestation and legal presumption); the persons who provided the sperm and the eggs (based on their respective genetic contributions); and the intended parent or parents (based on intention). This immediately yields up to six potential parents for the child, depending on the legal basis that is prioritized.

Yet multiple parenthood can also easily arise in the case of natural reproduction. Take the example of a mixed-sex couple who split up and continue to raise their biological child amicably and cooperatively with each other. It is very common for a new partner or partners to enter the family landscape and participate in parenting the child – perhaps to a larger degree than one of the legal parents. Yet for that new partner to acquire parental status, a previous legal parent must lose it, which might go against both the social reality of more than two people parenting the child and be against the wishes of all parties involved.

Recognizing multiple parenthood can offer protection to the child as well as the non-legally recognized parent. While the relevant legal debates are often meddled with concerns about the potential for greater conflict when more than two people are recognized as parents, research has shown that recognizing multiple parenthood can help resolve conflict and introduce more stability and protection for the child by providing legal recognition for a situation that is already happening on the ground.[21] Imagine a case where a child has been exclusively cared for since birth by the maternal aunt, while both the mother and the father (who split up with the mother shortly after birth) have been absent. If the father returns when the child is already a few years old and wishes to take over exclusive parenting over the child, there is nothing the maternal aunt can do to avoid this, even though she has been the only 'parent' the child has ever known. She might be able to claim some limited contact rights, but not much else, absent a legal framework that can recognize her claim to parenthood on par with that of the father's.

---

20 See C. Joslin and D. NeJaime, 'Multi-Parent Families, Real and Imagined' (2022) 90 *Fordham Law Review* 2561, 2567ff.

21 C. Joslin and D. NeJaime, above n. 20, p. 2582, who note that 'an examination of West Virginia case law shows that courts are confronted with families in which recognition of a third (or fourth) parent would promote, rather than undermine, children's interests. That is, multi-parent recognition can make the lives of the children in these cases more stable and less conflictual – exactly the opposite of what many commentators assume multi-parent recognition will yield'.

Although it is reasonable to assume that the current two-parent model will be able to sufficiently accommodate the realities of most families, these examples highlight the significance of a legal framework that allows the option of recognizing more than two legal parents. Across European jurisdictions, the law has so far prioritized the claims to legal parenthood of up to two people, at the expense of other potential parents.[22] Thus, different answers may be given in each jurisdiction. For example, when a female same-sex couple uses a friend's sperm to conceive, it will either be the female partner (who is not the birth mother) or the sperm donor who will be recognized in law as the second parent, but not both. Yet this is not the only way to deal with competing claims to parenthood. Several jurisdictions in the US and Canada have now introduced rules that allow recognition of legal parenthood across more than two people.[23] Employing a comparative approach to examine their respective legal frameworks can allow us to draw helpful conclusions about the different potential models on how to regulate multiple parenthood.[24] One key categorization is the rationale upon which recognition of multiple parenthood will rest. This can vary across three main strands: the functional approach, the 'best interests' approach and the 'private autonomy' approach.

3. THREE MODELS FOR REGULATING MULTIPLE PARENTHOOD

A comparative look into North American jurisdictions that regulate multiple parenthood in law[25] can lead us to identify three different approaches. The jurisdictions of Delaware and Maine in the US rely exclusively on the doctrine

---

22 See K. Baker, 'Bionormativity and the Construction of Parenthood' (2008) 42 *Georgia Law Review* 649, 671–91, for further arguments on why binary parenthood has prevailed in the US.

23 This chapter focuses on Delaware, Maine, California, Connecticut, Vermont and Washington in the US, and British Columbia and Ontario in Canada. It should also be noted that the 2017 Uniform Parentage Act includes an alternative that allows states to recognize multiple parents: see Uniform Parentage Act §609 (Unif. L. Comm'n 2017); S.B. 1133, 192d Gen. Ct. (Mass. 2021).

24 This chapter focuses on jurisdictions that regulate multiple *legal parenthood*. There is another way to deal with competing claims to parental status, which is to retain the two-parent paradigm, but recognize multiple holders of *parental responsibility*, as in the jurisdictions of England and Wales, and Finland. On the different conceptions of parental responsibility that allow English law to allocate it to more than two parties, see J.M. Scherpe, 'Parental Responsibility: To Consult or Consent, is that the Question?', above n. 16, pp. 637, 639–41. Abraham also distinguishes between 'egalitarian' (where 'all [multiparents] perceive themselves as having the same status, rights and obligations') and 'hierarchal' structures of multiple parenthood (where some individuals have a full parental status and others 'a more limited standing'): see H. Abraham, above n. 9, p. 407.

25 As opposed to those where more than two parents may be recognized by court decision: see, e.g., the case law examined by C. Joslin and D. NeJaime, above n. 20.

of 'de facto' parenthood to regulate multiple parenthood, which rests on a functional conception of parenthood.[26] This is close, but adequately distinct, to the approach adopted by the jurisdictions of California, Vermont, Washington and Connecticut, which focuses on the best interests of the child. Finally, the Canadian jurisdictions of British Columbia and Ontario have taken a completely different approach and introduced a multiple parenthood system that relies on private pre-conception agreements.

3.1. THE FUNCTIONAL APPROACH

The rationale of the functional approach is the recognition of an *existing parent-like relationship* between the child and a third party beyond the two legal parents. In that sense, this approach is retrospective, looking into the past and leading up to the present, in order to establish that a relationship exists which bears the hallmarks of a parent-child relationship. Whether or not that is the case is a substantial question that requires an evaluation of the facts, which is why a judicial determination is needed to confer de facto parenthood. In both Delaware[27] and Maine,[28] which are the two jurisdictions representative of this

---

26 The jurisdiction of the District of Columbia also recognizes a de facto parent in addition to two parents, but this recognition affects specific areas regarding custody, alimony and maintenance, does not confer full parenthood. See Code of the District of Columbia, Chapter 8A, §16–831.03 (2022).

27 Del. Code Ann. tit. 13, 8-201(c) (2021): 'De facto parent status is established if the Family Court determines that the de facto parent: (1) Has had the support and consent of the child's parent or parents who fostered the formation and establishment of a parent-like relationship between the child and the de facto parent; (2) Has exercised parental responsibility for the child as that term is defined in §1101 of this title; and (3) Has acted in a parental role for a length of time sufficient to have established a bonded and dependent relationship with the child that is parental in nature'.

28 Me. Stat. tit. 19-A §1853 (2) (2022): 'Preservation of parent-child relationship – Consistent with the establishment of parentage under this chapter, a court may determine that a child has more than 2 parents' and §1891 '1. De facto parentage. The court may adjudicate a person to be a de facto parent. 2. Standing to seek de facto parentage. … 3. Adjudication of de facto parent status. The court shall adjudicate a person to be a de facto parent if the court finds by clear and convincing evidence that the person has fully and completely undertaken a permanent, unequivocal, committed and responsible parental role in the child's life. Such a finding requires a determination by the court that: A. The person has resided with the child for a significant period of time; B. The person has engaged in consistent caretaking of the child; C. A bonded and dependent relationship has been established between the child and the person, the relationship was fostered or supported by another parent of the child and the person and the other parent have understood, acknowledged or accepted that or behaved as though the person is a parent of the child; D. The person has accepted full and permanent responsibilities as a parent of the child without expectation of financial compensation; and E. The continuing relationship between the person and the child is in the best interest of the child. 4. Orders. … 5. Other parents. The adjudication of a person under this subchapter as a de facto parent does not disestablish the parentage of any other parent'.

approach, it is the court that will determine whether the requirements for de facto parenthood are met.

In contrast to the best interests approach, which will be outlined below, the functional approach sets out strict requirements that must be met for a person to be recognized as a de facto parent.[29] These requirements include *substantial* conditions related to the nature of the relationship and the exercise of care over the child; a *temporal* condition related to the amount of time for which the relationship has existed; a '*parental consent*' condition related to the stance of the existing legal parent or parents with regard to the formation of this relationship; and a requirement that this recognition is in the *best interests* of the child.

The first set of requirements relates to the nature of the relationship developed between the parent and the child, which according to both jurisdictions must be 'bonded and dependent', echoing the law's understanding of what it means to be a parent. The Delaware code further requires that this bonded and dependent relationship be 'parental in nature', while the Maine statute goes further into detail in its wording, requiring that that the de facto parent 'has fully and completely undertaken a permanent, unequivocal, committed and responsible parental role in the child's life'. The de facto parent must have cared for the child – a requirement that is framed in terms of exercising parental responsibility over the child in the Delaware code. In that same vein, the Maine statute requires that the de facto parent must have engaged in 'consistent caretaking' of the child and must have 'accepted full and permanent responsibilities as a parent of the child without expectation of financial compensation'.

A second important condition is a temporal requirement that the relationship must have existed for a 'significant' or 'sufficient' amount of time. It is noteworthy that neither jurisdiction provides for a specific threshold, for example one year. Instead, they leave this evaluation to the court. This might better reflect the realities of de facto parenthood, where the de facto parent gradually assumes an increasingly parental role, making it difficult to pinpoint a specific date when the relationship transformed into a parental one. However, under the Maine statute there is a specific point of reference: the de facto parent must have *resided* with the child for a significant period of time. Under the Delaware code, which includes no such requirement, the temporal element is instead framed in terms of *acting in a parental role* for a length of time sufficient to establish a bonded, dependent and parental relationship with the child.

Finally, a third condition, and one that again sets the functional approach apart from the 'best interests' approach, is that this parent-child relationship must have been formed with the consent and support of another parent of the

[29] See, e.g., the wording of the Maine statute: 'The court shall adjudicate a person to be a de facto parent if the court finds *by clear and convincing evidence* that ...' (emphasis added).

child.[30] This requirement puts the existing parent in a powerful position, as they are in charge of who can be allowed to develop a parental relationship with their child, presumably adding a protective layer for the child. However, this is again formulated as a retrospective requirement, meaning that the parent might have now changed their mind and oppose the recognition of the de facto parent. It is notable that while this is an important requirement, it is the only one where the existence of a de facto parental relationship is mediated through the relationship of the de facto parent with another parent. There are no further requirements in either jurisdiction that the de facto parent be a partner or a relative of the parent, nor are there any limitations on who *cannot* be a de facto parent, for example relatives of the parent(s) who already have kinship to the child. There is also no explicit maximum number of parents that can be recognized by the court.

One issue that is handled differently in these two jurisdictions is the matter of shared residence between the de facto parent and the child. While the Maine statute requires that the de facto parent has *resided* with the child for a significant period of time, the Delaware code makes no such mention, allowing the courts to be more flexible in their determination. Finally, the Maine statute explicitly requires the courts to take into account the best interests of the child, while the Delaware code does not include such a provision.[31] Unlike within the 'best interests' approach, in the functional approach the best interests of the child is simply one of the elements considered by the court, rather than being the overarching consideration.

The functional approach focuses firmly on the reality on the ground, paying equal attention to all three parties involved: the de facto parent, the child and the existing legal parent(s). In order to establish functional parenthood, requirements that are related to all three must be met, including the exercise of functional parenthood by the de facto parent (and its constituent elements, notably a bonded and dependent relationship, and the exercise of care over the child); the best interests of the child; and the consent/support of the other parent(s). The functional approach affords the courts flexibility and increases protection for both child and de facto parent. However, while its inherently

---

[30] The Delaware code states that the de facto parent must have had 'the support and consent of the child's parent or parents who fostered the formation and establishment of a parent-like relationship between the child and the de facto parent'. The Maine statute requires that 'the relationship was fostered or supported by another parent of the child and the person and the other parent have understood, acknowledged or accepted that or behaved as though the person is a parent of the child'. The consent of one parent suffices, as the Maine statute provides for the opportunity for an 'adverse party, parent or legal guardian' to oppose the person who petitioned the court for recognition of their de facto parenthood.

[31] By contrast, the Delaware code makes explicit mention to the best interests of the child as a guiding principle for the court in the context of legal custody and residential arrangements – see Del. Code Ann. tit. 13, §722 (2021).

comparative nature can allow the courts the flexibility needed to recognize new ways to parent a child that are *similar enough* to those already recognized in law, it can also conversely serve to gatekeep and restrict our conceptions of parenthood *only to those that are already similar* to parenthood as we already know it.[32]

3.2. THE BEST INTERESTS APPROACH

The best interests approach is not conceptually completely unrelated to the functional approach. As was mentioned, the best interests of the child form part of the court's determination under the functional approach. However, in the best interests approach, this element is brought to the forefront and forms the single most important determination by the court. Therefore, one important distinction between the two approaches is that the various elements considered by the court are not strict requirements – as in the functional approach – but mere indicators to determine where the child's welfare lies. This includes the support and consent of the other parent(s), which means that under the best interests approach the existing legal parent(s) is no longer in such a powerful position as in the functional approach: they might have opposed the development of a parental relationship between the potential parent and the child from the start, but this is something that the court may simply take into account, and its ruling on whether to recognize parenthood will not rest on this. In fact, in none of the jurisdictions examined here as representative of the best interests approach is the consent or support of an existing parent explicitly required in order to establish multiple parenthood, albeit in the jurisdictions of Washington,[33] Vermont[34]

---

32 See A. Diduck, 'If Only We Can Find the Appropriate Terms to Use the Issue Will Be Solved: Law, Identity and Parenthood' (2007) 19 *Child and Family Law Quarterly* 458, for arguments on the risk of assimilation and normalization in the context of lesbian couples, which could also be applied to the case of multi-parent families. For example, she notes that 'lesbian parent families emphasise their normality, but while courts interpret that emphasis and claim to normality by promoting their formal equality with heterosexual families, they normalise them, pre-empting innovations in the legal imagination and inhibiting the possibility of forging new constructs' (at p. 480).

33 Wash. Rev. Code §26.26A.440(4)(f) (2022) 'In a proceeding to adjudicate parentage of an individual who claims to be a de facto parent of the child, the court shall adjudicate the individual who claims to be a de facto parent to be a parent of the child if the individual demonstrates by a preponderance of the evidence that: … (f) Another parent of the child fostered or supported the bonded and dependent relationship required under (e) of this subsection …'.

34 Vt. Stat. Ann. tit. 15C, §501 (2022) '(a)(1) In a proceeding to adjudicate the parentage of a person who claims to be a de facto parent of the child, if there is only one other person who is a parent or has a claim to parentage of the child, the court shall adjudicate the person who claims to be a de facto parent to be a parent of the child if the person demonstrates by clear and convincing evidence that … (F) the person and another parent of the child fostered or supported the bonded and dependent relationship required under subdivision (E) of this

and Connecticut[35] it is needed under the separate provisions that regulate de facto parenthood specifically. Rather than an equal consideration of all three parties under the functional approach, in the best interests approach it is the child and its welfare that is elevated above all else. Therefore, while in the jurisdictions examined here de facto parenthood can be one pathway to multiple parenthood[36] and relevant laws demonstrate similarities across the functional and the best interests approaches, it is feasible to categorize a specific jurisdiction as falling within one rather than the other.

The jurisdictions chosen here as representative of the best interests approach are California,[37] Vermont,[38] Connecticut[39] and Washington.[40] Out of those, California is the most clear example of the best interests approach, while Vermont, Connecticut and Washington can also be viewed as having mixed elements: all three regulate de facto parenthood in the same vein as under the functional approach, but have also introduced a broader provision that allows the courts to recognize more than two parents based on the best interests of the child, which does not refer exclusively to de facto parenthood.

The question of the best interests of the child is again left to the court, which may find that a child has more than two parents if that is in the best interests of the child (Vermont) or if recognizing only two parents would be detrimental to the child (California, Washington, Connecticut). Thus, the court under this

---

subdivision (1) … (b) In a proceeding to adjudicate the parentage of a person who claims to be a de facto parent of the child, if there is more than one other person who is a parent or has a claim to parentage of the child and the court determines that the requirements of subsection (a) of this section are met by clear and convincing evidence, the court shall adjudicate parentage under section 206 of this title, subject to other applicable limitations in this title'.

35 Connecticut Parentage Act Ch 818, §46b-490 (2022) 'Adjudicating claim of de facto parentage of child. (a) In a proceeding to adjudicate parentage of a person who claims to be a de facto parent of the child, if there is only one other person who is a parent or has a claim to parentage of the child, the court shall adjudicate the person who claims to be a de facto parent to be a parent of the child if the person demonstrates by clear and convincing evidence that: … (6) Another parent of the child fostered or supported the bonded and dependent relationship required under subdivision (5) of this subsection … (c) Subject to other limitations set forth in this section and section 46b-491, if, in a proceeding to adjudicate parentage of a person who claims to be a de facto parent of the child, there is more than one other person who is a parent or has a claim to parentage of the child and the court determines that the requirements of subsection (a) of this section are satisfied, the court shall adjudicate parentage under section 46b-475, provided the adjudication of a person as a de facto parent under this section shall not disestablish the parentage of any other parent, nor limit any other parent's rights under the laws of this state'.

36 See the very similar wording between regulating de facto parenthood under the Washington, Vermont and Connecticut laws, and the de facto parenthood provisions of Maine and Delaware.

37 California Code, Family Code – FAM §7612 (c) (2021).

38 Vt. Stat. Ann. tit. 15C, §206(b) (2022).

39 Connecticut Parentage Act Ch 818, §46b-475 (2022).

40 Wash. Rev. Code §26.26A.501 (2022).

approach has increased leeway, as it does not need to establish that specific requirements are met.[41] Instead, it must consider 'all relevant factors', which include the harm to the child 'if it is removed from a stable placement with an individual who has fulfilled the child's physical needs and psychological needs for care and affection and has assumed the role for a substantial period' (California, Washington, Connecticut).[42] The factors considered here are reminiscent of the functional approach, as the court will examine whether a stable caring relationship exists and whether the temporal aspect ('for a substantial period') is satisfied. However, the threshold is more flexible than under the functional approach, as this relationship is not explicitly framed in terms of being parent-like and is only considered as one factor in determining the child's welfare. Indeed, the court must follow a two-step test: first, whether not recognizing parenthood would mean removing the child from this stable caring relationship, and second, whether that would be harmful to the child.

The court does not, however, need to determine that any other existing parent(s) are unfit in order to find that removing the child would be to its detriment. This affirms the departure from the two-parent paradigm, where in order to establish parenthood of a third person, one of the existing parents would have to be stripped of that status, which would usually involve a determination of unfitness. Furthermore, as in the functional approach, no limitations are introduced as to who can be recognized as a parent, nor is there a maximum number of parents set out in law.

California law stops here, allowing courts a high degree of discretion. In contrast, the Vermont, Connecticut, and Washington jurisdictions include a checklist of further relevant factors that the court shall consider when adjudicating competing claims of parentage based on the best interests of the child. These factors include elements considered under the functional approach, albeit framed in broader terms: the nature of the relationship between the child and every individual; the harm to the child if the relationship is not recognized; and the length of time during which each individual assumed the role of parent of the child. Under the best interests approach, the age of the child, as well as 'other equitable factors' that would arise from the disruption of this relationship or the likelihood of *other* harm to the child are explicitly taken into account, which affirms the focus of this model on the child itself.[43] Finally, under the checklist, the basis of each individual's claim to parentage is also considered when deciding the best interests of the child. This confirms that, unlike under

41 Apart from those outlined in the respective provisions regulating a specific pathway to parenthood, e.g., the requirements to establish de facto parenthood referred to above.

42 By contrast, Vermont does not include such wording.

43 Adding emphasis, the Connecticut law repeats 'any other factor the court deems relevant to the child's best interests' as a further, separate factor.

the functional approach, de facto parenthood is not the only pathway to multiple parenthood under the best interests model.

3.3. THE PRIVATE AUTONOMY APPROACH

The third approach to regulating multiple parenthood examined in this chapter is drastically different to both the functional and the best interests approach, as it shifts the focus to private pre-conception parenthood agreements. Despite their differences, the jurisdictions of British Columbia[44] and of Ontario[45] in Canada are representative of this approach. Unlike the functional and best interests models, which were retrospective, the private autonomy approach outlined here is *prospective*, looking into the future of who will be a parent to the child in question. Under this approach, future parenthood is determined *before* conception of the child, and therefore there is no existing parenting reality to take into account. The parties draw up a private agreement which outlines who will be the legal parents of the child to be born. This agreement can include parties who agree to *not* be a legal parent, as in the case of Ontario law, where the person giving birth must be party to the agreement, agreeing either to *be* a legal parent together with the other parties or to *not be* a legal parent.

This highlights an important aspect of the private autonomy approach: while private autonomy lies at its core, it is not left unchecked. Limitations and safeguards are introduced to protect all parties, which extend to who can be party to the agreement, the maximum number of parents, and the scope of application of relevant provisions. Importantly, there are limitations on who can enter into a parental agreement. Yet instead of *negative* limitations on who *cannot* be part of the agreement, these are framed as *positive* limitations, i.e., requiring that certain persons *must* be parties to the agreement for it to be valid. Notably, this includes the birth parent under both jurisdictions. Under British Columbia law, the agreement must be made between the birth mother and an intended parent or parents, or between the birth mother, her spouse or spouse-like partner, and a donor, thus introducing a maximum number of up to three potential parents. While in the second case these limitations also conversely regulate who *can* be party to the agreement, in the first case there are no further limitations on who could be the intended parent(s).

Ontario law also deals with two distinct cases of pre-conception parenthood agreements by virtue of which more than two parents can be established, distinguishing between non-surrogacy[46] and surrogacy cases.[47] In both cases,

44 Family Law Act [SBC 2011] Ch. 25, Section 30.
45 All Families Are Equal Act (Parentage and Related Registrations Statute Law Amendment), 2016, S.O. 2016, c. 23 – Bill 28, Sections 9–11.
46 All Families Are Equal Act, Section 9.
47 All Families Are Equal Act, Sections 10–11.

the birth parent must be party to the agreement, agreeing *to be* a legal parent in non-surrogacy cases and agreeing *to not be* a legal parent in surrogacy cases.[48] Ontario law introduces a limit of up to four potential parents, which means that in surrogacy cases there are up to five parties to the agreement. However, in surrogacy cases the surrogate is still a parent at birth and must provide written consent relinquishing parenthood after the child is seven days old, thus providing a reflection period of one week within which the surrogate can change their mind. Therefore, during the first seven days the child effectively has five parents, and if the surrogate does not provide that consent, then the court can adjudicate parenthood according to the best interests of the child, which can include more than four parents.[49]

The law in both jurisdictions further regulates the scope of the agreement by introducing other limitations and safeguards, notably that the agreement must be made *before conception*. Yet one important difference is that, under British Columbia law, the private autonomy approach is only applied when a child is conceived through assisted reproduction. Thus, cases of natural reproduction or other pathways to parenthood such as adoption are excluded. By contrast, under Ontario law, pre-conception agreements can also be valid in natural reproduction cases.

A distinctive feature of the private autonomy approach is the process through which parenthood is established. The focus shifts from a substantive evaluation of an existing parent-child relationship under the functional and the best interests models, which should be undertaken by a judicial authority, to recognition of private agreements after checking that certain formalities laid out in law are met, which can be carried out by administrative authorities. If these formalities are not met or in case of unforeseen developments, the matter can be taken up before the courts.[50]

---

48 In non-surrogacy cases, the person providing the sperm in case of natural reproduction or the spouse of the birth parent in cases on assisted reproduction or artificial insemination must also be parties to the agreement. The birth parent's spouse may also provide written confirmation before the child is conceived that they do not wish to be a parent, in which case they do not need to be party to the agreement.

49 A surrogacy agreement is unenforceable under Ontario law, but can be used as evidence of the parties' intentions.

50 As Leckey points out with regard to Ontario's All Families Are Equal Act, while Ontario's law intended to provide administrative, non-judicial paths to multiple parenthood, families might still turn to courts when the new requirements for automatic recognition of a parental agreement are not met. In that case, given the pre-reform practice of judicial activism in recognizing diverse family forms in the absence of a statute that would regulate multiple parenthood, Ontario judges might still be inclined to recognize multiple parenthood outside the statute, taking the parental agreement that does not meet the law's requirements as proof of relevant intention to be a parent. Leckey advises against this, warning that 'Once the legislature replaces a framework "hostile to lived forms of family" with one opening accessible paths to law's recognition for diverse family forms, it may be advisable for judges to temper their creativity. Even judges committed to being antihomophobic, queer-affirmative,

4. CONCLUSIONS

The differences between the three models, and especially between the functional and the best interests approach on one hand, and the party autonomy approach on the other hand, raise interesting questions about the principles guiding the regulation of multiple parenthood, which also reveal different underlying conceptions of parenthood more generally. The first two approaches aim to align legal recognition with the social reality of an existing parental relationship on the ground, either by focusing on de facto parenthood or the best interests of the child. By contrast, in the party autonomy approach, no parental ties have formed yet, as legal parenthood is left up to the parties that draw up the pre-conception agreement. This highlights two levels of tension: one between regulation and regularization (or paternalism/interventionism and private autonomy), and one between predictability and flexibility.

The opposing terms of 'regulation' vs. 'regularization'[51] were introduced by John Eekelaar in the context of divorce law.[52] Under the 'regularization' approach, the law accepts that relationship breakdown will occur regardless of whether the legal process for divorce is more or less strict, and aims to regulate the process in a way that does not add to the harms involved and largely leaves it up to the parties to settle its consequences. By contrast, under the 'regulation' approach, divorce law assumes a more paternalistic role in the process by imposing stricter requirements and restrictions that reflect the state's view on the importance of marriage.

If we apply that same dichotomy in the context of the laws regulating multiple parenthood, then we could come up with a spectrum that reflects the law's understanding of what it means to be a parent. The functional approach would reflect the most intense form of regulation, as the law imposes a checklist of strict requirement to be met, and thus a substantial judicial determination is necessary. The best interests approach would still fall under regulation, albeit one where the courts are given more leeway by following the overarching guiding principle of the child's best interests. Finally, the private autonomy approach would reflect 'regularization', where the law largely leaves it up to the parties to determine who will be the legal parents, and introduces limited restrictions and safeguards.

Where each jurisdiction chooses to position its rules on regulating multiple parenthood within that spectrum will reflect its underlying assumptions about

and alert to feminist concerns may wisely channel these commitments through the legislative text'. See R. Leckey, 'One Parent, Three Parents: Judges and Ontario's All Families Are Equal Act, 2016' (2019) 33(3) *International Journal of Law, Policy and the Family* 298.

51 Abraham describes a similar dichotomy by using the terms 'regulation' and 'recognition': see H. Abraham, above n. 9, 408.

52 See J. Eekelaar, *Regulating Divorce*, Clarendon Press, 1991, p. 142ff.

parenthood: is legal parenthood a matter that can in large part be left up to private agreement and intention, or should the state play a substantial role in outlining what a legal parent looks like in practice? This will also determine the degree to which the state will intervene in the process, which will be reflected in the capacity of the state authority designated to deal with the issue – judicial (in jurisdictions that lean towards 'regulation') or administrative (in jurisdictions that lean towards 'regularization'). Framing the issue in terms of regulation vs regularization also highlights that regardless of where the law stands, individuals can develop *parental* relationships to children without being recognized as legal parents, as the lived experiences of queer parents have unequivocally demonstrated.

The second, related level of tension is that between predictability and flexibility. The private autonomy approach lends itself to more predictable and thus more secure outcomes with respect to who will be the legal parents of the child to be born. However, it cannot accommodate developments that happen further down the road in a child's life, and allow for the recognition of new parental relationships that come into play. Conversely, jurisdictions that favour regulation can be seen as providing more security for the child, by limiting and regulating who can be recognized as a legal parent, as opposed to jurisdictions that rely on private autonomy, which can provide more flexibility in that respect. The dilemma between security and flexibility can thus be seen as a false one in many respects, as relevant considerations can vary according to the perspective prioritized.

What remains essential, however, is that the approach adopted to recognize multiple parenthood caters to both security and flexibility – not only for the child, but for all parties involved. While the jurisdictions examined in this chapter demonstrate different ways to regulate multiple parenthood, laws can combine elements from all three: for example, by both honouring pre-conception agreements and recognizing de facto parenthood. The choice will ultimately reflect the current conceptions of parenthood that underlie family law in each jurisdiction.

WHEN FILIATION FAILS

Adoption as a Fallback Mechanism for Modern Family Forms?

Christiane VON BARY

1. INTRODUCTION

Adoption has long been used to create a legal parent–child relationship in order to help adults who cannot have biological children overcome childlessness and to provide care for children.[1] It is a legal mechanism which exists in most countries.[2] Historically, the focus was mainly on the needs and wishes

---

1 This chapter only addresses the adoption of children and does not discuss adult adoption, which is possible in many countries but concerns a different situation that is not determined by a child in need of day-to-day care.

2 The exception being many countries with an Islamic legal tradition where adoption is forbidden for religious reasons. Instead, those countries provide for 'kafala', a functional equivalent without a change of full legal status. See P. OREJUDO PRIETO DE LOS MOZOS, 'Adoption' in J. BASEDOW, G. RÜHL, F. FERRARI and P. DE MIGUEL ASENSIO (eds), *Encyclopedia*

of the adults and allowing them to establish an heir through adoption.[3] This is for example reflected in the fact that the original German Civil Code only permitted the adoption of a child if the adult had no children of their own and was more than 50 years of age.[4] Today, the focus has shifted towards an approach which puts the needs of the child in the centre.[5] The primary purpose of an adoption now is to give a child a permanent home when the birth parents cannot fulfil this role. For various reasons on both the side of adoptive parents and birth parents the number of adoptions has been decreasing in Europe since the 1970s.[6] Amongst those reasons are decreased stigma regarding non-marital children, better access to birth control and the possibilities of fertility medicine. Legal hurdles have also had an effect, especially on the decline of intercountry adoptions. In particular the successful 1993 Hague Convention on Intercountry Adoption[7] has set up a restrictive legal framework to protect children and their families from child trafficking.

However, adoption still plays an important role today in ensuring that children can legally be fully integrated into a new family, which increasingly often is a stepfamily. Additionally, adoption has lately assumed a new function, which this chapter focuses on: contrary to the origins of adoption, it is under some circumstances used to legally integrate children into the family they are born into and were intended to be born into. Since adoption usually creates a legal parent–child relationship equal to the one established through parenthood,[8] it has emerged as a substitute in cases where the law does not allow for the allocation of legal parenthood at birth through any other way. This is true in particular for same-sex couples – provided that adoption is open to them – and couples using a surrogate mother to carry their child. The once clear line between adoption and parenthood therefore is becoming increasingly blurred.[9]

---

of Private International Law, Edward Elgar, Cheltenham 2017, pp. 13–21, at p. 14; M. Rohe, *Das islamische Recht*, C.H. Beck, München 2009, p. 29.

3 K. O'Halloran, *The Politics of Adoption*, 3rd ed., Springer, Dordrecht 2015, p. 6 f. See also for example the explanation to the draft of the German Civil Code: B. Mudgan, *Die gesamten Materialien zum Bürgerlichen Gesetzbuch für das Deutsche Reich*, 1899, Part IV, p. 952.

4 See §§ 1741, 1744 German Civil Code 1896.

5 J.M. Scherpe, *The Present and Future of European Family Law*, Edward Elgar, Cheltenham 2016, p. 86.

6 J. Mignot, 'Child Adoption in Western Europe, 1900–2015' <https://halshs.archives-ouvertes.fr/halshs-02008838> accessed 25.04.2022.

7 Convention of 29 May 1993 on Protection of Children and Co-operation in Respect of Intercountry Adoption. The convention has been adopted by 104 countries so far; for a status table see <https://www.hcch.net/en/instruments/conventions/status-table/?cid=69> accessed 25.04.2022.

8 For details, see below, section 3.1.

9 Similarly for the distinction between surrogacy and adoption, K. Trimmings and P. Beaumont, 'International surrogacy arrangements: an urgent need for legal regulation at the international level' (2011) *Journal of Private International Law* 627, 638.

This chapter explores when and how adoption is used to establish a legal parent-child relationship in modern family forms and whether adoption is a suitable mechanism to solve the problems these families face when having children. Initially, the situations in which adoption is used because legal parenthood cannot be acquired in any other way are discussed. Then, turning to national adoption law, this chapter explores how adoption law does and does not account for the circumstances of increasingly diverse family forms. After looking at the national context – albeit with a comparative perspective – the focus shifts to the problems in international cases, looking at questions of recognition and private international law. The chapter ends by suggesting criteria to determine how to delineate between adoption and acquiring parenthood by law.

2. THE ROLE OF ADOPTION IN MODERN FAMILY FORMS

Traditionally, creating a parent–child relationship through filiation has followed the pattern of what was considered the 'normal' family: a different-sex married couple and their children who are genetically related to them. Thus, the law was designed to allocate legal parenthood in these cases. A growing number of countries have started to adapt the law of parenthood to modern family forms. Other countries have resisted granting any protection to families outside of the traditional norm. This includes no legal recognition of same-sex partnerships and no possibility of adoption for these couples.[10] Sometimes this problem is circumvented by an adoption by a single person, even if they live with a same-sex partner.[11] In these countries, using adoption law in the way analysed in this chapter is especially difficult, if not impossible. Both ends of the spectrum – the most and the least progressive countries – mostly fall outside of the scope of this investigation. The focus instead is on

---

10 J.M. Scherpe, above n. 5, p. 87. In Italy, for example, adoption is not explicitly open to same-sex couples because this was rejected during the legislative procedure resulting in the Civil Partnership Act (Legge 20 maggio 2016, n. 76 Regolamentazione delle unioni civili tra persone dello stesso sesso e disciplina delle convivenze), which introduced a registered partnership for same-sex couples (see A. Pera, 'The "Law in Context" for (Stepchild) Adoption in Same-Sex Couples: The Italian Models' in C. Rogerson, M. Antokolskaia, J. Miles, P. Parkinson and M. Vonk (eds), *Family Law and Family Realities*, Eleven International Publishing, The Hague 2019, pp. 187–202, at p. 191). However, Art. 44(1)(d) of the Adoption Act (Legge 4 maggio 1983, n. 184 Diritto del minore ad una famiglia), a provision on adoption in special cases, has been used by courts, including the Corte di Cassazione (22.06.2016, no. 12962), to allow for stepchild adoption for same-sex couples.

11 See, e.g., C. Fenton-Glynn, 'Adoption in a European perspective' in J.M. Scherpe (ed.), *European Family Law Volume III*, Edward Elgar, Cheltenham 2016, pp. 311–40, at p. 329.

the many countries that still largely follow the traditional model but have started to adapt to modern family forms in some regards. Usually, same-sex partnerships are accepted but same-sex parenthood is only recognized to a limited degree. Some forms of artificial reproduction are possible but surrogacy is not permitted.

Although the details are more complex and vary between jurisdictions,[12] for the purposes of this investigation, a very simplified explanation of the traditional rules of allocating parenthood at birth, which the countries addressed in this chapter still follow, suffices. The legal mother is the woman who gives birth to the child.[13] Determining fatherhood has traditionally not been as straightforward and the law generally provides for more than one route to becoming a legal father. Many countries follow a so-called marital presumption, meaning that the husband of the mother is the legal father of the child.[14] Additionally, fatherhood can be established through either a declaration of recognition by the father,[15] sometimes only with the consent of the mother,[16] or by a court decision which often involves proving genetic fatherhood.

These general principles of establishing parenthood are facing challenges where assisted reproduction and modern family forms are concerned. While the traditional rules are modelled after the genetic ties most commonly present for children of married different-sex couples, a genetic connection is not always strictly necessary. When different-sex couples resort to assisted reproduction, in most cases with the exception of surrogacy, they can acquire legal parenthood under the traditional framework despite a lack of genetic ties: the woman giving birth after an egg donation is the legal mother, the man who is married to her will be the legal father even if donated sperm was used, and a recognition does usually not require a proof of genetic ties.

The same, however, is not equally true for same-sex couples who have children and couples who rely on a surrogate to carry their child. Despite the societal development towards a greater acceptance of diverse family forms, equal treatment is still a work in progress, especially concerning children in these families. Therefore, in these cases, the adults are often not able to acquire legal parenthood at birth even though they decided to have a child together and from the beginning intended to become parents of the child together. Although in many countries, laws are changing and increasingly offer protection for same-

---

12 For an in-depth comparative approach to parenthood, see C. Fenton-Glynn (ed.), *Comparative Parenthood*, Cambridge, Intersentia (forthcoming).

13 See N. Dethloff, *Familienrecht*, 32nd ed., C.H. Beck, Munich 2018, §10 para. 105.

14 P. Reuß, *Theorie eines Elternschaftsrechts*, Duncker & Humblot, Berlin 2018, pp. 305 ff.

15 N. Dethloff, above n. 13, §10 para. 107.

16 N. Dethloff, above n. 13, §10 para. 105.

sex relationships, this is still not true in other countries.[17] And even if the relationship between same-sex partners is legally recognized, same-sex parenting is not necessarily equally accepted. Additionally, surrogacy, which is often used by male same-sex couples but also by other couples where a pregnancy by one of the partners is medically not possible or not desired, remains a controversial topic.

Following the traditional rules of acquiring parenthood, for female same-sex couples, only the woman giving birth to the child is a legal parent. Even if same-sex partnerships are possible, the marital presumption does not always extend to a female partner of the mother.[18] Male same-sex couples must rely on a surrogate to carry their child. If the surrogate is not married or if there is no marital presumption, one of the intended fathers can recognize the child as his own. The other partner, however, cannot acquire legal parenthood. The same applies if a different-sex couple uses a surrogate: the woman giving birth to the child, i.e., the surrogate, generally becomes the legal mother of the child and thus has to be replaced by one of the intended parents, which is usually not possible under traditional parenthood rules.[19] In all of these cases, at least one of the intended parents cannot become a legal parent under the traditional parenthood rules which only leaves adoption to achieve this result. However, this means that the respective national adoption law must be followed.

3. SUBSTANTIVE ADOPTION LAW

Looking at substantive adoption law and the effects and prerequisites of an adoption, it becomes clear why adoption plays a role in modern family forms but also why adoption usually does not provide for an appropriate fallback mechanism when filiation cannot be established through the law of parenthood.

---

17 Only looking at EU Member States, there are still six countries without any kind of protection for same-sex couples: Bulgaria, Latvia, Lithuania, Poland, Rumania and Slovakia.

18 E.g,. in Germany, see BGH, 10.10.2018, XII ZB 231/18, *Zeitschrift für das gesamte Familienrecht (FamRZ)* 2018, 1919, although this might change soon due to a current challenge before the Constitutional Court. In Greece, a registered partnership is possible but the marital presumption does not cover these relationships. Extending the marital presumption to female same-sex couples is, however, increasingly common and exists, e.g., in Austria (§144 ABGB), Belgium (Art. 325/2 Code civil belge), Denmark (§27 Børneloven), England and Wales (Sec. 42 ff. HFEA 2008), the Netherlands (Art. 1:198 BW), Norway (§3 Barneloven), and Sweden (§9 Föräldrabalk).

19 Countries which allow surrogacy usually provide for a mechanism to ensure that intended parents can become legal parents. For examples see the chapters on Greece, Israel, South Africa, New Zealand, Portugal and Iceland in J.M. Scherpe, C. Fenton-Glynn and T. Kaan (eds), *Eastern and Western Perspectives on Surrogacy*, Intersentia, Cambridge 2019.

3.1. EFFECTS OF AN ADOPTION

Adoption can be used as a substitute for the rules of parenthood because the legal effect of an adoption is often the same as after the allocation of parenthood by law. In many countries, the adoption of a minor leads to the full integration of the child into the new family and the adopted child is treated like any other child of the family.[20] Additionally, all ties to the birth parents are severed, including succession rights.[21] However, one significant difference remains even with a full adoption: parenthood allocated by law is regularly established at the time of the birth or with a retroactive effect from this time. Therefore, the parent–child relationship exists from the beginning of the child's life. This is not the case under adoption law: the effect of the adoption only starts with its finalization and generally does not have retroactive effect.

In some countries, the effects of an adoption can be more limited: the child gains new parents but a connection to the birth parents remains. Often, there are two different kinds of adoption:[22] a full adoption and a simple adoption. This is for example the case in France, where a simple adoption[23] does not sever the ties between child and birth family but grants additional rights to adoptive parents.[24] In Austria, the effects of an adoption are always limited. While the adoptive parents gain full legal status[25] the ties to the birth parents are never completely severed concerning financial interests:[26] the adopted child retains a maintenance claim against the birth parents and vice versa, although the liability is subordinate compared to the one of and towards the adoptive family.[27] The succession rights also remain intact.[28] When adoption is used to substitute the rules of acquiring parenthood at birth, the closer the effects of the adoption come to the full status established by legal parenthood, the better it is. Thus, a full adoption suits the needs of the family better.[29]

---

20 See, e.g., Croatia (Art. 197 Obiteljski zakon), Denmark (§16 Bek af lov om adoption), Greece (Art. 1561 Civil Code), Ireland (Sec. 58 Adoption Act 2010), Italy (Art. 27 Legge 04.05.1983, no. 184 Diritto del minore ad una famiglia), Netherlands (Art. 1:229 Burgerlijk Wetboek), Portugal (Art. 1986 Código Civil), Spain (Art. 178 Código Civil).

21 For an explicit regulation of the termination of succession rights, see, e.g., Croatia (Art. 199 Obiteljski zakon), Denmark (§16 Bek af lov om adoption).

22 E.g., in France and Belgium.

23 Adoption simple, Art. 364(1) Code civil français. The full adoption is called 'adoption plénière', Art. 356(1) Code civil français.

24 Especially permanent parental responsibility, Art. 365 Code civil français.

25 Art. 197 ABGB (Austria).

26 C. Voithofer, 'Eltern-Kind-Verhältnisse im Spannungsfeld genetischer und sozialer Beziehungen: Ein Streifzug durch das österreichische Familienrecht' (2016) *Praxis des Familienrechts (FamPra.ch)* 422, 434.

27 Art. 198 ABGB.

28 Art. 199 ABGB.

29 For Belgian law explicitly see G. Verschelden and J. Verhellen, 'Belgium' in K. Trimmings and P. Beaumont (eds.), *International Surrogacy Arrangements*, Hart Publishing, Oxford 2013, pp. 49–84 at p. 72 f.

A common scenario in modern family forms is that only one parent can acquire legal parenthood at birth through the rules on parenthood. In this case, a stepparent adoption helps the second parent to gain legal parenthood: the child has and retains one legal parent but the second parent is added. Stepparent adoptions are usually full adoptions and therefore not undisputed in typical stepfamily situations where a biological parent is replaced by a stepparent.[30] However, in the case of modern family forms, where the second parent has always acted as and was always intended to be the second parent and only needs the help of adoption law to acquire this status legally, those concerns do not apply. This is reflected in French law where stepchild adoptions usually cannot be full adoptions to preserve the tie to the other biological parent. Exceptions apply – among other cases – when a child only has one legal parent either through the law of parenthood or through previous adoption by a single person.[31]

3.2. PREREQUISITES OF AN ADOPTION

Although the resulting parental status is the same or at least very similar through adoption and the law of parenthood, the prerequisites vary considerably. While adoption is used as a fallback mechanism to create legal parenthood under certain circumstances today, this development was not something intended originally. Therefore, the law is generally not adapted to these scenarios. Going through adoption and having to comply with the requirements raises questions of equality and discrimination.

3.2.1. General Prerequisites

The typical case of an adoption for which the law needs to provide an appropriate mechanism is a child born to birth parents who cannot care for the child and who therefore place their child with another family that they most often will not have known before. Usually, an agency – mostly run by the State or State approved to ensure child trafficking is ruled out[32] – will provide the service of facilitating the meeting between birth and adoptive parents.

Since an adoption, in essence, means choosing parents for a child, it is important to find people who can take care of the child and support the child's development emotionally, educationally and financially, at least until the child

30 For reasons why stepchild adoptions can be criticized see, e.g., R. FRANK, 'Die Stiefkindadoption' (2010) *Das Standesamt (StAZ)* 324, 325 f.

31 See Art. 345-1 Code civil français.

32 See, e.g., for Germany §2 Adoptionsvermittlungsgesetz.

comes of age but ideally for a lifetime. Therefore, from a substantive point, there is a general consensus in Europe that an adoption is only possible if it is in the best interest of the child,[33] making this the main substantive prerequisite of an adoption in most countries. Relevant considerations concern the current situation of the child as well as the suitability of the adoptive parents. Since someone must decide what the best interest of the child is in each individual case, in most countries, adoption requires the involvement of a court.[34] Usually, the court will obtain information on the situation by hearing the adults concerned and – depending on the age – also the child. Additionally, social services are often involved. In Germany, for example, the court must obtain a statement from the youth welfare office.[35] To prepare this statement, the youth welfare office asks the adoptive parent(s) to provide documentation on questions such as health, financial situation, criminal history or living situation. Then, a social worker visits the family at home. In Spain, a declaration of suitability is required which includes a psychosocial assessment[36] where similar factors are considered.[37]

Although almost all jurisdictions agree on looking at the best interest of the child, this does not mean that there is a comparable consensus about what the best interest of the child is and how it is determined in practice. Thus, it can depend on the personal and professional experience and perspective of the person who makes the decision. Sometimes, personal prejudice against certain family forms may influence the procedure or a decision. Since the decision is based on a prognosis for the future it is necessarily based on a prediction. Thus, although the best interest of the child is a child-centred criterion and in principle appropriate, it also leads to a considerable amount of uncertainty and potential bias.

In some countries, an adoption requires a certain minimum waiting or trial period where the adoptive parents care for the child but the adoption is not yet formalized. Since there are very limited options to dissolve an adoption, a waiting period is intended to ensure that the adoption is successful. But a waiting period adds to the delay which the requirement of a court involvement

---

33 J.M. Scherpe, above n. 5, p. 86. See the explicit regulation, e.g., in §194 ABGB (Austria), §1741 BGB (Germany), Art. 1:227(3) BW (Netherlands).

34 N. Dethloff, above n. 13, §15 para. 81.

35 §189 Gesetz über das Verfahren in Familiensachen und in den Angelegenheiten der freiwilligen Gerichtsbarkeit (FamFG).

36 Art. 176 Código civil.

37 The details are not regulated on the federal level and vary. For an example of the factors considered in Madrid, see Art. 58 Ley 6/1995, de 28 de marzo, de Garantías de los Derechos de la Infancia y la Adolescencia en la Comunidad de Madrid.

already entails. For example, in Italy, a waiting period of one year is mandatory.[38] In the Czech Republic, there is a trial period of at least nine months.[39] During this time, the child usually lives with the adoptive parents but since the adoption is not final, a change in circumstances – like a separation of the adoptive parents – can have serious consequences.[40] This leads to prolonged insecurity, which is especially problematic when the child has always lived with and was always intended to be a common child of a couple.

The further requirements of an adoption usually do not lead to particular problems for modern family forms. Usually, the consent of several parties is necessary: the birth parent(s), the adoptive parents and the child, depending on the age either through a parent or guardian or themselves. In modern families, usually all parties involved are in agreement about who the parents of the child should be, meaning the consent is given. Additionally, in some countries, there are age requirements, which can both be a minimum and a maximum age and/or an age gap. This is intended to guarantee that it is possible for adoptee and adoptive parent(s) to form a typical parent–child relationship. National laws also diverge on the question whether unmarried couples can adopt a child.[41] This usually applies to different-sex and same-sex unmarried partners who then cannot rely on adoption if the rules on parenthood do not allow them to acquire legal parenthood.

3.2.2. *Specific Rules for Modern Family Forms*

Some national adoption laws include provisions which lead to particular consequences for modern family forms or specifically take their needs into account. While this most often leads to less strict prerequisites, the opposite can also be true. For example, in Germany, §1741(1)2 BGB provides that a person who has participated in an illegal or immoral child arrangement or has mandated or rewarded a third person to do so shall only be allowed to adopt the child if adoption is necessary to protect the best interest of the child. This provision is intended to prevent child trafficking by imposing a stricter requirement on a subsequent adoption: it is not sufficient if the adoption is conducive to the best interest of the child but it has to be necessary to protect the child. Some courts have applied this standard to adoptions after surrogacy[42] and the official

---

38 Art. 25 Legge Nr. 184 Diritto del minore ad una famiglia.

39 The trial period itself lasts at least six months, Art. 829(2) Občanský zákoník, but can start at the earliest three months after the birth of the child, Art. 823(2) Občanský zákoník.

40 See also below, section 3.3.

41 J.M. Scherpe, above n. 5, p. 87.

42 AG Düsseldorf, 19.11.2010, 96 XVI 21/09; AG Hamm, 22.02.2011, XVI 192/08; LG Düsseldorf 15.03.2012, 25 T 758/10.

recommendations of the umbrella organization of youth welfare offices still argue for an application.[43] However, most courts[44] and academics[45] now – rightly so – do not support stricter requirements for an adoption after surrogacy.

In the Netherlands, however, female same-sex couples can rely on Art. 1:227(4) Burgerlijk Wetboek (BW) to grant them easier access to adoption in certain cases. This provision from 2009 still exists although co-motherhood was introduced in 2014.[46] If the child was born into a relationship between the legal parent and the 'adoptor' after assisted reproduction with sperm from an anonymous donor, the adoption is granted unless it is evidently not in the interest of the child. The burden to show that the adoption is in the best interest of the child is therefore lower, giving female same-sex parents easier access to adoption.[47] Additionally, Art. 1:230(2) BW provides for the retroactive effect of the adoption to the time of birth if the adoption was requested before birth. This constitutes an exception to the general rule that an adoption takes effect on the day the court decision becomes final. Such a provision is especially important if the mother giving birth dies before or shortly after the birth of the child because the adoption can still go ahead in these cases.[48]

Differences can also concern the proceedings. For example, in Germany there is a requirement to undergo counselling before a stepchild adoption.[49] However, this requirement is waived for cases in which at the time of birth of the child the 'adoptor' is either married to or in a stable relationship the legal parent of the child.[50]

---

43 Empfehlungen zur Adoptionsvermittlung der Bundesarbeitsgemeinschaft Landesjugendämter, 7th ed. 2014, <http://www.bagljae.de/downloads/120_empfehlungen-zur-adoptionsvermittlung_2014.pdf> accessed 25.04.2022.

44 LG Frankfurt a.M., 03.08.2012, 2-09 T 50/11; OLG Düsseldorf, 17.03.2017, II-1 UF 10/16; OLG München, 12.02.2018, 33 UF 1152/17; OLG Frankfurt a.M., 28.02.2019, 1 UF 71/18.

45 A. Botthoff and A. Diel, 'Voraussetzungen für die (Stiefkind-)Adoption eines Kindes nach Inanspruchnahme einer Leihmutter' (2013) *StAZ* 211; N. Dethloff, 'Leihmütter, Wunscheltern und ihre Kinder' (2014) *Juristenzeitung (JZ)* 922, 931; M. Löhnig, in *BeckOGK*, C.H. Beck, Munich 2022, §1741 BGB para. 47; H. Maurer, in *Münchener Kommentar zum Bürgerlichen Gesetzbuch Band 10*, 8th ed., C.H. Beck, Munich 2020, §1741 para. 149. For an application of §1741(1)2 BGB see C. Thomale, *Mietmutterschaft*, Mohr Siebeck, Tübingen 2015, p. 16.

46 For information on the introduction of co-motherhood in the Netherlands, see I. Curry-Sumner and M. Vonk, 'Dutch Co-Motherhood in 2014' (2014) *International Survey of Family Law* 361.

47 W. Schrama, M. Antokolskaia and G. Ruitenberg, *Familierecht*, 4th ed., Boom juridisch, Den Haag 2021, p. 280.

48 M. Vonk, 'Same-sex parents in the Netherlands' in E. Bouvier de Rubia and A. Voinnesson (eds), *Homoparentalité? Approche comparative*, vol. 18, 2012, pp. 13–40, at pp. 34 f.

49 §9a(1) Adoptionsvermittlungsgesetz.

50 §9a(4), (5) Adoptionsvermittlungsgesetz.

3.3. ADOPTION PROCEEDINGS AS DISCRIMINATION

Whereas the effects of an adoption and acquiring legal parenthood through the rules of parenthood are usually the same, the requirements are markedly different. With an adoption, the prospective parents are evaluated and the State assesses whether the adoption is in the best interest of the child. Parents in traditional family forms do not have to undergo such an evaluation if they have biological children or if they resort to artificial reproduction with donor material. In fact, such an assessment – sometimes referred to as parental licensing – would likely violate constitutional and human rights.[51] However, families who must resort to adoption because the rules of parenthood do not currently apply to them have to accept such an evaluation. Additionally, an adoption requires judicial or administrative proceedings which means that it takes time for an adoption to be processed. Sometimes the costs associated with this process can also be significant.[52] Further, before the adoption is final, the person already assumes the role of a parent but has no legal rights. In return, the child does not have a maintenance claim. Especially problematic are cases where the parents separate or one of them dies before the adoption is final. In these situations, no parental connection has been established and in case of death it can no longer be established. This leads to the child not having inheritance rights or rights to potential benefits like survivor's pension or insurance. In the case of separation of the parents, a joint adoption might become legally impossible[53] or deemed not to be in the best interest of the child because of the less stable household situation. The necessity of an adoption thus places an additional burden on families who cannot rely on the law of parenthood. Because those families are ones which break from traditional norms relating to sexuality, family formation and gender, this becomes a question of equality and discrimination.[54]

However, not every different treatment also amounts to a violation of rights. While the European Court of Human Rights (ECtHR) repeatedly found an interference with the rights to respect of private and family life and freedom from discrimination under Articles 8 and 14 of the European Convention on Human Rights, this interference was regularly held not to be disproportionate. In connection with surrogacy, the Court has frequently affirmed that it is sufficient

51 For a violation of Arts 2 and 6 of the German Constitution, see D. Coester-Waltjen, 'Überlegungen zur Notwendigkeit einer Reform des Abstammungsrechts' (2021) *Zeitschrift für die gesamte Privatrechtswissenschaft (ZfPW)* 129, 142 f.

52 See, e.g., for the US D. NeJaime, 'The Nature of Parenthood' (2017), 126 *Yale Law Journal* 2260, 2317.

53 This was e.g. the case in the decision of the ECtHR, *Valdís Fjölnisdóttir and others v. Iceland*, 18.05.2021, no. 71552/17.

54 D. NeJaime, above n. 52, p. 2323 ff.

if legal parenthood can be acquired through an effective and sufficiently fast mechanism.[55] In practice, this mechanism usually is an adoption,[56] although in recent decisions, the ECtHR held that a foster care agreement[57] or parental responsibility[58] can also suffice. Thus, it seemed that the Convention only protects the lived reality of the family rather than the legal status of parenthood. However, in its latest decision, the ECtHR explicitly held that not recognising a legal parent child relationship by refusing adoption of a child born through surrogacy violates the right to private life of the child.[59] This change might pave the way for a violation of the Convention in other cases but is still built on adoption as a means of establishing a parent-child relationship. Additionally, the Court allows the States a wide margin of appreciation, which presents a significant hurdle to establishing a violation of the Convention. This wide margin of appreciation is based on varying views on the issues at hand and therefore at least partly on political reasons. The specific question of whether an adoption in itself can be a discriminatory requirement has not been examined by the court. While this is understandable from a pragmatic standpoint given the limitations of the power of the Court, it still falls short of a full consideration of the rights of people living in modern family forms.

However, it is possible that national constitutional law follows a stricter approach. In Germany, the Constitutional Court is currently considering such questions.[60] Lower courts have considered it to be a violation of the right to equal treatment under Article 3 to not allocate parenthood to married female same-sex partners. The question is whether it can be justified to treat spouses of women giving birth differently based on whether they are men or women. Under the current law, a husband of a woman giving birth can become the father of the child without adoption even if he is not genetically related to the child but the wife of the woman giving birth of the child cannot.

A justification previously brought forward for this difference in treatment was the best interest of the child, i.e., the consideration that a child would be better off having two parents of a different sex or a home where it was not in danger of being discriminated against because of traditional values pervading in society. However, there is no empirical evidence that

55 *ECtHR Advisory Opinion*, 10.04.2019, request no. P16-2018-001, para. 54; ECtHR, *C and E v. France*, 19.11.2019, no. 1462/18 and no. 17348/18, para. 42; ECtHR, *D v. France*, 16.07.2020, no. 11288/18, para. 64.

56 See especially the advisory opinion in a case involving surrogacy, *ECtHR Advisory Opinion*, 10.04.2019, no. P16-2018-001.

57 ECtHR, *Valdís Fjölnisdóttir and others v. Iceland*, 18.05.2021, no. 71552/17.

58 ECtHR, *C.E. and others v. France*, 24.03.2022, no. 29775/18 and 29693/19.

59 ECtHR, *K.K. and Others v. Denmark*, 06.12.2022, no. 25212/21.

60 Several courts have suspended proceedings and referred the problem to the Constitutional Court, e.g., OLG Celle, 24.03.2021, 21 UF 146/20; KG Berlin, 24.03.2021, 3 UF 1122/20; AG München, 11.11.2021, 542 F 6701/21.

these arguments are true,[61] excluding the best interest of the child as a justification.[62] Additionally, in modern families, the child usually already lives with the adult(s) who want to adopt the child meaning that waiting for the legal approval does not protect the child during this time even if this should in exceptional cases be necessary. On the contrary, the insecurity for parents and children persists in the meantime, which can have harmful consequences.[63] Relying on purely genetic ties is also not satisfactory because the marital presumption does not require the man to be the genetic father. On the contrary, in the case of reverse egg donation, the wife of the woman giving birth can be the genetic mother without this having any effect on her acquiring legal parenthood. Thus, a justification of this unequal treatment seems elusive, meaning that it violates the Constitution.

This exact question has not yet been considered by the ECtHR. In the case of *D v. France*, it was only brought forward at a later stage and was found inadmissible.[64] It will be interesting to see how this plays out in the future and it might provide a promising avenue to pursue before the ECtHR.

4. INTERNATIONAL CONTEXT

At a national level, using adoption as a fallback mechanism reveals certain problems. Looking at cases with an international dimension adds to the complexity but also reveals that in some cases, adoption can have advantages over acquiring parenthood by law. As a starting point, it is necessary to differentiate between three different situations: the procedural recognition of a foreign decision; a recognition based on EU law; and the assessment of a situation with a foreign element according to the applicable law.

4.1. PROCEDURAL RECOGNITION

If there is a foreign decision that can be recognized by procedural means, this takes priority and is usually easier because the standard of review is limited to

61 R.H. Farr and C.J. Patterson, 'Coparenting Among Lesbian, Gay, and Heterosexual Couples: Associations with Adopted Children's Outcomes' (2013) 84 *Child Development* 1226; S. Golombok, *Modern Families*, Cambridge University Press, Cambridge 2015, p. 198 f.

62 P. Reuß, 'Das Abstammungsrecht auf dem verfassungsrechtlichen Prüfstand' (2021) *Zeitschrift für das gesamte Familienrecht (FamRZ)* 824; E. Schumann, 'Elternschaft nach Keimzellspende und Embryoadoption' (2014) *Medizinrecht* 736, 745.

63 See, e.g., for same-sex parents in the US, A. Gash and J. Raiskin, 'Parenting without Protection: How Legal Status Ambiguity Affects Lesbian and Gay Parenthood' (2018) 43 *Law & Social Inquiry* 82.

64 ECtHR, *D v. France*, 16.07.2020, no. 11288/18, para. 81 ff.

certain grounds of refusal. However, there needs to be a decision by a foreign court to go through this process. This is where differences between acquiring parental status through adoption and the rules of parenthood occur:[65] an adoption is usually based on a court order,[66] which means that a procedural recognition is possible. If parenthood is allocated by law, a birth certificate provides an official record of this status which is often also entered into a registry. Although a birth certificate is an official document, it usually is not recognizable by procedural means as it does not have the same binding legal effect as a court decision. This has often been a problem in surrogacy cases.[67] The country where the surrogacy takes place provides for the intended parents to become legal parents and issues a birth certificate. Upon return home, the intended parents aim for recognition of the birth certificate, which is not always possible. For example, in Germany, the provision[68] for procedural recognition of a foreign decision does not apply to birth certificates.[69] A similar differentiation exists in Belgium.[70] Other countries, for example the Netherlands,[71] recognize birth certificates through a separate procedure. In France, a transcription – which leads to the inscription in the birth registry and therefore resembles a recognition – of a foreign birth certificate used to be impossible.[72] In 2019, the *Cour de cassation* changed its opinion, allowing a transcription.[73] A change of Art. 47 Code civil,[74] which regulates the effect of foreign civil status documents in France, was intended to reverse the most recent decisions of the *Cour de cassation*, meaning that an adoption would once

65 An illustrative example is a decision from the UK High Court of Justice Family Division, *Re Q (A Child) (Parental Order: Domicile)* [2014] EWHC 1307 (Fam): the adoption by the intended mother was recognized but the allocation of parenthood by law of the intended (and genetic) father was not.

66 See above, section 3.2.1.

67 However, there are cases where parenthood is based on a court decision after surrogacy, e.g., under the law of California, see BGH, 10.12.2014, XII ZB 463/13.

68 §109 Gesetz über das Verfahren in Familiensachen und in den Angelegenheiten der freiwilligen Gerichtsbarkeit (FamFG).

69 BGH, 20.03.2019, XII ZB 320/17.

70 G. Verschelden and J. Verhellen, 'Belgium' in K. Trimmings and P. Beaumont (eds), *International Surrogacy Arrangements*, Hart Publishing, Oxford 2013, pp. 49–84, at p. 69 f.

71 I. Curry-Sumner and M. Vonk, 'The Netherlands' in K. Trimmings and P. Beaumont (eds), *International Surrogacy Arrangements*, Hart Publishing, Oxford 2013, pp. 273–94, at p. 286.

72 Cour de Cassation, 1st Civil Chamber, 06.04.2011, n°10-19053, n°09-66486 and n°09-17130; Cour de cassation, 13.09.2013, n°12-18315 and n°12-30138.

73 Cour de cassation, 1st Civil Chamber, 18.12.2019, n°18-11815 and n°18-12337, recently confirmed by Cour de cassation, 1st Civil Chamber, 13.01.2021, n°19-17929.

74 Art. 7 of loi n° 2021-1017 du 2 août 2021 relative à la bioéthique added a new last sentence: 'Celle-ci [l'acte de l'état civil] est appréciée au regard de la loi française', which translates to 'It [the civil status act] is assessed in the light of French law' (translation by the author).

again become necessary;[75] however, so far this legislative change only seems to have created further confusion because the wording of the new addition to the provision is incoherent.[76] It will be interesting to see how the *Cour de cassation* reacts to the new legislation.

That the recognition of an adoption is easier than accepting parenthood based on foreign law because an adoption is based on a court decision might seem arbitrary but can have far-reaching consequences. For example, in the Netherlands, female same-sex couples sometimes decide to use adoption rather than establishing co-motherhood and one of the reasons advanced is that they fear that the latter would not be accepted abroad.[77] One factor favouring this decision might also be that adoption for female same-sex parents is made easy in the Netherlands.[78] Some families have even asked the court to dissolve the recognition of co-motherhood to then go through a stepchild adoption. A child who was a minor at the time of the recognition by the co-mother can challenge this relationship if the co-mother – as is normally the case – is not genetically related to the child. A special guardian (*bijzondere curator*) can file an application for the minor child. The special guardian only files the application if it is in the best interest of the child but if an application is filed, the order is usually granted.[79] One reason for the application being in the best interest of the child is the better acceptance abroad of a subsequent adoption.[80]

If a procedural recognition is possible, the most relevant ground for a refusal of recognition for the purposes of this chapter, which exists in almost all jurisdictions, is a violation of public policy. However, the standard of review in a procedural recognition is still lower[81] than the full review under private international law. In Germany, for example, courts have not found foreign decisions allocating parenthood after surrogacy to violate public policy although

---

75 C. Bidaud, 'La force probante des actes de l'état civil étrangers modifiée par la loi bioéthique: du sens à donner à l'exigence de conformité des faits à la réalité «appréciée au regard de la loi française» ...,' (2022) *Revue critique de droit international privé* 35, 36 f.

76 C. Bidaud, above n. 74, pp. 35, 38 ff.

77 See the arguments brought forward in the cases cited below in fns 79, 80.

78 See above, section 3.2.2.

79 Rechtbank Overijssel, 19.05.2016, C/08/174066, ECLI:NL:RBOVE:2016:2134; Rechtbank Den Haag, 22.09.2016, C/09/503074, ECLI:NL:RBDHA:2016:5263; Rechtbank Noord-Holland, 10.10.2018, C/15/255549, ECLI:NL:RBNHO:2018:8762.

80 Rechtbank Den Haag, 22.09.2016, C/09/503074, ECLI:NL:RBDHA:2016:5263. In another case (Rechtbank Overijssel, 19.05.2016, C/08/174066, ECLI:NL:RBOVE:2016:2134), it also sufficed to argue that the child should not later – after turning 18 – be forced to decide if they want to challenge the recognition and therefore an adoption would be preferable.

81 This so-called effet atténué is based on the fact that a court decision already commands a certain trust and therefore rejecting the recognition must meet a higher threshold. For German law see, e.g., J. von Hein, in F. Säcker, R. Rixecker, H. Oetker and B. Limperg, *Münchener Kommentar zum Bürgerlichen Gesetzbuch Band 12*, 8th ed., C.H. Beck, Munich 2020, Art. 6 EGBGB para. 110 ff.

surrogacy is not permitted.[82] The German Federal Supreme Court has, however, not yet decided on a case involving surrogacy without a genetic connection of the intended parents to the child – the case that most closely resembles the situation of an adoption.[83] The higher regional court of Berlin did not see a reason to weigh the interests differently in cases without a genetic connection of the intended parents.[84] As a decision on public policy requires weighing the different interests and needs for protection in the individual situation, the best interest of the child – which regularly is to stay permanently with the intended parents – is of great significance. However, countries which do not accept modern family forms in any way will most likely also refuse recognition. The public policy exception is based on national values. Therefore, a varying acceptance of modern family forms can easily be justified.

4.2. RECOGNITION BASED ON EU LAW

In the EU, there has been a discussion about the recognition of birth certificates based on EU law, namely on freedom of movement under Article 21 of the Treaty on the Functioning of the European Union (TFEU). In the *Pancharevo* case,[85] the Court of Justice of the European Union decided that, at least for purposes of free movement and family reunification, all EU Member States must recognize the parent–child relationship established in another Member State. So far, it is still unclear if this decision mandates a full recognition of the parent–child relationship in all areas of the law or if it remains limited to the ability to live and move together within the EU.[86] If EU law truly leads to a full recognition within the EU, which is unlikely, this levels the difference between the procedural recognition of adoption orders and the private international law treatment of birth certificates and acquiring parenthood through the rules of parenthood. In this case, in an intra-EU international context, there would be no advantage to adoption for this reason.

---

82 BGH, 10.12.2014, XII ZB 463/13.

83 T. Helms, 'Co-Elternschaft im IPR' (2023) *Praxis des internationalen Privat- und Verfahrensrechts (IPRax)* 232, 236. A first decision by a lower instance court has now applied a best-interest-of-the-child-test and thus essentially the standard for an adoption in the case of a recognition after surrogacy without a genetic connection to either intended parent but recognised the foreign decision, AG Sinsheim, 15.05.2023, 20 F 278/22.

84 KG Berlin, 21.01.2020, 1 W 47/19.

85 ECJ, C-490/20, *V.M.A. v. Stolichna obshtina, rayon 'Pancharevo'*, ECLI:EU:C:2021:1008. Very similar also ECJ, C-2/21, *Rzecznik Prw Obywatelskich*.

86 J.O. Flindt, 'Anmerkung zu EuGH C-490/20' (2022) *FamRZ* 286, 288; A. Tryfonidou, *The Cross-Border Recognition of the Parent-Child Relationship in Rainbow Families under EU Law: A Critical View of the ECJ's V.M.A. ruling* <https://europeanlawblog.eu/2021/12/21/the-cross-border-recognition-of-the-parent-child-relationship-in-rainbow-families-under-eu-law-a-critical-view-of-the-ecjs-v-m-a-ruling> accessed 25.04.2022.

However, since surrogacy is most often accessed outside of the EU as it is prohibited in most of the EU Member States – only Greece and Portugal offer access to surrogacy under certain limited conditions – the differentiation remains relevant. The same is true for parents with a connection to a non-EU Member State who want to improve the likelihood of recognition in all relevant jurisdictions.

4.3. PRIVATE INTERNATIONAL LAW

If a recognition is not possible, the facts of the case are assessed anew in the country where the question whether a parent–child relationship exists poses itself. The first step is then to determine which law is applicable under conflict-of-law rules. This requires choosing the correct conflict-of-laws rule.

Since private international law is routinely concerned with foreign law and its different rules, the provisions and their scope of application need to be flexible. A functional analysis is necessary to ensure that foreign elements are evaluated correctly. Since adoption is used as a functional equivalent to allocating parenthood at birth in modern family forms, choosing the correct conflict-of-laws rule is not as easy as it might seem at first glance. It has been argued that foreign provisions on same-sex parenthood should fall under the conflict-of-law rules on adoption and only biologically possible parent–child connections should be qualified as parenthood.[87] In Germany, it was suggested that an explicit amendment with a similar effect should be included in the private international law of parenthood.[88] The classification on the private international law level (adoption) would then deviate from the classification in the country of origin (parenthood). As such, this is not entirely uncommon and follows accepted private international law methodology.[89] However, since classification has to follow a functional approach,[90] the question remains whether adoption really is the right category for all cases where parent(s) and child lack a genetic

87 M. Andrae, 'Die gesetzliche Zuordnung des Kindes nach ausländischem Recht bei lesbischer institutioneller Partnerschaft' (2015) *StAZ* 163, 168 ff.; C. Thomale, *Mietmutterschaft*, Mohr Siebeck, Tübingen 2015, p. 90.

88 This was suggested (and never implemented) as an addition to the private international law rule for parenthood in a new Art. 19(5) EGBGB, see H.-P. Mansel, 'Reform des internationalen Abstammungs- und Adoptionsrechts des EGBGB' (2015) *IPRax* 185.

89 A famous example would be the qualification of the statute of limitations as substantive law in civil law countries rather than procedural law as it is usually done in common law countries.

90 See, e.g., J. Kropholler, *Internationales Privatrecht*, 6th ed., Mohr Siebeck, Tübingen 2006, p. 126 ff. For a general overview on the problem of classification see also S. Bariatti, 'Classification' in J. Basedow, G. Rühl, F. Ferrari and P. de Miguel Asensio, *Encyclopedia of Private International Law*, above n. 2.

relationship. This leads back to the necessity to distinguish between adoption and parenthood.

5. DISTINGUISHING ADOPTION AND PARENTHOOD

On a national level, distinguishing between adoption and parenthood is mostly a normative question because the rules are mandatory and if the prerequisites of parenthood are not met, only adoption remains an option. However, in private international law, the question of delineation arises in practice. Reproductive technologies have allowed people who are not genetically related to the child to become the original parents, making it challenging to distinguish clearly between situations where adoption is appropriate and where filiation should be established by law at birth. Situations involving same-sex parents and surrogacy show how adoption is used in cases where filiation might seem more appropriate. But the opposite can also occur:[91] if a child does not yet have a legal father, any man – in practice, usually the new partner of the mother – can recognize the child. A genetic relationship is not necessary and neither is an assessment of the best interest of the child although this situation is very similar to the typical case of a stepchild adoption.[92] Looking at surrogacy, the intended father also benefits from this situation as he can often recognize the child as his own, sometimes with the consent of the birth mother, i.e., the surrogate, which is especially remarkable if he is not the genetic father.[93]

To differentiate between the two phenomena, it is necessary to ascertain the core of what makes them distinctive. The biggest difference is that a careful evaluation of the prospective parents before an adoption is mandatory whereas nothing comparable exists in case of allocating parenthood by law at birth. In the end, this means that the law follows the rule rather than the exception: usually, genetic parents will take good care of the child. Therefore, the law is based on the assumption that this is the case. In turn, when parents are unable or unwilling to care for the child or if they endanger the welfare of the child, they refute this assumption. Consequently, the state has the right – and the duty – to intervene. Then, it is necessary to choose between different possible adoptive parents and the state has a duty to ensure the best interest of the child, which

---

91 R. Frank, *Grenzen der Adoption*, Metzner Verlag, Frankfurt a.M., 1978, pp. 98 ff. calls this 'concealed stepchild adoption'.

92 See R. Frank, 'Art. 8 EMRK und die Anfechtung wahrheitswidriger Vaterschaftsanerkennungen durch den biologischen Vater (§1600 Abs. 2 BGB)' (2021) *Zeitschrift für das gesamte Familienrecht (FamRZ)* 1081, 1086.

93 T. Helms, 'Co-Elternschaft im IPR' (2023) *IPRax* 232, 236 f.

justifies a close assessment. Modern families, however, should be afforded the same assumption – the same trust – as traditional families because they can care for a child just as well as those families. Everything else comes back to a discrimination against modern family forms.

Therefore, the main difference between adoption and allocation of parenthood by law at birth lies in the timeline: adoptive parents become parents to a child without being involved in the conception of the child. The parent–child relationship only develops after the birth parents decide that they cannot take care of the child. The law of parenthood allocates parenthood for children whose parents have been party to the conception of the child, whether through their own biological or genetic contribution or through their wish to care for the child. Genetics play a role but in many of the critical cases, it is not the deciding factor. The marital presumption does not require a genetic connection and due to medical advancement, neither does giving birth to the child. Therefore, a genetic connection is only one way of being involved from the beginning.

Identifying the timeline as the relevant criterion fits well with the fact that the allocation of parenthood and an adoption usually take effect at a different time, reflecting this delineation. The law of parenthood regularly designates parents from the time of birth or with retroactive effect to the time of birth. This is true not only for the automatic allocation of parenthood by law but mostly also for a recognition or challenge of parenthood which requires a declaration.[94] Since the allocation of parenthood results in a permanent status which has consequences in many other areas such as parental responsibility, maintenance or nationality, it is of particular importance that this relationship is defined as soon as possible.[95] In contrast, adoption usually only has an effect for the future.[96]

From a normative perspective, this means that changing adoption law to fit modern family forms is not the best solution to the problem of legal recognition of parental status in these families.[97] On the contrary, changes should be made to the law of parenthood. Any reform of adoption law would have to consider the needs of the more typical situation of an adoption. In these cases, an evaluation of the best interest of the child is generally an appropriate solution because a child is brought into the family from the outside. In the end, there would have to be two different kinds of adoption: one for children born into the family with the same or at least very similar requirements to allocating parenthood

94 P. Reuß, *Theorie eines Elternschaftsrechts*, above n. 14, pp. 167 ff.

95 See, e.g., the expert recommendations for a reform of the law of parenthood in Germany <https://www.bmj.de/SharedDocs/Downloads/DE/PDF/Berichte/07042017_AK_Abstimmung_Abschlussbericht.pdf> accessed 25.04.2022, p. 24.

96 See above, section 3.1.

97 In contrast, C. Thomale, *Mietmutterschaft*, Mohr Siebeck, Tübingen 2015, p. 95 ff. argues for a change of the adoption procedure.

by law, and one for children where the birth parents cannot fulfil their role as parents, similar to today's provisions. While possible, this does not seem to be a very efficient and easily understandable solution. However, some changes to adoption law – such as ensuring a consistent, efficient and fast procedure – could be beneficial for all adoptions.

6. CONCLUSION

Since the law of parenthood is the more appropriate route for assigning parenthood also for modern family forms, adoption is only a stopgap in the absence of a reform of the law of parenthood rather than a good substitute. In many ways, using adoption creates the impression of a pragmatic temporary solution to the issues arising from children growing up in ever more diverse family forms. However, while it is better than nothing, even calling adoption a real solution seems inappropriate considering the discriminatory nature of the prerequisites and the potential danger for the welfare of the child due to a delay in the protection of the parent–child relationship.

Therefore, a reform of the law of parenthood must remain the primary objective. Such a reform is an ambitious and difficult project, which can only be discussed here very rudimentarily.[98] Solutions which address the needs of diverse families will have to give more room to the autonomy of the parents because the increasing diversity does not allow for a one size fits all generalization used by the law in the past. Considering that the welfare of the child is at stake, deregulation is not a solution either. Rather, parents will have to be able to choose between more different options.

Additionally, in many ways a more functional approach to parenthood seems to gain traction. Looking at parenthood from the perspective of the child and considering who is responsible for the day-to-day care and the actual task of raising the child leads to this approach: the person who fills the social and psychological role of the parent is entitled to protection by the law.[99] This could be a stepparent, a same-sex partner or any other primary caregiver, in principle regardless of a genetic connection. Especially in the US, the recognition of so-called de facto parents as full legal parents is increasingly common.[100] This

---

98 See also the contributions of D. Lima (Chapter 6 in this volume) and K. Rokas (Chapter 5 in this volume).

99 For a comparative approach on how this does and does not happen, C. Huntington, C.G. Joslin and C. von Bary (eds), *Social Parenthood in Comparative Perspective*, NYU Press, New York 2023.

100 Such a recognition originates in equitable or common law doctrines and varies from State to State. For a description of the requirements see, e.g., *Parentage of L.B.*, 122 P.3d 161, 176 f. (Wash. 2005); *Smith v. Guest*, 16 A.3d 920, 931 (Del. 2010). Some States have also codified

further blurs the line between parenthood and adoption – although in a different and more permanent way than addressed in this chapter. Rather than using adoption as a substitute, certain elements traditionally found only in adoption law like an evaluation of the individual case based on the best interest of the child,[101] are used to determine parenthood. Additionally, since being a parent depends on an evaluation of whether someone acts as a parent, it does not necessarily mean that parenthood is assigned at birth and remains the same throughout the entire life. Thus, this is to a certain degree at odds with a stable and permanent status of parenthood and instead follows the more flexible idea of parental responsibility. Nevertheless, looking at the function of a parent can provide a solution to the needs of modern family forms because it means looking at the lived reality of the family. However, it is necessary to be careful not to perpetuate the situation that only modern family forms need to go through an evaluation of their fitness to parent by adding this requirement to the law of parenthood, amounting to an indirect discrimination.

rules on de facto parents, e.g., Delaware (Delaware Code title 13, §8-201(c)) or Vermont (Vermont Statutes title 15C, §501).

101 See, e.g., Sec. 609(7) Uniform Parentage Act 2017.

PART III

QUEER IDENTITIES, QUEER FAMILIES

GENDER IDENTITY

A Comparative European Perspective

Sandra DUFFY

Across the European continent, the legal recognition of the gender of transgender persons has long been a fragmented regime, with States offering varying degrees of protection to applicants for legal gender recognition. This has never been as pressing or evident as in the present day, where social movements in many jurisdictions present a concerted and worrying backlash to the progress which has been made in transgender law. This reactionary backlash to so-called 'gender ideology' threatens the steps which have been taken in many States toward more accessible and less onerous procedures for legal gender recognition. From the United Kingdom to Hungary and beyond, transgender rights face a strong opposition from those who believe that gender, and gender identity, are a figment of a left-wing ideology which threatens traditional conservative paradigms of binary sex roles and cisheteropatriarchal family forms.

Beginning with a discussion of gender/identity and its regulation in the legal sphere, this chapter will go on to discuss the current situation of legal gender recognition from a comparative European perspective. Using up-to-date examples of legislation and jurisprudence from across the continent, it will provide a picture of the state of transgender recognition in Europe as of the time of writing in mid-2022. Following an overview of gender recognition law in general, it will examine the European Court of Human Rights jurisprudence which established access to legal gender recognition as a protected right under the European Convention on Human Rights (ECHR). Since the 2002 case of *Goodwin and I. v. United Kingdom*,[1] it became compulsory for Council of Europe member States to introduce legislation allowing for the legal recognition of trans persons. This case, and those which have followed it, have occasioned a spate of new and updated legislation across the Council's membership, with almost every member State now operating a functional system of administrative gender recognition procedures. This first section will then examine the judgments which have followed the *Goodwin* decision, and which have made steps toward the depathologization of transgender identity in European law. Next, the chapter will examine two common barriers to legal gender recognition in European jurisdictions: age, and (non-)binary identity status. The final section of the chapter will discuss social movements pertaining to gender identity across the continent, and how they influence law-making processes.

Although transgender rights have become a contested topic of late in the media and in the public marketplace of ideas, with sensationalized rhetoric rendering the issue divisive and emotive, it is vital to remember that transgender persons are still a small and marginalized minority. Frequently deprived of socioeconomic rights such as access to healthcare and to an adequate standard of living, transgender persons rely on the law to ensure that their lives are not further compromised by the refusal to issue them correct identity documentation to protect them from forced 'outing', which can lead to dangerous situations, or an inability to marry or to found a family. The scope of this chapter does not allow for a discussion of all human rights violations to which transgender persons are liable, choosing instead to focus on legal gender recognition as the most standardized and comparable metric of transgender rights across the continent. Legal gender recognition can be seen as a reflection of the level of social citizenship of transgender persons in a particular State,[2] displaying the extent to which they are legally recognized as participants in the social sphere. However, it is also vital to remember that 'administrative systems in general are sites of production and implementation of racism, xenophobia, sexism, transphobia, homophobia, and ableism under the guise of neutrality',[3] and to interrogate carefully who is included, versus who is excluded, under each system of recognition.

It is not proposed to examine, for instance, the healthcare systems of each country in Europe except where it is pertinent to the legal status of

1 *Goodwin and I v. United Kingdom*, no. 28957/95, ECHR 2002-VI.

2 See S. Hines, *Gender Diversity, Recognition and Citizenship: Towards a Politics of Difference*, Palgrave Macmillan, London 2013.

3 D. Spade, *Normal Life: Administrative Violence, Critical Trans Politics, and the Limits of Law*, Duke University Press, Durham 2015, p. 73.

transgender persons, although it is to be noted that access to healthcare is a frequent barrier to the enjoyment of human rights for this demographic. Lastly, it is important to note that progress with regard to transgender rights has historically been hard-won and is often liable to be erased or reversed dependent on the prevailing philosophy of a particular government of a jurisdiction. It is therefore of paramount importance that we retain a focus on the significance, but also the fragility, of advances in transgender recognition in the European context.

1. GENDER IDENTITY AND GENDER RECOGNITION LAWS

Gender recognition laws are legislation which allow for the legal recognition of the true, lived gender of a transgender person. This is done through updates to the birth registry and birth certificate of the person, as well as updating secondary identity documentation such as passport or driver's licence. Gender recognition laws can have a variety of stipulations present within the text of the legislation, but in its simplest form, legal gender recognition is an administrative process which can be actioned on the request of the applicant. In jurisdictions which operate 'self-identification' procedures, no further input is needed before the administrative operations can take place. However, many States require medicolegal obstacles to be overcome before the registry and documentation can be updated.

Entries to a jurisdiction's register of births are predicated on an assignation of sex, made according to the observation of a baby's external sex characteristics at birth. It is generally assumed that if a baby is seen to have a vagina, they will be assigned female; if they have a penis, they will be registered as male. In a minority of cases, babies will be seen to have intersex sex characteristics. Intersex characteristics occur when a baby is born with chromosomal differences (e.g., an XXY chromosomal configuration), and can affect primary and secondary sex characteristics of the person, including internal and external physical presentation. In almost all European jurisdictions, a choice is made at birth as to which sex/gender the child will be assigned. This sex assignation of intersex children is often accompanied by medical procedures to conform the child's genitalia to the assigned sex, which is considered coercive due to the child's age, lack of understanding, and subsequent inability to give consent. The consent of the parents to the practice is irrelevant when it is the child's bodily autonomy which is being infringed upon. In Europe, the first State to outlaw these non-consensual practices was Malta, in its Gender Identity, Gender Expression, and Sex Characteristics Act 2015.

The Maltese Act provides that 'it shall be unlawful for medical practitioners or other professionals to conduct any sex assignment treatment and/or surgical intervention on the sex characteristics of a minor, which treatment and/or intervention can be deferred until the person to be treated can provide informed consent'.[4] Intersex status is not the same as gender identity, but the two are inextricably linked due to the medicalized nature of both in law and society; the struggle for intersex autonomy and transgender autonomy are interlinked.

Gender is commonly understood, drawing on the work of Judith Butler,[5] to be a socially constructed combination of characteristics, expression and relational roles. Butler describes gender as a series of performative acts. Performativity is 'a regularized and constrained repetition of norms'.[6] Gender can therefore neither be seen as a choice, nor as an inherent aspect of humanity – it is a socially constructed system of acts, which have been given the meaning of producing 'male' or 'female' identity through their repetition. The repetition of social actions also means that gender must be thought of as being 'constrained by … what remains radically unthinkable'.[7] Gender, as the 'cultural meanings that the sexed body assumes', belies the theory of biological essentialism – the assumption that social gender roles will map neatly onto bodies sexed male or female. Gender theory also problematizes the notion of biological sex in and of itself: if the characteristics that we call male or female are productive of the male or female subject, then it follows that that categorization is not an inherent human characteristic but another socially constructed system of organization. It is destabilizing to traditional concepts of binary sex norms to consider sex as being socially constructed: however, if the process of sex assignation is observed, it can be seen that this is precisely what occurs. Sex assignment is generally socially considered to map onto gender identity and expression: that is to say, if a child is assigned female, she will be assumed to grow up to be a girl and, later, a woman, fulfilling the roles which society has mapped out for girls. If this happens, the girl is considered to be cisgender. If, however, the child assigned female grows up to identify with the masculine gender or a non-binary gender, they would be considered to be transgender. It is thereby possible to think of sex and gender (or sex/gender)[8]

---

4 Gender Identity, Gender Expression, and Sex Characteristics Act 2015 (Malta), Chapter 540, 14.04.2015, Art. 14.1.

5 See J. Butler, *Gender Trouble*, Routledge, Abingdon 1990; J. Butler, *Bodies That Matter*, Routledge, Abingdon 1994.

6 J. Butler, *Bodies that Matter*, above n. 5, p. 60.

7 ibid., p. 59.

8 See Z. Davy, *Sex-Gender and Self-Determination: Policy Developments in Law, Health and Pedagogical Contexts*, Policy Press, Bristol 2021.

as being congruent or parallel concepts – both socially constructed systems of categorization with similar expectations to be placed upon the person.

Transgender persons, or trans persons,[9] are therefore those who identify with a sex/gender incongruent with that which they were assigned at birth. The gender of identification can be a binary identity (male or female); a non-binary identity (any of a spectrum of identities lying outside the male/female binary); or an agender identity (where the person does not relate to any gender identity). Trans persons may choose to undergo medical or surgical interventions, such as hormone replacement therapy or vaginoplasty, to conform their physical presentation to their internally felt gender identity, or they may not. It is not essential to social transgender identity to have undergone medical gender-affirming interventions. Frequently, trans persons experience gender dysphoria: a state of distress caused by non-conformity of outward physical presentation and gender expression with internally felt gender identity. Medical or psychological interventions can help to alleviate gender dysphoria, as can access to social support, appropriate clothing and other supports like vocal training. Likewise, access to legal gender recognition can also be key to alleviating social gender dysphoria by allowing trans persons to participate as full social citizens of their State.

An individual's experience of, and relationship to, their gender identity is an extremely personal aspect of their being. However, sex/gender becomes public property in its coercive regulation by law. The first time it is recorded is, as discussed, at birth. This assignment is recorded on the birth certificate of the individual and in the jurisdiction's state registry. It forms the basis for their legal classification throughout life. Passports, driver's licences, census forms: many forms of legal documentation require or request a sex/gender marker for identification. For the majority of people, who are cisgender and whose gender identity is therefore congruent with their sex assigned at birth, this does not pose a problem. However, for trans and/or non-binary persons, a lack of legal documentation in their correct gender can lead to personal, legal or administrative problems. A trans woman's birth certificate marked 'male', for example, could lead to its bearer being unable to marry another male-assigned person in a legal system where marriage equality is not yet present. Furthermore, if a trans person 'passes' (to 'pass' is slang for being seen as a cis person of that gender; to 'blend in' unobtrusively) in their lived gender, to force them to present official identity documents which do not match their gender presentation can lead them to be forcibly outed and could potentially put them in danger from transphobic officials or others.

9 'Trans' is considered to be an abbreviation and umbrella term which includes all transgender persons, non-binary persons, agender persons and all those falling into the gender-variant category.

The historical approach to legal gender recognition in Europe has been fragmented and piecemeal, with jurisdictions opting to legislate in their own time and according to their own wishes. Earlier iterations of gender recognition laws also frequently included onerous and invasive medical or surgical requirements for the verification of identity, up to and including permanent sterilization. It was not until the 2002 case of *Goodwin and I. v. United Kingdom*, before the European Court of Human Rights, that a lack of legal gender recognition legislation within a State became recognized as a violation of human rights.

2. THE CASE LAW: TO *GOODWIN* AND BEYOND

Throughout the 1980s and 1990s, a series of cases before the European Court of Human Rights challenged the United Kingdom's lack of legal recognition for transgender persons. Beginning with *Rees v. United Kingdom* in 1986, this line of jurisprudence built an ever-more convincing case for legal gender recognition as a human right. The case of *Rees* was taken by a transgender man, Mark Rees, who alleged a violation of his human rights as he could not legally marry a woman in the United Kingdom due to not being recognized as male on his birth certificate. The Court found in favour of the United Kingdom in this case, holding that the recognition of transgender persons fell within a State's margin of appreciation. The margin of appreciation represents the 'leeway' which is given to States in choosing how they implement the rights presented in the ECHR. From *Rees* onwards, a sequence of litigants alleged that their inability to change their birth certificates to reflect their true gender was a violation of their Article 8 ECHR right to a private life, and, in some cases, their Article 12 ECHR right to family life and Article 14 ECHR right to freedom from discrimination.[10] The Court denied all applications previous to *Goodwin*, holding that the matter of access to legal gender recognition continued to fall within the margin of appreciation given to the State, involving, as it did, administrative as well as legislative concerns. The Court also continued to hold that there was not enough of a legislative consensus across the continent to justify imposing a requirement to legislate for legal gender recognition.

Goodwin and I. v. United Kingdom is a pivotal case in trans law, marking as it did the first time the Court found that a State's refusal to allow transgender persons to update their birth certificates was a violation of Article 8 ECHR. Part of its reasoning hung upon a developing broad international trend[11] toward

---

10 *Cossey v. United Kingdom*, no. 10843/84, ECHR 1990; *X, Y, and Z v. United Kingdom* no. 21830/93 ECHR 1997-II; *Sheffield and Horsham v. United Kingdom* nos. 22985/93 and 23390/94, ECHR 1998-V.

11 *Goodwin and I v. United Kingdom*, above n. 1, para. 84.

the implementation of gender recognition legislation, including the fact that 33 out of 37 then-member States of the Council of Europe had adopted some facility for gender marker change on birth certificates. It also had regard to the situation in the United Kingdom itself. Recalling its decision in *X, Y, and Z v. United Kingdom*, it commented that where a State allows and even facilitates the medical and physical elements of a person's transition, it is discordant to not allow them 'the final and culminating step in the long and difficult process':[12] legal recognition. It considered the question of whether there would be any detriment to the public interest from allowing trans persons to change their legal gender, and concluded that there would be '[n]o concrete or substantial hardship or detriment to the public interest ... the Court considers that society may reasonably be expected to tolerate a certain inconvenience to enable individuals to live in dignity and worth in accordance with the sexual identity chosen by them at great personal cost'.[13]

It held that, on that basis, there was no longer such a broad margin of appreciation available to the United Kingdom and that therefore, there had been a violation of Goodwin's Article 8 ECHR right to privacy in the United Kingdom's refusal to allow her to update her birth certificate to reflect her female gender, as well as a violation of her Article 12 ECHR right to marry. Gender recognition laws which allowed for birth registry updates therefore became compulsory across the member States of the Council of Europe. The *Goodwin* judgment did not, however, place restrictions or obligations on States when it came to the formulation of those laws. This meant that States were free to impose whatever conditions they chose on potential applicants for legal gender recognition, up to and including sterilization or permanent and irreversible surgical interventions tantamount to sterilization. In almost all cases, even those which did not go so far, there were pathologized requirements for medical or psychological diagnoses imposed on applicants.

In the 2015 case of *Y.Y. v. Turkey*,[14] the European Court of Human Rights heard an applicant from a Turkish national challenging the Turkish Courts' requirement that he undergo sterilization before he could access legal gender recognition procedures which included a surgical intervention. The Court found that this was an unreasonable requirement. The facts of *Y.Y.* are very specific, meaning that the unreasonableness threshold in this case applied only to the medical pathway that the applicant was on, having been prevented from accessing the surgeries he needed in order to have his gender legally recognized as he was not sterilized. However, as Dunne notes,[15] that the Court was able to

12 ibid., para. 78.

13 ibid., para. 91.

14 *Y.Y. v. Turkey*, no. 14793/08, ECHR 2015.

15 P. Dunne, 'YY v Turkey: Infertility as a Pre-Condition for Gender Confirmation Surgery' (2015) 23 *Medical Law Review* 646.

find sterilization unnecessary in a medical pathway was a hopeful sign for their willingness to do so in a legal gender recognition administrative pathway. Dunne also cites the case of *V.C. v. Slovakia*, where the Court stated that 'sterilisation constitutes a major interference with a person's reproductive health states' and that non-consensual sterilization is 'incompatible with the requirement of respect for human freedom and dignity, one of the fundamental principles on which the Convention is based'.[16]

Y.Y. would become direct precedent for the next major turning point in the Court's jurisprudence, the landmark case of *A.P., Garcon, and Nicot v. France*.[17] In the *A.P.* case, three French transgender women challenged the then-law in the State which required trans persons to undergo irreversible physical interventions, mostly interpreted as gender-affirming surgical procedures with the (side-)effect of sterilization. Referring to a broad range of domestic and international sources, the Court considered the applicants' Article 8 ECHR challenges to the requirement for sterilization. It held that the main question in the case was whether the French government had enough reason to require 'irreversible change in appearance' as a precondition for legal gender recognition.[18] The Court saw this condition as a conflict between the applicants' right to personal identity and their right to bodily integrity, which was not a fair balance for the State to have struck between the interests of the individual and the public interest in which the law was intended to operate. Therefore, it held that making access to legal gender recognition contingent on sterilization procedures was a breach of Article 8 ECHR. The Court has more recently upheld this judgment in the case of *X and Y v. Romania*[19] in 2021, wherein two trans men challenged Romania's sterilization requirement for legal gender recognition.

A.P. and *X and Y* mark a step toward the depathologization of gender recognition laws in the European context. Depathologization – the removal of medical aspects of a law or laws – would in this case involve the removal of all medical barriers to legal gender recognition, such as a requirement for surgery, hormone therapy or a medical or psychological diagnosis. However, the Court did not go this far, explicitly stating in *A.P.* that it was permissible within Article 8 ECHR to require medical proof that an individual had 'gender identity disorder' before they could apply for legal gender recognition.[20] The Court found that there was a 'quasi-unanimity' between member States of the Council of Europe that this was a valid requirement, and it was not a disproportionate interference in the private lives of individuals. Therefore, *A.P., Garcon, and*

16 ibid., p. 651.
17 *A.P., Garcon, and Nicot v. France* no. 79885/12, 52471/13, and 52596/13, ECHR 2017.
18 ibid., para. 120.
19 *X and Y v. Romania*, no. 2145/16 and 20607/16, ECHR 2021-IV.
20 *A.P., Garcon, and Nicot v France*, above n. 17, para. 144.

Nicot may have removed the need for sterility before legal gender recognition can be accessed, but it did not alter the pathologized status of transgender identity in the eyes of the Court. Although, in her submissions in the case, Garcon enters a challenge to the requirement to prove a diagnosis of gender identity disorder, the Court uses a consensus approach to find that 'a psychiatric diagnosis features among the prerequisites for legal recognition of transgender persons' gender identity in the vast majority of the forty Contracting Parties [to the ECHR] which allow such recognition, with only four of them having enacted legislation laying down a recognition procedure which excludes such a diagnosis'.[21] Queer readings of the *A.P.* judgment find it disappointing for a number of reasons. As Theilen writes, 'changing a person's birth certificate does not constitute true "gender recognition" if the person is considered mentally ill ... The ECtHR itself cites "human dignity," "human freedom," and "personal autonomy" as the basis of the right to gender identity ... such values cannot be reconciled with trans pathologisation'.[22] However, it is interesting to note the Court's wording in the *A.P.* judgment, which does not close the door fully on further consideration of depathologization at a later date. *Goodwin,* it is to be recalled, was partially decided on the identification of a growing consensus that legal gender recognition was a human right. As more States move toward self-determination of gender, will the Court move with them?

3. GENDER RECOGNITION LAWS AND LIMITATIONS

The structure of gender recognition laws across Europe has historically varied greatly. One of the earliest laws in force was the German Transsexuellengesetz (TSG) of 1980, which at the time was referred to as '"the most progressive law in the world" and the "most human and comprehensive of all solutions ... so far in any state under the rule of law"'.[23] However, as time has passed, sections of the TSG fell behind in terms of updated human rights standards, and a report was commissioned in 2016 which recommended its reform.[24] In many cases, early gender recognition laws have been found to be archaic or obsolete in terms of current human rights obligations and standards. Legal requirements such as attaining the age of majority or divorcing one's spouse, and medical requirements such as surgical or hormonal interventions, have been found

21 ibid., para. 139.

22 J. Theilen, 'Depathologisation of Transgenderism and International Human Rights Law' (2014) 14 *Human Rights Law Review* 327, 334.

23 *Report on Reform of the Transsexuals Act (Transexuellengesetz) (Short version in English)*, German Federal Ministry for Family Affairs, Senior Citizens, Women and Youth (2016), p. 5.

24 ibid.

to contravene the rights of trans persons seeking recognition. In this section, this chapter explores some of the requirements which still remain in force in European gender recognition laws.

The most liberal form of gender recognition law is one based on self-determination. Self-determination, or self-identification/self-ID, refers to a statutory or administrative regime wherein the request and avowal of the applicant is the only trigger for the legal processes to begin. Self-determination has been recognized by the United Nations Independent Expert on Sexual Orientation and Gender Identity as the 'gold standard' for gender recognition legislation.[25] It is the only system which has been upheld by international human rights law as being compliant with the human rights of trans persons to bodily integrity, privacy and dignity. Approximately 10 countries across Europe currently operate a system of self-determination. Among the earliest adopters were Malta[26] and Ireland.[27]

Self-determination stands in stark contrast to systems such as that of the United Kingdom,[28] which imposes heavy requirements on applicants for legal gender recognition. Applicants in the United Kingdom must supply two letters from doctors or psychologists diagnosing them with gender dysphoria; live for two years 'out' in their true gender before the application is considered; obtain the consent of their spouse, if they have one; and go before a Gender Recognition Panel who will determine the success of the application. By contrast, in Ireland, a request to the Registrar General by the applicant, and the payment of a nominal fee, are all that are required to have one's gender marker updated. Some common requirements featured in gender recognition laws are age limits, (non-)binary identity status, and pathologized or medical requirements.

3.1. PATHOLOGIZATION

As has been previously discussed, the case of *A.P., Garcon, and Nicot v. France* ended the legality of requiring permanent medical interventions to the level of sterilization across the member States of the Council of Europe; however, it did not go so far as to require complete depathologization of transgender identity with regard to legal gender recognition. Trans identity therefore retains the stigma of being addressed as a medical and psychological condition in the laws of many European countries.

25 Report of the United Nations Independent Expert on protection against violence and discrimination based on sexual orientation and gender identity, V. Madrigal-Borloz, 'The law of inclusion', A/HRC/47/27, 03.06.2021, para. 87.

26 Gender Identity, Gender Expression, and Sex Characteristics Act 2015, above n. 4.

27 Gender Recognition Act 2015, Ireland, Act no. 25 of 2015, 22.07.2015.

28 Gender Recognition Act 2004, United Kingdom, Chapter 7, 01.07.2004.

Gender variance has been removed from the 'mental and behavioural disorders' section of the International Classification of Diseases produced by the World Health Organization[29] and replaced with an entry on 'gender incongruence' in the 'conditions related to sexual health' section.[30] It has also been reclassified in the Diagnostic and Statistical Manual of Mental Disorders 5 as 'gender dysphoria' rather than 'gender identity disorder'. These are welcome moves toward the removal of psychological criteria from trans identities. Commenting on these developments, Victor Madrigal-Borloz, UN Independent Expert on Sexual Orientation and Gender Identity, wrote,

> this reclassification will have a significant impact on the wrong perception of some forms of gender as a pathology, will promote the visibility of those forms of gender and will allow individuals to access better health care … [P]athologization has had a deep impact on public policy, legislation and jurisprudence, thus penetrating all realms of State action in all regions of the world and permeating the collective conscience.[31]

'Reducing and eliminating medical evidence requirements for gender reclassification', writes Spade, 'directly addresses trans people's survival issues, especially low-income people, youth, and people of color who are disproportionately deprived of healthcare access'.[32] Some European jurisdictions are moving toward the removal of pathologized requirements from their gender recognition laws, including all of those which currently operate a self-determination regime.

In many European jurisdictions, however, fully pathologized requirements are extant for applicants for legal gender recognition. In Czechia,[33] legal gender recognition is still qualified by sterilization, despite the ruling in *A.P.* Before legal gender recognition can be applied, the applicant must undergo gender-affirming surgical procedures which prevent reproductive function and change the appearance of the genitals.[34] In order to undergo this surgical treatment, a

---

29 'A major win for transgender rights: UN health agency drops "gender identity disorder", as official diagnosis', United Nations News <https://news.un.org/en/story/2019/05/1039531> accessed 10.06.2022.

30 International Classification of Diseases, ICD-11, sub-heading 17.

31 UN Independent Expert on Sexual Orientation and Gender Identity, Report to the General Assembly, (2018) A/73/152, para. 14.

32 D. Spade, above n. 3, p. 91.

33 For an overview on trans identity in the Czech context, see P. Agha, '"True Sex": The Law and Confirmation of One's Sex' in E. Brems, P. Cannoot and T. Moonen (eds), *Protecting Trans Rights in the Age of Gender Self-Determination*, vol. 1, Intersentia, Cambridge 2020, pp. 145–70, at p. 145; Z. Králíčková, 'The Civil Status of Trans Persons in the Czech Republic' in I.C. Jaramillo Sierra and L. Carlson (eds), *Trans Rights and Wrongs: A Comparative Study of Legal Reform Concerning Trans Persons*, Springer, New York 2021, pp. 77–96, at p. 77.

34 Czech Civil Code, Act No. 89/2012 of 3rd February 2012, Coll., Art. 29.

person must be found by an 'expert commission' to have a 'sexual identification disorder'.[35] In Romania, there is no official procedure for legal gender recognition outside of a court process as detailed in the Civil Code,[36] but it is reported that judges will impose conditions up to and including sterilization on applicants.[37]

In Italy, pathologization is more uncertain. In 2015, and later in 2017, the Constitutional Court struck down the need for surgery amounting to sterilization as a requirement for legal gender recognition. However, they 'explicitly, and categorically, ruled out' self-determination as a means of operation.[38] Although surgery was no longer required, the Courts

> emphasized that, in order to obtain gender recognition, applicants must transform the 'psychological, behavioral, and physical components of gender identity' and acquire those of the gender with which they identify ... individuals must behave and appear in accordance with, and show the psychological traits of, the (binary) gender for which they claim a legal recognition ... The Court strongly reaffirmed this doctrine in 2017. Italian courts are called to implement this doctrine.[39]

Therefore, a psychological 'transformation' must be observed – but what does this entail? It is unclear whether a diagnostic requirement would be put in place, or whether this is at the discretion of the judge. This lack of clarity is off-putting and concerning to potential applicants.

3.2. AGE

In general, where legal gender recognition processes exist, they are open to binary-identified adults over the age of 18. Having attained the age of majority is seen as a basic prerequisite for the exercise of personal autonomy in this area. In Turkey, for example, Article 40 of the Civil Code[40] limits the availability of

---

35 Czech Specific Health Services Act, Act No. 373/2011 of 6th November 2011, Coll., Art. 21.

36 Romania, Law no. 287/2009 on the Civil Code, 17.07.2009, Arts 98–103.

37 'Romania', Rainbow Europe Map, ILGA Europe <https://www.rainbow-europe.org/#8655/0/0> accessed 10.06.2022. For an overview of trans identity in the Romanian context, see D.A. Deteşeanu and C.M. Nicolescu, 'The Civil Status of Trans Persons under the Romanian Legal System' in I.C. Jaramillo Sierra and L. Carlson (eds), *Trans Rights and Wrongs: A Comparative Study of Legal Reform Concerning Trans Persons*, Springer, New York 2021, pp. 33–48, at p. 119.

38 S. Osella, 'Reinforcing the Binary and Disciplining the Subject: The Constitutional Right to Gender Recognition in the Italian Case Law' (2022) *International Journal of Constitutional Law* 465.

39 Osella, above n. 38, p. 456.

40 Turkey, Civil Code 2001, 22.11.2001, Series 5 Vol. 41, Art. 40.

legal gender recognition to persons who are over the age of 18, transgender – certified by a psychological report – and unmarried. A requirement to be 18 is also in place in Finland,[41] Sweden[42] and Denmark.[43]

However, in many jurisdictions, legal gender recognition is becoming available to minors under the age of 18 (in most cases, with conditions placed on age limits or parental or guardian consent). In Spain, the Constitutional Court ruled in 2019 that minors should be allowed to access legal gender recognition procedures on an equal basis with adults, meaning that a court process was no longer required.[44] In Germany, it is possible for a minor over the age of 14 to access legal gender recognition procedures as long as medical authorization is present, and if parental consent is not acquired then the Family Courts can make an order in the child's best interests.[45] In Ireland, it is possible for a 16 or 17 year old to access legal gender recognition with parental consent since 2019; however, it is not available to minors under the age of 16.[46] Under the 2017 Belgian law, a child can apply for legal gender recognition from the age of 16 provided they have the opinion of a psychiatrist that they are capable of making the decision – however, this does not need to include a diagnosis of gender dysphoria.[47]

However, in Norway, children aged six and over can apply for legal gender recognition provided they have the consent of both parents, or the consent of one parent and a court order that gender marker change is in the best interests of the child.[48] Interestingly, the Norwegian law also allows for gender marker change for children under the age of six if it is medically certified that the child is intersex. The application must be made by the child's parents, but the views of the child are to be taken into account if they are determined to be capable.[49]

It would seem that, following the best interests of the child approach, taking the view of the child into account would allow for the most human rights-compliant legislative processes in this area.[50] As the United Nations Independent Expert on Sexual Orientation and Gender Identity stated in 2018:

> States should take the best interests of the child as a primary consideration and respect the child's right to express views in accordance with the age and maturity of

41 Finland, Act on legal recognition of the gender of transsexuals, no. 563/2002.
42 Gender Recognition Act (1972:119) as reformed in 2012.
43 Law No. 752 of 25.06.2014.
44 Spain, Tribunal Constitucional, Pleno. Sentencia 99/2019, 18.07.2019, 'BOE' núm. 192, de 12 de agosto de 2019, páginas 89782 a 89810.
45 Germany, Civil Status Act, 2007, 19.02.2007, Bundesgesetzblatt Jahrgang 2007 Teil I Nr. 5.
46 Gender Recognition Act 2015, above n. 27.
47 Belgium, Transgender Regime Reform Act, 25.06.2017, para. 3.11.
48 Norway, Act on Change of Legal Gender, ACT-2016-06-17-46, para. 4.
49 ibid.
50 See further F.R. Ammaturo and M.F. Moscati, 'Children's Rights and Gender Identity: A New Frontier of Children's Protagonism?' (2021) 39(2) *Nordic Journal of Human Rights* 146.

the child, in line with the Convention on the Rights of the Child and, in particular, in keeping with the safeguards established pursuant to article 19 of the Convention, which must not be excessive or discriminatory in relation to other safeguards that give recognition to the autonomy and decisional power of children of a certain age in other areas. States should also fulfil their obligation to ensure to the maximum extent possible the survival and development of the child and the creation of an environment that respects human dignity.[51]

3.3. (NON-)BINARY IDENTITY STATUS

Although legal gender recognition is, as has been discussed, commonplace in Europe at the time of writing, it is in general restricted to persons who identify within the male/female binary. Non-binary persons, who do not identify within the binary categories of male and female, are often either omitted from legislation completely; have their legal identification relegated to secondary documents such as driver's licences; or have to go through lengthy court procedures in order to have their status recognized. Non-binary is not a 'third gender' class; rather, it is a broad spectrum umbrella term which covers a plurality of genders.[52] Some non-binary persons identify solely as non-binary, while others use more specific labels such as genderqueer,[53] agender,[54] bigender,[55] etc. This renders legislating for non-binary recognition more difficult, as will be explored further later.

As of mid-2022, the only country in Europe with full non-binary recognition based on self-determination is Iceland.[56] Their law, introduced in 2019 and operational as of 2021, allows for 'neutral registration of gender'.[57] This factor alone would make it potentially the most progressive legislation on the subject in Europe, but it also provides, in Article 3, that:

> Every individual enjoys, in accordance with age and maturity, an unrestricted right to:
>
> 1. define their gender,
> 2. recognition of gender, gender identity and gender expression,

51 Report of the UN Independent Expert on Sexual Orientation and Gender Identity to the General Assembly, A/73/152, 'Laws of Inclusion', para. 35; These concerns were repeated in his complementary report, 'Practices of Exclusion', A/76/152.

52 See B. Vincent, *Non-Binary Genders: Navigating Communities, Identities, and Healthcare*, Policy Press, Bristol 2020, in particular Chapter 1, 'Reviewing Non-Binary'.

53 A subcategory of non-binary identity which tries to 'queer' or subvert gender roles and expectations.

54 Agender persons do not identify with or experience any particular gender identity.

55 Bigender persons identify with two genders, whether binary or non-binary.

56 Iceland, Act on Sexual Autonomy, 80/2019, 18.06.2019, Art. 3.

57 ibid., Art.6. This means that a person can be registered in a 'neutral' (non-male and non-female) gender.

3. to develop their personality according to their own sexuality,
4. physical immunity and autonomy over changes in gender characteristics.[58]

This wording is in line with the Yogyakarta Principles, which is the leading document on the human rights of persons relating to sexual orientation, gender identity and expression, and sex characteristics. The Act on Sexual Autonomy also allows for legal gender recognition and change of legal name for children under the age of 18 with the consent of their parents. If one or more parents do not approve of the application, the child can appear before an Expert Committee to determine if it is in their best interests to have the application accepted.[59]

Other European jurisdictions have taken some steps toward the recognition of identities outside the male/female binary. In Germany, non-binary recognition is possible under Section 45b of the Personenstandsgesetz,[60] but on the condition of medical certification of an identity other than that assigned at birth. This does not need to be a psychiatric diagnosis, however. It is also possible for an intersex child to have their birth registration marked as 'diverse' or left blank. In Malta, a similar provision applies to intersex children, who can have their birth certificates marked with an X marker.[61]

However, several European junctions with some measure of non-binary legal gender recognition restrict that recognition to secondary documentation such as passports or driving licences. This is the case in Denmark, where access to non-binary markers is restricted to passports only and is accessed via administrative procedures which are limited and difficult to use.[62] In the Netherlands, court proceedings have held since 2018 that non-binary persons should be allowed to use X markers in their national identity cards, but only in 2021 did the Amsterdam High Court allow for retroactive amendment of a birth certificate to include an X marker. This has not yet, as of May 2022, been codified in law. In the United Kingdom, a petition to allow for non-binary legal gender recognition on passports was denied by the Supreme Court in 2021.[63] Christie Elan-Cane, who is non-gendered, announced per[64] intention to take per case to the European Court of Human Rights.[65] In response to the judgment, Gonzalez-Salzburg

---

58 ibid., Art.3.
59 ibid., Art.5.
60 Germany, Civil Status Act 2007, above n. 45.
61 Gender Identity, Gender Expression, and Sex Characteristics Act 2015, above n. 4.
62 'Denmark', *Rainbow Europe 2022*, ILGA-Europe <http://www.rainbow-europe.org> accessed 19.05.22.
63 *R (on the application of Elan-Cane) v Secretary of State for the Home Department* [2021] UKSC 56.
64 Elan-Cane uses per/perself pronouns.
65 'Gender-neutral passports: Campaigner Christie Elan-Cane loses Supreme Court case', BBC News, 15.12.2021 <https://www.bbc.co.uk/news/uk-59667786> accessed 19.05.2022.

argued that the United Kingdom had 'lost an invaluable opportunity to ease one of the many components of the regulatory network that sustain the UK's binary-only gender policy'.[66]

Non-binary legal gender recognition faces a number of problems, both administrative and theoretical. To begin with, governments have argued that their state registries are not set up to handle three identity categories, with the associated administrative and financial difficulties that an overhaul of registry systems would bring. Allowing for non-binary identification or X markers on birth certificates, as well as on secondary identity documents such as passports, would create an entirely new juridical category of persons. Developing this theme, it has also been argued that allowing non-binary identity markers in law would disrupt existing and traditional legal figures such as the 'mother', 'father' and the gendered child figure at the heart of the system of baby registration. In particular, the concern has been raised that it would complicate systems of family law regarding succession and parental claims.

However, these arguments need not spell an end to the possibility of non-binary legal gender recognition. The administrative arguments are similar to those used by successive United Kingdom governments in cases such as *Rees v. United Kingdom*, *Cossey v. United Kingdom*, etc., at the European Court of Human Rights, and which were roundly struck down in *Goodwin*. The Court held that it no longer fell within the government's margin of appreciation to not allow for legal gender recognition, and that there was not a fair balance struck between the applicant's interest and the public interest in not updating systems of administration.

Of course, non-binary legal gender recognition prima facie faces a huge problem: there is no one 'non-binary' gender. Non-binary, as elucidated above, is not a 'third gender' category, it is an umbrella term. As Ashley writes,

> in offering a single letter to those who are neither men nor women, 'X' gender markers place the umbrella of non-binary on the same level as the specific identities of man and woman … A third gender marker option is progress, but not enough of it. By offering a single box to all non-binary people, the internal differences of non-binary communities are suppressed.[67]

---

66 D. Gonzalez-Salzberg, 'The Supreme Court Refused to Order the Legal Recognition of Elan-Cane's Non-Gendered Identity', *Oxford Human Rights Hub Blog*, 19.12.2021. <https://ohrh.law.ox.ac.uk/the-supreme-court-refused-to-order-the-legal-recognition-of-elan-canes-non-gendered-identity> accessed 10.06.2022.

67 F. Ashley, '"X" Why? Gender markers and non-binary transgender people' in I.C. Jaramillo Sierra and L. Carlson (eds), *Trans Rights and Wrongs: A Comparative Study of Legal Reform Concerning Trans Persons*, Springer, New York 2021, pp. 33–48, at p. 38.

Likewise, Davis adds that 'The homogenizing effects of the x marker are not only evident in the extent to which the category obscures differences among non-binary people but also in the extent to which it problematically conflates non-binary gender and intersex status, instead subsuming them within one undifferentiated category'.[68] They go on to argue that 'the x marker thus not only functions to contain the apparent threat posed by non-binary trans people and people with intersex to the stability and coherence of the gender binary, but in doing so dismisses as irrelevant the range of actual experiences within this apparently homogenous group'.[69] It is therefore clear to see that non-binary recognition is not without its difficulties. This chapter does not intend to propose a solution to these difficulties, as it is not evident that one can be found outside of gender decertification.[70] However, by contrast, it is likewise important to note that for some non-binary people, the availability of an X gender marker to differentiate them from the categories of male and female is both welcome and validating.[71]

4. CONCLUSION: SOCIAL MOVEMENTS – PROGRESS OR REGRESSION?

Although legal developments in the European context with regard to gender recognition have in general been progressive, an increasing backlash to this progress exists in terms of media, political and social discourse.[72] From the United Kingdom,[73] nicknamed 'TERF Island'[74] by some commentators, to the

---

68 D.A. Davis, 'The Normativity of Recognition: Non-Binary Gender Markers in Australian Law and Policy' in V. Demos and M. Texler Segal (eds), *Advances in Gender Research*, vol. 24 (Emerald Publishing Limited 2017).

69 ibid., p. 238.

70 D. Cooper, R. Emerton, E. Grabham, H.J.H. Newman, E. Peel, F. Renz and J. Smith, 'Abolishing legal sex status: The challenge and consequences of gender related law reform' (2022) Future of Legal Gender Project, Final Report, King's College London, UK.

71 H.J.H. Newman and E. Peel, '"An Impossible Dream"? Non-Binary People's Perceptions of Legal Gender Status and Reform in the UK' (2022) *Psychology & Sexuality* 1, 15.

72 See generally A. Graff and E. Korolczuk, *Anti-Gender Politics in the Populist Moment*, Routledge, Abingdon 2022.

73 C. McLean 'The Growth of the Anti-Transgender Movement in the United Kingdom. The Silent Radicalization of the British Electorate' (2021) 51(6) *International Journal of Sociology* 473.

74 'TERF' is the acronym for 'Trans-Exclusionary Radical Feminist'. Originally applied to adherents of a particular strand of radical feminism which did not acknowledge the womanhood of transgender women, it has colloquially become the standard term for persons expressing anti-trans viewpoints, whether or not they espouse any form of feminism. It is debated whether the usage is derogatory in common parlance, or merely factual description. See further 'TERF Wars: An Introduction' in B. Vincent, S. Erikainen and R. Pearce (eds), *TERF Wars: Feminism and the Fight for Transgender Futures*, Sage Publications, London 2020.

far-right politics of Victor Orbán's Hungary[75] and the anti-'gender ideology' rhetoric espoused by Poland[76] and Bulgaria[77] (among others), conservative fearmongering about the effects of legal gender recognition and the wider movement to recognize sex/gender as socially constructed categories rather than immutable biological facts has gained considerable ground in recent years.

Constructing gender/identity as an 'ideology' allows for a political framing wherein people, and especially young people, are 'indoctrinated' into its 'belief system'. As Tranfić writes in his study of Croatia, 'gender ideology' is 'a term concocted at the heart of the Vatican'[78] whereby gender is 'denounced as an inauthentic value system, or a "covert political strategy and conspiracy of deviants and minorities"'.[79] This belief, taken from the religious right, has been adopted by a variety of actors across the continent. In the United Kingdom in particular, it has been taken up by a coalition of ostensibly left-wing soi-disant feminists, who label themselves 'gender critical',[80] and hard-right conservatives. These beliefs came to the forefront in particular with regard to the public consultation on the future of the Gender Recognition Act 2004, in 2017/2018 and have been particularly influential in public debate, including at the highest political levels.[81] This has no doubt hampered progress in the area of transgender rights, including the now-scrapped reform of the 2004 Act.[82]

These worrying currents in social discourse cast a shadow over the progress which has been made in liberalizing gender recognition laws across Europe. In their article on Slovakia,[83] Maďarová and Valkovičová pose the question

75 'Viktor Orbán wins fourth consecutive term as Hungary's prime minister', *The Guardian*, 03.04.2022.

76 K. Konopka, M. Prusik and M. Szulawski, 'Two Sexes, Two Genders Only: Measuring Attitudes toward Transgender Individuals in Poland' (2020) 82 *Sex Roles* 600.

77 M. Ilcheva, 'Bulgaria and the Istanbul convention: law, politics and propaganda vs. the rights of victims of gender-based violence' (2020) 3(1) *Open Journal for Legal Studies* 49.

78 See also P. Gusmeroli and L. Trappolin, 'Narratives of Catholic Women against "Gender Ideology" in Italian Schools: Defending Childhood, Struggling with Pluralism' (2021) 23 *European Societies* 513.

79 I. Tranfić, 'Framing "Gender Ideology": Religious Populism in the Croatian Catholic Church' [2022] *Identities* 1.

80 A. Zanghellini, 'Philosophical Problems With the Gender-Critical Feminist Argument Against Trans Inclusion' (2020) 10 *SAGE Open*.

81 S. Hines, 'Sex Wars and (Trans) Gender Panics: Identity and Body Politics in Contemporary UK Feminism' in B. Vincent, S. Erikainen and R. Pearce (eds), *TERF Wars: Feminism and the Fight for Transgender Futures*, above n. 74.

82 Government Equalities Office, 'Government responds to Gender Recognition Act consultation', 22.09.2020 <https://www.gov.uk/government/news/government-responds-to-gender-recognition-act-consultation> accessed 10.06.2022.

83 Z. Maďarová and V. Valkovičová, 'Is Feminism Doomed? Feminist Praxis in the Times of "Gender Ideology" in Slovakia' (2021) 28 *European Journal of Women's Studies* 274.

'Is feminism doomed? ... in the times of "gender ideology"'.[84] While it is perhaps not so bleak as that, it is certain that there is significant opposition to trans-inclusive feminism from various actors in Europe and a concerted effort to push back on reforms which have liberalized access to legal gender recognition across the continent. As lawyers concerned with the rights of individuals to autonomy and to the formation of relationships, this is a worrying development to watch.

This chapter has aimed to give an overview of the current status of gender identity in comparative European legal and political perspective, looking to the past, present and future. It aims to present a hopeful picture filled with possibilities for advancements in the rights of transgender persons across the continent. However, it is clear that the path ahead is not free of obstacles – and this chapter attempts to signpost those also.

[84] See also V. Valkovičová and P. Meier, '"Everyone Has the Right to Their Opinion": "Gender Ideology" Rhetoric and Epistemic Struggles in Slovak Policymaking' (2022) 29(3) Social Politics: International Studies in Gender, State & Society 1080.

SAME-SEX COUPLES AND EU PRIVATE INTERNATIONAL LAW AFTER *COMAN*

José María LORENZO VILLAVERDE

1. INTRODUCTION

In 2018, the Court of Justice of the European Union (CJEU) delivered its long-awaited judgment in Case C-673/16 *Relu Adrian Coman and Others v. Inspectoratul General pentru Imigrări and Ministerul Afacerilor Interne* (hereinafter, '*Coman*').[1] This decision, preceded by the Opinion of Advocate General Wathelet,[2] concerns Directive 2004/38/EC on freedom of movement of citizens and their families (hereinafter, 'Directive 2004/38/EC' or 'the Directive').[3] The main judgment's conclusion is that the term 'spouse' in the Directive includes same-sex married partners within its scope.[4]

While *Coman* is limited to Directive 2004/38/EC, the aim of this chapter is to explore its potential impact on EU private international law in family matters. In particular, this chapter addresses the Brussels II bis Recast regulation (hereinafter, 'the Recast Regulation')[5] and the regulations on matrimonial property[6] and the property consequences of registered partnerships[7] (hereinafter, 'the Property Regulations' when referring to both of them or 'the Matrimonial Property Regulation' and 'the Regulation on Property Consequences of Registered Partnerships' when discussing them separately). Moreover, it discusses the limits of and opportunities arising from the judgment in relation to the protection of same-sex couples in cross-border situations in the EU.

2. HAPPILY MARRIED, LET'S MOVE TO ROMANIA!

While working at the EU Parliament, Mr Coman, a Romanian and a United States citizen, married a United States national, Mr Hamilton, in

---

1 Case C-673/16, *Relu Adrian Coman and others v. Inspectoratul General pentru Imigrări and Ministerul Afacerilor Interne*, ECLI:EU:C:2018:385.

2 Case C-673/16, *Relu Adrian Coman and others v. Inspectoratul General pentru Imigrări and Ministerul Afacerilor Interne*, Opinion of the Advocate General Mr Wathelet, ECLI:EU:C:2018:2.

3 Directive 2004/38/EC of the European Parliament and of the Council of 29 April 2004 on the right of citizens of the Union and their family members to move and reside freely within the territory of the Member States amending Regulation (EEC) No 1612/68 and repealing Directives 64/221/EEC, 68/360/EEC, 72/194/EEC, 73/148/EEC, 75/34/EEC, 75/35/EEC, 90/364/EEC, 90/365/EEC and 93/96/EEC [2004] OJ L158/77.

4 ibid., Article 2(2)(a). The terms 'same-sex marriage'/'gender-neutral marriage' will be used interchangeably in this chapter, acknowledging that the notion of sex refers to a biological category while gender refers to a social construct, see A. Schuster, 'Gender and Beyond: Disaggregating Legal Categories' in A. Schuster (ed.), *Equality and Justice: Sexual Orientation and Gender Identity in the XXI Century*, Editrice Universitaria Udinese srl, Udine 2011, pp. 21–39, at pp. 31 et seq.

5 Council Regulation (EU) 2019/1111 of 25 June 2019 on jurisdiction, the recognition and enforcement of decisions in matrimonial matters and the matters of parental responsibility, and on international child abduction [2019] OJ L178/1.

6 Council Regulation (EU) 2016/1103 of 24 June 2016 implementing enhanced cooperation in the area of jurisdiction, applicable law and the recognition and enforcement of decisions in matters of matrimonial property regimes [2016] OJ L183/1.

7 Council Regulation (EU) 2016/1104 of 24 June 2016 implementing enhanced cooperation in the area of jurisdiction, applicable law and the recognition and enforcement of decisions in matters of the property consequences of registered partnerships [2016] OJ L 183/30.

Belgium. In 2012, they decided to move to Romania as spouses pursuant to Directive 2004/38/EC, thinking this would allow Mr Hamilton to reside in Romania for more than three months. Their application was rejected based on the fact that the Romanian Civil Code prohibits the celebration of marriages between people of the same sex in Romania and explicitly rules out the recognition of such marriages contracted abroad.[8] The couple, supported by the LGBT+ association Accept appealed this decision before the Court of First Instance on grounds of the unconstitutionality of the relevant provisions of the Civil Code.[9] The Court of First Instance requested that the Constitutional Court decide whether the Civil Code complied with the constitution. The Constitutional Court understood this as a matter of interpretation of Directive 2004/38/EC in conjunction with the prohibition against discrimination on grounds of sexual orientation[10] and consequently referred the question to the CJEU for a preliminary ruling.

The Constitutional Court asked whether the term 'spouse' in Directive 2004/38/EC, in light of Articles 7, 9, 21 and 45 of the Charter of Fundamental Rights of the EU (CFREU),[11] included the case of a same-sex, non-EU-citizen spouse lawfully married to a EU citizen on the basis of the law of a Member State different from the host Member State.[12] In case of a positive answer, the Court queried whether the host Member State was obliged to grant the right of residence as a spouse pursuant to Article 2(2)(a) of the Directive.[13] Finally, should the notion of 'spouse' not necessarily comprise a gender-neutral marriage, the Constitutional Court asked if it was to be defined as a 'durable relationship' under Article 3(2)(b),[14] in which case the host State would only be obliged to facilitate the entry and residence of a Union citizen's spouse.

The CJEU concluded that the term 'spouse' in the Directive necessarily embraces same-sex spouses. In consequence, no Member State can refuse to grant entry and residence to the spouse of an EU citizen exercising the right to free movement in the EU. This also applies to Union citizens returning to their country of nationality after residing in another Member State under Article 21 of the Treaty on the Functioning of the EU (TFEU).[15]

---

8 Articles 227(1) and (2) of the Romanian Civil Code.

9 Wathelet's Opinion, above n. 2, para. 17.

10 ibid., para. 18.

11 Charter of Fundamental Rights of the European Union [2016] OJ C202/389.

12 Request for a preliminary ruling from the Curtea Constituțională a României (Romania) lodged on 30 December 2016 – Relu Adrian Coman, Robert Clabourn Hamilton, Asociația Accept v. Inspectoratul General pentru Imigrări, Ministerul Afacerilor Interne, Consiliul Național pentru Combaterea Discriminării (Case C-673/16) [2017] OJ C104/29, question 1.

13 ibid., question 2.

14 ibid., questions 3 and 4.

15 Consolidated Version of the Treaty on the Functioning of the European Union [2016] OJ C 202/1; *Coman* judgment, above n. 1, paras 24 and 25.

There is little doubt that the *Coman* case is a ground-breaking judgment for the rights of same-sex couples in the EU. It also represents an example of strategic litigation.[16] Additionally, it exemplifies a divide in the EU between countries with legal policies in favour of strengthening the rights of same-sex couples and LGBT+ rights in general (e.g., Belgium, the Netherlands, Spain, Portugal, Malta or the Scandinavian countries) and those with no or even hostile legal policies towards same-sex relationships (currently, Romania, Poland, Lithuania, Bulgaria, Latvia and Slovakia do not allow marriage or provide a registration scheme for same-sex couples).[17] This divide can be drawn easily on the European map by tracing a line between Western European and Central-Eastern European countries. Some of the latter have taken steps backward on LGBT+ rights in recent years. So-called 'LGBT+ ideology-free zones' have emerged in various Polish municipalities and, together with the current Polish government's active stance against LGBT+ rights, have become a concern at the EU level.[18] Hungary has also generated concern due to the backlash experienced since the Orbán government came into office.[19] After the *Coman* judgment, a referendum was called in Romania to amend the constitution in order to restrict marriage to different-sex couples and thus rule out any introduction of gender-neutral marriages in Romanian law. But as the turnout was only 21.1 per cent, lower than the required 30 per cent threshold, the referendum failed.[20]

In some Central-Eastern European countries, the *Coman* judgment has drawn reactions aimed against strengthening LGBT+ rights and against the work of EU institutions in this regard.[21] However, their impact should not be exaggerated. In various of these Member States, legal policies contrary to legislating on same-sex couples had been effected much earlier, through constitutional amendments to

---

16 J. Rijpma, 'You Gotta Let Love Move: ECJ 5 June 2018, Case C-673/16, Coman, Hamilton, Accept v Inspectoratul General pentru Imigrări' (2019) 15(2) *European Constitutional Law Review* 324, 330.

17 Further on the legal position of same-sex couples in Central and Eastern European countries, see, inter alia, L. Vaigé, '"Listening to the Winds" of Europeanisation? The Example of Cross-Border Recognition of Same-Sex Family Relationships in Poland' (2020) 7(1) *Oslo Law Review* 46 et seq.; A. Wysocka-Bar, 'Enhanced cooperation in property matters in the EU and non-participating Member States' (2019) 20 *ERA Forum* 189 et seq.

18 See the European Parliament resolution of 17 September 2020 on the proposal for a Council decision on the determination of a clear risk of a serious breach by the Republic of Poland of the rule of law (COM(2017) 0835 – 2017/0360R(NLE)), OJ C 385/317.

19 European Parliament resolution of 8 July 2021 on breaches of EU law and of the rights of LGBTIQ citizens in Hungary as a result of the legal changes adopted by the Hungarian Parliament (2021/2780(RSP)), OJ C 2022/218.

20 <http://referendum2018.bec.ro/wp-content/uploads/2018/10/prezenta_16.01.pdf> accessed 16.07.2022.

21 T. Mukau, 'European Court of Justice Says "I Do" to Expanding the Acquis Communitaire on Free Movement Rights to Include Same-Sex Marriage' (2020) 34 *Georgetown Immigration Law Journal* 733, 778.

shield the so-called 'traditional' family based on different-sex marriages. Such policies have underlain some 'conservative' Central-Eastern European countries' non-participation in the Property Regulations.[22] The impact of *Coman* among the Romanian population was in fact limited, as evidenced by the low turnout for the referendum on a constitutional amendment. In any event, political reactions against the CJEU's decisions should not deter the Court from ensuring compliance with the Treaties, the secondary legislation and the rights and freedoms enshrined in them.

The *Coman* case exemplifies something else, too, however: the use of substantive family law notions like 'spouse' or 'marriage' in EU legal instruments that deal with other areas of law such as Directive 2004/38/EC. Substantive family law is not within the competence of the EU. However, the EU may develop legislation on private international law in family matters pursuant to Article 81(3) TFEU. This competence is limited; it must follow a special legislative procedure requiring unanimity of the Council and prior consultation with the European Parliament. Once more, an East–West divide on LGBT+ rights is perceptible in the recent Property Regulations in this area. In the 2021 CJEU judgment *V.M.A. v. Stolichna obshtina, rayon 'Pancharevo'* (hereinafter, '*V.M.A.* case'),[23] which largely follows the path cleared in *Coman*, purely family law notions are again used in a case involving Directive 2004/38/EC.

2.1. *COMAN* AS A GROUND-BREAKING JUDGMENT

The following section discusses the main achievements of *Coman*, which reinforce freedom of movement and LGBT+ rights in the EU.

2.1.1. *Enhancing Freedom of Movement*

By affirming that that the term 'spouse' in Directive 2004/38/EC is to be interpreted as gender-neutral, *Coman* represents a step forward in enhancing the rights of same-sex married couples in the EU. It has been claimed that the legal effects of the decision are limited.[24] Indeed, it only covers same-sex married couples of whom one spouse is not an EU national; if both are EU citizens, then each would in principle enjoy freedom of movement rights on their own. However, *Coman* would also be relevant if one of the spouses, despite being a Union citizen, did not fulfil any of the other requirements the Directive sets

22 See above n. 5 and n. 6. See also A. Wysocka-Bar, above n. 17, p. 191.

23 Case C-490/20, *V.M.A. v. Stolichna obshtina, rayon 'Pancharevo'*, ECLI:EU:C:2021:1008.

24 A. Spalding, 'Where Next after *Coman*?' (2019) 21 *European Journal of Migration and Law* 117, 123.

forth.[25] In any case, regardless of the number of same-sex couples benefitting from the judgment, its symbolism must not be underestimated.

Some differences between the judgment and the Advocate General's Opinion are worth noting: Wathelet's Opinion is more ambitious, because it discusses the case not only as one of freedom of movement but also as one of discrimination on grounds of sexual orientation; indeed, the CJEU's decision mostly overlooks the latter.[26] It is striking that Wathelet reproduces Article 21 CFREU under the headings 'legal context' and 'EU law' whereas the Charter is missing from the corresponding heading in the judgment.

Wathelet's Opinion mentions dignity, equality and the ways the concept of 'spouse' is connected to various fundamental rights.[27] It also dedicates several paragraphs to how the case is linked to the right to family life and to the case-law of the European Court of Human Rights (ECtHR).[28] It clearly points out that 'a definition of the term "spouse" that was limited to heterosexual marriage would inevitably give rise to situations involving discrimination on grounds of sexual orientation'.[29] The CJEU only reproduces recital 31 of the Directive as a reference to the CFREU and timidly discusses the right to family life.[30]

The CJEU continued to employ this approach in the *V.M.A.* judgment,[31] which dealt with same-sex parentage and the presentation of a Spanish birth certificate in Bulgaria for the purpose of transcribing the parentage of the child and for the child to acquire Bulgarian citizenship. Despite the fact that the Bulgarian authorities refused to issue a certificate of citizenship because both parents, a married couple, were women, the CJEU did not address discrimination on the grounds of sexual orientation. Instead, it discussed the case on the basis of the right to free movement and the best interests of the child.[32] This contrasts with its approach in the 'surnames' cases *García Avello v. Belgian State*[33] and *Grunkin-Paul v. Standesamt Niebüll*,[34] in which the Court

---

25 Article 7 of Directive 2004/38/EC. See T. Mukau, above n. 21, pp. 750–51.

26 A. Tryfonidou and R. Wintemute, *Obstacles to the Free Movement of Rainbow Families in the EU*, Policy Department for Citizens' Rights and Constitutional Affairs, Directorate-General for Internal Policies of the European Parliament, European Union, 2021, p. 41; A. Tryfonidou, *An analysis of the ECJ ruling in Case C-673/16 Coman. The right of same-sex spouses under EU Law to move freely between EU Member States*, Network of European LGBTIQ families associations NELFA AiSBL, 2019, p. 5, <http://nelfa.org/inprogress/wp-content/uploads/2019/01/NELFA-Tryfonidou-report-Coman-final-NEW.pdf> accessed 16.07.2022; A. Spalding, above n. 24, pp. 123, 136.

27 Wathelet's Opinion, above n. 2, paras 2, 34, 55.

28 ibid., paras 59–67.

29 ibid., para. 75.

30 *Coman* judgment, above n. 1, paras 47–50.

31 *V.M.A.* judgment, above n. 23.

32 ibid., paras 43–52, 56, 58–59, 63–65, 69.

33 Case C-148/02, *Carlos Garcia Avello v. Belgian State*, ECLI:EU:C:2003:539.

34 Case C-353/06, *Stefan Grunkin and Dorothee Regina Paul v. Standesamt Niebüll*, ECLI:EU:C:2008:559.

recognized discrimination on the grounds of nationality. Why nationality and not sexual orientation? One would have expected the CJEU in *Coman* to discuss sexual orientation discrimination, in particular because the referring court had expressly asked about a potential violation of Article 21 CFREU.[35] The decision fell short of providing a complete answer to the questions posed.

In any event, the decision in *Coman* adopts a clear *favor circulationis* stance. Both the CJEU and the Advocate General rejected arguments of public policy and of respect for national identity as justifications for the authorities' denial of entry and residence to a same-sex spouse in light of Directive 2004/38/EC.[36] Thus, where various interpretations of the Directive are possible, the one that best reinforces freedom of movement should be favoured.

The decision in *Coman* is an open gate for further strengthening LGBT+ rights (in particular, the legal situation of same-sex couples) in Europe. The *V.M.A.* judgment largely followed in its footsteps. It remains to be seen whether similar cases before the CJEU will be addressed in the future from a sexual orientation discrimination perspective rather than merely from a free movement one.

2.1.2. *The Autonomous Interpretation of 'Spouse'*

The main outcome of *Coman* is that the term 'spouse' in Directive 2004/38/EC is to be interpreted autonomously from national laws, and that it comprises same-sex spouses. First, the Opinion underscores that unlike Article 2(2)(b), Article 2(2)(a) makes no reference to the law of the Member State.[37] Absent such a reference, an autonomous definition must prevail.[38] Second, if the definition of a 'spouse' were left to each Member State, it would undermine the purposes of freedom of movement and of uniformity of criteria. An autonomous definition reinforces the *favor circulationis* approach discussed above and strengthens the effectiveness of EU law. Third, the CJEU follows a dynamic interpretation; Wathelet's Opinion reminds us that when the Directive was passed back in 2004, the definition of 'spouse' was intentionally left open to account for future developments.[39]

Indeed, the number of Member States that had enacted legislation on gender-neutral marriage had increased from two in 2004 to 13 in 2018. Some of the literature is of the view that the 'historical' and the 'dynamic' interpretations should be identical because the passage of time since 2004 has been slight, with

---

35 Above n. 11.

36 Wathelet's Opinion, above n. 2, paras 39, 40, 74, 75; *Coman* judgment, above n. 1, paras 42–44.

37 Wathelet's Opinion, above n. 2, para. 33; *Coman* judgment, above n. 1, para. 36.

38 Wathelet's Opinion, above n. 2, para. 34 and case-law cited there.

39 ibid., paras 51–52.

the consequence that 'spouse' should be restricted to different-sex marriages.[40] This author can hardly share such an understanding. To paraphrase a well-known saying, a week can be a long time in legal policy and even more the 14 years from 2004 until *Coman*. Certainly, this applies to LGBT+ legal policy. Changes have taken place, and quickly, not least in terms of the level of societal support for same-sex relationships. Currently, those EU countries with no legislation in place to protect same-sex couples are the minority.

In reality, the CJEU in *Coman* does not elaborate an autonomous EU concept of 'spouse'. The Court does not detail the requirements of capacity or formal requirements to marry, for example. It only states that a 'spouse', as the term appears in the Directive, must comprise same-sex spouses. In terms of the question posed, this is a coherent position. However, it also means that the situation with respect to other kinds of marriages – ones potentially not foreseen or allowed under the national civil law of the host Member State – will remain uncertain. It cannot be ruled out that there will be further decisions on the interpretation of 'spouse' in the Directive in the future.

Finally, what is the scope of this autonomous interpretation? As mentioned, it is expected that, if no reference to national laws is made, an EU autonomous interpretation of 'spouse' and 'marriage' should be followed; however, this author does not see why such an autonomous interpretation should be restricted to some EU legal instruments and not applied to others. Whether such an interpretation can be extended to EU private international law regulations will be discussed later.

2.1.3. Observing EU Law

The CJEU is interpreting a family law notion in a non-family law instrument. As so often repeated, substantive family law remains within the competence of the Member States. However, it is unavoidable that family law terms are also used in other areas of law, such as in social security, taxation, health, migration etc.

There is an interplay between the principle of hierarchy and the principle of competence. The CJEU in *Coman* reiterates the primacy of EU law, which must also be observed even when a Member State is exercising its own competence.[41] Wathelet recalls that 'the fact that marriage – in the sense exclusively of the union of a man and a woman – is enshrined in certain national constitutions cannot alter that approach'.[42] The primacy of EU law has been settled in Community law since the *Costa v. ENEL* decision of 1964.[43] Scholars like Stehlík opine otherwise,

---

40 V. Stehlík, 'The CJEU crossing the Rubicon on the same-sex marriages? Commentary on Coman case' (2018) 18(2) *International and Comparative Law Review* 85, 92.

41 Coman judgment, above n. 1, para. 38; Wathelet's Opinion, above n. 2, para. 37.

42 Wathelet's Opinion, above n. 2, para. 39.

43 Case 6-64, *Flaminio Costa v. ENEL*, ECLI:EU:C:1964:66.

arguing that the CJEU when dealing with migration matters should strike a balance so as not to undermine national constitutions and public policy.[44] Such an understanding, which turns the argument upside down by calling for the observance of national constitutions, is at odds with the primacy of EU law and can hardly be accepted in the case at hand. Otherwise, the principle of primacy of EU law as well as its effectiveness could be seriously compromised through domestic legislation or changes in national constitutions no matter whether they are intended as departures from or challenges to EU law.

2.2. LIMITS OF THE JUDGMENT AND SOME DOUBTS

Having examined the main achievements of *Coman*, can Mr Coman and Mr Hamilton in fact happily live as spouses in Romania? This section discusses the limitations of the *Coman* judgment for same-sex couples and freedom of movement in the EU.

2.2.1. We are in Romania; What Now?

In various paragraphs, the Court reiterates that the autonomous interpretation of 'spouse' is for the sole purpose of entry and residence under Directive 2004/38/EC.[45] Mr Hamilton can reside in Romania and live together with Mr Coman. What happens when they file a tax return, or if one of them falls ill or passes away? Or if they decide to split up? The Court in *Coman* seemingly wishes to underline that its judgment does not infringe on national competence for family law and that its significance cannot go beyond the scope of the case.

The practical consequence is that the marriage has not actually been 'recognized'. 'Recognition' is a typical private international law term often used beyond private international law in different meanings, which can be misleading.[46] While cross-border limping civil status is a well-known phenomenon in private international law, Bogdan has explained that it is uncommon for a marriage to be recognized in the one country for some purposes and not for others.[47] But in fact this is not so rare: it happens when *ordre public atténué* is applied, as can be the case when a polygamous marriage is not recognized as such but some of its effects are (e.g., regarding the distribution of a pension between surviving

44 V. Stehlík, above n. 40, p. 97.

45 *Coman* judgment, above n. 1, paras 36, 40, 45 and 46.

46 The confusion of the term is explained in detail by L. Vaigé, above n. 17, pp. 50 et seq.

47 M. Bogdan, 'The relevance of family status created abroad for the freedom of movement in the EU' (2020) 4 *Acta Universitatis Carolinae – Iuridica* 85, 91.

spouses).[48] In relation to *Coman* and same-sex marriages, one could speak of a special kind of 'top-down' *ordre public atténué*. Thus, relying on *ordre public* under Directive 2004/38/EC (i.e., entry and residence of same-sex married couples) is ruled out. However, concerning legal effects in their exclusive areas of competence, national authorities could perhaps rely on *ordre public*.

This fragmented result remains problematic, however. One could argue that the non-recognition of a same-sex spouse beyond mere entry and residence (e.g., in family matters) still hinders freedom of movement.[49] After all, the Court has pointed out that freedom of movement enables citizens to 'lead a normal family life' in the host Member State.[50] Can Mr Coman and Mr Hamilton lead a normal family life in Romania if they can live together but not inherit from each other, organize their property or simply be regarded as a couple before the Romanian legal system? Freedom of movement is one of the EU fundamental freedoms, and the right to family life is enshrined in Article 7 CFREU and Article 8 of the European Convention of Human Rights (ECHR).[51] Same-sex couples fall within the notion of 'family life'.[52]

2.2.2. *Registered Partnerships, ubi sunt?*

Coman deals with Article 2(2)(a) of the Directive. It does not apply to registered partnerships under Article 2(2)(b). Pursuant to this provision, the partner registered on the basis of the law of a Member State is a family member if the host EU country considers registered partnerships as 'equivalent to marriage' in accordance with the conditions set forth in its law.

The restrictiveness of the wording is considerable. First, it is limited to registered partnerships contracted in a Member State, and thus partnerships registered outside the EU are seemingly excluded even if such registered partnerships have been recognized in the Member State from which the couple has moved to the host Member State. Second, it is not sufficient that the host Member State provide a registration scheme (in fact, the provision does not require it); rather, registered partnerships must be treated as 'equivalent to

---

48 Carrascosa González distinguishes between 'core' and 'peripheral' legal effects, see J. Carrascosa González, 'Orden público internacional y externalidades negativas' (2008) 2065 *Boletín del Ministerio de Justicia* 2351, 2370.

49 In a similar vein, D. Martiny, 'The impact of the EU private international law instruments on European family law' in J.M. Scherpe (ed.), *European Family Law. Volume I*, Elgar Publishing, Chetelham 2016, p. 265.

50 Case C-127/08, *Blaise Baheten Metock and others v. Minister for Justice, Equality and Law Reform*, ECLI:EU:C:2008:449, para. 62; *Coman* judgment, above n. 1, para. 32; *V.M.A.* judgment, above n. 24, para. 47.

51 Convention for the Protection of Human Rights and Fundamental Freedoms, signed in Rome 04.11.1950, entering into force 03.09.1953.

52 See *Shalk and Kopf v. Austria*, no. 30141/04 §§94-95 ECHR 2010-IV.

marriage'. What does 'equivalent to marriage' stand for? An autonomous interpretation would be welcome. Furthermore, the interpretation of the term 'marriage' should follow the autonomous interpretation of 'spouse' in Article 2(2)(a). Otherwise, a host Member State could potentially deny entry and residence to a registered partner as not in a relationship 'equivalent to marriage' solely because its national laws only regulate different-sex marriages.

Finally, because the CFREU must be interpreted in line with the ECHR, the case-law of the ECtHR should be taken into account.[53] The ECtHR has discussed registered partnerships in a number of judgments. This chapter addresses the relevance of ECtHR case-law to EU law later, when it delves into the EU's private international law regulations.

2.2.3. *The Autonomous Interpretation of Marriage and Genuine Residence*

A first reading of the *Coman* decision may give the misleading impression that it is limited to marriages contracted in another EU Member State,[54] which can only be explained because in the *Coman* case the marriage was entered into in Belgium, an EU country. As Wathelet points out, Directive 2004/38/EC does not contain such requirement.[55] That *Coman* is not limited to marriages contracted in another EU Member State is reinforced by the fact that, unlike Article 2(2)(a), Article 2(2)(b) of the Directive indeed requires the registered partnership to be contracted in a Member State. Furthermore, since the CJEU talks about a relationship 'created or strengthened' (i.e., not necessarily 'created') in another Member State,[56] it is logical to conclude that the Court does not exclude the possibility that the marriage has been celebrated outside the EU.[57]

Another unclarified question is what having 'genuine residence' in another Member State means. Unfortunately, the Court does not define 'genuine residence', and this lack of definition could potentially jeopardize the outcome of *Coman*. In principle, a residence of more than three months should suffice; and in any case, 'genuine residence' does not appear to correspond exactly to the notion of 'habitual residence' in private international law.

---

53 Articles 52(3) and 53 CFREU.

54 *Coman* judgment, above n. 1, paras 35–36, 39, 45, 52, 56.

55 Wathelet's Opinion, above n. 2, para. 49. See also *Metock* judgment, above n. 50, paras 81, 99.

56 *Coman* judgment, above n. 1, paras 51, 53.

57 A different perspective is held, e.g., by M. Ní Shúilleabháin who considers (and criticizes) that the CJEU in *Coman* requires the couple to be lawfully married in a Member State, M. Ní Shúilleabháin, 'Cross-Border (Non-) Recognition of Marriage and Registered Partnership: Free Movement and EU Private International Law' in J.M. Scherpe and E. Bargelli (eds), *The Interaction between Family Law, Succession Law and Private International Law. Adapting to Change*, Intersentia, Cambridge 2021, pp. 13–34, at pp. 26–27. In the author's understanding, the underlying assumption that the CJEU demands the marriage to be concluded in a Member State is wrong, as the alternative 'created or strengthened' expressly mentioned in the judgment indicates.

2.2.4. *Obstacles to Implementing Coman on the Ground*

The practice of some Member States also originates problems for the adequate implementation of *Coman*. In a study commissioned by the European Parliament, based on a questionnaire circulated among Member States, Tryfonidou and Wintemute describe several challenges encountered by same-sex spouses when exercising their freedom of movement.[58] Since Romania continued denying a residence permit to Mr Hamilton after *Coman*, the European Parliament sent a letter requesting the European Commission to take action.[59] The mentioned study also notes a practice of characterizing a same-sex spouse as a registered partner for purposes of Article 2(2)(a) in EU countries that lack legislation on gender-neutral marriage but that do provide for civil unions or have registration schemes.[60] In the author's understanding, this is contrary to the *Coman* judgment,[61] even if the consequences of such a characterization are the same: granting the residence. The judgment focuses on the word 'spouse' in Article 2(2)(a) and constructs an autonomous interpretation of the concept. Hence, *Coman* has already established a characterization under the Directive of same-sex marriage as 'marriage' that host Member States should respect. Borrowing private international law terminology into this freedom of movement case, one could speak of a characterization *ex lege fori*, in which the *lex fori* is EU (case) law.

3. EU PRIVATE INTERNATIONAL LAW IN FAMILY MATTERS

What influence may *Coman* have on cross-border family law in the EU? In the last 20 years, several regulations have been passed on cross-border family law, some of them based on enhanced cooperation in which only some Member States participate.[62] The purpose of EU private international law is to coordinate

58 A. Tryfonidou and R. Wintemute, above n. 26, pp. 42 et seq.

59 Letter of the European Parliament LGBTI Intergroup to the European Commission: *(Non-)Implementation of the Coman & Hamilton case 4 years after the CJEU decision* (7 June 2022) <https://lgbti-ep.eu/2022/06/07/meps-write-to-president-von-der-leyen-on-coman-hamiltons-4-year-non-implementation-anniversary> accessed 15.06.2022.

60 Following Tryfonidou and Wintemute's study, only Estonia and Croatia seem to regard same-sex spouses as spouses for the Directive's purposes, A. Tryfonidou and R. Wintemute, above n. 26, p. 44.

61 Tryfonidou and Wintemute say that, even if not expressly required by the judgment itself, such 'downgrading' is not acceptable in EU law in light of Article 21 CFREU, A. Tryfonidou and R. Wintemute, above n. 26, p. 45. In the author's understanding it is already contrary to the *ratio decidendi* of the *Coman* decision itself.

62 For a vision of the various regulations, see D. Martiny, above n. 49, pp. 263 et seq.

the diversity of substantive family law across EU countries. The picture of EU law in cross-border family matters is nevertheless fragmented, both in terms of what matters are regulated and the number of EU countries participating in each regulation. This chapter discusses the possible impact of *Coman* on EU private international law by focusing on the Recast Regulation[63] and the Property Regulations.[64]

3.1. BRIEF INTRODUCTION TO THE RECAST REGULATION AND THE PROPERTY REGULATIONS

All Member States with the exception of Denmark participate in the Recast Regulation.[65] It concerns two distinct areas: matrimonial matters and matters of parental responsibility. This chapter deals with the former. As this is a regulation on jurisdiction, recognition and enforcement, choice of law is excluded from its scope.

The Recast Regulation is part of the EU's overall development in the areas of freedom, security and justice, in which 'mutual trust in one another's justice systems should be further enhanced' and 'the free movement of persons and access to justice is ensured'.[66] The Recast Regulation nowhere provides an autonomous definition of marriage. The regulation simply remains silent. The forms contained in the annexes have been drafted in a gender-neutral fashion.

Unlike the Recast Regulation, both Property Regulations were passed under the enhanced cooperation mechanism.[67] They also respond to the objective of ensuring 'free movement of persons' and 'the compatibility of the rules applicable in the Member States concerning conflicts of laws and of jurisdiction'.[68] Both exclude from their scope the preliminary question of the existence, validity or recognition of a marriage or registered partnership.[69] A main difference between the Matrimonial Property Regulation and the Regulation on Property Consequences of Registered Partnerships is that the former does not define 'marriage' while the latter provides an autonomous definition of

63 Brussels II bis Recast, above n. 5.

64 Matrimonial Property Regulation and Property Regulation for Registered Partnerships, above n. 6 and n. 7.

65 Protocol No. 22 to the Treaty on the Functioning of the European Union, on the Position of Denmark [2016] OJ C 202/298.

66 Brussels II bis Recast, above n. 5, recital 3.

67 Currently: Belgium, Bulgaria, the Czech Republic, Cyprus, Germany, Greece, Spain, France, Croatia, Italy, Luxembourg, Malta, the Netherlands, Austria, Portugal, Slovenia, Finland and Sweden.

68 Both Property Regulations, above n. 6 and n. 7, recitals 1 and 2.

69 ibid., recitals 21 and Article 1(2).

'registered partnerships'.[70] Pursuant to both Property Regulations, Member State authorities can set aside foreign law or refuse to recognize a decision of a foreign court if it is 'manifestly incompatible' with their *ordre public*. However, authorities are prevented from relying on *ordre public* if it would be contrary to the CFREU, in particular Article 21 on non-discrimination.[71]

The wind of the Property Regulations concerning same-sex relationships blows hot and cold. On the one hand, they allow a Member State to decline jurisdiction, e.g., if it does not consider same-sex marriages to be valid or has not legislated on registered partnerships. They regulate *ordre public* exceptions and refer to national law on the definition of marriage. On the other hand, ordre public cannot be invoked if it is contrary to the CFREU. The original 2011 European Commission proposal was more far-reaching.[72]

3.2. CAN *COMAN* AFFECT THE INTERPRETATION OF THE REGULATIONS ON CROSS-BORDER FAMILY MATTERS?

3.2.1. Coman *is not a Private International Law Case, but ...*

It should be borne in mind that *Coman* is not a private international law case. It concerns free movement in the EU internal market. However, these limits are, as already discussed, blurred when it comes to family law terminology. With *Coman* we find ourselves at the intersection between EU migration law, private international law, family law and human rights. The Romanian authorities in *Coman* rested their position on Romania's Civil Code. The Sofia Administrative Court in *V.M.A.* likewise referred to the 'Bulgarian legal literature on family and inheritance law'[73] in relation to parentage.

Similarly, where typical private international law notions such as recognition, *ordre public* or *renvoi* are used in the *Coman* judgment, it is also in the context of EU free movement.[74] It has been suggested that the CJEU acts as a family law court in an 'incidental' manner.[75] The inclusion of family law notions in non-family law EU instruments is necessary to enable them to operate properly.

70 Matrimonial Property Regulation, above n. 6, recital 16; Property Regulation for Registered Partnerships, above n. 7, Article 3.

71 Matrimonial Property Regulation, above n. 6, recital 54; Property Regulation for Registered Partnerships, above n. 7, Recital 53.

72 A. Wysocka-Bar, above n. 17, pp. 191 et seq.

73 *V.M.A.* judgment, above n. 23, para. 28.

74 *Coman* judgment, above n. 1, paras 42, 44–46; Wathelet's Opinion, above n. 2, paras 33, 58, 99.

75 G. de Baere and K. Gutman, 'The impact of the European Union and the European Court of Justice on European family law' in J. M. Scherpe (ed.), *European Family Law Volume I. The Impact of Institutions and Organisations on European Family Law*, Elgar Publishing, Chetelham, 2016, p. 33.

The notion of 'civil status' deserves a few words. The CJEU reminds us that civil status is within the competence of national law.[76] However, based on the TFEU, *V.M.A.* underlines the 'freedom conferred on all Union citizens to move and reside within the territories of the Member States, by recognizing, for that purpose, the civil status of persons that has been established in another Member State in accordance with the law of that other Member State'.[77] *V.M.A.* refers to civil status in a clearer way than *Coman*. Even if these words aim to ensure freedom of movement, it would be going too far to conclude at this stage that such a statement could directly apply to EU cross-border family law regulations. The limits set forth in *Coman* regarding civil status and 'recognition' only for residence purposes are nevertheless problematic in terms of legal certainty. The consequences of limping marriages should not be underestimated. Let us imagine that Mr Coman and Mr Hamilton, while living in Romania, separated de facto without dissolving their marriage bond. Since Romania is not obliged to recognize their civil status as spouses (beyond Directive 2004/38/EC) and does not characterize their marriage as a registered partnership either, could one of them marry a woman in Romania without previously dissolving their Belgian marriage? In such scenario, we would witness a 'cross-border bigamous marriage' with undesired consequences for the parties, including for third parties. This certainly jeopardizes the purposes of the principle of freedom of movement in the EU.

3.2.2. *An Autonomous Concept versus Definition by National Law*

The most relevant breakthrough in *Coman* is the EU's autonomous interpretation of 'spouse' (and hence, of 'marriage') such that it embraces same-sex spouses.

The question is whether this autonomous interpretation can be extended to the previously mentioned EU private international law regulations.[78] A distinction is to be drawn between the Recast Regulation and the Matrimonial Property Regulation. The former does not define marriage, as explained in section 3.1., but it does not leave it to national laws, either. Even if *Coman* itself is limited to the 'sole purpose' of Directive 2004/38/EC, this does not give a reason not to 'adopt' the definition provided in *Coman* into the Recast Regulation. The following arguments support this position. First, it is settled EU

---

76 *Coman* judgment, above n. 1, para. 37; Wathelet's Opinion, above n. 2, para. 36.

77 *V.M.A.* judgment, above n. 23, para. 52.

78 P. Jiménez Blanco mentions that the autonomous interpretation in *Coman* extends to national administrative authorities dealing with residence permits, but not civil authorities, P. Jiménez Blanco, 'La movilidad transfronteriza de matrimonios entre personas del mismo sexo: la UE da un paso (1): Sentencia del Tribunal de Justicia de 5 de junio de 2018, asunto C-673/18: Coman' (2018) 61 *La Ley Unión Europea*, para. 9. In what follows it is argued that this may not necessarily always be the case.

case-law that in absence of an express reference to national law, an autonomous interpretation is needed.[79] If the Recast Regulation does not define the concept autonomously, what other autonomous interpretation should be followed but the one in *Coman*? This choice coheres with a systematic understanding of EU law. Second, mention of a continuity between the Recast Regulation and its predecessors[80] is not an obstacle for a dynamic interpretation of the Recast Regulation, similar to the one carried out regarding Directive 2004/38/EC. If this dynamic interpretation is possible in the same legal instrument, *a fortiori* it should be possible for two consecutive instruments. Third, both the Recast Regulation and Directive 2004/38/EC share the aim of enhancing EU free movement, and such an interpretation would increase the number of EU citizens benefitting from the Recast Regulation. Finally, the argument that some of the 'conservative' EU countries with constitutional bans against same-sex marriage would not understand why they should set aside their constitutions because of EU private international law[81] can hardly be supported. One should call to mind the principle of the supremacy of EU law: Member States, by their very membership, are bound to it.[82] Becoming part of the EU entails a political decision, with all that this means in terms of compliance with EU law.

Still, the consequences of interpreting 'marriage' in the Recast Regulation in line with *Coman* remain unclear. Let us imagine a same-sex couple applying for divorce in a Member State with a constitutional ban on same-sex marriages. What choice-of-law rule would the court apply, e.g., regarding matrimonial property? If the Member State is not part of the Property Regulations, it would apply its own private international law rules and likely resort to *ordre public*. The Matrimonial Property Regulation, as we have seen, does not apply to the existence or the validity of the underlying marriage and offers ways for a national court to decline jurisdiction or claim *ordre public*. This takes us to the role of ordre public and fundamental rights in the EU regulations.

3.2.3. Ordre Public *and the Charter of Fundamental Rights of the EU*

Ordre public is meant to be an exception in private international law.[83] Private international law presupposes a level of acceptance of foreign laws, decisions

---

79 Wathelet's Opinion, above n. 2, para. 34.

80 Brussels II bis Recast, above n. 5, recital 90. See on this matter M. Brosch and C. M. Mariottini, *EUFAMS II, Facilitating cross-border family life: Towards a common European understanding. Report on the International Exchange Seminar*, Max Planck Institute for Procedural Law, Luxembourg, 2019 <http://www2.ipr.uni-heidelberg.de/eufams/index-Dateien/microsites/download.php?art=projektbericht&id=17> accessed 15.06.2022, pp. 6–7.

81 M. Brosch and C. M. Mariottini, above n. 80, p. 11.

82 See also Wathelet's Opinion, above n. 2, para. 39.

83 D. Martiny, above n. 49, p. 278; M. Bogdan, *Private International Law as Component of the Law of the Forum* BRILL, Leiden, 2012, p. 222.

and institutions that differ from those of, or do not even exist in, the forum. The purpose of *ordre public* is to protect those fundamental principles and values of the forum which would otherwise be undermined by applying a specific foreign legal provision or by recognizing a foreign decision or institution. If a forum were to resort frequently to *ordre public*, an excessive application of *lex fori* would result, jeopardizing the very nature of private international law.[84] Thus, *ordre public* is a very last resort exception.

That the EU private international law regulations include clauses on *ordre public* evidences both diversity among Member States and a reluctance on their part to give up such exceptions.[85] It is clearly framed as an exception nonetheless. The expression used is 'manifestly incompatible with' the *ordre public* of the forum. The CJEU has also underlined the restrictive character of the concept.[86] Moreover, the existence and validity of a same-sex marriage under these EU regulations comes as a preliminary question, and following Philip, the role of *ordre public* in preliminary questions is expected to be narrower.[87]

The Property Regulations establish another limit to *ordre public*: it cannot be claimed if it contradicts the CFREU, in particular Article 21. Although included in the recitals rather than in the normative part of the text, the aim of restricting *ordre public* based on fundamental rights is clear. As we have seen, the CFREU is to be interpreted in line with the ECHR. Given the fact that the CFREU and the ECHR apply to all EU countries, when can a court of a Member State resort to an *ordre public* exception in conflict with the CFREU and the ECHR? Same-sex couples are protected by the right to family life even if the ECtHR has not, to date, interpreted Article 12 ECHR as mandating gender-neutral marriage laws. The above does not oblige EU Member States to define marriage broadly enough to comprise same-sex spouses when there is express reference to their national laws, but it does narrow down the sphere in which the already restrictive notion of *ordre public* may be invoked.

The strictly limited understanding of *ordre public* does not prevent courts from turning to other private international law techniques (e.g., characterization) to avoid the recognition or application of undesirable foreign law.[88] In the EU's Matrimonial Property Regulation, a marriage is characterized (as a preliminary question) pursuant to the law of the forum. One could easily conclude that such techniques in the end amount to the application, through the back door, of an '*ordre public* in disguise'.

84 M. Bogdan, above n. 83, p. 222; L. Vaigé, above n. 17, p. 53.

85 In this vein, see G. Zarra, *Imperativeness in Private International Law. A View from Europe*, Asser Press, The Hague, 2022, p. 109.

86 See, for all, *V.M.A.* judgment above n. 23, para. 55.

87 A. Philip, *Dansk international privat -og procesret*, Juristforbundets Forlag, Copenhagen, 1976, p. 68.

88 See, mainly focusing on the Swedish experience, M. Bogdan, above n. 83, p. 254.

Finally, could the autonomous characterization of marriage in *Coman* bring about an EU-level *ordre public* in relation to 'spouse' and 'marriage'? If it does, Romania's refusal to grant entry and residence would not only violate Directive 2004/38/EC but it would also contradict an EU *ordre public* developed in CJEU case-law. In accordance with the approach advocated in this chapter, the same can be said regarding other EU legal instruments when they make no reference to national laws.

3.2.4. Characterization of Registered Partnerships

The Regulation on Property Consequences of Registered Partnerships defines 'registered partnership' as the regime governing the common life of two people, with its registration being mandatory under the law that governs it.[89] This notion is gender-neutral and aims to distinguish registered partnerships from de facto relationships. Furthermore, this definition departs from Article 2(2)(b) of Directive 2004/38/EC, which calls for the registered partnership to be considered 'equivalent to marriage' (whatever that means) in the host Member State. The Regulation on Property Consequences of Registered Partnerships focuses on the formal requirement of registration rather than on the breadth of the legal effects of registration. Such a definition contemplates the diversity of nomenclatures and of the legal consequences of registration schemes across EU countries. This autonomous definition basically avoids the risk of a foreign registered partnership not being characterized as such even when an EU jurisdiction provides a registration scheme or civil union under its own system. A dynamic interpretation as well as the coherence and uniform application of EU law tends to prevent the expression 'equivalent to marriage' in Directive 2004/38/EC from making the definition of 'registered partnership' narrower than it is in the Regulation on Property Consequences of Registered Partnerships. The CJEU has yet to pronounce on this matter.

What is also important here is the limit on the operation of *ordre public* the CFREU entails. *Coman* does not pertain to registered partnerships, but ECtHR case-law can shed some light on the limits of fundamental rights to *ordre public*. First, a registration scheme cannot be limited to different-sex couples.[90] Second, in *Oliari and others v. Italy* and *Orlandi and others v. Italy*, the ECtHR found that the failure to provide a 'specific legal framework' to protect same-sex relationships was contrary to the ECHR.[91] Third, the ECtHR refers to

89 Property Regulation for Registered Partnerships, above n. 7, Article 3(1).

90 *Vallianatos and others v. Greece*, nos 29381/09 and 32684/09, §89–92, ECHR 2013-IV, paras 91, 92.

91 *Oliari and others v. Italy*, nos 18766/11 and 36030/11, §185 ECHR 2015, paras 167, 185; *Orlandi and others v. Italy*, nos 26431/12; 26742/12; 44057/12 and 60088/12, §210 ECHR 2017, paras 192, 199, 210.

registered partnerships or civil unions, and it can be inferred that mere cohabitation agreements would not suffice.[92] If these ECtHR's decisions can be extrapolated beyond the Italian context, they cast doubt on whether EU Member States are in compliance with the ECHR (and CFREU) if they lack legislation either on gender-neutral marriage or on any type of registration or civil union scheme for same-sex couples.

4. FINAL REMARKS: 'COMMUNICATING VESSELS'

Coman is a landmark decision concerning both the legal situation of same-sex couples and freedom of movement in the EU. It involves a step towards enhanced autonomy of EU law vis-à-vis national law, thus favouring a uniform application of Directive 2004/38/EC. This chapter has argued that the autonomous interpretation of 'spouse' in *Coman* can be extended beyond Directive 2004/38/EC to cover other EU legal instruments, such as the EU regulations on cross-border family matters when there is no express reference to national marriage laws.

Coman evidences the interrelationship of national and EU law and various other areas of law (public law and private law; migration law; private international law; and family law). There are 'communicating vessels' among these areas of law and spheres of competence as they permeate and influence each other. It is necessary to use typical family law notions such as 'spouse' or 'marriage' instrumentally in fields within EU's competence such as free movement. Without utilizing these family law concepts, the EU legal instruments under discussion would not be able to operate. Their provisions, as interpreted by the CJEU, potentially affect other areas of EU law such as the private international law regulations on cross-border family matters, which for their part will also likely influence national (family) law. In consequence, there emerges a circle of 'communicating vessels' among areas of law, spheres of competence and hierarchical levels. It functions both ways, and so accordingly national substantive family law may potentially affect EU law, and so on, initiating a 'circle of communicating vessels' the other way around.

The connection between, e.g., Directive 2004/38/EC and EU cross-border family law instruments should be seen as natural, both aiming to enhance freedom of movement of persons and families across the Union. Some authors and 'conservative' Member States have argued that the CJEU's autonomous interpretation of 'spouse' in Directive 2004/38/EC quite likely involves an

[92] See *Oliari* judgment, above n. 91, paras 168, 169, 172, 174.

intrusion into national competence for substantive family law.[93] However, this argument also goes the other way. In *Coman*, the Romanian authorities turned to article 277 of their Civil Code to deny residence to Mr Hamilton. Similarly, the Bulgarian Court in *V.M.A.* refers to the 'Bulgarian legal literature on family and inheritance law'.[94] Can it not be considered intrusive to rely on national family law to restrict the scope and application of an EU legal instrument in a matter within the EU's competence? And on the other side of the spectrum, more 'progressive' EU countries with gender-neutral marriage laws could argue that a restrictive approach to family law concepts in EU instruments to satisfy 'conservative' stances on same-sex relationships negatively affects the scope of their own national family law. An explanation of the 'circle of communicating vessels' cannot be uncoupled from the legal policy background across Europe. The balance of national laws evidences that the EU countries with neither gender-neutral marriage laws nor civil unions for same-sex couples are a minority nowadays. If the picture were different, the outcome in *Coman* would probably not have been the same.

Finally, should we not wonder whether too much pressure is being placed on EU institutions, which Eurosceptics often dismissively refer to simply as 'Brussels'? Wathelet mentions the differing positions the EU Commission and Parliament on one hand and the more conservative stance the Council took on the other, back in 2004 during the passage of Directive 2004/38/EC.[95] The Council, in the end, represents the national States and has often been a brake on widening EU competence and on more ambitious approaches of the Parliament or the Commission. Cases such as the ones this chapter discusses demonstrate that the more competence the EU holds, the better protected citizens moving across the EU will be. In an increasingly globalized Europe, freedom of movement of persons and families within the EU is likely to keep expanding. LGBT+ persons are Union citizens because they are nationals of a Member State, which includes nationals of one reluctant to legislate on same-sex couples.

---

93 Stehlík, above n. 40, p. 91. These arguments were raised by the Romanian, Polish, Hungarian and Latvian governments in the *Coman* case, see Wathelet's Opinion, above n. 2, para. 31.

94 *V.M.A.* judgment, above n. 23, para. 28.

95 Wathelet's Opinion, above n. 2, para. 51.

TRANS(FORMING) FATHERHOOD? EUROPEAN LEGAL APPROACHES TO 'SEAHORSE FATHERHOOD'

Alice MARGARIA*

1. STORIES OF SEAHORSE FATHERS

When the time felt right for Thomas and his (then) wife, Nancy, to have a baby, they decided to do something which was 'completely unprecedented':[1] Thomas – a trans[2] man who had kept his reproductive organs – would carry the pregnancy, and Nancy would breastfeed the baby. In Thomas' words, 'he would be the father, and Nancy would be the mother'.[3] After Thomas Beatie (and perhaps even before), other trans men have decided to start a family by carrying their own babies, and have shared their extraordinary birth and parenting experiences. The

* This work was supported by the University Research Priority Programme 'Human Reproduction Reloaded', University of Zurich.

1 T. BEATIE, *Labour of Love: The Story of One's Man Extraordinary Pregnancy*, Seal Press, Berkeley 2009, p. 5.

2 In this chapter, the term 'trans' is used to refer to people whose gender identity differs from the gender assigned at birth.

3 T. BEATIE, above n. 1, p. 8.

documentary *Seahorse*,[4] for instance, tells the story of how Freddy McConnell became a father and 'how, as a trans man, [he] chose pregnancy and birth in order to do that'.[5] Another trans man whose birthing experience has become known is that of Yuval Topper-Erez who, in 2011, gained widespread media attention as the first trans man to give birth in Israel. Moved by the desire to contribute to 'the normalisation of trans and non-binary people giving birth',[6] he decided to publicly share powerful pictures of his third (home) birth, which took place in England in 2019.

These are certainly stories of changing families, and – although to a significant lesser extent – of changing family laws. Over the last decade, an increasing number of court cases have arisen out of transmasculine[7] experiences of pregnancy and birth. In spite of being able to become fathers *in practice*,[8] from a legal perspective, the registration of their births and, therefore, the attribution of legal parenthood have been a source of controversy in most western jurisdictions. Legal actors have raised the question of what parental status trans birthing men should be assigned: Should they be considered the child's 'mother', 'father', or simply 'parent' for the purposes of birth registration?

Focusing on European national jurisdictions, this chapter will identify and critically analyse two main, existing approaches to addressing these questions. Section 2 will elaborate on the so far prevalent approach, which will be termed 'gender mis-alignment' in this chapter.[9] Grounded in the rule *mater semper certa est*, this approach regulates legal parenthood as separate from legal gender. It follows that, in those jurisdictions adopting 'gender mis-alignment', a seahorse

---

4 A trailer, reviews and links useful to watch it can be found here: <https://seahorsefilm.com> (Grain Media, 2019). The reason for choosing Seahorse as a title has to do with seahorses being the only species in which males get pregnant and give birth. Drawing from the title of this documentary, the terms 'seahorse father' and 'seahorse fatherhood' will be used throughout the text to refer to trans men who carry and give birth to their children, and to their parenting experiences more broadly.

5 F. McConnell, '"If all men got pregnant, it'd be taken so much more seriously" – behind the scenes of Seahorse', *YouTube* at <https://www.youtube.com/watch?v=bu6fQIZN3c0> (0:25).

6 Facebook page of Yuval Topper-Erez: <https://www.facebook.com/media/set/?set=a.10160905869264619&type=3>.

7 'Transmasculine' refers to people who were assigned the female gender at birth, but identify with the male gender.

8 This does not come without challenges. McConnell, for instance, experienced the process not as '[him] having a baby or pregnancy', but like 'a much more fundamental, total loss of [him]self' (0:13); S. Marcus Ware, 'Boldly Going Where Few Men Have Gone Before: One Trans Man's Experience' in R. Epstein (ed.), *Who's My Daddy? And Other Writings about Queer Parenting*, Sumach Press, Toronto 2009, pp. 65–72; T. Kirczenow MacDonald, M. Walks, M. Biener and A. Kibbe, 'Disrupting the Norms: Reproduction, Gender Identity, Gender Dysphoria, and Intersectionality' (2021) 22(1–2) *International Journal of Transgender Health* 18.

9 'Gender mis-alignment' as well as 'gender alignment' are inspired by S. McGuinness and A. Alghrani, 'Gender and Parenthood: The Case for Realignment' (2008) 16 *Medical Law Review* 261.

father is assigned the status of legal 'mother' for the purposes of birth registration even if he is legally male. In section 3, the attention will shift to the second approach, i.e., 'gender alignment', which provides for parental status in line with legal gender. Under this second approach, a seahorse father is registered as 'father' on the child's birth certificate. Through a legislative reform which entered into force in 2019,[10] Sweden was the first (certainly European) jurisdiction to embrace 'gender alignment'. Other Nordic countries have taken the same path over the last years. In addition to offering concrete illustrations, the analysis will also shed light on the (gendered) assumptions underlying each approach and reflect on the image(s) of 'the father' resulting from their application. By way of conclusion, section 4 will consider and share some reflections on the adoption of a potential third approach: that of 'degendering legal parenthood'.

2. GENDER MIS-ALIGNMENT

2.1. THE TENACIOUS HOLD OF THE RULE *MATER SEMPER CERTA EST*

In western jurisdictions, the attribution of legal motherhood has traditionally followed the Roman law principle *mater semper certa est*, according to which a mother is the person who gives birth. In other words, the biological processes of gestation and childbirth are the grounds for determining who is a child's legal mother. *Mater semper certa est* remains 'one of the most immutable facts' of (European) family laws,[11] even in times of changing family realities. This explains, for instance, why many intended parents struggle to obtain legal recognition of their family ties with their children born from transnational surrogacy and, even before, why surrogacy is prohibited in many European jurisdictions.[12] As one can imagine, the tenacious hold of the rule *mater semper certa est* may pose legal challenges to seahorse fathers too: in most European countries, indeed, registry personnel and judges invoke this rule to justify their refusal to register trans birthing men as 'fathers' and, in so doing, assign parental status as independent from and inconsistent with legal gender.

This approach to regulating seahorse fatherhood will be illustrated by delving into the abovementioned case of Freddy McConnell, which landed

[10] Lag om ändring i föräldrabalken [Act on Amendment of the Parental Code] 2018:1279.

[11] Z. Mahmoud and E.C. Romanis, 'On Gestation and Motherhood' (2022) *Medical Law Review* fwac030, <https://doi.org/10.1093/medlaw/fwac030>.

[12] On surrogacy, see K. Rokas (Chapter 5 in this volume).

before English courts in 2019–2020.[13] He was assigned female gender at birth and transitioned to live as a man at the age of 22. He always knew he wanted to have children and, in 2016, he suspended testosterone treatment in preparation for fertility treatment. In April 2017, he was granted a Gender Recognition certificate affirming his male gender. A few days later, Freddy underwent intrauterine insemination treatment using donor sperm at a licensed clinic, subsequently became pregnant and gave birth to his first child in January 2018. After his child was born, the Registry Office informed Freddy that he would have to be registered as the child's mother. Since he wished to be registered as 'father' or, alternatively, 'parent', Freddy sought judicial review of the Registrar's decision, albeit in vain. The High Court of Justice held that, as a matter of English law, being a mother 'is the status afforded to a person who undergoes the physical and biological process of carrying a pregnancy and giving birth', and therefore concluded that McConnell must be registered as 'mother' on his child's birth certificate. This ruling was upheld by the Court of Appeal,[14] and the UK Supreme Court denied permission to appeal because McConnell's application did 'not raise an arguable point of law'.[15]

2.2. THE NEED FOR CERTAINTY IN FAMILY LAW

The English courts' decision to register McConnell as 'mother' is based on two interrelated lines of reasoning.[16] The first resonates with a perceived need to ensure 'certainty in family law'.[17] Agreeing with the Government, English courts identified 'the need to have an administratively coherent and certain scheme for the registration of births' as one of the legitimate societal aims pursued by the requirement to register persons who give birth – McConnell in this case – as 'mother'.[18]

---

13 The following factual account is taken from the text of the High Court's decision in *Re TT and YY* [2019] EWHC 2384, 25 September 2019. For a more comprehensive and personal reconstruction of McConnell's experience, watch the documentary *Seahorse*. He gave birth to his second child in 2022.

14 *R (McConnell and YY) v. Registrar General* [2020] EWCA Civ 559, 29 April 2020.

15 9 November 2020.

16 The term 'English courts' is used in this chapter when discussing arguments advanced by both the High Court and the Court of Appeal. Whilst reaching the same conclusion on the same grounds, the High Court's decision shows a greater 'willingness to reconsider fundamental notions of family law' whilst the Court of Appeal adopts 'a fairly circumscribed and orthodox approach to statutory interpretation'. See P.D. Bremner, 'Birth registration: "coherent and certain" or "an occasion for exquisite embarrassment and confusion"?' (2020) 42(4) *Journal of Social Welfare and Family Law* 524, 525.

17 P. Dunne, 'Transgender Sterilisation Requirements in Europe' (2017) 25(4) *Medical Law Review* 554, 564.

18 *Re TT and YY*, above n. 13, para. 227; *R (McConnell and YY) v. Registrar General*, above n. 14, para. 58.

This line of reasoning is far from novel within the context of state approaches to regulating trans identities, more generally. The ability of procreation post-transition to 'destabilise Europe's family law systems' has long been a concern for judges and legislatures even before cases like the one of McConnell emerged, in discussions around gender recognition laws.[19] In particular, the need to preserve legal certainty and stability has represented a core rationale for imposing sterilization requirements for legal gender recognition. This was the main justification advanced, for instance, by the German Federal Government which supported the maintenance of the sterilization requirement originally included in the Transsexuals Act 1980, whose constitutionality was at stake in 2011. The Government grounded its position in 'the supposed incompatibility of trans reproduction with a family law system based on child-bearing women and sperm-producing men'.[20] The same rationale arguably underpins legislative provisions, such as Section 12 of the UK Gender Recognition Act,[21] which explicitly rule out any effect of legal gender recognition on existing family relationships. Even if the prospective applicability of similar provisions (i.e., their applicability to 'future' relationships concerning children born after transition) may eventually be cause of disagreement in court,[22] the purpose underlying their introduction is to control and limit – to the extent possible – the degree of legal uncertainty regarding parental status and obligations created by trans procreation.

2.3. THE CHILD'S RIGHT TO A MOTHER

The second, related, justification for confirming the Registry's decision put forward by English courts pertains to 'the need for the rights and interests of others to be respected', especially the child's right to know the identity of the person who carried them.[23] Referring to the European Court of Human Rights (ECtHR) case-law, the High Court acknowledges that Article 8 of the European Convention on Human Rights (ECHR) protects *inter alia* the right to establish the substance of one's identity which includes 'the right to know who gave birth to them' as a 'core element'.[24]

---

19 P. Dunne, above n. 17, p. 564.

20 ibid. Federal Constitutional Court of Germany, 1 BvR 3295/07 (11 January 2011).

21 Section 12 GRA: 'The fact that a person's gender has become the acquired gender under this Act does not affect the status of the person as the father or mother of a child'. Other examples are section 19, Gender Recognition Act 2015 (Ireland); section 3(2), Gender Identity, Gender Expression and Sex Characteristics Act 2015 (Malta).

22 *Re TT and YY*, above n. 13, para. 280; *R (McConnell and YY) v. Registrar General*, above n. 14, paras 29–33.

23 *Re TT and YY*, above n. 13, para. 227.

24 ibid., para. 256.

Like the need for certainty in family law, also this second line of argument ties in with commonly advanced justifications for sterilization requirements. If trans individuals who are legally recognized in their (preferred) gender can (nonetheless) procreate – so the argument goes – children will be confused about their genetic origins and deprived of important family relationships.[25] This concern transpires also from the reasoning of the High Court, according to which, if Freddy was registered as 'father' or 'parent', his child 'will not have, and will never have had, a mother as a matter of law, he will only have a father'.[26] This scenario would, so the High Court continues, be detrimental and contrary to the child's best interests.[27]

This argument appears flawed and problematic because of two reasons. First, as argued by Dunne, a child's ability to trace their genetic origins will not be hindered merely because they were born from a trans man.[28] Rather, it might even be argued that, in cases where children know that their birth parent is a trans man and – like in the case of McConnell – there is no other parent involved, it is obvious that a sperm donation was necessary.[29] In similar circumstances, as Dunne puts it, 'children are already on notice about third-party intervention' and therefore are better placed to search for information when allowed to do so by law.[30]

Second, it remains unclear why the protection of the child's right to know one's origins requires the use of the particular term 'mother'. As emphasized by Fenton-Glynn, McConnell did not object to the registration of his birthing role, but to 'the use of a highly gendered term to do so'.[31] As this author has argued elsewhere, English courts seem to endorse an *ad hoc* interpretation of the child's right to know.[32] By referring to the views taken by Parliament when designing the current birth registration scheme, the Court of Appeal holds that 'every child should have a mother and should be able to discover who their mother was, because that is in the child's best interests'.[33] The right to know one's origins is therefore 'reduced' to a more specific right to know one's mother, and the outcome sought by the applicants is considered to breach more profoundly a 'right to a mother' which every child supposedly has.[34] As observed by the Court of Appeal, the application of the *mater semper certa est* rule has important effects

---

25 P. Dunne, above n. 17, p. 564.
26 *Re TT and YY*, above n. 13, para. 258.
27 ibid.
28 P. Dunne, above n. 17, p. 566.
29 ibid.
30 ibid.
31 C. Fenton-Glynn, 'Deconstructing Parenthood: What Makes a "Mother"?' (2020) *Cambridge Law Journal* 34, 37.
32 A. Margaria, 'Trans Men Giving Birth and Reflections on Fatherhood: What to Expect?' (2020) 34 *International Journal of Law, Policy and the Family* 225, 233.
33 *R (McConnell and YY) v. Registrar General*, above n. 14, para. 86.
34 A. Margaria, above n. 32, p. 233.

in practice: it does indeed ensure that someone has parental responsibility for a newborn child from the very moment of birth.[35] At the same time, by mandating the registration of the person who gives birth as 'mother', the legal system reinforces the gendered notion that, at the moment of birth, the person who is ready and able to be responsible for the care of a newborn child is who we call 'mother'.[36]

In their reasoning, English courts paid attention also to some adverse consequences arising from the incongruence between the lived and legal realities of McConnell and his child. The Court of Appeal, in particular, acknowledged that requiring a trans person to declare in an official document that 'their gender is not their current gender but the gender assigned at birth' amounts to 'a significant interference with a person's sense of their own identity' as well as with the right to respect for family life of both McConnell and his child.[37] By registering McConnell as 'mother', 'the state describes their relationship … as being that of mother and son; whereas, as a matter of social life, their relationship is that of father and son'.[38] In spite of acknowledging so, domestic courts concluded that the public interest in maintaining an administratively coherent and certain birth registration system and the best interests of children 'very substantially outweighed' any difficulty experienced by McConnell and his child.[39] In light of the above, McConnell's designation as 'mother' was confirmed as correct under English law.[40]

2.4. RESTATING CONVENTIONAL FATHERHOOD

The position endorsed by English courts leads therefore to a mis-alignment between legal gender and parental status. The High Court is of the explicit view that being a 'mother' (or a 'father') is to be understood irrespective of any

35 *R (McConnell and YY) v. Registrar General*, above n. 14, para. 64.

36 A. Margaria, above n. 32, p. 235. On birth registration as a channel through which notions and arrangements of care are created and supported, see A. Margaria, 'When the Personal Becomes Political: Rethinking Legal Fatherhood' (2022) 20(3) *International Journal of Constitutional Law* <https://doi.org/10.1093/icon/moac076>.

37 *R (McConnell and YY) v. Registrar General*, above n. 14, para. 55. This remark refers more specifically to the long-form birth certificate which, different from the short-form, includes particulars about parentage. The Court of Appeal underlines that the resulting incongruence is cause of interference even if, in practice, McConnell would be required to produce the long-form birth certificate only on a limited number of occasions, thus implying that disclosure would be a rare occasion. See also *Re TT and YY*, above n. 13, para. 272.

38 ibid.

39 *Re TT and YY*, above n. 13, para. 272.

40 McConnell had also requested domestic courts to raise a declaration of incompatibility on the grounds that birth registration rules breach his and his child's rights under Article 8, alone and in conjunction with Article 14 ECHR. Domestic courts also rejected this part of his claims.

consideration of legal gender and, therefore in law, there can be 'male mothers' and 'female fathers'.[41] Whilst representing 'the first step in the legal undoing of binary understandings of reproduction and gender, sex and the body'[42] this ruling – at the same time – 'seems to privilege a certain [conventional] portrayal of 'family' life'.[43] As Davis notes, indeed, 'a child can only have a mother and father (correctly identified) by being born to a cisgendered, heterosexual woman, and her male partner'.[44] Therefore, if on the one hand, the High Court can be perceived as revising and disconnecting legal motherhood from the traditionally sex/gendered body, on the other hand, it radiates conventional messages on what it means to be a (legal) father today.[45]

English courts seem to suggest that, in order to be legally registered as 'father', a person needs to contribute to reproduction as a 'male' (or at least not as a 'female') and, therefore, be assigned male gender at birth.[46] By giving priority to birth-assigned gender when determining a seahorse father's parental status, the law reconstitutes the biological link between sperm and fatherhood. This, in turn, privileges a cis[47] reality, where 'one's sex, gender identity and identification as mother/father neatly align'.[48]

The image of 'the father' emerging from the decisions at hand is conventional also inasmuch as it maintains a mediated character. As historically mandated by the so-called 'marital presumption', the father of a child born during marriage is the mother's husband. Moulded upon this assumption, western legal regulation has conventionally constructed (legal) fatherhood as a derivative of the relationship between (cis and heterosexual) parents. It follows from this perspective that what makes someone a legal father is his marital or partner status, more than the (potential) existence of direct and autonomous emotional bonds between him and his child.[49] English courts do not destabilize these

41 *Re TT and YY*, above n. 13, para. 251.

42 R. Pearce, S. Hines, C. Pfeffer, D. W. Riggs, E. Ruspini and F. Ray White, 'Of trans fathers and male mothers – the importance of centering experience', *Trans Pregnancy Blog*, 5 December 2019 at <https://transpregnancy.leeds.ac.uk/2019/09/26/of-trans-fathers-and-male-mothers-the-importance-of-centering-experience>.

43 L. Davis, 'Re TT and YY: when a "Father" is a "Mother"', *BioNews* 1018, 7 October 2019 at <https://www.progress.org.uk/re-tt-and-yy-when-a-father-is-a-mother>; [conventional] is the author's addition. See also C. Fenton-Glynn, above n. 31, at p. 36.

44 L. Davis, above n. 43.

45 A. Margaria, above n. 32, p. 237.

46 ibid. 'Therefore' is used to convey the idea that people who contribute sperm to conception have been generally assigned male gender at birth by virtue of their genitalia.

47 The adjective 'cis' (or 'cisgender') is the opposite of 'trans' (or 'transgender') and is therefore used to describe the correspondence of gender identity and birth-assigned gender.

48 L. Karaian, 'Pregnant Men: Repronormativity, Critical Trans Theory and the Re(conceive) ing of Sex and Pregnancy in Law' (2013) 22(2) *Social and Legal Studies* 211, 213.

49 A. Margaria, *The Construction of Fatherhood: The Jurisprudence of the European Court of Human Rights*, Cambridge University Press, Cambridge 2019, p. 14.

notions. Rather, in the rulings at hand, fatherhood continues to be indirectly constructed as in need of a (female) connector to be legally relevant.[50] Given his direct tie with his child – so English courts seem to suggest – Freddy can 'only' be 'mother'.[51] Therefore, unlike provided by section 9(1) of the Gender Recognition Act,[52] a trans man who gives birth is 'not a real man' or a man 'for all legal purposes' even if his legal gender indicates him to be, and therefore he is not a man deserving and capable to become a father.[53]

Gender mis-alignment is, to date, the prevalent approach for regulating seahorse fatherhood in Europe. Cases similar to that of McConnell have arisen before domestic courts and led to identical outcomes in a variety of jurisdictions, including Germany, Norway and Poland.[54] Following the application of a German seahorse father (O.H.), the issue of birth registration following transmasculine pregnancy and birth has also reached the ECtHR.[55] O.H., who had changed his legal gender from 'female' to 'male' in 2011, was registered under his previous deadname as 'mother' of his child, G.H., who was born in 2013. Having exhausted national remedies,[56] O.H. and G.H. submitted that the former's registration as 'mother' clashes with their perception of their relationship, and requires them to frequently disclose O.H.'s trans identity.[57] In April 2023, the ECtHR ruled that gender mis-alignment does not violate the applicants' right to respect for private and family life (Article 8 ECHR).

---

50 A. Margaria, above n. 32, p. 237.

51 ibid.

52 Section 9(1): 'Where a full gender recognition certificate is issued to a person, the person's gender becomes *for all purposes* the acquired gender (so that, if the acquired gender is the male gender, the person's sex becomes that of a man and, if it is the female gender, the person's sex becomes that of a woman)'. Emphasis added by the author.

53 A. Margaria, above n. 32, p. 237. See also G. Baars, 'Queer Cases Unmake Gendered Law, or, Fucking Law's Gendering Function' (2019) 45(1) *Australian Feminist Law Journal* 15, 41.

54 On Norway, see A. Sørlie, 'Governing (Trans) Parenthood – The Tenacious Hold of Biological Connection and Heterosexuality' in D. Otto (ed.), *Queering International Law: Possibilities, Alliances, Complicities, Risks*, Routledge, Abingdon and New York 2018, pp. 171–90. On Poland, see M. Szeroczynska, 'Między Dobrem Dziecka a Litera Prawa – Ustalenie Treści Aktu Urodzenia Dziecka Urodzonego Przez Trans-Ojca. Rozważania Na Tle Postanowienia Sadu Apelacyjnego We Wrocławiu Z Dnia 7 Marca 2016 R., Sygn. I Axa 1830/15' ['Between the Welfare of the Child and the Letter of the Law – Establishing the Content of a Birth Certificate for a Child Born of a Trans Father. Considerations based on the Decision of the Court of Appeal in Wroclaw of 7 March 2016, Ref. I Aca 1830/15] (2017) *Ius Novum* pp. 182–93. On Germany, see, e.g., A. Margaria, above n. 32.

55 *O.H. and G.H. v. Germany*, Applications Nos. 53568/18 and 54741/18, 4 April 2023. Another case was decided on the same day: *A.H. and Others v. Germany*, Application No. 7246/20. In the latter, a trans woman who begot her child was registered as 'father' and under her male deadname. Also in this case, no violation was found on the same grounds as in *O.H. and G.H.*

56 AG Berlin, 13 December 2013–71 III 254/13; Kammergericht Berlin, 30 October 2014–1 W 48/14; BGH, 6 September 2017 – XXI ZB 660/14. The Federal Court of Justice reached the same decision in a more recent decision: 26 January 2022 – XII ZB 127/19.

57 *O.H. and G.H. v. Germany*, above n. 55, para 76.

3. GENDER ALIGNMENT

3.1. RECENT DEVELOPMENTS IN SWEDEN

In a small but growing number of European jurisdictions, the regulation of legal parenthood has been recently adjusted to meet the needs of contemporary families. Sweden was the first to introduce new provisions which explicitly contemplate trans parenthood and assign parental status in accordance with legal gender.[58] Trans men who give birth to their children in Sweden, therefore, are registered as 'fathers'.[59] This section will briefly discuss the genesis of the abovementioned reform, the resulting image of legal fatherhood as well as some persisting challenges.

In 2013, the sterilization requirement was removed from Swedish legislation.[60] Infertility ceased to be a precondition to access legal gender recognition, and trans people could to an increasing extent also have biological children after (legal) transition. In the reform process, the implications of trans procreation for family law were not given much thought;[61] the Government considered it reasonable for the Parental Code 1949 to continue to apply (in its original form).[62] Soon after, however, the need for a concomitant reform of parentage provisions became an inescapable reality. The Swedish Tax Agency, which is responsible for *inter alia* birth registration, refused to register trans parents in accordance with their legal gender. This gave rise to litigation before domestic administrative courts and, subsequently, to the Government's opening of a public investigation aimed to reform the Parental Code 1949.[63]

The first case was brought by a seahorse father who had been registered as 'mother' by the Swedish Tax Agency, and requested to have his parental status changed to 'father'.[64] The applicant pointed out that his registration as 'mother'

---

58 See above n. 10.

59 This is the reason why McConnell had initially planned to give birth to his second child in Sweden. See V. Parsons, 'British trans man must give birth abroad to be legally recognised as his baby's dad', *Pink News*, 21 October 2021 at <https://www.pinknews.co.uk/2021/10/21/trans-dad-freddy-mcconnell-sweden>.

60 See D. Alaattinoğlu, *The Path of the Law: The Establishment, Abolition and Remedy of Involuntary Sterilisation and Castration in Sweden, Norway and Finland*' (PhD diss., European University Institute, Florence, 2019), Chapter 4; D. Alaattinoğlu and R. Rubio-Marín, 'Redress for Involuntarily Sterilised Trans People in Sweden against Evolving Human Rights Standards: A Critical Appraisal' (2019) 19(4) *Human Rights Law Review* 705.

61 Swedish Government Bill Prop. 2012/13:107.

62 ibid., pp. 19–20.

63 See Justitiedepartementet [The Swedish Ministry of Justice], *Olika vägar till föräldraskap [Different Routes to Parenthood]*, SOU 2016:11, 21.

64 Stockholm Administrative District Court, Case No 24685-13, 14 April 2014. Annex 1 of the judgment is confidential and has been accessed and quoted with the permission of the applicant. Another case followed, concerning a trans man who had given birth to his child *before* changing legal gender, and confirmed the outcome and the principles established

breached his and his child's right to respect for private and family life, and amounted to discrimination on the grounds of gender identity. His legal status of 'mother' meant that his trans identity would no longer be confidential, and – so he continued – invalidated his right to legal gender recognition.[65] Contesting the applicant's complaint, the Swedish Tax Agency explained that his designation as 'mother' followed the *mater semper certa est* rule and was therefore grounded in the fact that he had given birth.[66] Similarly to what the High Court will then argue in the case of McConnell, the Tax Agency went on to clarify that parental status is disconnected from legal gender: under domestic law, neither the person giving birth nor a child's mother necessarily needs to be a woman.[67] The Tax Agency further noted that, in case the applicant was registered as 'father', the child would have had 'two fathers and no mother' – a situation which, the Tax Agency observed, had no legal basis in Swedish law.[68]

Given that, at the time, the Parental Code did not include any provision applicable to the situation at hand, the Administrative Court of First Instance chose to fill the legislative gap through a human rights-compliant application of domestic law.[69] Referring to the ECtHR case-law, the domestic court emphasized that Article 8 ECHR requires States to recognize amendments of legal gender with full legal force.[70] The public interest to maintain a coherent and clear birth registration system was also acknowledged but, differently from the views of English courts, considered not to be hindered by the registration of the applicant as 'father'.[71] The interests of the child were also part of the equation. According to the Swedish Administrative Court, Articles 3 and 4 of the UN Convention on the Rights of the Child confer on States an obligation not to place the child in a vulnerable position threatening their personal integrity.[72] In light of these considerations, the court held that the applicant had to be registered as 'father' on the child's birth certificate.[73] The position taken by Swedish administrative courts was subsequently 'codified' as part of a wider reform of the Parental

in the first. For a more comprehensive analysis of both cases and the Swedish approach, more broadly, see D. Alaattinoğlu and A. Margaria, 'Trans Parents and the Gendered Law: Critical Reflections on the Swedish Regulation' (2023) 21(2) *International Journal of Constitutional Law* 603–24.

65 Stockholm Administrative District Court, above n. 64, Annex 1.

66 ibid., Annex 1, at p. 2.

67 ibid., Annex 1, at pp. 2–3.

68 ibid., Annex 1, at p. 3. In this specific case, the applicant father was married to a man, who was registered as 'father' at birth.

69 ibid., Annex 1, at p. 4.

70 ibid.

71 ibid., Annex 1, at p. 5.

72 ibid., Annex 1, at pp. 3 and 5.

73 The ruling contained also an order for the Tax Agency to revise their registration practice. This led to an appeal before the Administrative Court of Second Instance, which reached the same conclusion as the First Instance Court on identical legal grounds. See Stockholm Administrative Court of Appeal, Case No. 3201-14, 9 July 2015.

Code which was passed by the Swedish Parliament in 2018. The current rule concerning the attribution of parental status provides that a trans man who gives birth is registered as 'father' of his child.

3.2. DEPARTING FROM CONVENTIONAL FATHERHOOD? PERSISTING CHALLENGES

The image of the father which emerges from this ruling and following legislative reform significantly departs from a conventional understanding of fatherhood. Being recognized as a legal father does not require a 'typically male' biological connection, nor being cis. It also follows that the father-child tie assumes legal relevance on its own, without the need for a mother to act as a legal connector. Constructing fatherhood as a direct tie, in turn, contributes to foregrounding care as relevant to make someone a legal father. This represents a further departure from conventional (legal) fatherhood, which tends to reduce a father's role in the child's upbringing to mere economic provision, in line with a traditional gender division of labour. Ruling in favour of seahorse fathers conveys the important message that 'men, and even more controversially trans men, are able to care and that trans men are not mothers, if they do (care)'.[74] From this perspective, therefore, the Swedish approach can be perceived not only as trans-friendly, but – more deeply – as having the power to disestablish conventional and dualistic beliefs about opposite sexes, gender and parenting.

That being said, reasons to be critical persist. The Swedish approach is 'inclusive, yet particularising'.[75] The reformed Parental Code does indeed provide that a man who gives birth is registered as his child's legal father, but his legal position is otherwise considered as that of a mother.[76] As discussed during the *travaux préaratoires*, mothers and fathers enjoy different legal positions under Swedish law – for instance, as regards the child's nationality, insurance and guardianship.[77] Hence, treating trans fathers as 'mothers' for purposes other than parental status is meant to ensure that they retain some of the (more comprehensive) rights and benefits which are available to legal mothers, with the purpose of avoiding discrimination on the grounds of gender identity. In spite of the underlying laudable intentions, this regulation in fact constructs trans parenthood as a separate, hybrid legal category.[78] Differently from cis parents, who enjoy a unitary legal status, trans parents' legal existence is fragmented and determined by both their (inconsistent) birth-assigned and legal genders.

---

74 A. Margaria, above n. 32, p. 245.
75 D. Alaattinoğlu and A. Margaria, above n. 64.
76 Parental Code 1949:381, Chapter 1 §11.
77 Justitiedepartementet [The Swedish Ministry of Justice], above n. 63, 605.
78 D. Alaattinoğlu and A. Margaria, above n. 64.

Another problematic aspect of the Swedish approach concerns the non-automatic application of the presumption of paternity/maternity. In cases where one parent has changed their legal gender, the status of 'mother'/'father' of the person not giving birth is not presumed, regardless of whether the couple is married or not. Rather, the wife/husband of the seahorse father has to obtain a special administrative acknowledgement or court order in order to acquire their parental status.[79] Whilst recognizing parental status according to legal gender, therefore, the reformed Swedish provisions end up according differential treatment to trans and cis parents.[80] Trans parents are left in a position where they are forced to disclose sensitive information to Government officials and third parties, thus exposing them to the risk of discrimination.[81]

The seemingly contradictory effects of the Swedish approach testify to the challenge(s) of regulating trans parenthood in gendered, cis- and heteronormative legal systems, more broadly. Gender alignment – as practised in Sweden, at least – does find trans parents *some* place within the existing regulation of parenthood. Yet, it does so without questioning the regulation's underlying rationales – essentially, the preservation of binary, conventional, gender categories – with the overall outcome of perpetuating patterns of discrimination. In other words, the Swedish legislator has expanded the boundaries of legal parenthood to include trans parents, but it has done so using an 'assimilationist approach':[82] the 'sexual family'[83] was taken as the starting point for carving out space for emerging family types and practices.

When it was introduced, the reform of the Parental Code made Sweden a European *première*, and gender alignment a 'globally original' approach for regulating seahorse fatherhood.[84] Whilst remaining exceptional, this approach has been adopted by other Nordic countries in recent times. Iceland, for example, introduced a legislative reform in 2021 which is similar to the Swedish

79 Parental Code 1949:381, Chapter 1 §§10, 12–14. This legislative amendment meant that the parental position for trans people was legally weakened, as before the reform of the Parental Code, the presumption for cis couples applied by analogy to trans parents.

80 D. Alaattinoğlu and A. Margaria, above n. 64.

81 This point of criticism has been raised also by the Equality Ombudsperson of Sweden. See Swedish Government Bill 2017/18:155, 59. In 2020, the Swedish Government appointed a committee responsible for exploring ways to reform and make the law on parenthood more inclusive. This committee's findings are included in the report *Alla tiders föräldraskap – ett stärkt skydd för barns familjeliv [Parentage of All Times – Strengthened Protection for Children's Family Life]*, released on 30 June 2022 and available here: <https://www.regeringen.se/rattsliga-dokument/statens-offentliga-utredningar/2022/06/sou202238>.

82 C. Fenton-Glynn, above n. 31, p. 36. She uses this term in relation to the UK Human Fertilisation and Embryology Act 2008.

83 M. Albertson Fineman, *The Neutered Mother, the Sexual Family and Other Twentieth Century Strategies*, Routledge, 1995, Chapter 6.

84 D. Alaattinoğlu and A. Margaria, above n. 64.

one.[85] As of April 2022, also in Denmark, legal parenthood is assigned in line with gender identity.[86]

4. A THIRD APPROACH: DEGENDERING LEGAL PARENTHOOD?

In recent debates concerning the parental status of trans parents, several scholars have advocated for replacing the gendered legal categories of 'mother' and 'father' with the gender-neutral category of 'parent'.[87] Degendering legal parenthood would certainly bring several advantages. To mention a few, in the specific context of trans parenthood, it would solve the issue of whether parental status should be assigned according to either legal gender or birth-assigned gender, once and for all. Providing for a standardized status of 'parent' would also meet the needs of non-binary parents. At a broader level, degendering legal parenthood would contribute to reducing the legal and cultural powers of heteronormativity.[88]

That being said, there are also reasons for being sceptical of the resolutive potential of degendering legal parenthood. Some crucial questions to be asked are: is birth registration 'only' a matter of filiation law or is it connected to broader questions around care and gender equality? Does degendering legal parenthood

[85] Lög 49/2021 um breytingu á barnalögum, (kynrænt sjálfræði) [Act 49/2021 Amending the Children's Act (gender autonomy)].

[86] Lov nr 227 af 15.02.2022 om ændring af børneloven, navneloven og forskellige andre love [Act on Amendment of the Children's Act, the Name Act and Several Other Acts].

[87] See, e.g., J.M. Scherpe and P. Dunne, 'The Legal Status of Transsexual and Transgender Persons – Comparative Analysis and Recommendations' in J.M. Scherpe (ed.), *The Legal Status of Transsexual and Transgender Persons*, Intersentia, Cambridge 2015, pp. 615–663, at p. 659; M. van den Brink and J. Tigchelaar, 'The Equality of the (Non)transparent: Women Who Father Children' in M. van den Brink, S. Burri and J. Goldschmidt (eds), *Equality and Human Rights: Nothing But Trouble? Liber Amicorum Titia Loenen*, Netherlands Institute of Human Rights, Utrecht 2015, pp. 247–260, at p. 259; S. McGuinness and A. Alghrani, above n. 9, p. 282. This possibility was also discussed by English courts in the case of McConnell. The Court of Appeal, in particular, held that replacing 'mother' with 'parent' (or 'gestational parent') 'would amount to judicial legislation' (*R. (McConnell and YY) v. Registrar General*, above n. 14, para. 35). One renowned example of a jurisdiction adopting gender-neutral language in legislation on parenthood is Ontario. See R. Leckey. 'One Parent, Three Parents: Judges and Ontario's All Families Are Equal Act, 2016' (2019) 33(3) *International Journal of Law, Policy and the Family* 298–315.

[88] A. Margaria, above n. 32, p. 245. Degendering legal parenthood is connected to broader efforts towards abolishing legal gender as a whole. On the benefits and challenges of 'decertification', see D. Cooper, R. Emerton, E. Grabham, H.J.H. Newman, E. Peel, F. Renz and J. Smith, *Abolishing Sex Legal Status: The Challenge and Consequences of Gender Related Law Reform* (2022) Future of Legal Gender Project. Final Report. King's College London, UK, at <https://www.kcl.ac.uk/law/research/future-of-legal-gender-abolishing-legal-sex-status-full-report.pdf>.

amount to a merely semantic move? Or can it also, more substantially impact the way care is conceptualized and organized in practice? Asking these questions opens the way for fundamental reflections on the actual shifts that replacing the terms 'mother' and 'father' with 'parent' would bring about, and on whether time is ripe for such an approach.

There is indeed no doubt that 'mother' and 'father' remain 'inextricably gendered in social use',[89] and it is quite unlikely that requiring the registration of mothers and fathers as 'parents' on their children's birth certificates would, on its own, have any immediate effect beyond changing legal categories. If the ultimate purpose is to disestablish dualistic beliefs about opposite sexes, degendering parenthood reforms should be accompanied by efforts towards degendering care. In other words, a *substantive* degendering of legal parenthood requires detaching care from traditional gender structures and, therefore, making care a responsibility and ability of all genders.[90] As mentioned in section 3, cases brought by seahorse fathers serve the opportunity to degender care on a proverbial silver plate. By confronting legal frameworks with realities which depart from conventional legal fatherhood, the legal claims of seahorse fathers bring the (new) element of care to the table, potentially raising it to the level of father-child legal connector.

This shows that what may appear as a case on (the specific issue of) birth registration, is actually connected to (broader) structural inequalities. Legal approaches to regulate seahorse fatherhood tell us not only about the struggles of family laws to evolve with social change, but also about a broader legal readiness (or lack thereof) to challenge long-held assumptions around gender and care underlying filiation rules and the legal system as a whole. The transformative potential of cases involving seahorse fathers, therefore, extends well beyond the domain of family law, and involves how notions of care are legally (re)shaped towards more equal societies.

---

89 C. Fenton-Glynn, above n. 31, p. 37.

90 D. Alaattinoğlu and A. Margaria, above n. 64.

PART IV

PROTECTION OF VULNERABLE FAMILY MEMBERS

CROSS-BORDER CHILD PROTECTION CASES BETWEEN FINLAND AND CENTRAL-EASTERN EUROPEAN STATES INCLUDING RUSSIA

Sanna Mustasaari

1. INTRODUCTION

The interrelationship of human rights and private international law continues to challenge practitioners and researchers.[1] In the field of transnational or cross-border child protection, the human rights of children depend on the functioning of the legal framework providing for the collaboration between local authorities of different countries. In the decades following the famous *Boll* case in the International Court of Justice in 1958,[2] the complexities of transnational child protection and the importance of the field from a human rights perspective have gained only limited attention in literature.[3] As Ruth Lamont, a leading scholar in the field, points out, European family law originated from the need to facilitate free movement, and even though recent years have seen attention being paid to the rights of the child within the EU, children as victims of abuse or neglect within the family sphere are still not a clear focus of concern in European family law.[4] This chapter addresses this somewhat understudied topic from the perspective of cross-border child protection cases between Finland and Central-Eastern European States, including Russia.[5]

The legal framework created to harmonize private international rules that govern cross-border child protection rests mainly on three instruments.[6] Within

---

1 J. Fawcett, M. Ní Shúilleabhain and S. Shah, *Human rights and private international law*, Oxford University Press, Oxford 2016, pp. 1–4.

2 *Netherlands v. Sweden* [1958] ICJ 8. See K. Lipstein, 'The Hague Conventions on Private International Law, Public Law and Public Policy' [1959] 8 *International and Comparative Law Quarterly* 506; M. Jänterä-Jareborg and K. Boele-Woelki, 'Protecting Children Against Detrimental Family Environments Under the 1996 Hague Convention and Brussells IIbis Regulation' in K. Boele-Woelki, T. Einhorn, D. Girsberger and S. Symeonides (eds), *Convergence and Divergence in Private International Law – liber amicorum Kurt Siehr*, Schulthess, Zürich 2010, pp. 125–56.

3 R. Lamont, 'The Development of Child Protection Across International Borders for Children at Risk of Harm' in G. Douglas, M. Murch and V. Stephens (eds), *International and national perspectives on child and family law: Essays in Honour of Nigel Lowe*, Intersentia, Cambridge 2018, pp. 233–45; see also S. Mustasaari, S. Adamo, A. Bredal, J. Hiitola, J. Köhler-Olson and N. Stybnarova (eds) 'Transnational Childhoods, Transnational Rights?' [2022] 4 *Child Family Law Quarterly* 34 (Special Issue).

4 R. Lamont, 'Risk, Borders and Children's Rights: Child Protection and EU Law' in M.J. Öberg and A. Tryfonidou (eds), *The Family in EU Law*, Cambridge University Press, forthcoming 2023.

5 Contemporary scholarship prefers the term 'Central-Eastern Europe' over, for example, Eastern Europe, as opposing east and west comes with unintended connotations to the Cold War era. Central-Eastern European countries (CEE countries) are EU member states which were socialist states and part of the former Eastern bloc. They include Bulgaria, Czech Republic, Estonia, Hungary, Lithuania, Latvia, Poland, Romania, Slovenia, and Slovakia. However, in this chapter, the cases between Finland and Estonia are excluded as Estonia stands out in terms of the intensity of collaboration between local authorities and CAs, as well as in relation to its 'Europeanization', see L. Vaige, *Cross-Border Recognition of Formalized Same-Sex Relationships*, Intersentia, Cambridge 2022.

6 R. Espinosa Calabuig and L. Carballo Piñeiro, 'Child Protection in European Family Law' in T. Pfeiffer, Q.C. Lobach and T. Rapp (eds), *Facilitating Cross-Border Family*

the EU, child protection is primarily ensured by Brussels II ter Regulation which has replaced the Brussels II bis Regulation as of 1 August 2022.[7] In addition to the Regulation, all EU Member States have ratified the 1980 Hague Child Abduction Convention, and the 1996 Hague Child Protection Convention.[8] Russia acceded to the 1980 Convention in 2011 and the 1996 Convention in 2013. All of these instruments base the jurisdiction to issue protective measures on the habitual residence of the child.[9] They also establish a system of Central Authorities, which operate on the national level and are responsible for sharing good practice and information on national laws and practices and for cooperating in cross-border cases.[10]

Taking a child into public care and placing the child out of home in a foster family or residential institution interferes with family life, and when such a measure concerns a child of foreign nationality, or a child with other firm links to a foreign State, questions arise as to which State's authorities should issue protective measures as well as which measures are in the best interests of the child.[11] In order to analyze the dynamics and functioning of cross-border child protection, shed light on the historical background and differences between Eastern and Western approaches to child protection and contextualize the contemporary politicization of cross-border child cases,[12] this chapter draws

---

Life – Towards a Common European Understanding: EU Fams II and Beyond, Heidelberg University Publishing, Heidelberg 2021, pp. 49–90.

7 Council Regulation (EU) 2019/1111 of 25 June 2019 on jurisdiction, the recognition and enforcement of decisions in matrimonial matters and the matters of parental responsibility, and on international child abduction. Regulation 2019/1111 replaces Council Regulation (EC) No 2201/2003 of 27 November 2003 concerning jurisdiction and the recognition and enforcement of judgments in matrimonial matters and the matters of parental responsibility, commonly known as Brussels II a (or Brussels II bis).

8 Convention of 19 October 1996 on Jurisdiction, Applicable Law, Recognition, Enforcement and Co-operation in Respect of Parental Responsibility and Measures for the Protection of Children; Convention of 25 October 1980 on the Civil Aspects of International Child Abduction.

9 E.g., Article 7 of Brussels II ter, Article 5 of the Hague 1996 Child Protection Convention, Article 4 of the Hague 1980 Child Abduction Convention.

10 M. Župan, C. Hoehn and U. Kluth, 'Central Authority Cooperation under the Brussels II TER Regulation' (2020/2021) 22 *Yearbook of Private International Law* 183; R. Lamont, 'Central Authorities and the European Judicial Network: Mainstreaming Children's Rights into Cross-border Cooperation in EU Family Law' in H. Stalford and I. Iusmen (eds), *The EU as a Children's Rights Actor: Law, Policy and Structural Dimensions*, Barbara Budrich Publishers, 2016, pp. 77–100; Practical Handbook on the Operation of the 1996 Hague Child Protection Convention, The Hague Conference on Private International Law Permanent Bureau.

11 R. Lamont, 'Care Proceedings with a European Dimension under Brussels IIa: Jurisdiction, Mutual Trust and the Best Interests of the Child' (2016) 28 *Child and Family Law Quarterly* 67.

12 K. Haugevik and C. Basberg Neumann, 'Reputation crisis management and the state: Theorising containment as diplomatic mode' (2021) 27 *European Journal of International Relations* 708.

on 29 child protection cases with links to Russia or Central-Eastern European States that were handled by the Finnish Central Authority and examines six of them more closely.

Social services, including child protection, are organized locally, and family law is generally perceived as national in character and closely related to the religious, cultural and legal history of the country.[13] On the one hand, the challenges in cooperation can at least partly be explained with reference to different cultural conceptions of the family in Central-Eastern and Western European States, as well as different historical and cultural ideas about the role of state welfare institutions in providing care for vulnerable family members, and migration patterns from Russia and Central-Eastern European countries to Western Europe. On the other hand, however, the media coverage and the fact that the cases were operationalized for the purpose of enhancing certain political goals should not be overlooked. Images and media representations of family and the rights of the child may be mobilized for diverse purposes, including an ideological and informational war. The broader questions that this tension brings to fore relate to the capacity of private international law to function as a form of global governance as well as the classical but urgently topical issue of the principle of mutual trust as basis of cross-border collaboration in contemporary Europe.

The purpose of this chapter is not to provide an evaluation of the compliance of the States with the Hague Conventions or Brussels II bis.[14] Instead, the three themes emerging from the cases are addressed: politicization of international child cases; issues relating to return of children wrongfully removed from the State of habitual residence or retained from returning there; and placements of children across borders. The chapter will proceed as follows. Section 2 describes the research material and introduces the cases. Section 3 addresses the differences of the legal concepts and interpretations between Russia and Central-Eastern and Western European States as well as the legacy of child protection in former socialist States. Section 4 explores, from the perspective of mutual trust, the sensitive issue of politicization of the concept of family and the rights of the child by looking at how the cases have been hijacked as part of information war and to enhance the goals of certain populist politicians and movements. Section 5 will conclude with a discussion on the challenges and possible venues for dialogue to overcome divergencies and facilitate collaboration in the politically intense times in Europe.

---

13 M. Antokolskaia, 'Harmonisation of substantive family law in Europe: Myths and reality' (2010) 22 *Child and Family Law Quarterly* 397, 399.

14 M. Norros, *Judicial Cooperation in Civil Matters with Russia and Methods of Evaluation*, Kikimora Publications, Helsinki 2009.

2. RESEARCH BACKGROUND AND DATA

2.1. RESEARCH BACKGROUND

This chapter draws on data collected in the research project '*Children Abroad: A Relational Analysis of Finnish Child Protection and Welfare in Transnational Contexts [CARELA]*', especially the 193 requests related to child protection from the years 2012–2020 and 53 requests related to child abduction from the years 2016–2018 that were handled by the Finnish Ministry of Justice as the Finnish Central Authority (CA) under the Hague Conventions of 1980 and 1996 as well as the Brussels II bis Regulation. In addition, staff handling international child protection cases and other key personnel in the CA and the Ministry of Foreign affairs were interviewed.

While the volume of cases is increasing, the numbers in the Finnish CA are low when compared internationally.[15] The child protection cases concerned 188 families and 282 children, representing all age groups and both sexes without any significant difference (see Figure 1).

Figure 1. Finnish Central Authority: Child Protection Cases 2012–2020

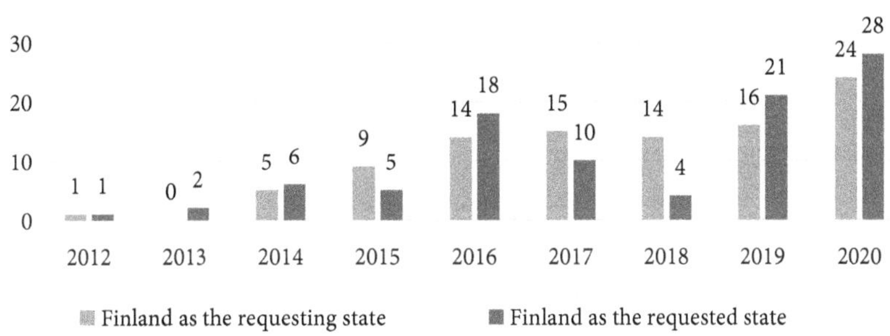

Source: Produced by the author.

The data does not include all cross-border child protection cases handled by Finnish authorities during the period examined period, because local child protection authorities in municipalities and cities may have established direct contact and communicated with the local authorities in other countries without involving CAs. This perhaps explains, for example, the small number of requests

15 For example, Wright analysed 100 English care cases with an international dimension between 2015 and 2018, see M. Wright, 'Care Proceedings and International Kinship Care' [2022] 4 *Child and Family Law Quarterly* 34; and Kruger's study included 443 child abduction cases open at the Belgian CA in 2007 and 2008, see T. Kruger, *International Child Abduction: The Inadequacies of the Law*, Hart Publishing, Oxford 2011.

from the neighbouring country Sweden.[16] In this respect, the situation has changed as of 1 August 2022. Brussels II ter introduces a centralized way of communication, as at least the first requests have to be made via the Central Authorities rather than directly from a local authority in one country to a local authority in another.[17]

Every request coming into the CA is registered in the electronic case management system and given a diary number and a handler. All actions and documents related to the case are recorded in the system and follow the case throughout the process, until the case is closed and archived. Until the end of 2020, all documents were printed so that the physical document bundle contained all the material submitted to the CA relating to a case. The material submitted to the CA varies a great deal depending on the case. In some cases, the case file may contain a lot of material, such as child welfare reports and court rulings with translations. In other cases, the file might only consist of a short e-mail inquiry, for example, about whether relatives of a child residing in another country can be found in the Finnish population information system.

In general the problems families face in cross-border contexts seem similar to those usually faced in child protection work: substance use, mental health problems and in many cases indications of intimate partner violence, although some specific case types do emerge from the data.[18] Particular geographical and migratory contexts are distinguishable, such as the mobility of ethnic majority Finns to the Spanish region of Costa del Sol; work-related mobility between Estonia and Finland; and mobility of families between Finland, Russia and Central-Eastern European States.

The detail in which the situation of a child and a family is described in the case file varies from case to case. This disparity of the data means that no far-reaching conclusions can be made about the children, the families or how the authorities work. For example, estimations on the numbers of cases of violence against the child or parental substance use that endangers the child's development cannot be made drawing on this material alone. Similarly, this data does not provide for a sound analysis on, for example, discourses in which authorities define and evaluate parenthood in cross-border contexts or make sense of their own obligations. The practices of child welfare and protection actors have been critically examined in the literature. Studies demonstrate, for example, how norms regarding 'good enough' parenting are gendered and how

16 Finnish authorities requested assistance from their Swedish colleagues via the CA in 11 cases and in one case a request came from Sweden, while in 47 cases the request came from the Estonian CA or vice versa.

17 Article 78 of Brussels II ter; M. Župan, C. Hoehn and U. Kluth, above n. 10.

18 S. Mustasaari, 'Children abroad: A relational analysis of cross-border child protection cases in the Finnish Central Authority' [2022] 4 *Child and Family Law Quarterly* 34.

culture may come to play in risk assessments.[19] Although this discussion is of utmost importance, it is of limited relevance here as the care orders made by the Finnish authorities were not scrutinized for this study. Instead, the data offers a bird's-eye view of the activities of authorities in the field of cross-border child protection as well as particular challenges pertaining to this field. The study thus contributes to the emerging research field pertaining to transnational child welfare and protection and especially to the socio-legal research on the Regulation and the two Hague Conventions.

In total, 29 cases in the data involved Russia and Central-Eastern European States.[20] Estonia is excluded from these 29 cases, as it stands out in terms of the intensity of collaboration between local authorities and CAs as well as in relation to its 'Europeanization'.[21] The cases are categorized on the basis of the interaction between CAs and not, for example, on the basis of the nationality of the child or the parents. Consequently, only those cases in which the corresponding CA is from Russia or a Central-Eastern European State are included. A much larger number of the children and families in the study are of Eastern European background. The number of families with Russian background is obviously high as the Russian speaking population is the largest minority group in Finland.[22] Of these 29 cases, six are introduced in this chapter. The cases discussed in the chapter are anonymized so that individuals may not be identified.[23] Details (such as the ages or gender of the children or number of siblings) that might lead to a risk of individuals being recognized have been modified to secure anonymization, and in some cases the State is left unspecified for the same reason.

---

19 J. Hiitola, *Hallittu vanhemmuus: Sukupuoli, luokka ja etnisyys huostaanottoasiakirjoissa* University of Tampere 2015, available at <https://trepo.tuni.fi/handle/10024/96664> accessed 20.08.2022; K. Sandberg and S. Hofman, 'Care Placements of Children Outside their Parental Home – Concerns of Culture' in M. Jänterä-Jareborg (ed.), *The Child's Interests in Conflict: The Intersections between Society, Family, Faith and Culture*, Intersentia, Cambridge 2016, pp. 73–84; R. Haga, 'Somali parents in Sweden: Navigating parenting and wellbeing' in M. Tiilikainen, M. Al-Sharmani and S. Mustasaari (eds), *Wellbeing of Transnational Muslim Families: Marriage, Law and Gender*, Routledge, Taylor & Francis, London 2019, pp. 112–28.

20 Lithuania 7, Romania 6, Russia 5, Poland 4, Latvia 3, Czech Republic 1, Slovakia 1, Hungary 1, Ukraine 1.

21 L. Vaige, above n. 5.

22 87552 individuals (31.12.2021) i.e., 1.6 per cent of Finnish residents speak Russian as their mother tongue, see <https://www.tilastokeskus.fi/tup/suoluk/suoluk_vaesto.html#vaesto-kielen-mukaan> accessed 15.07.2022. In other Nordic countries, Russian minorities are much smaller, amounting to approximately 31000 individuals in Sweden, and 2300 in Norway, see <https://www.ssb.no/en/statbank/table/05183/tableViewLayout1> accessed 15.07.2022.

23 In the analysis, other research materials containing personal data, such as court cases or media material were not combined with the material collected from the CA files.

2.2. INTRODUCING THE CASES

2.2.1. *Politicization of International Child Disputes*

Dealing with cross-border cases requires skill and courtesy in communication, and the style of communication could be described as diplomatic in almost all cases analysed for this study. However, of all the cases, the only ones that became politicized and expanded to the level of diplomatic relations, were related to Russia and Central-Eastern European States. In some cases, the parent or parents actively sought media attention as part of the custody battle.[24]

2.2.1.1. Case 1

The case concerned a family in which one of the parents was Finnish and the other parent from a Central-Eastern European State.[25] The children were habitually resident in Finland and had lived their whole life in Finland. A deep conflict between the divorced parents resulted in a complicated custody battle, and later, to the placing of the children into institutional care. The embassy of the Central-Eastern European State got involved and sent a *note verbale* to the Finnish ministry of Foreign Affairs asking for the children to be sent to the Central-Eastern European State to live with their grandparents. There was pressure from the politicians and media of that State that the ambassador, as a representative of the State, should find a solution to this case. The dynamics of the case resembled another case from Norway that led to large scale demonstrations.[26]

2.2.1.2. Case 2

The case concerned a nine-year-old child, who had been abducted abroad by one of the parents.[27] The child had spent four years abroad before a return order was issued by a foreign court and the child returned to Finland. A Finnish court had decided that the Finnish parent was the sole custodian of the child with whom the child should live, while the other parent's rights were restricted. The other parent no longer had the right to receive information about the child. After the custody and child abduction processes were completed, the foreign CA requested, on the request of the other parent, a report on the circumstances of

---

24 See also E. Stang, 'Resistance and protest against Norwegian child welfare services on Facebook – different perceptions of child-centring' [2018] 8 *Nordic Social Work Research* 273, 275.

25 Case code CE1-4.

26 K. Haugevik and C. Basberg Neumann, 'Reputation crisis management and the state: Theorising containment as diplomatic mode' [2021] 27 *European Journal of International Relations* 708.

27 Case code 8.

the child. However, as the requesting parent no longer was the guardian or had any information rights regarding the child, the child welfare authorities refrained from giving any information about the circumstances of the child. This resulted in a *note verbale* from the foreign embassy, in which the embassy stated that the child was wrongfully removed to Finland (although a return order existed), asked for more information about the case, and requested that a meeting should be arranged in which the representatives of the foreign embassy would meet the child. The Finnish Ministry of Justice responded to the note by emphasizing that the custodian decides about all matters relating to a child, and that the Ministry has no jurisdiction over family life and family cases or competence to interfere in individual cases.

Both Brussels II bis and the Hague Child Protection Convention of 1996 establish mechanisms for the transfer of jurisdiction and placement of the child in another Member State. Interestingly, these mechanisms were not adhered to in Case 1 nor in Case 2.

2.2.2. Children Taken Wrongfully to Another State

A particular issue with Russia has to do with the fact that children are rarely, if ever, returned from Russia, even when the child was habitually resident in Finland or when taking of the child from Finland to Russia was clearly wrongful. This has been a continuous theme also in the European Court of Human Rights.[28]

2.2.2.1. Case 3

The case concerned children under the age of seven and their pre-teenager sibling.[29] The children had been taken into care urgently and placed out of home. However, the parents had been given permission to take the children to Russia for a custody hearing, on the condition that they would be returned to their foster home after the trip. The children never returned to Finland. Later, the Russian CA requested that the jurisdiction should be transferred to Russia under Article 9 of the Hague 1996 Convention. The request was eventually

---

[28] See, e.g., *Khanamirova v. Russia*, no. 21353/10, ECHR 2011; *Pakhomova v. Russia*, no. 22935/11, ECHR 2014; *Vladimir Ushakov v. Russia*, no. 15122/17, ECHR 2019; M. Zamboni, 'Implementation of the Judgements of the European Court of Human Rights: Russia, European Implementation Network', 2021, available at <https://static1.squarespace.com/static/55815c4fe4b077ee5306577f/t/60885b57b2684c205bcc9cc6/1619549031001/EIN+report+on+ECtHR+implementation+in+Russia_2021_english+version.pdf> accessed 15.07.2022; T. van Hof, 'Vladimir Ushakov V. Russia – The 1980 Hague Convention, the child's best interests and gender biases' *Strasbourg Observers* 21 August 2019 <https://strasbourgobservers.com/2019/08/21/vladimir-ushakov-v-russia-the-1980-hague-convention-the-childs-best-interests-and-gender-biases> accessed 15.07.2022.

[29] Case code CE 12.

accepted by the Finnish authorities. The case became politicized on the level of diplomatic relations between Russia and Finland.

2.2.2.2. Case 4

The case concerned children under the age of five and their pre-teenager sibling.[30] The children had been taken into care and placed out of home as an emergency protection measure, and later a longer care order was issued by a Finnish court. The family had a long history with child protection in Finland and another Nordic country; the basic care of the children was neglected; the family had lived in a camping area in winter; and the parents had severe and long-lasting problems with substance use. The mother took the children to Russia and left them there to live with a relative who could not and would not care for them. After a request made by the Finnish child welfare authorities via the CAs, the local Russian authorities made an emergency placement of the children in a local children's home because the children were not taken care of. The local Russian authority agreed that the children were habitually resident in Finland and that it was in the best interest of the children to return to Finland where they would continue to live in foster care. The transfer to Finland was prepared in collaboration between the Finnish and Russian authorities. However, the official decision on the return needed to be confirmed by the Russian Basic and Vocational Education Committee. The Committee decided to return the children to the parents, who had stated to the Committee that they had applied for child support, rented a house and were looking for work. After the decision of the Committee, the numerous inquiries made by the Finnish CA to the Russian CA were left unanswered.

2.2.3. *Placements across Borders*

2.2.3.1. Case 5

The case concerned a newborn baby who was placed in a foster family straight after birth.[31] The mother did not want to see the child after the birth and the identity of the father was unknown. The mother had contacted the social authorities in Finland only a few weeks before the due date, and asked for financial support to get a flight ticket back to her country of nationality to give birth there. She could not be assisted to travel back, as the labour was too close, and flying would have been a risk at that late stage of pregnancy. She told the authorities that she came to Finland to meet a friend but ran out of money and could not return home. She learned about the pregnancy at a late stage, and her

[30] Case code CE 10–11.

[31] Case code CE 15.

plan was to give the child up for adoption. After the birth, she did not want to receive support and left the hospital. After that she could no longer be reached by the social workers.

The Finnish child welfare authorities decided that given the cultural and genetic connections of the child, it would be in the best interest of the child to grow up in the mother's country of origin. They based their official request on Articles 55 and 15 of Brussels II bis. The relatives of the mother were asked if they wanted to take the child, but a volunteer foster family was not found. The plan was that the foreign authorities would find a suitable adoptive family for the child, and the foster mother would take the child there and stay with the child in the country for a few days. However, the adoption plan did not proceed, and after two years, the child was still in Finland. The child was called by a nickname as the decision on the child's name had been left pending the adoption. The child had started day care and was learning Finnish as their first language. Eventually the request was withdrawn, as the transfer to the new environment was no longer considered to be in the best interest of the child.

2.2.3.2. Case 6

The case concerned a pre-teenager who had been urgently taken into care and placed out of home.[32] The growth and development of the child were severely jeopardized by the living conditions with the mother, who suffered of alcoholism. The Finnish local child welfare authorities requested the authorities of the Central-Eastern European State in which the child had previously lived and the child's father still lived, to investigate the possibility of the child to move there to live with the father, including the potential living conditions, the father's life situation and his ability to provide for the child. The report delivered via the CAs confirmed that the father would be happy to have the child live with him, and that the living conditions were considered good. The child moved to live with the father in the Central-Eastern European State.

3. LEGAL, CULTURAL AND HISTORICAL BACKGROUNDS OF THE TENSIONS IN INTERNATIONAL CHILD LAW

3.1. DIVERGENT LEGAL CONCEPTS AND INTERPRETATIONS

As part of global governance, private international law seeks to make international collaboration between States easier through harmonizing rules

32 Case code CE 25.

concerning jurisdiction and applicable law. As responses of national legal systems to children at risk in the family are, as Lamont observes, 'heavily informed by (potentially very) localised cultures and practices',[33] it is important to understand the differences between the legal concepts and their interpretations between Western European States and Russia and Central-Eastern European States, as well as the historical legacies and contemporary developments of child protection in the former communist and socialist regimes.

Child welfare models can be categorized roughly into those that focus on offering support and promoting the welfare of the family and those that focus on categorizing families into risk families.[34] Russia and many former communist and socialist States traditionally belonged to the latter category; support for parenting was rarely available, and when the authorities intervened, the parents often lost their rights in court and family reunification was not possible.

Concepts and practices of custody and child protection measures vary considerably between legal systems. Legal scholar Olga Khazova describes the differences between the Russian legal concepts regarding habitual residence and parental rights and the ones used in the Hague Conventions that might have concrete consequences as to how Russian courts and lawyers understand and apply the rules. For example, no separate concepts of 'parenthood' and 'custody' exist under Russian law, and consequently, parents cannot be considered 'custodial' or 'non-custodial' parents.[35] This means that a care order and placement of a child into care can have dramatically different consequences in Russia and many of the Western European countries. For example, in Finland, the taking of children into care and out-of-home placement are never intended as permanent solutions, and the goal is always for the child to return to live with the parents. In Russia, the decision to remove parental rights has consequences of more permanent nature; the child can, for example, be given up for adoption without consulting the biological parents.[36] Such differences can obviously contribute to misunderstandings in child disputes between the countries,

---

33 R. Lamont, above n. 4, p. 8; see also R. Lamont, above n. 11.

34 N. Gilbert, N. Parton and M. Skivenes, 'Introduction' in N. Gilbert, N. Parton and M. Skivenes (eds), *Child Protection Systems: International Trends and Orientations*, Oxford University Press, Oxford 2011, pp. 3–14.

35 O. Khazova, 'Russia's Accession to the Hague Convention on Civil Aspects of International Child Abduction 1980: New Challenges for Family Law and Practice' [2014] 48 *Family Law Quarterly* 253.

36 However, recent research points to the tendency in Norway and Denmark to favour adoption, event without the consent from the birth parents, over long-term care. A. Mørk, K. Sandberg, T. Schultz and H. Hartoft, 'A Conflict between the Best Interests of the Child and the Right to Respect for Family Life? Non-Consensual Adoption in Denmark and Norway as an Example of the Difficulties in Balancing Different Considerations' (2022) *International Journal of Law, Policy and The Family* 2022. Published online 20 September 2022, available at <https://academic.oup.com/lawfam/article/36/1/ebac019/6706743> accessed 15.10.2022.

especially when media gets involved.[37] In addition, the 1996 Convention seems to be poorly known by the competent authorities.[38]

Eastern and Western European States also seem to interpret the Vienna Convention on Consular Relations[39] differently. According to Article 5 (h-i) of the Vienna Convention on Consular Relations, consular functions include safeguarding, within the limits imposed by the laws and regulations of the receiving State, the interests of minors and other persons lacking full capacity who are nationals of the sending State, particularly where any guardianship or trusteeship is required with respect to such persons. Subject to the practices and procedures obtaining in the receiving State, consular functions may also include representing or arranging appropriate representation for nationals of the sending State before the tribunals and other authorities of the receiving State. As an interviewee explains:

> Even though Brussels IIbis Regulation and Hague Conventions talk about habitual residence in relation to jurisdiction, in Eastern Europe nationality is still considered a strong connection, and in Eastern European States it is sometimes felt that, regardless of jurisdiction regulations, they have the right and duty to protect their nationals on the basis of consular legislation. So the element of protecting the nationals is strong, and we have the Vienna Convention on Consular Relations, which regulates consular duties and authorizes, among other things, the contact with a national. This raises questions such as, for example, does the consular have access to court proceedings in child protection cases. We think very differently in Western Europe compared to Eastern Europe about whether the Vienna Convention establishes an obligation to notify the state of nationality of the appointment of a guardian or a trusted man in child protection cases. In Western Europe and especially the Nordic countries we have a consensus that it does not cover child protection measures. That is, if an Eastern European child is taken into public care in Finland, the embassy of the child's State of nationality will not be notified about the care order and the placement of the child. This follows from the absolute confidentiality regulations, but also from our interpretation that it is not a question of appointing a trustee or a guardian. There is disagreement about this, and Eastern Europeans think that they should also be informed under the Vienna Convention.[40]

---

37 M. Jäppinen and M. Kulmala, 'Uusi lastenkoditon Venäjä?' (2015) *Idäntutkimus* 58. Available at <https://journal.fi/idantutkimus/article/view/78087/38990> accessed 22.05.2022.

38 A. Abashidze, A. Solntsev, A. Koneva, D. Gugunskiy and N. Grigorieva, 'Current Issues of Application of Hague Child Protection Convention of 1996 on National Level' *Mediterranean Journal of Social Sciences* 6 [2015] 289, available at <https://www.richtmann.org/journal/index.php/mjss/article/view/7379> accessed 15.07.2022.

39 Vienna Convention on Consular Relations 24 April 1963. United Nations, Treaty Series, vol. 596, p. 261.

40 Interviewee code CE 5. Translation from Finnish by SM.

As demonstrated in Cases 1, 2 and 3, the authorities of the involved Central-Eastern European States did not (in some cases initially, in some cases at all) formally request the transfer of jurisdiction or the placement of the child abroad, although both Hague 1996 and Brussels II bis provide rules for this purpose.[41] Rather, the preferred way to proceed seemed to be through meetings held at embassies or at high level between ministers, and *note verbales.*

3.2. LEGACY OF THE POST-SOCIALIST CHILD PROTECTION SYSTEMS

In addition to the differences between the systems, legal concepts and interpretations of consular legislation, the cultural and political centrality of the extended family in Central-Eastern European States may result in different views concerning the care arrangements of a child. In Central-Eastern Europe it is common that grandparents provide child care. For instance, many of the 4.5 million Romanian citizens who moved abroad for work after the country's accession to the EU had to leave their children behind to be taken care of by the grandparents.[42] Moreover, there is a long shadow of the Soviet and socialist ideology of collective care and upbringing. In accordance with the idea of the paternalist state as the primary caregiver, care in state residential facilities was regarded as an ideal environment where good citizens and future workers would be raised.[43]

In Romania, the state policies on reproduction and institutionalized child welfare under the Ceausescu regime had notoriously drastic consequences. Abortion was prohibited in the country in 1966, and the State required that each family produce four or five children to further Ceausescu's megalomaniac ambition of ruling over a populous nation.[44] A significant number of Romanian parents had to give their babies to orphanages when the State failed to provide them opportunities to take care of the child at home. As the families depended on the State for the very basics of life, many parents simply did not have the

---

41 Articles 15 and 56 of Brussels II bis, Articles 8 and 9 of Hague 1996. The new Brussels II ter introduces more detailed rules; Article 82 para. 3 allows other Member States to intervene in domestic family procedures by indicating a close connection of the child to its State; M. Župan, C. Hoehn and U. Kluth, above n. 10.

42 I. Horváth and R. Anghel, 'Migration and Its Consequences for Romania' [2009] 58 *Südosteuropa* 386.

43 S. An and M. Kulmala, 'Global deinstitutionalisation policy in the post-Soviet space: A comparison of child-welfare reforms in Russia and Kazakhstan' (2021) 21 *Global Social Policy* 51.

44 L. Turcescu and L. Stan, 'Religion, Politics and Sexuality in Romania' (2005) *Europe-Asia Studies* 291; G. Kligman, *The Politics of Duplicity: Controlling Reproduction in Ceausescu's Romania*, University of California Press, Berkeley 1998.

means to take care of the babies which the State required women to give birth to.[45]

After the revolution, about 170,000 orphans were found in Romanian orphanages. The conditions in which children lived in these institutions were horrendous. Mortality rates were generally high, as were, for example, caregiver ratios with one caregiver to as many as 12 to 15 babies, and one caregiver to 20 to 25 toddlers. In some rural institutions, children were chained to the beds.[46]

For Romanians, the history of the Ceausescu era represents both individual tragedies and collective trauma, and a lack of trust towards state-provided child protection both in Romania and abroad.[47] Moreover, with a high level of street children, Romania continues to be a destination for child abuse tourism.[48] This background might at least partly explain the distrust toward foreign authorities and the polemics related to child protection cases involving Romanian families.[49]

In Russia, the rise of the neo-traditionalist thinking in the 2000s and the emphasis on family values has been reflected in the development of the child protection system. In the 2010s, official Russia began to speak in favour of traditional family values, and the government began to fundamentally reform its child protection system. 'The party of power', United Russia (*Yedinaya Rossiya*), launched the 'Russia Needs Every Child' programme, and the ambitious goal of another programme, the 'Russia Without Orphans' programme was that a foster family would be found for nine out of 10 children placed outside the home.[50] The key principle of the reforms is the child's right to live and grow up in the family. Children's wellbeing is therefore thought to come first and foremost

---

45 G. Kligman, above n. 44, p. 225.

46 C. Nelson, N. Fox and C. Zeanah, *Romania's Abandoned Children: Deprivation, Brain Development, and the Struggle for Recovery*, Harvard University Press, Cambridge 2014, p. 51; A. Powell, '"Breathtakingly awful": HMS professor's work details devastating toll of Romanian orphanages' *Harvard Gazette* 05.10.2010, available at <https://news.harvard.edu/gazette/story/2010/10/breathtakingly-awful> accessed 15.07.2022.

47 C. Nelson et al., above n. 46.

48 M. Gamble, 'Sexual Exploitation and Abuse of Street Children in Romania: Catalysts of Vulnerability and Challenges in Recovery', Second Annual Interdisciplinary Conference on Human Trafficking, 2010, available at <https://core.ac.uk/download/pdf/17239888.pdf> accessed 15.07.2022.

49 Romanian child protection cases have been debated in the media, e.g., the Norwegian child protection case which led to widespread protests against Norway in Romania. *BBC News* 14 April 2016, available at <https://www.bbc.com/news/magazine-36026458> accessed 15.07.2022; see also J. Doughty, 'The best interests of children and the mutual trust principle that goes both ways' [2015] 38 *Journal of Social Welfare and Family Law* 333; K. Haugevik and C. Basberg Neumann, 'Reputation crisis management and the state: Theorising containment as diplomatic mode' [2021] 27 *European Journal of International Relations* 708, 710; E. Stang, above n. 24; and R. Lamont, above n. 3.

50 M. Jäppinen and M. Kulmala, above n. 37.

within the private sphere.[51] In the political discourse, it is often stated that the state should not interfere in the private sphere of the family. In addition, the nationalist agenda of Putin's regime has set strict limitations to international adoptions from Russia and heavily prioritizes domestic adoptions.

The reforms have fundamentally shifted the ideological premises behind both Romanian and Russian child welfare.[52] They also reflect global trends in child welfare, such as deinstitutionalization of care, and their local adaptation.[53] In Romania, the changes have been basic.[54] Improving children's conditions and strengthening their rights was also a condition of Romania's EU membership; the infamous childcare institutions needed to be reformed before accession negotiations would proceed.[55] However, in a broader view, these developments are still quite recent.

In Russia, the ongoing re-organization of the institutional design is being implemented throughout the country as a top priority of the government, and at speed; major reforms that have been under way for decades elsewhere are going to be implemented in a few years.[56] As the sociologists and social work researchers Meri Kulmala, Maija Jäppinen, Anna Tarasenko and Anna Pivovarova point out:

> top-down modes of reform definitely create many tensions in the implementation at the lower levels. Under such pressures in the current increasingly authoritarian political environment and with the heavy legacy of residential care in large institutions, the reform is resulting in multiple unintended, even paradoxical, consequences of 'good intentions'.[57]

The tensions between the authorities are visible in Case 4, in which the local authorities agreed that the circumstances in which the children lived were detrimental and that the children's best interests would be to return to Finland, but the Committee refused to confirm the return to Finland and instead returned the children to live with their parents.

---

51 M. Kulmala, M. Jäppinen, A. Tarasenko and A. Pivovarova, 'Introduction: Russian child welfare reform and institutional change' in M. Kulmala, M. Jäppinen, A. Tarasenko and A. Pivovarova (eds), *Reforming Child Welfare in the Post-Soviet Space: Institutional Change in Russia*, Abingdon, Routledge 2021, pp. 3–19, at p. 3.

52 ibid.

53 S. An and M. Kulmala, above n. 43, p. 51.

54 In the 2000s, several social reforms were initiated to improve the situation of children in Romania: the National Agency for the Protection of Children's Rights was established; the national child protection strategy was formulated; increases were made to the child welfare allocation; and the government began its own foster system and to pass a law prohibiting institutionalization of children younger than age 2, see C. Nelson, N. Fox and C. Zeanah, above n. 46.

55 See <https://www.europarl.europa.eu/enlargement/briefings/3a2_en.htm> accessed 15.07.2022.

56 M. Kulmala, M. Jäppinen, A.Tarasenko and A. Pivovarova, above n. 51.

57 ibid., p. 3.

4. POLITICIZATION OF INTERNATIONAL CHILD LAW

4.1. INTERNATIONAL CHILD CASES IN PUTIN'S RUSSIA

In addition to the understandable challenges caused by the numerous differences and gaps between national child protection and welfare systems, international child cases have become politicized for specific purposes in new ways in the 2010s and 2020s. During Putin's era, the official narrative in Russia has focused on the 'legacy of the past, i.e. the struggle against the West which does not respect and recognise Russia as a global player in the international setting'.[58] International child cases are hijacked to support Putinism and authoritarian politics, and thus become mobilized in information war. This also has consequences elsewhere in Eastern Europe, where the cases are being used by right-wing populists.

The 26 years of Russian membership in the Council of Europe and European Convention on Human Rights recently ended as the Committee of Ministers of the Council of European Council decided on 16 March 2022, that the Russian Federation ceases to be a member of the Council of Europe.[59] On the previous day, the Parliamentary Assembly had unanimously adopted an Opinion which considered that the Russian Federation can no longer be a member due to the unjustified military aggression against Ukraine. On the same day, the Russian Government had declared that it was withdrawing from the Council of Europe and denounced the European Convention on Human Rights.[60] This marked a significant point on Russia's path towards authoritarian rule and away from democracy and the rule of law, although the relations between Russia and the Council of Europe always were marked by a profound contradiction.[61] Russia amended neither its practice nor its legislation following European Court of

58 M. Morini, 'Myths and realities of Putinism in post-truth politics' in S. Giusti and E. Piras (eds), *Democracy and Fake News: Information Manipulation and Post-Truth Politics*, Routledge, London 2021, pp. 132–42, at p. 134.

59 Russia's role in the founding of the International Court of Justice, in the wake of the first World War, was remarkable, see R. Higgins, 'The ICJ, the ECJ, and the Integrity of International Law' [2003] 50 *International and Comparative Law Quarterly* 1.

60 Opinion of the Parliamentary Assembly 300 (2022) <https://pace.coe.int/en/files/29885/html> accessed 15.07.2022.

61 W. Pomeranz, 'Uneasy Partners: Russia and the European Court of Human Rights' Human Rights Brief [2012] 17, 17; see also S. Marochkin, 'ECtHR and the Russian Constitutional Court: Duet or Duel?' in L. Mälksoo and W. Benedek (eds), *Russia and the European Court of Human Rights: The Strasbourg Effect*, Cambridge University Press, Cambridge 2017, pp. 93–124, at pp. 123–4 (Lauri Mälksoo & Wolfgang Benedek eds., 2018); J-P. Massias, 'Russia and the Council of Europe: Ten Years Wasted?' *IFRI Research Programme Russia/NIS* 2007, available at <https://www.ifri.org/sites/default/files/atoms/files/ifri_CE_massias_ang_jan2007.pdf> accessed 15.07.2022; D. Kurnosov, 'Russia without Strasbourg and Strasbourg without Russia: A Preliminary Outlook' Strasbourg Observers (20.09.2022) available at <https://strasbourgobservers.com/2022/09/20/russia-without-strasbourg-and-strasbourg-without-russia-a-preliminary-outlook> accessed 25.09.2022.

Human Rights judgments, for example on domestic violence,[62] and the dissenting opinions by the Russian judge of the Court have fuelled fierce criticism.[63]

The rise of Putinism and imperialistic fantasies marked a considerably stronger emphasis on neo-traditionalism and the high value attributed to the family by the state.[64] According to the official narrative, Finland along with Western Europe represent a degenerate culture where homosexuals destroy the family institution and the authorities arbitrarily intervene in the lives of families.[65] The main narrative spread in the Russian media is simple: Finnish social services systematically and without grounds issue care orders to take the children of Russian parents and place them in children's homes that resemble concentration camps or give them up for adoption to same-sex couples. In this sense, the media attention received by child protection cases fits the broader Russian agenda very well. However, the narrative according to which children of foreign background would be 'kidnapped' from their families and placed in Finnish residential institutions or foster homes is not confirmed by this study. In contrary, as Cases 5 and 6 show, Finnish authorities seem to be quite well aware of the benefits of finding an adoptive home in the country of origin or returning the child to live with the parent in another country.

Stories about the persecution of Russian families are circulated on the Russian state radio and television company VGTRK (the Kremlin's main propaganda and disinformation broker), Russia Today, Sputnik, Pravda and other media. Political scientists Corneliu Bjola and Krysianna Papadakis note that these family cases emerged in the late 2000s, with 2014 marking a turning point in the intensity of Russian disinformation. One purpose of the disinformation was to prevent the Finnish government from taking a critical position against the Russian policies in Ukraine.[66]

---

62 R. McQuigg, 'The European Court of Human Rights and Domestic Violence: Volodina v. Russia' [2021] 10 *International Human Rights Law Review* 155.

63 See, e.g., L. Lavrysen, 'Bayev and Others v. Russia: on Judge Dedov's outrageously homophobic dissent' *Strasbourg Observers* (13.07.2017) available at <https://strasbourgobservers.com/2017/07/13/bayev-and-others-v-russia-on-judge-dedovs-outrageously-homophobic-dissent> accessed 15.07.2022; K. Dzehtsiarou and G. Esakov, 'Russian Roulette? Selection of the Judicial Candidates to the European Court from Russia' in *Strasbourg Observers* (7 December 2020) available at <https://strasbourgobservers.com/2020/12/07/russian-roulette-selection-of-the-judicial-candidates-to-the-european-court-from-russia> accessed 15.07.2022.

64 A. Sorainen, A. Avdeeva and A. Zhabenko, 'Strategies of non-normative families, parenting and reproduction in neo-traditional Russia' [2017] 6 *Families, Relationships and Societies* 471.

65 M. Kulmala, M. Jäppinen, A. Tarasenko and A. Pivovarova, above n. 51.

66 C. Bjola and K. Papadakis, 'Digital propaganda, counterpublics, and the disruption of the public sphere: The Finnish approach to building digital resilience' in T. Pfeiffer, T. Clack and R. Johnson (eds), *The world information war: western resilience, campaigning, and cognitive effects*, Routledge, London 2021, pp. 186–213, at p. 186.

Russia utilizes various actors and networks in its information war. A key figure in the Finnish-Russian cases has been Johan Bäckman, an informal leader of the pro-Kremlin Finnish counterpublic, who positions himself as a 'human rights activist' (*pravozaščitnik*), defender of the rights of the Russian minority group in Finland, a publisher, a political researcher and a doctor or docent in criminology. He approaches Russian media and offers to be interviewed as an expert in the field and has actively spread false information for years in the Russian media.[67] Already in 2012, Bäckman declared, on his speaking tour in Russia, that 'Finnish child welfare is political terror' and that 'the number one theme of our Lutheran Church is the blessing of gay unions'.[68] Recently, he was sentenced in the criminal court for persecution of the journalist Jessikka Aro, who has written about the Russian online trolls and other elements of the information war.

Propaganda has long roots in the history, and it has always been part of the apparatus used in conflicts. Child cases are operationalized in this classic way to serve the propaganda machinery and to manipulate the views and attitudes of the people in a pre-determined direction, that of the traditional family values. However, the contemporary propaganda goes beyond this to 'induce people into a state of self-defeating and endemic scepticism by undermining the very criteria on the basis of which they develop their cognitive abilities to make sense, interpret, and shape social reality'.[69] Along with other hybrid warfare measures the aim of fake news is to weaken contemporary democracies. Putinism finds allies and support in populist agendas, which may make it attractive in the eyes of some Western populist leaders.[70]

4.2. CHILD CASES AND POPULIST AGENDAS

The international legal framework generated by the Hague Conventions and the Brussels II bis/ter Regulation builds on the principle of mutual trust, which means that States should trust the evaluations made by the authorities who have jurisdiction and act within their competence.[71] Cemented in EU law, the principle of mutual trust is also the basis of efficient collaboration in the Hague

67 O. Salovaara, 'Venäjän uskollinen mediasoturi' *Helsingin Sanomat* 10.07.2022. The newspaper uses material from a collaborative project in investigative journalism coordinated by Occrp, a network of journalists specializing in crime and corruption, and the American publication *Intercept*. It covers more than 90 emails sent by Bäckman in 2014–2020 to VGTRK.

68 E. Yli-Ojanperä, 'Dosentti lietsoo Venäjällä epäluuloa lasten huostaanotoista Suomessa' *YLE* 15.10.2012 available at <https://yle.fi/aihe/artikkeli/2012/10/15/dosentti-lietsoo-venajalla-epaluuloa-lasten-huostaanotoista-suomessa> accessed 15.07.2022.

69 C. Bjola and K. Papadakis, above n. 66, p. 186.

70 M. Morini, above n. 58, p. 139.

71 R. Lamont, above n. 11.

Conventions.[72] The principle stands in clear opposition to nationalist and anti-European agendas of populist groups in Europe.

Cross-border child cases are useful for populists in the era of post-truth politics, because the possibilities of authorities to correct disinformation are limited as the law prevents the authorities from commenting on individual cases. Populism and Putinism are interconnected both ideologically and historically. Propaganda was central to the public sphere in all former socialist States, and disinformation was widely spread.

In Romania, the Ceausescu regime used symbolic violence to manipulate people's minds to internalize and play along with the totalitarian order. In her influential study, sociologist Gail Kligman explains how the lies and disinformation were essential in maintaining the former socialist Romanian State and how the intertwining of propaganda and reproductive policies resulted in the penetration of the state into the most private area of the citizens' lives, which 'served as effective mechanism for integrating individuals into the functioning of socialist society'.[73]

In recent years, Romanian right-wing nationalists have used child protection cases of Romanian children abroad to support their anti-European and anti-egalitarian agendas. The parents may even spread filmed material relating to legal procedures or actively seek attention and support from nationalist media forums.[74] Some (right-wing populist) politicians may use these cases as a way to strengthen their agendas and gain visibility, for example before national elections.[75]

A demonstration in front of the Finnish embassy in Bucharest in February 2020 featured banners such as 'Down with the Nazis!' and 'Stop the destruction of the Romanian family' and claims such as: 'You realise which Europe we want to be in, in which Europe they want us to go – a Europe that turns Islam into a culture, that places value on homosexuality, but which condemns children's love for their mother.'[76]

In the light of these developments, the question about the future of integration and collaboration between the East and the West seems all the more urgent: How can the principle of mutual trust underpinning harmonized

---

72 R. Lamont, above n. 11; Stockholm Programme, 'An open and secure Europe serving and protecting citizens' [2010] OJ C 115.

73 G. Kligman, above n. 44, p. 14.

74 For cases between the UK and Central-Eastern European States that received similar kind of media attention and became debated in populist terms, see R. Lamont, above n. 11, p. 83.

75 See Resonant voices, 17.09.2020 <https://resonantvoices.info/romanian-right-turns-finnish-custody-fight-into-anti-western-propaganda> accessed 15.07.2022; see also <https://tribuna.us/finland-and-the-smicala-children-abducted-by-the-state-is-that-the-future-of-child-protection-in-europe> accessed 15.07.2022.

76 Resonant voices, 17.09.2020 <https://resonantvoices.info/romanian-right-turns-finnish-custody-fight-into-anti-western-propaganda> accessed 15.07.2022.

legal frameworks, be it through Brussels II ter or the Hague Conventions, be maintained? Despite the inevitably eroding effect of the development described here, the shared legal framework may still offer means to enhance protection in cross-border cases.

Legal scholars Ralf Michaels and Karen Knop and anthropologist Annelise Riles suggest a move from politics to technique, without denying the politics. According to them, conflict of laws as technique is not about formalism but 'a way of doing things, in relative oblivion to outcomes, and indeed (for the time being) politics',[77] and as such it requires an 'as if' mode. Legal discourse can succeed only as a fictitious discourse – in awareness of the politics, but held, for the time being, as if the politics did not exist. Perhaps one such useful fiction is the principle of mutual trust, which, as Lamont points out, 'is designed to obscure the difference between national substantive laws'.[78]

While Russia might be out of reach, at least for the time being, of efficient inter-State collaboration, the focus must lie heavily on enhancing the integration between the rest of Central-Eastern Europe and Western Europe.[79] This requires educational and collaboration programmes on the grassroot-level, and probably also resources allocated both to the CAs and the local authorities.

5. CONCLUSIONS: ENHANCING LEGITIMACY AND RAISING AWARENESS OF INTERNATIONAL CHILD LAW

Drawing on the child protection cases handled by the Finnish Central Authority, this chapter examined challenges of collaboration between Finland, and more generally Western European States, and Central-Eastern European States, including Russia. The cases demonstrate that the functioning of the legal framework in cross-border child protection and the principle of mutual trust leaves much to hope for in relation to certain Member States of the EU and Russia as a Hague 1996 Convention State. It was found that legal, cultural and historical reasons explain much of the hindrances of the collaboration between East and West.

---

77 R. Michaels, 'Post-critical Private International Law: From politics to technique' in H. Muir Watt and D. Fernández Arroyo (eds), *Private International Law and Global Governance*, Oxford University Press, Oxford 2014, pp. 54–70, at p. 66.

78 R. Lamont, above n. 11, p. 82.

79 In 2015, Russia seemed to be well on the way to implementing the Hague Conventions of 1980 and 1996. It remains to be seen if Russia will at some point return to this track. See A. Abashidze, D. Gugunskiy, A. Koneva, M. Simonova and A. Solntsev, 'Current Problems of Interstate Cooperation of Russian Federation for the Protection of Children in Case of Disputes between Parents Living in Different States' [2015] 11 *Asian Social Science* 337.

Central to the de facto efficiency of any international convention or norm is the ability of the convention to reach the awareness of the local administration and to convince the local authorities of the legitimacy of the international norms. 'Vernacularization', i.e., the process of making international norms culturally acceptable and understandable,[80] requires continuous work toward making the norms known and accepted. 'Mutual trust' can be a useful fiction in this endeavour.

The most urgent challenges concern anti-democratic and anti-European developments taking place in Russia and elsewhere in Europe. The nationalist and totalitarian Putinist regime does not follow the obligations arising from the international conventions it has ratified, nor has it invested efforts to educate local administration about the Convention concepts and mechanisms. The contemporary 'post-truth era' represents a dangerous surge of populism with implications also in the field of private international law. In spite of these challenges, and partly because of them, there is work to be done in this field toward enhancing legitimacy and awareness of international child law.

80 S. Merry and P. Levitt, 'The Vernacularization of Women's Human Rights' in S. Hopgood, J. Snyder and L. Vinjamuri (eds), *Human Rights Futures*, Cambridge University Press, Cambridge 2017, pp. 213–36.

THE CHALLENGES OF THE HAGUE CONVENTION ON INTERNATIONAL CHILD ABDUCTION

Cases Involving Domestic and Family Violence

Onyója Momoh

1. INTRODUCTION

It is undoubtedly by intentional design that the preamble to the 1980 Hague Convention on the Civil Aspect of International Child Abduction begins by reflecting on the paramount importance of the interests of children.[1] This

[1] The 1980 Hague Convention on the Civil Aspects of International Child Abduction (hereafter 'the Hague Convention'). Preamble: which provides that signatory States are 'firmly

'ground-breaking instrument'[2] tackles the issue of cross-border parental child abduction and its harmful effects on children by seeking to secure their prompt return to their country of habitual residence. The rapidity of this process is essential in order to match the needs of a child's sense of time.[3] In many ways, invoking the Hague Convention can be seen as a measure of protection of its own right. Hague Convention return proceedings are not intended to indulge in the merits of custody battles, they are 'summary proceedings where the issues are succinctly defined and the evidence confined to those issues'.[4] The premise of this mandatory return mechanism[5] comes from the underlying rationale that the court in the child's home country is best placed to make substantive decisions concerning their welfare, therefore restoring the *status quo ante*.[6] What is more, in some ways, is that the Hague Convention plays a vital role in upholding the integrity of the national laws of its Contracting States. Of course, the cross-border movement of children is an area much too delicate to be regulated by just national laws.[7] The Hague Convention enshrines the legislative foothold in which parental child abduction cases are determined in private international law.[8] It is envisaged that the return may well be temporary until matters relating to the welfare of the child are decided by the courts where the child is habitually resident. However, despite this treaty, it cannot be said that the problem of international child abduction has lessened, particularly because our modern and ever evolving channels of international movement

---

convinced that the interests of children are of paramount importance in matters relating to their custody'. It has 101 Contracting States as of 31 May 2022.

2 P. Beaumont and P. McEleavy, *The Hague Convention on International Child Abduction*, Oxford University Press, Oxford 1999, p. 4; P. Beaumont and P. McEleavy, *Anton's Private International Law*, 3rd ed., W. Green, e-book 2011, p. 816.

3 See G.A.L. Droz, 'A Comment on the Role of the Hague Conference on Private International Law' (1994) 57(3) *Law and Contemporary Problems* 8. See also *Re S (Abduction: Intolerable Situation: Beth Din)* [2000] 1 FLR 454 (Connell J).

4 *Re S (Abduction: Intolerable Situation: Beth Din)* [2000] 1 FLR 454, Fam Law 234 per Connell J. See also Permanent Bureau, 'Guide to Good Practice under the HCCH Convention of 25 October 1980 on the Civil Aspects of International Child Abduction – Part VI – Article 13(1)(b)' HCCH, 2020, p. 36.

5 R. Schuz, *The Hague Child Abduction Convention: A Critical Analysis*, Hart Publishing, Oxford 2013, pp. 270–71, see also generally 'defence to mandatory return' pp. 223–44.

6 P. Beaumont and P. McEleavy, *Anton's Private International Law*, 3rd ed., W. Green, e-book 2011, p. 818.

7 A. Briggs, *The Conflict of Laws*, 2nd ed., Oxford University Press, Oxford 2008, pp. 357–58.

8 In the UK for example, the Child Abduction and Custody Act 1985 brings the Hague Convention into UK law and gives effect to the Convention. See also Lord L. Collins of Mapesbury and J. Harris QC (ed.), *Dicey, Morris and Collins on the Conflict of Laws*, vol. 2, 15th ed., Sweet & Maxwell, London 2012, p. 1157; E.B. Crawford and J.M. Carruthers, *International Private Law: A Scots Perspective*, 4th ed., W. Green, Edinburgh 2015, p. 473; J. Fawcett and J.M. Carruthers, *Cheshire, North & Fawcett: Private International Law*, 14th ed., Oxford University Press, Oxford 2008, pp. 1103–08.

have led to increasing incidences of child abduction.[9] Added to this, statistical information confirms that the majority of child abductions are committed by mothers with Article 13(1)(b) grave risk of harm exception often raised, suggesting that one of the reasons for the increase in child abduction is the motivation to flee domestic violence.[10] Where the child is concerned, whilst it is generally accepted that a child's future is best determined by the courts in the child's home country, the idea that a child may be returned to 'uncertain fates remain[s] controversial'.[11]

Although the Hague Convention's objective is to ensure a prompt return of wrongfully removed or retained children, in some instances a departure from this principle may be justified. Accordingly, Article 12(1) of the Hague Convention provides the mechanism that requires a return order to be made

---

9 N. Lowe, S. Armstrong and A. Mathias, 'A Statistical Analysis of Applications made in 1999 under the Hague Convention of 25 October 1980 on the Civil Aspects of International Child Abduction' (March 2001) Permanent Bureau of the Hague Conference on Private International Law, The Hague 2001; N. Lowe, E. Atkinson, K. Horosova and S. Patterson, 'A Statistical Analysis of Applications Made in 2003 under the Hague Convention of 25 October 1980 on the Civil Aspects of International Child Abduction' Part I & II (October 2006) & 2007 Update Part II & II (September 2008) Permanent Bureau of the Hague Conference on Private International Law, The Hague 2008; and N. Lowe, 'A Statistical Analysis of Applications Made in 2008 under the Hague Convention of 25 October 1980 on the Civil Aspects of International Child Abduction, Part I, Global Report' (November 2011) Permanent Bureau of the Hague Conference on Private International Law, The Hague 2011, Part II – Regional Report (November 2011) Permanent Bureau of the Hague Conference on Private International Law, The Hague 2011 and Part III – National Reports (May 2011) Permanent Bureau of the Hague Conference on Private International Law, The Hague 2011. N. Lowe and V. Stephens, 'A Statistical Analysis of Applications Made in 2015 under the Hague Convention of 25 October 1980 on the Civil Aspects of International Child Abduction, Part I – Regional (revised) (September 2017), Permanent Bureau of the Hague Conference on Private International Law, The Hague 2017; Part II – Global Report (September 2017), Permanent Bureau of the Hague Conference on Private International Law, The Hague 2017; Part III – National Reports (July 2018), Permanent Bureau of the Hague Conference on Private International Law, The Hague 2018. See Part I – Global Report (November 2011), paras 10, 11, 14 which summarized that a total of 2,705 children were involved in the 1,961 return applications and 360 access applications; compared with the 2003 survey, there had been a 45 per cent increase in return applications and a 40 per cent increase in access applications. The findings of the above statistical analyses (1999, 2003 and 2008) are available at <http://www.hcch.net/index_en.php?act=conventions.publications&dtid=32&cid=24> accessed 31.05.2022. The surveys were conducted by the Centre of International Family Law Studies at Cardiff University Law School (under the Directorship of Professor Nigel Lowe) in collaboration with the Permanent Bureau of the Hague Conference on Private International Law.

10 See section 3.1. below on the changing face of the perceived abductor. The Best Practice Guide – Protection of Abducting Mothers in Return Proceedings (hereafter 'POAM Best Practice Guide'), s. 2.1.1.

11 P. Beaumont and P. McEleavy, *Anton's Private International Law*, 3rd ed., W. Green, Edinburgh 2011, p. 816. See also J. Fawcett and J.M. Carruthers, *Cheshire, North & Fawcett: Private International Law*, 14th ed., Oxford University Press, Oxford 2008, pp. 1114–17 on 'grave risks of harm'.

when a child has been wrongfully removed or retained, and less than one year has elapsed. The exceptions to the mandatory return mechanism are contained in Articles 12, 13 and 20[12] of the Hague Convention. In cases involving domestic and family violence, the Article 13(1)(b) 'grave risk of harm' exception is frequently relied upon and will be the main focus in this chapter. The approach to Hague Convention return cases involving domestic violence has evolved to recognize that children accompanied by primary carers who have fled from abuse and maltreatment should not be expected to return without adequate, effective and enforceable protective measures. In particular, giving effect to the protection of children and their primary carers in cross-border cases has been the subject of much discussion at late.[13]

This chapter explores prevailing challenges in Hague Convention proceedings in cases involving domestic and family violence and, where applicable, examining current and future efforts to overcome these challenges. The content of the chapter is divided into two parts. The first part will assess harm in cases involving domestic and family violence and, in particular, the challenges in recognizing how interpreted and applied under Article 13(1)(a) (intimidatory tactics), Article 13(1)(b) (grave risk of harm) or Article 20 (human rights violations). The second part will examine protective measures in return proceedings and the challenges in ensuring their adequacy and enforceability.

---

12 Articles 12 and 20 contain exceptions to the Hague Convention rule. Article 12 may be relied upon to argue in favour of a non-return order if more than 12 months have elapsed since the abduction and it can be shown that the child is now settled in the new environment. Article 20 provides that a return may be refused where the protection of human rights and fundamental freedoms is at risk.

13 See, e.g., the Hague Conference on Private International Law, 'Guide to Good Practice under the HCCH Convention of 25 October 1980 on the Civil Aspects of International Child Abduction – Part VI – Article 13(1)(b)', 2020 (hereafter 'HCCH Guide'), available at <https://assets.hcch.net/docs/225b44d3-5c6b-4a14-8f5b-57cb370c497f.pdf> accessed 25.05.2022. See also activities under the auspices of the POAM project. POAM (Protection of Abducting Mothers in Return proceedings) is a project funded by the European Union's Rights, Equality and Citizenship programme 2014-202 under grant agreement No 810373. POAM explored the intersection between domestic violence and international parental child abduction within the EU. In particular, the project focused on the operation of the Regulation 606/2013 on Mutual Recognition of Protection Measures in Civil Matters and the Directive 2011/99/EU on the European Protection Order in the context of return proceedings involving allegations of domestic violence under the 1980 Hague Convention on the Civil Aspects of International Child Abduction and the Council Regulation (EC) No. 2201/2003 of 27 November 2003 Concerning Jurisdiction and the Recognition and Enforcement of Judgments in Matrimonial Matters and the Matters of Parental Responsibility, repealing Regulation (EC) No. 1347/2000 ('Brussels IIa Regulation'. See also O. Momoh, 'The need for cross-border protective measures in return proceedings' in K. Trimmings, A. Dutta, C. Honorati and M. Zupan (eds), *Domestic Violence and Parental Child Abduction*, 1st ed., Intersentia, Cambridge 2022, pp. 67–81.

2. ASSESSING HARM IN CASES INVOLVING DOMESTIC AND FAMILY VIOLENCE

The harmful effects of domestic violence may stem from abuse perpetrated on the child or by exposure to the abuse. In international child abduction cases, domestic violence was identified as a matter in need of urgent attention,[14] especially in relation to Article 13(1)(b).[15] Indeed, to ignore the issue would be 'inconsistent with and liable to undermine polices adopted in many countries to combat domestic violence'.[16] It underpins the argument that there are possible weaknesses in the Hague Convention to adequately protect victims[17] of domestic violence caught up in cross-border proceedings.[18] Debatably, such weaknesses span from the lack of sufficient recognition of the issue during the drafting of the Hague Convention, to the absence of any specific comprehensive statistics on how many Hague Convention cases, across jurisdictions, involve allegations or findings of domestic violence at this time.[19]

For the purposes of this chapter, the definition of domestic violence (to include family violence) is derived primarily[20] from Article 3(b) of the Council of Europe Convention on Prevention and Combating Violence against Women and Domestic Violence, Istanbul, 11.V.2011 (the Istanbul Convention).

---

14 Permanent Bureau of the Hague Conference, 'Domestic and Family Violence and the Article 13 '"Grave Risk"' Exception in the Operation of the Hague Convention of 25 October 1980 on the Civil Aspects of International Child Abduction: A Reflection Paper' (May 2011) para. 1 <https://assets.hcch.net/upload/wop/abduct2011pd09e.pdf> accessed 30.05.2022.

15 ibid., in the context of defences under the Hague Convention, domestic and family violence received particular attention at the Sixth Special Commission Meeting in June 2011. The discussion was based on a Reflection Paper drawn up by the Permanent Bureau recommending that 'further work be undertaken to promote consistency in the interpretation and application of Article 13(1) *b)* in relation to allegations of domestic and family violence'. See chap. 3 on discussions regarding the Special Commission and their recommendations.

16 R. Schuz, *The Hague Child Abduction Convention: A Critical Analysis*, Hart Publishing, Oxford 2013, p. 314.

17 The victims include the parent and/or the child. Whilst the Hague Convention is concerned with the welfare of the child, it is argued that children can be direct or indirect victims of domestic violence (the latter is premised on domestic violence witnessed by children).

18 R. Schuz, 'Thirty Years of the Hague Convention: A Children's Rights Perspective' in A. Diduck, N. Peleg and H. Reece, *Law in Society: Reflections on Children, Family, Culture and Philosophy: Essays in Honour of Michael Freeman*, Brill Nijhoff, Leiden 2015, pp. 607–33, at p. 607.

19 Permanent Bureau of the Hague Conference, 'Domestic and Family Violence and the Article 13 "Grave Risk" Exception in the Operation of the Hague Convention of 25 October 1980 on the Civil Aspects of International Child Abduction: A Reflection Paper' (May 2011), para. 3.

20 Also noting the definition of 'domestic and family violence' in the Permanent Bureau, 'Guide to Good Practice under the HCCH Convention of 25 October 1980 on the Civil Aspects of International Child Abduction – Part VI – Article 13(1)(b)' HCCH, 2020, [11].

Domestic violence is defined there as 'all acts of physical, sexual, psychological or economic violence that occur within the family or domestic unit or between former or current spouses or partners, whether or not the perpetrator shares or has shared the same residence with the victim'. Domestic violence remains an international problem.[21] Accordingly, for the purposes of this chapter, the focus is on the link between domestic violence and the harm suffered by children who are exposed to such violence.[22] It should be pointed out that this chapter recognizes that domestic violence can affect any gender or familial structure. However, in the context of international child abduction, the evaluation is based on domestic violence against women (and children) as in the majority of cases, allegations are against fathers as the perpetrators of violence towards the mother.[23] As Freeman explains, the problems of domestic violence 'cannot be solved or ameliorated until they are properly understood'.[24] Therefore, primary carer parents may be identified as vulnerable persons requiring protection, alongside their children. In recent times, in particular efforts from the Hague Conference and case law, there have been general developments recognizing (i) the grave risk of harm from the impact of domestic violence witnessed by the child; (ii) the grave risk of harm from the resulting separation of a parent who feels unable to return due to fear of the left-behind parent; (iii) that protective measures for the parent are in effect or by extension measures that protect the child. However, there is still much ground to cover.

---

21 As evidenced by a variety of research papers prepared for The Council of Europe Parliamentary Recommendations in the drafting of the Istanbul Convention including the following: Recommendation 1450 (2000) on Violence against women in Europe, Recommendation 1817 (2007) on Parliaments united in combating domestic violence against women: mid-term assessment of the Campaign, Recommendation 1891 (2009) on Migrant women: at particular risk from domestic violence, Recommendation 1905 (2010) on Children who witness domestic violence, Recommendation 260(2009) Combating domestic violence against women, and Resolution 279 (2009) Combating domestic violence against women of the Congress of Local and Regional Authorities of the Council of Europe. See also N. Lowe and G. Douglas, *Bromley's Family Law*, 11th ed., Oxford University Press, Oxford 2015, pp. 164–210.

22 Article 19(1) of the United Nations, Convention on the Rights of the Child 1989 (UNCRC) specifies that 'State Parties shall take all appropriate legislative, administrative, social and educational measures to protect the child from all forms of physical or mental violence'. Subsequently, the UN Committee on the Rights of the Child clarified that mental violence referred to 'psychological maltreatment, mental abuse, verbal and emotional abuse or neglect' which included 'exposure to domestic violence': UN Committee on the Rights of the Child, General comment No.13(2011): The right of the child to freedom from all forms of violence (2011) 9 <http://www.refworld.org/docid/4e6da4922.html> accessed 14.05.2022.

23 The majority of cases in a given sample: Permanent Bureau of the Hague Conference, 'Domestic and Family Violence and the Article 13 "Grave Risk" Exception in the Operation of the Hague Convention of 25 October 1980 on the Civil Aspects of International Child Abduction: A Reflection Paper' (May 2011), para. 49.

24 M. Freeman, 'Michael Freeman and Domestic Violence' in A. Diduck, N. Peleg and H. Reece, *Law in Society: Reflections on Children, Family, Culture and Philosophy: Essays in Honour of Michael Freeman*, Brill Nijhoff, Leiden 2015, pp. 309–29, at p. 310.

2.1. THE CHANGING FACE OF THE PERCEIVED ABDUCTOR

The drafting of Article 13(1)(b) in the late 1970s was premised on stereotypical abductors being non-custodial fathers. One of the documents available to the delegates at the Fourteenth Session of the Hague Conference was the Summary of findings by the International Social Services (ISS).[25] The report found that fathers were abducting more than mothers.[26] It revealed that in 80 cases, the father (or the father's relatives) were the abductor, in comparison to 18 cases where it was the mother or her relative. Notably, however, it was indicated in the report by the German ISS branch that the findings should be approached cautiously as it does not necessarily mean that mothers abduct less often than fathers, instead mothers were not always immediately recognized as having abducted the child.[27] Nonetheless, Dyer's report[28] describes a likely motive as 'frustration on the part of the non-custodial parent when unjustifiably deprived of the right of visitation with the child'[29] and thereafter the report refers to a father, as opposed to a mother, with whom a child was entrusted for visitation.[30] Thus, it was believed that fathers would be the ones unhappy with the outcome of the custodial decision and therefore likely to abduct, whilst mothers were more likely to obtain custody of the child(ren).[31] The Explanatory Report, in its analysis of the potential abductors in Hague Convention cases, emphasizes this gender bias.[32] It notes that:

> since the idea of 'family' was more or less wide, depending on the different cultural conceptions which surrounded it, it was felt better to hold a wide view which would, for example, allow removals by a grandfather or an adoptive father to be characterized as child abduction, in accordance with the Convention's use of that term.[33]

---

25 Permanent Bureau of the Hague Conference, Summary of Findings on a Questionnaire studied by International Social Service (*Preliminary Document No 3 of February 1979)* Actes et Documents of the XIVth Session (Child Abduction), pp. 130–43.

26 ibid., p. 136.

27 ibid., p. 134.

28 A preliminary document produced for the Fourteenth Session of the Hague Conference.

29 A. Dyer, 'Report on International Child Abduction by One Parent Legal Kidnapping', Preliminary Document No 1 of August 1978, III Hague Conference on Private International Law, Acts and Documents of the XIVth Session (Child Abduction) (1980) pp. 12, 19.

30 ibid., p. 21.

31 P. Beaumont and P. McEleavy, *The Hague Convention on International Child Abduction*, Oxford University Press, Oxford 1999, pp. 13–15. See also E.B. Crawford and J.M. Carruthers, *International Private Law: A Scots Perspective*, 4th ed., W. Green, Edinburgh 2015, 496; P. Beaumont and P. McEleavy, *Anton's Private International Law*, 3rd ed., W. Green, Edinburgh 2011, p. 817.

32 M.H. Weiner, 'The potential and challenges of transnational litigation for feminist concerned about domestic violence here and abroad' (2003) 11(2) *Journal of Gender, Social Policy & the Law* 799.

33 E. Pérez-Vera, 'Explanatory Report on the 1980 Hague Child Abduction Convention, Acts and Documents of the Fourteenth Session' (1982) para. 81.

The examples given do not refer to a grandmother or adoptive mother, thereby highlighting that the preparation of the Hague Convention was on the basis of a male potential abductor. As discussed, the emergent picture that the majority of abductors were mothers in Hague return cases was only identified post-drafting of the Hague Convention.[34] These situations often include mothers who have decided to leave a foreign country following the break-up of their relationship with the child's father. In some cases, their decision to leave is motivated by the need to flee from domestic violence. With this sociological change in the profile of the typical abductor came the tension that arises from addressing domestic violence allegations in a provision that is expected to be interpreted in a restrictive fashion.[35] The public image that fathers were more likely to abduct children was underlined as a troubling feature of the Article 13(1)(b) grave risk of harm exception.[36] It has been construed as 'gender politics', in that this has come to affect how the exceptions and obligations under the Hague Convention are interpreted. Silberman opines that this has gone as far as to jeopardize the effectiveness of the Hague Convention.[37] This view was echoed by Kaye who highlighted serious concerns over the dangers of overlooking 'circumstances surrounding abductions' that were 'inevitably gendered'.[38] Freeman also argued that the Hague Convention needs to 'operate in a gender sensitive manner'[39] and has called for 'additional consideration of this underlying fact'[40] in examining the grave risk of harm and for the Article 13(1)(b) threshold to be treated differently[41] where the primary carer is the taking parent. Ripley disagrees with this notion, commenting that the 'increase in primary-carer abductions

---

34 N. Lowe et al.'s findings that show a majority of taking parents were mothers: 69 per cent in 2008, 68 per cent in 2003 and 69 per cent in 1999.

35 E. Pérez-Vera, 'Explanatory Report on the 1980 Hague Child Abduction Convention, Acts and Documents of the Fourteenth Session' (1982) available at <https://assets.hcch.net/upload/expl28.pdf> at para. 34. This Report records the expectation that the interpretation of the exception of Article 13 (1)(b) should be in a 'restrictive fashion'.

36 L. Silberman, 'Patching Up the Abduction Convention: A Call for a New International Protocol and a Suggestion for Amendments to ICARA' (2003) 38 *Texas International Law Journal* 44.

37 L. Silberman, 'The Hague Child Abduction Convention Turns Twenty: Gender Politics and Other Issues' (2000) 33 *New York University Journal of International Law & Politics* 221.

38 M. Kaye, 'The Hague convention and the flight from domestic violence: How women and children are being returned by coach and four' (1999) 13(2) *International Journal of Law, Policy and the Family* 191.

39 M. Freeman, 'Primary Carers and the Hague Child Abduction Convention' (2001) *International Family Law* 42.

40 M. Freeman, 'In the Best Interests of Internationally Abducted Children? – Plural, Singular, Neither or Both?' (2002) *International Family Law* 77.

41 M. Freeman, 'Primary Carers and the Hague Child Abduction Convention' (2001) *International Family Law* 42, 140.

does not … justify the use of a different threshold'.[42] Arguably, the terminology provided under the Article 13(1)(b) exception remains adequate in applying to cases involving allegations of domestic violence as it has enabled flexibility in interpretation and application, albeit such flexibility has led to the varying approaches amongst Contracting States.[43] A core issue is the lack of a mechanism within the Hague Convention to properly to ameliorate the grave risk of harm by facilitating the safe return of children.[44] A wider problem was the lack of consistency among Contracting States in the approach to the interpretation and application of Article 13(1)(b) in cases involving domestic violence. The Hague Conference has sought to address this problem by setting up a Working Group to produce a Guide to Good Practice on Article 13(1)(b).[45] That Guide was published in 2020.[46]

2.2. RECOGNIZING INTIMIDATORY TACTICS UNDER ARTICLE 13(1)(A)

Intimidatory tactics in litigation and court trials is not unfamiliar. Hague Convention return proceedings are not exempt from this, especially in cases involving domestic violence where the issue of coercive and controlling behaviour is at play. In this context, intimidatory tactics may arise as part of a pattern of post-separation abuse. Article 13(1)(a) provides grounds for refusing a return if the court is satisfied that at the time of the wrongful removal, the left-behind parent was not exercising custody rights. In circumstances were the applicant knowingly or is found to have knowingly mounted litigation when it is determined that custody rights were not being exercised or where the applicant had consented to or acquiesced to the removal/retention, this could amount to intimidatory tactics.

---

42 P. Ripley, 'A Defence of the Established Approach to the Grave Risk Exception in the Hague Child Abduction Convention' (2008) 4(3) *Journal of Private International Law* 459.

43 O. Momoh, 'The Interpretation and Application of Article 13(1) b) of the Hague Child Abduction Convention in Cases Involving Domestic Violence: Revisiting X v. Latvia and the Principle of "Effective Examination"' (2019) 15 *Journal of Private International Law* 626, 633.

44 See Mr Justice Moylan, 'The Strengths and Weaknesses of the Hague Convention: a 'Child-Centric' view from an English Judge' (2010) *International Family Law* 78, 84: examining whether enough is done for returned children where Article 13(1)(b) defences were raised.

45 Permanent Bureau of the Hague Conference, Conclusions and Recommendations adopted by the Special Commission on the Practical Operation of the 1980 and 1996 Hague Conventions (1–10 June 2011), para. 123.

46 Permanent Bureau, 'Guide to Good Practice under the HCCH Convention of 25 October 1980 on the Civil Aspects of International Child Abduction – Part VI – Article 13(1)(b)' HCCH, 2020.

Weiner has argued that in considering domestic violence cases under the Hague Convention and the exceptions raised by taking parents, it must include the 'broader systemic pattern of gender socialization'[47] and 'coercive control'.[48] Kubitschek reiterates that the use of litigation by a perpetrator is a form of coercive control over battered women,[49] and therefore enabling perpetrators to use the Hague Convention as a tool of abuse.[50] Where domestic violence is concerned, intimidatory tactics, abusive litigation or legal bullying can be a form of coercive and controlling behaviour which is abusive.[51] Psychological and emotional harm are consequences of coercive and controlling behaviour for the victim that cannot be understated, though one might see how evidential difficulties may arise in persuading the court that these tactics are being employed. In the changing landscape of the recognition of the various ways in which domestic abuse may present itself, it will be a challenge to effectively address this. Encouragingly, the Guide to Good Practice on Article 13(1)(b)[52] recognizes that to harm a parent, whether physically or psychologically could constitute a grave risk of harm to a child,[53] but much like the high threshold of Article 13(1)(b) cases, the Guide notes that this recognition occurs in 'exceptional circumstances'.[54] There is a distinction, as clearly the Guide is concerned with Article 13(1)(b), but by virtue of acknowledging the psychological harm to a parent as capable of causing a grave risk to the child, there is no reason why the source of that harm cannot stem from intimidatory and abusive litigation. Similarly, there is no reason why such harm cannot also be pleaded under Article 13(1)(b).

---

47 M.H. Weiner, 'The potential and challenges of transnational litigation for feminist concerned about domestic violence here and abroad' (2003) 11(2) *Journal of Gender, Social Policy & the Law* 760, 787, citing E.M. Schneider, 'Battered Women & Feminist Lawmaking' Yale University Press 2000, p. 230.

48 ibid.

49 C.A. Kubitschek, 'Failure of the Hague Abduction Convention to Address Domestic Violence and its Consequences' (2014) 9 *The Journal of Comparative Law* 113, citing S.L. Miller and N.L. Smolter, "'Paper Abuse': When All Else Fails, Batterers Use Procedural Stalking, *Violence Against Women*, XVII (May 2011) 637.

50 ibid.

51 Ministry of Justice, England and Wales, Practice Direction 12J – Child Arrangements & Contact Order: Domestic Violence and Harm, para. 3 <https://www.justice.gov.uk/downloads/fjr/pd12J.pdf>.

52 Permanent Bureau, 'Guide to Good Practice under the HCCH Convention of 25 October 1980 on the Civil Aspects of International Child Abduction – Part VI – Article 13(1)(b)', HCCH, 2020.

53 Permanent Bureau, 'Guide to Good Practice under the HCCH Convention of 25 October 1980 on the Civil Aspects of International Child Abduction – Part VI – Article 13(1)(b)', HCCH, 2020, [28].

54 ibid.

2.3. THE GRAVE RISK OF HARM UNDER ARTICLE 13(1)(B)

A child's exposure to domestic violence can constitute a grave risk of harm. The HCCH Guide to Good Practice confidently reflects this stance. The Honourable Diana Bryant AO, QC, Chair of the Working Group on the Guide states that 'scientific literature has established that, in some cases, exposure to violence itself creates a grave risk to the child, as can the taking parent's inability to care for the child as a result of the violence. The drafters of the Guide were also of that view'.[55] Article 13(1)(b) of the Hague Convention provides that the competent authority is not bound to return a child if it is established that there is a grave risk that return would expose the child to physical or psychological harm or otherwise place the child in an intolerable situation. A taking parent may invoke Article 13(1)(b) on the grounds of domestic violence; usually perpetrated on that parent and witnessed by the child. Nevertheless, the grave risk of harm should be specific to the child[56] not the parent, although witnessing domestic violence alone is sufficiently traumatizing to cause harm to children.[57] The recognition and acceptance that children exposed to domestic violence are victims of abuse has been growing for some time.[58] The challenge is ensuring the interpretation and application of Article 13(1)(b) in a manner that consistently takes into account the abuse of a parent and children being exposed to the grave risk of harm by the harmful effects of witnessing the abuse. Of course, in considering the grave risk of harm, Article 13(1)(b) is not just about the child's 'immediate future'[59] it is also about 'looking into the future: the situation as it would be if the child were to be returned forthwith to her home country'.[60]

---

55 D. Bryant AO, QC, Response to Professors Rhona Schuz and Merle H. Weiner ('the authors'), 'A mistake waiting to happen: the failure to correct the Guide to Good Practice on Article 13(1)(b)' [2020] IFL 207. Cf. Rhona Schuz and Merle Weiner, A mistake waiting to happen: the failure to correct the *Guide to Good Practice on Article 13(1)(b)*, [2020] IFL 87.

56 *Re S (Abduction: Custody)* [2002] EWCA Civ 908; *Re S (A Child) (Abduction: Grave Risk of Harm)* [2002] 1 WLR 3355, Ward LJ [3366].

57 ibid., [3370].

58 Council of Europe Treaty Series 210, 'Explanatory Report to the Council of Europe Convention on preventing and combating violence against women and domestic violence, Istanbul, 11.v.2011, para. 27 (hereafter 'Istanbul Convention Explanatory Report') <https://rm.coe.int/168008482e> accessed 12 May 2022. See also H. Hughes, 'Impact of Spouse Abuse on Children of Battered Women: Implications for Practice' (1992) 2(12) Violence Update 1, 9–11; C. Mirrlees-Black, 'Domestic Violence: Findings from the BCS Self-Completion Questionnaire, Home Office Research Study 191', Home Office, London 1999, p. 41.

59 *Re E (Children)* [2011] UKSC 27, [35]: stating that the court is concerned not only with the child's immediate future, because the need for effective protection may persist.

60 ibid.

2.3.1. The Approach to the Assessment of the Grave Risk of Harm

Two main distinct approaches have been identified in cases where domestic violence is raised under the grave risk of harm exception:[61] (i) 'the evaluative assessment approach', where the disputed facts relevant to the allegations of domestic violence are tested by the court, considering all available documentary evidence and at times oral accounts; and (ii) 'the protective measures approach',[62] where the court assumes that the allegations of domestic violence are true, and taking the allegations at their highest without assessing their merits, the court determines whether there are adequate protective measures to ameliorate the grave risk. The latter approach appears to place primary focus on assessing the suitability of protective measures before or as a substitute for investigating the disputed facts.

The recently completed POAM project and published Best Practice Guide endorses the evaluative assessment approach[63] over the protective measures approach. Importantly, the evaluative assessment is preferred in the HCCH Guide to Good Practice on Article 13(1)(b).[64] The evaluative assessment approach is considered more appropriate in cases involving domestic violence. This may remain a controversial position as English case law has demonstrated.[65] Indeed, the Guide acknowledges that in some jurisdictions, courts 'begin by asking: are there adequate and effective measures of protection available'.[66] Suffice it to say,

---

61 Permanent Bureau of the Hague Conference, 'Guide to Good Practice under the Convention of 25 October 1980 on the Civil Aspects of International Child Abduction: Part VI Article 13(1)(b)', HCCH, 2020. For more discussion on the approaches to the assessment of grave risk, see POAM Best Practice Guide s. 5.1.2, O. Momoh, 'The interpretation and application of Article 13(1) b) of the Hague Child Abduction Convention in cases involving domestic violence: Revisiting X v Latvia and the principle of "effective examination"' (2019) 15(3) *Journal of Private International Law* 626; K. Trimmings and O. Momoh, 'Intersection between Domestic Violence and International Parental Child Abduction: Protection of Abducting Mothers in Return Proceedings' (2021) 35(1) *International Journal of Law, Policy and the Family* 1, 8. See also POAM National Report – UK at p. 3.2. The report further notes that 'additionally, isolated incidences of alternative approaches have been recorded, although these remain largely non-theorized and conceptually underdeveloped'.

62 See, e.g., *Re E (Children) (Abduction: Custody Appeal)* [2011] UKSC 27.

63 O. Momoh, 'The interpretation and application of Article 13(1) b) of the Hague Child Abduction Convention in cases involving domestic violence: Revisiting X v Latvia and the principle of "effective examination"' (2019) 15(3) *Journal of Private International Law* 626, 638–43.

64 Permanent Bureau of the Hague Conference, 'Guide to Good Practice under the Convention of 25 October 1980 on the Civil Aspects of International Child Abduction: Part VI Article 13(1)(b)', HCCH, 2020, p. 31.

65 POAM National Report – UK, case law analysis <https://research.abdn.ac.uk/wp-content/uploads/sites/15/2020/02/National-report_UK.pdf> accessed 31.05.2022.

66 Permanent Bureau of the Hague Conference, 'Guide to Good Practice under the Convention of 25 October 1980 on the Civil Aspects of International Child Abduction: Part VI Article 13(1)(b)', HCCH, 2020, p. 33.

compelling arguments in favour of the evaluative approach include the point that to reliably assess the 'grave risk of harm' and effectiveness of protective measures, the merits of the domestic violence alleged needs to be evaluated, so as not to put 'the cart before the horse' by considering 'protective measures to mitigate risk before that risk has been established and assessed'.[67] Therefore, it is yet to be seen whether there will be an intentional shift towards the evaluative assessment approach endorsed by the Guide or whether judicial autonomy will continue to prevail with consequences on such cases. In these circumstances, if such guidance is afforded little regard to promote consistency, then the challenge remains.

2.3.2. *Evidential Difficulties*

The highest rate of non-reported violence is attributed to gender-based violence.[68] Evidential challenges are part and parcel of Hague return proceedings because two key features make it so; first, dealing with cross-border proceedings where the events alleged happened in another country, and second dealing with domestic violence which often happens behind closed doors, and may go unreported. In some instances, a taking parent may have some evidence which may include one or a combination of the following, non-harassment order, custody orders, protective orders such as 'non-molestation' order, 'ouster' orders, police reports, medical reports, reports from an educational setting, or perhaps criminal or other injunctive proceedings dealing with abusive behaviour. As part of the POAM Best Practice Guide,[69] an evidence map was developed to aid the approach to dealing with the challenges that arise in seeking to evaluate the merits of the allegations raised, and whether they amount to a grave risk of harm.

The POAM Best Practice Guide considers support that may be available from Central Authorities, which in itself may be a challenge,[70] and proposes a way forward in cases were evidence is scarce or difficult to obtain in a cross-border setting. In assessing the existence of a grave risk of harm (and/or the merits

---

[67] A. Barnett, 'Draft Guide to Good Practice on Article 13(1)(b) of the Hague Convention on International Child Abduction – a perspective from England and Wales', p. 18, in *Eight Letters Submitted to the United States Department of State and the Permanent Bureau of the Hague Conference on Private International Law about a Draft Guide for Article 13(1)b) and Related Draft Documents that were circulated for comment prior to the October 2017 meeting of the Seventh Special Commission on the 1980 Hague Child Abduction Convention at The Hague*, <https://law.ucdavis.edu/faculty/bruch/files/Letters-re-Hague-Convention.pdf>.

[68] R. Manjoo and J. Jones (eds), *The Legal Protection of Women From Violence. Normative Gaps in International Law*, Routledge, Boca Raton 2018; R. Shreeves and M. Prpic, *Violence against women in the EU. State of play*, European Parliamentary Research Service, 2019, p. 3.

[69] The Best Practice Guide – Protection of Abducting Mothers in Return Proceedings, s. 5.1.3.3: 'Evidence Roadmap', 'Oral Evidence', 'Navigating the Evidence Type'.

[70] POAM Best Practice Guide, s. 5.1.3.3.

of the disputed allegations of domestic violence), the POAM Guide[71] observes that courts may consider (1) documentary evidence, (2) affidavit evidence from the parties, (3) affidavit evidence from witnesses, (4) to commission an expert report from a child psychologist, (5) to meet with the child in person, (6) to commission an expert report to examine the mother's mental health, (7) limited oral evidence or as part of a composite fact-finding or finding-of-fact hearing(s). The HCCH Guide to Good Practice does not comprehensively address evidential difficulties and how one tackles this, but it does reflect on good practice in instructing an expert and producing a report to the court in a timely fashion, taking into account the potential of oral evidence from that expert.[72]

2.4. HUMAN RIGHTS VIOLATION UNDER ARTICLE 20

Article 20 may be evoked on the basis that the abuse suffered violates human rights and fundamental freedoms, thus giving way to refusing the return of a child on this basis. The complexities of cases that require the courts to consider the interplay between obligations of the State under the Hague Convention and human rights and fundamental freedoms under the 1951 Refugee Convention is a challenge for the Hague Convention.[73] For instance, it can be argued that domestic violence is a form of persecution, an argument that may gain ground particularly in cases that deals with the interplay between the Hague Convention and the 1951 Refugee Convention. The Refugee Convention seeks to protect those entitled to asylum from refoulment to the country from which they have sought refuge[74] or other country where life is threatened.[75] Women fall under a particular social group within the meaning of Article 1A of the Refugee Convention. It may be argued that a mother has fled a country where her human rights had been violated in contravention with Article 3 (freedom from torture,

---

71 POAM Best Practice Guide, s. 5.1.3.1, figure 5 'Evidence Roadmap'.

72 Permanent Bureau of the Hague Conference, 'Guide to Good Practice under the HCCH Convention of 25 October 1980 on the Civil Aspects of International Child Abduction – Part VI – Article 13(1)(b)', HCCH, 2020, pp. 57–58.

73 A. Fiorini, 'The Protection of the Best Interests of Migrant Children – Private International Law Perspectives' in G. Biagioni and F. Ippolito (eds), *Migrant Children in the XXI Century: Selected Issues of Public and Private International Law*, 'La ricerca del diretto' Series (Editoriale Scientifica, Naples 2016), pp. 379–417 and L. Carpaneto, 'The Recognition of Protection Measures Affecting Migrant Children' in G. Biagioni and F. Ippolito (eds), *Migrant Children in the XXI Centrury: Selected Issues of Public and Private International Law*, 'La ricerca del diretto' Series (Editoriale Scientifica, Naples 2016), pp. 419–57, at pp. 425–34. See also *G (Appellant) v. G (Respondent)* [2021] UKSC 9.

74 Article 33 (Prohibition of Expulsion or Return), the Geneva Refugee Convention 1951.

75 The Refugee Convention, 1951, The Travaux Preparatoires Analysed with a Commentary by Dr Paul Weis <https://www.unhcr.org/media/refugee-convention-1951-travaux-preparatoires-analysed-commentary-dr-paul-weis> accessed 31.05.2022.

inhuman or degrading treatment), Article 8 (family and private life) and/or Protocol 1, and even Article 1 (peaceful enjoyment of property). Settled case law on the matter is ample, going back to English House of Lords decisions.[76]

In some instances, one may argue that the failure or impossibility of the State to protect the victim is a part of the human rights violations which give rise to the evoking of the Article 20 exception. In *Blondin v. Dubois* the US second Circuit upheld the district court's findings of domestic abuse and noted that the particular circumstances of the case made protective measures inadequate. The mother's allegations of domestic abuse included physical and emotional abuse throughout the marriage, perpetrated on both her and the children (step-son and daughter). The mother asserted that on two occasions, she left the home with the children, including one in which she spent eight or nine months in a battered women's shelter but upon reconciliation on both occasions, the violence resumed. The court found that, although capable and willing, the French authorities face an 'impossible task'[77] in ensuring that the children would not be exposed to a grave risk of harm resulting from a recurring traumatic stress disorder. The expert report and testimony of the child psychiatrist and psychologist had concluded that the children associated France with their father's abuse and the trauma suffered, and therefore returning them would almost certainly evoke the traumatic stress disorder that they had suffered. In addition to a situation like *Blondin*, other circumstances might include where the father has repeatedly violated protective orders.[78] In *Walsh v. Walsh*[79] the First Circuit refused a return order in circumstances where the father's perpetual disobedience of orders meant that any protective measures would be ineffective. Similarly, as emphasized in *State Central Authority, Secretary to the Department of Human Services v. Mander*,[80] the assessment of whether protective measures were adequate included considering the left-behind father's behaviour, such as whether there had been a history of disobeying orders and violating undertakings in the home country. In this case, it was found that neither undertakings offered by the father nor a barring order made by the district court would be sufficient given his 'history of violating orders issued by any court, Irish or American'.[81]

---

76 *Islam (A.P.) v. Secretary of State for the Home Department Regina v. Immigration Appeal Tribunal and Another Ex Parte Shah (A.P.) (Conjoined Appeals)* 25 March 1999; *SN & HM and 3 Dependants (Divorced Women – Risk on Return) Pakistan v. Secretary of State for the Home Department, CG* [2004] UKIAT 283; *FS (Domestic Violence – SN and HM – OGN) Pakistan v. Secretary of State for the Home Department, CG* [2006] UKAIT 23.

77 *Blondin v. Blondin* 283 F.3d 153 (2nd Cir. 2001) para. B.

78 *Achakzad v. Zemaryalai* [2011] W.D.F.L. 2, 20.07.2010.

79 *Walsh v. Walsh* 221 F.3d 204, 221 (1st Cir. 2000).

80 *State Central Authority, Secretary to the Department of Human Services v. Mander*, No. (P) MLF1179 of 2003, p. 25 (INCADAT database).

81 ibid.

Taking such circumstances into account and reflecting on Lord Hoffmann's dicta in *SN & HM*, one may argue that these are human rights violations that 'cannot be ignored merely on the ground that this would imply criticism of the legal or social arrangements in another country'.[82] Well-founded fear engages a subjective and objective element: a fear of persecution with an objectively justifiable basis. The serious harm is the domestic violence and other violent and criminal acts that may be perpetrated by the left-behind parent; and the failure of the state to protect may be seen from the lack of effective measures of protection or failure to adequately follow up on complaints made. In essence, for the purposes of the Refugee Convention, women who are subject to domestic violence are a particular social group. Once the court is satisfied that the mother is at risk of domestic violence, her gender is a protected characteristic for which arguably human rights violations may occur, thereby engaging Article 20 of the Hague Convention, which by extension impacts the child.

3. PROTECTIVE MEASURES IN RETURN PROCEEDINGS

Perhaps one of the biggest challenges in Hague return cases involving domestic violence is the absence of direct jurisdictional power to make enforceable protective measures. This is particularly so in cases where the court is considering whether adequate and effective protective measures would enable the safe return of the child. In cases where the domestic violence is directed towards a parent and witnessed by the child, there is a gap in the protection of a primary carer parent who wishes to accompany the child back to their country of habitual residence. The HCCH Guide to Good Practice recognizes that a grave risk may exist for a child from harm directed towards a taking parent.[83] Thus, notwithstanding that the Hague Conference has for some time recognized that 'the protection of the child may also sometimes require steps to be taken to protect an accompanying parent',[84] the mechanism for such protection does not exist under the Hague Convention. As the POAM project has examined, quite aside from the use of mirror orders, Hague return courts may look to two core instruments to establish international jurisdiction to issue protective

---

82 *SN & HM (Divorced Women – Risk on Return) Pakistan CG* [2004] UKIAT 283, para. 34.

83 Permanent Bureau, 'Guide to Good Practice under the HCCH Convention of 25 October 1980 on the Civil Aspects of International Child Abduction – Part VI – Article 13(1)(b)', HCCH, 2020, p. 26.

84 Hague Conference on Private International Law, Conclusions and Recommendations of the Fifth Meeting of the Special Commission (2006), para. 1.1.12, <https://assets.hcch.net/upload/concl28sc5_e.pdf>.

measures. These two instruments are Brussels Ia,[85] Brussels IIa[86] and the 1996 Hague Convention.[87] The POAM Best Practice Guide sets out in much detail the pathways to establishing jurisdictions, cross-border circulation and applicable law.[88]

In intra-EU cases, turning to the Recast Regulation, firstly it is of note that 'international child abduction' has been added to its title, giving focus to the utility of this instrument in international child abduction cases. Secondly, the Recast Regulation continues to retain key provisions relating to jurisdiction such as Article 15[89] and Article 27(3).[90]

Interestingly, the Recast Regulation includes a provision in the preamble that is arguably adaptable to situations where protective measures are required for the parent. The Recast Regulation reflects on the need for provisional protective measures in international child abduction cases 'aimed' at protecting the child.[91] It further provides that protective measures may include a child being allowed to 'stay with the abducting parent who is the primary carer'[92] until custody decisions are made following their return. The provision acknowledges that the adequacy of such measures to protect the child would depend on the 'concrete grave risk'[93] that the child has been exposed to. It follows that: (a) an accompanying primary parent is recognized as a measure of protection; (b) that measure of protection is subject to an assessment as to its adequacy; and (c) there is an expectation that the safety of that accompanying parent is part of measures 'aimed' at the child.

Of note, paragraph 45 in the Recast Regulation introduces the word 'concrete' vis-à-vis the grave risk. This is a new development that may be cause for concern. The term concrete is often connected with the adequacy of protection measures, not the other way round. This is expressly stated in the Brussels IIa Practice Guide.[94] To describe the grave risk as 'concrete' is surely to reverse the burden and standard for establishing measures of protection, adding 'gloss'[95] to the

---

85 Regulation (EU) No. 1215/2012 of the European Parliament and of the Council of 12 December 2012 on jurisdiction and the recognition and enforcement of judgments in civil and commercial matters, Article 7(2).

86 Now based on the Recast Regulation, Articles 15, 27.

87 POAM Best Practice Guide'), see 'pathways' in s. 5.

88 ibid., s. 5.2.1.

89 Previously Article 20 of Brussels IIa.

90 Previously Article 11(4) of Brussels IIa.

91 Recast Regulation, para. 59.

92 Recast Regulation, para. 45.

93 ibid.

94 Practice Guide for the Application of the new Brussels II Regulation (2005) para 2.2. Available at <https://op.europa.eu/en/publication-detail/-/publication/f7d39509-3f10-4ae2-b993-53ac6b9f93ed> accessed 31.05.2022. Brussels IIa, Practice Guide, p. 55. See also Anatol Dutta, 'Cross-border protection measures in the European Union' (2016) 12(1) *Journal of Private International Law* 180.

95 *Re E (Children)* [2011] UKSC 27, para. 31.

interpretation *and* application of Article 13(1)(b) that ought not to be, when one reflects on Baroness Hale's dicta in the Supreme Court decision in *Re E (Children)*, that Article 13(1)(b) should be applied sensibly.

3.1. EU INSTRUMENTS

3.1.1. Regulation 606/2013 on Mutual Recognition of Protection Measures in Civil Matters

The Regulation 606/2013 on mutual recognition of protection measures in civil matters ('Protection Measures Regulation') can be utilized to facilitate the protection of returning children and their mothers in child abduction cases committed against the background of domestic violence. The Protective Measures Regulation is based on Article 81 of the Treaty on the Functioning of the European Union (TFEU). Article 81 provides for the mutual recognition of civil protection measures across the EU by establishing 'rules for a simple and rapid mechanism for the recognition of protection measures ordered in a Member State in civil matters'.[96] Restrictions can be placed on the person causing risk, with a view to safeguarding the protected person's physical or psychological integrity.[97] The recognition of the protection measure is automatic, meaning that 'a protection measure ordered in a Member State shall be recognised in the other Member States without any special procedure being required and shall be enforceable without a declaration of enforceability being required'.[98] The protected person can bring enforcement proceedings in the Member State addressed if necessary, and the enforcement, including the sanctions and procedures relating to the breach of the protection order, are left to the law of that Member State.[99] The POAM project sheds light on the usefulness and utility of the Protective Measures Regulation, the extensive evaluative exercise during this project has led to a Best Practice Guide which provides helpful guidance on how the Protective Measures Regulation can work in practice. In some ways, it addresses a key challenge for the Hague Convention: the absence of a methodology that address the consequences of the exceptions to return. Having said this, the take up and increased utility of the Protective Measures Regulation is untested. It is not only its utility that is vital, but also the confidence that circulation, mutual recognition and enforcement will indeed take place once it reaches the Member State that the child has been returned to. Another challenge is that the Protective

96 Regulation 606/2013, Article 1.
97 Regulation 606/2013, Article 3(1).
98 Protection Measures Regulation, Article 4(1).
99 Protection Measures Regulation, Article 4(5).

Measures Regulation does not contain rules on applicable law or international jurisdiction. However, this issue is also comprehensively examined in the POAM Best Practice Guide,[100] whereby international jurisdiction can be established under Brussels IIa (now the Recast Regulation), the 1996 Hague Convention or even Brussels Ia, with the applicable law being the *lex fori* in all circumstances.

3.1.2. Directive 2011/99/EU on the European Protection Order

The mutual recognition procedure under the Directive 2011/99/EU on the European Protection Order ('the Directive') is given effect by implementation into national legislative frameworks. The Directive is based on Article 82(1) TFEU, on judicial cooperation in criminal matters. The aim of the Directive is to facilitate the mutual recognition of criminal protection orders made in the 'issuing State' to be recognized in the 'executing State'.[101] Pursuant to Article 2 of the Directive, a protection measure 'means a decision in criminal matters adopted in the issuing State in accordance with its national law and procedures ….'[102] This limits its utility in civil matters, in this instance international child abduction cases involving domestic violence. Where the Directive is applicable, Article 5 provides for a range of measures of protection that could apply in cases involving domestic violence; for example, a case where previous allegations of abuse resulted in criminal proceedings such as assault, battery or grievous bodily harm in the executing State. Article 5 reiterates the need for existing measures of protection under national law. The POAM Best Practice Guide recognizes the use of the Directive as measures of protection in the context of international parental child abduction but advocates for the Protective Measures Regulation as the preferred option where the choice presents itself.[103] This is because where the Hague return court seeks to utilize the Directive, it would not be possible to engage this instrument if the abuse is not/has not yet been criminalized in the executing State and/or there is no existing protecting measure under national law.

3.2. THE 1996 HAGUE CHILD PROTECTION CONVENTION

The 1996 Hague Convention has sought to fill the aforementioned 'gap' by providing the jurisdiction to issue measures based on the presence of the child in the territory of the State of refuge. To this end, the court dealing with the

100 POAM Best Practice Guide, s. 5.
101 Directive 2011/99, Article 2.
102 ibid.
103 POAM Best Practice Guide, s. 4.4.

return application would be the competent court to exercise the utility of this provision.[104]

Article 11 of the 1996 Hague Convention enables the court in 'all cases of urgency' to take 'necessary measures' of protection on the premise that the child is present in that jurisdiction at the time such measures are taken. In addition, it is expected that the provision under Article 11 enables measures taken to be recognized in all the Contracting States.[105] Article 11 allows the court in 'all cases of urgency' to take 'necessary measures' of protection on the premise that the child is present in that jurisdiction at the time such measures are taken. Firstly, the requirement that the case has to be urgent is clearly established in cases where a return is imminent in the face of established grave risk of harm. There is no definition of urgency;[106] whereas on the one hand it has been stated that the concept of urgency should be interpreted strictly,[107] on the other hand, it is difficult to envisage that in an abduction case, the court would not consider it urgent.[108]

Article 23 (1) of the 1996 Convention sets out a rule of recognition whereby 'measures taken by the authorities of a Contracting State shall be recognised by operation of law in all other Contracting States'. However, pursuant to Article 23(2), such measures may be challenged on six grounds and recognition may be refused.[109] The term recognition 'by operation of law' means that the measures can be recognized in the requested State and have effect without the commencement of proceedings.[110] The measure to be recognized can be evidenced by way of written documentation or in urgent cases, by telephone.[111] Once the enforceable measure is taken in one Contracting State, Article 26(1) provides that such a measure shall 'upon request by an interested party, be declared enforceable

---

104 See the POAM Best Practice Guide, s. 5.2.1.1 'Pathway 3'.

105 See P. Lagarde, 'Explanatory Report on the 1996 Hague Child Protection Convention' II (1998) 534–605, para. 72 (hereafter 'Lagarde Report'). See also POAM Best Practice Guide, s. 5.2.1.1 'Pathway 2'.

106 P. Lagarde, ibid., para. 68.

107 Permanent Bureau of the Hague Conference, Practical Handbook on the operation of the Hague Convention of 19 October 1996 on Jurisdiction, Applicable Law, recognition, Enforcement and Co-operation in respect of Parental responsibility and Measures of the Protection of Child (2014) para. 63 (hereafter 'Practical Handbook on the 1996 Convention') <https://assets.hcch.net/upload/handbook34en.pdf>.

108 *Re J (A Child) (Reunite International Abduction Centre and others intervening)* [2015] UKSC 70; [2015] 3 WLR 1827, per Baroness Hale, at [39]. See also Edward Devereux, '*Re J*: the 1996 Hague Convention in the Supreme Court' (2016) *International Family Law* 21.

109 Article 23(2) provides an exhaustive list of the grounds in which recognition may be refused.

110 Permanent Bureau of the Hague Conference, Practical Handbook on the operation of the Hague Convention of 19 October 1996 on Jurisdiction, Applicable Law, Recognition, Enforcement and Co-operation in Respect of Parental Responsibility and Measures of the Protection of Child (2014) 103.

111 ibid.

or registered for the purpose of enforcement in that other State according to the procedure provided in the law of the latter State'. Article 26(2) envisages that the procedure of declaration of enforceability and registration, which is governed by the law of the State of enforcement, must be 'simple and rapid'. However, it is also possible for such declaration to be refused on one of the grounds on which recognition can be denied pursuant to Article 23(2). Thereafter, Article 28 provides that once the measure has been declared enforceable or registered for enforcement, it has to be enforced as if it had been taken by the authorities of the State of enforcement. The actual enforcement takes place 'in accordance with the law of the requested State to the extent provided by such law, taking into consideration the best interests of the child'.[112]

In essence, in child abduction cases, the 1996 Hague Convention supports and supplements[113] the 1980 Convention[114] by addressing the lacuna that exists in the latter in relation to mechanism to ensure a safe return of a child and left-behind parent. In this respect, the 1996 Convention is capable of ensuring that children are adequately safeguarded where a return order is made. However, a challenge is that there are only 53 Contracting States to the 1996 Hague Convention, just over half of those party to the 1980 Hague Convection, therefore limiting the scope of its applicability. Nevertheless, where applicable protective orders can be made under Article 11 of the 1996 Convention and enforced under Article 23,[115] the 1996 Convention is particularly useful in circumstances where a return order is made.[116] Even where intra-EU cases are concerned, although

112 1996 Hague Child Protection Convention, Article 28.

113 ibid. It is also said to have inspired some of the rules under Brussels II *bis*, such as Article 15: T. Kruger and L. Samyn, 'Brussels II bis: successes and suggested improvements' (2016) 12 *Journal of Private International Law* 132, 150 discussing the interaction between Brussels II *bis* and the 1996 Convention.

114 See N. Lowe, 'The Impact of the 1996 Convention on International Child Abduction', Division 5, Chapter 5, *Clarke Hall & Morrison on Children*, Butterworths, London 2017, p. 882: It is further stated that its 'clear purpose' is to 'secure the primacy' of the Hague Convention. See also N. Lowe, 'The Applicable Laws Provisions of the 1996 Hague Convention on the Protection of Children and the Impact of the Convention on International Child Abduction' (2010) *International Family Law* 51; Permanent Bureau of the Hague Conference, Practical Handbook on the operation of the Hague Convention of 19 October 1996 on Jurisdiction, Applicable Law, Recognition, Enforcement and Co-operation in respect of Parental Responsibility and Measures of the Protection of Child (2014) <https://assets.hcch.net/upload/handbook34en.pdf>.

115 See discussion below on *Re Y (A Child) (Abduction: Undertakings Given for Return of Child)* [2013] EWCA Civ 129, [2013] 2 FLR 649 where undertakings given were enforceable under the 1996 Convention. See also Article 50 of the 1996 Convention provides that it 'shall not affect the application' of the Hague Convention and that it can be 'invoked for the purposes of obtaining the return of a child who has been wrongfully removed or retained or of organising access rights'.

116 Article 50 also provides that nothing precludes the provisions of the 1996 Convention from being invoked for the purposes of obtaining the return of the child.

the Recast Regulation takes priority over the 1996 Convention, it does not mean that the latter has no relevance.[117]

3.3. A GLOBAL CROSS-BORDER REGIME

In March 2011, the Hague Council on General Affairs and Policy of the Conference ('the Council') agenda included consideration of 'the topic of recognition of foreign civil protection orders made, for example, in the context of domestic violence cases'.[118] The objective is to develop a multilateral mechanism to assure protection of 'at risk' parents returning with their child. It is envisaged that this would enable the recognition and enforcement of any protection order in the country of return and thereby addressing the current gap in a 'global cross-border regime'.[119] Notably, the scope on its applicability imposes less conditions in comparison to the 1996 Hague Convention.[120] The proposed treaty suggests qualifying words including 'serious reasons' existing as to the 'risk to a person's physical and/or psychological 'integrity or liberty'.[121] The idea envisages a regime that is able to recognize and enforce measures including 'no contact' orders and 'stay-away' orders, although referred to as 'exclusion', 'eviction' or 'non-molestation' orders to protect against stalking and harassment.[122] This anticipated instrument would no doubt ameliorate some of the challenges that exists in the cross-border circulation, recognition and enforcement of protective measures in Hague return proceedings. As highlighted in the preliminary document, such measures are to be 'preventative and temporary' and in 'accordance with its national law'.[123]

---

117 N. Lowe, 'The Impact of the 1996 Convention on International Child Abduction', Division 5, Chapter 5, *Clarke Hall & Morrison on Children*, Butterworths, London 2017, p. 879. See, however, chap. 3.4(iv) which discusses the draft proposals for the recast of Brussels II *bis* in respect of EU Member States. Compare the proposed addition to enable measures taken by one Member State to be recognized and enforceable in all other Member States: 22. On Article 11 of the 1996 Convention and the relationship with EU law, see also P. Beaumont, L. Walker and J. Holliday, 'Conflicts of EU courts on child abduction: the reality of Article 11(6)–(8) Brussels IIa proceedings across the EU' (2016) 12(2) *Journal of Private International Law* 219.

118 Permanent Bureau of the Hague Conference, 'Recognition and Enforcement of Foreign Civil Protection Orders: A Preliminary Note' (March 2012) para. 1 <https://assets.hcch.net/docs/dec27663-d385-4919-9fa1-32b69ac89e4d.pdf>.

119 ibid., para. 8.

120 E.g., 'urgency' and 'necessary'.

121 Permanent Bureau of the Hague Conference, 'Recognition and Enforcement of Foreign Civil Protection Orders: A Preliminary Note' (March 2012) para. 1. <https://assets.hcch.net/docs/dec27663-d385-4919-9fa1-32b69ac89e4d.pdf> para. 28.

122 ibid., paras 8–16.

123 ibid.

4. CONCLUSION

The harmful consequences of domestic and family violence towards a child, or exposure to the abuse, can constitute a grave risk of harm. This acknowledgement is amply reinforced by international human rights instruments such as the UNCRC and the Istanbul Convention, as well as the observations in the HCCH Guide to Good Practice on Article 13(1)(b). As the definition of domestic and family violence has evolved over time – going beyond the traditional physical aspects of abuse – so too has its complexities. This is amplified by factors such as the inconsistencies in the interpretation and application of the grave risk of harm,[124] and evidential difficulties in assessing the factual allegations raised. There are also the disparities in hearing children in return proceedings and the manner in which they are heard, especially in cases involving domestic violence. Further, in the absence of direct jurisdictional power under the Hague Convention to make enforceable protective measures, engaging EU instruments or the 1996 Hague Convention is not without its challenges. Thus, the legal mechanisms and their application as measures of protection in cases of domestic violence has room for improvement. Perhaps the anticipated global cross-border regime is the most hopeful solution.

Although Article 13(1)(b) is the most prevalent exception relied upon in cases involving allegations of domestic and family violence, this chapter brings to focus other grounds for refusal that may be established with similar facts. For example, Article 13(1)(a) in respect of intimidatory tactics which goes to the heart of coercive and controlling abusive behaviour, and Article 20 by protecting the fundamental rights of accompanying parents, and by extension their children. As discussed, the protected characteristics of women as a particular social group within the meaning of the Refugee Convention may create the need for protection in circumstances where a well-founded fear as a victim of domestic violence is established in a particular case.

The harm from the abduction of children must be weighed against the harm from exposure to or suffering domestic and family violence. Finding solutions to the challenges of the Hague Convention in cases involving domestic violence cannot be a 'one model fits all' situation. However, it is important to strike a careful and fair balance between policy considerations and the interests of children. The remedying of international child abduction must make room, fully and unapologetically, for the interests of children caught up in cross-border proceedings involving domestic and family violence.

---

124 O. Momoh, 'The Interpretation and Application of Article 13(1) b) of the Hague Child Abduction Convention in Cases Involving Domestic Violence: Revisiting X v. Latvia and the Principle of "Effective Examination"' (2019) 15 *Journal of Private International Law* 626.

VIOLENCE AS NATIONAL HERITAGE?

The EU and CoE Strategies on Violence against Women and Domestic Violence

Laima VAIGĖ*

* ORCID ID: 0000-0002-3938-3657.

1. INTRODUCTION

In 2011, the Council of Europe (CoE) opened for signature the Convention on Preventing and Combating Violence against Women and Domestic Violence (the Istanbul Convention). It was the first time that the prohibition of violence against women and domestic violence became a treaty norm in Europe. The Convention has faced a significant backlash – a process driven by global anti-gender movements. The backlash culminated with Turkey withdrawing from the Istanbul Convention in 2021. Many Eastern European States either refused ratification, threatened to withdraw, or signed the Istanbul Convention with broad and arguably impermissible reservations, referring to their national identities.

Why are explicit treaty norms tackling violence against women and domestic violence viewed as contradicting States' national identities? Are there differences in European supranational strategies tackling violence, and why has the EU strategy caused less opposition at the national level? This chapter examines these questions. The strategies for tackling violence against women and domestic violence in the CoE and the EU are compared in search of answers. The text also offers an explanation as to why the strategies have been received so differently.

This chapter uses the approach 'What's the problem represented to be?' (WPR) by Carol Bacchi[1] to compare the framings of the problem in the Istanbul Convention and the EU law tackling violence against women and domestic violence. The WPR approach is a critical tool that allows problems in public policies to be illuminated, including problems that are implied in silences and assumptions. The six key questions of the WRP approach are (here, simplified):

1. What's the problem represented to be?
2. What assumptions underpin this representation?
3. How has this representation come about?
4. What is left unproblematic in this problem representation?
5. What effects are produced by this representation?
6. How has it been (or how could it be) questioned, disrupted and replaced?

The outline of the text is as follows. The chapter first introduces the key documents at the CoE and the EU level, which will be used as examples of the CoE and EU policies on tackling violence against women and domestic violence

---

1 C. Bacchi, 'Why Study Problematizations? Making Politics Visible' (2012) 2(1) *Open Journal of Political Science* 1.

(section 2). Section 3 focuses on comparing framings of the problem while going through six key questions of the WPR approach. Section 4 discusses why some Member States had a problem in accepting the Istanbul Convention but tolerate the EU law on this matter. In section 5, the prospect of combining the strategies is discussed. The chapter finishes with short conclusions and an outlook in section 6.

2. SUPRANATIONAL EUROPEAN STRATEGIES TACKLING VIOLENCE AGAINST WOMEN AND DOMESTIC VIOLENCE

2.1. THE ISTANBUL CONVENTION

The Istanbul Convention is an international treaty specifically designed for combating and preventing violence against women and domestic violence.[2] It is the very first regional treaty *in Europe* that tackles violence. The first regional treaty on violence against women globally, the Inter-American Convention on the Prevention, Punishment and Eradication of Violence against Women (Convention of Belém do Pará), was adopted in 1994 by the Organization of American States. The Istanbul Convention is 'more comprehensive' than regional treaties in this area but also 'significantly reinforces' these regional efforts.[3]

The Convention states at the start that 'women and girls are exposed to a higher risk of gender-based violence than men' but at the same time it provides that 'domestic violence affects women disproportionately, and that men may *also* be victims of domestic violence'.[4] Hence, the Istanbul Convention builds on the previous global and regional documents but takes a step away from essentialization of violence[5] as always constituting a case of discrimination experienced by women. That has been the case under the 1979 Convention for Elimination of all Forms of Discrimination against women (CEDAW), which

---

2 Council of Europe Convention on Preventing and Combating Violence against Women and Domestic Violence (CETS No. 210).

3 Para. 6 in Explanatory Report on CETS 210 – Violence against Women and Domestic Violence.

4 Preamble of the Istanbul Convention. My emphasis.

5 See, for instance, P. Scully, 'Vulnerable Women: a Critical Reflection on Human Rights Discourse and Sexual Violence' (2009) 23 *Emory International Law Review* 113; J. Goldscheid, 'Gender Neutrality, the "Violence against Women" Frame, and Transformative Reform' (2013–2014) 82 *UMKC Law Review* 623, 623–66.

due to its scope and aim, that is, the fight against discrimination, can only address violence as a *form of* discrimination against women.[6]

Although the CEDAW Convention does not mention violence against women in its text, it has always been on the mind of experts in this area, and in 1992, the CEDAW Committee[7] adopted General Recommendation No. 19 on violence against women.[8] In 2017, it adopted General Recommendation No. 35 on gender-based violence against women.[9] In contrast to the Istanbul Convention, General Recommendations are not legally binding and do not have such a significant legal status as an international treaty. In both Recommendations, violence is a form of discrimination against women.

The Istanbul Convention can be seen as tackling two problems: violence against women, which is still seen as a form of discrimination, and domestic violence, which is partially detached from the framework of sex discrimination. Domestic violence is defined as:

> all acts of physical, sexual, psychological or economic violence that occur within the family or domestic unit or between former or current spouses or partners, whether or not the perpetrator shares or has shared the same residence with the victim.[10]

Due to this broad definition and the possible application to men, the Convention could even be accused of 'implying that domestic violence is unrelated to the structural issues of violence against women'.[11] Nevertheless, the Istanbul Convention retains a rather strong gender analysis discourse and interrelation with the CEDAW. It describes violence against women as follows:

> violence against women is one of the crucial social mechanisms by which women are forced into a subordinate position compared with men.[12]

---

6 Certain researchers suggested partially de-gendering the frame, and others argued against this suggestion as losing the focus on women. D. Rosenblum, 'Unsex CEDAW, or What's Wrong with Women's Rights' (2011) 20 *Columbian Journal of Gender & Law* 98. B.E. Hernandez-Truyol, 'Unsex CEDAW? NO! Super-Sex It!' (2011) 20 *Columbian Journal of Gender & Law* 195.

7 The CEDAW Committee is the body responsible for monitoring the CEDAW Convention.

8 General Recommendation No. 19: Violence against women, adopted by the CEDAW Committee in 1992, 11th session.

9 The later General Recommendations of the CEDAW Committee in fact include LBT women, and intersex women, see for instance General Recommendation No. 35, para 12. General Recommendation No. 35 on gender-based violence against women, updating general recommendation No. 19, 14.07.2017, CEDAW/C/GC/35.

10 Article 3(b) of the Istanbul Convention.

11 R. McQuigg, 'A Contextual Analysis of the Council of Europe's Convention on Preventing and Combating Violence against Women' (2012) *International Human Rights Law Review* 370.

12 Preamble of the Istanbul Convention.

Women are victims of gender-based violence in accordance with the Istanbul Convention.[13] The concept 'gender' in this Convention relates only to two genders, female (women) and male (men):

> the socially constructed roles, behaviours, activities and attributes that a given society considers appropriate for women and men.[14]

The opponents of the Convention suggest that gender roles are not 'socially constructed' but inherent in the different natures of women and men. Political campaigns against the Convention have been led in Eastern parts of Europe for the last decade.[15] At the time of adoption, the Istanbul Convention was already being criticized by the Russian Federation and the Holy See (Vatican) – both suspicious of the so-called 'gender agenda for law'.[16] The backlash against the Convention culminated with Turkey withdrawing from the Istanbul Convention in 2021.

In the future, the Istanbul Convention could be interpreted to fully 'unleash the gender equality potential'[17] by the Group of Experts on Action against Violence against Women and Domestic Violence (GREVIO).[18] This potential is repeatedly reinforced by the interconnections between the Istanbul Convention, the CEDAW and the 1950 European Convention on Human Rights (ECHR). The latter documents, the CEDAW and the ECHR, have been interpreted in a solid body of case-law[19] which allows a better understanding of the Istanbul Convention.

---

13 The Preamble of the Convention stresses the 'structural nature of violence against women as gender-based violence'. Article 2(2) states: 'Parties shall pay particular attention to women victims of gender-based violence in implementing the provisions of this Convention.'

14 Article 3(c) of the Istanbul Convention.

15 See, for instance, a paper on political campaign against the Convention in Bulgaria, M. Ilcheva, 'Bulgaria and the Istanbul Convention – Law, Politics and Propaganda vs. the Rights of Victims of Gender-based Violence' (2020) 3(1) *Open Journal for Legal Studies* 49.

16 M.A. Case, 'After Gender the Destruction of Man – The Vatican's Nightmare Vision of the Gender Agenda for Law' (2011) 31(3) *Pace Law Review* 802. Address of Vladimir Putin of 19.09.2013 (Valdai Forum), calling for the defence of Christian family values.

17 L. Peroni, 'Unleashing the Gender Equality Potential of the Istanbul Convention' in *International Law and Violence Against Women, Europe and the Istanbul Convention*, Routledge, 2020, pp. 43–56.

18 The GREVIO is appointed as a monitoring body of the Istanbul Convention, Article 66 of the Istanbul Convention.

19 The ECHR is interpreted in binding judgments that need to be implemented by States to whom they are addressed, whereas the CEDAW Committee's assessments are recommendatory.

2.2. EU LAW TACKLING VIOLENCE AGAINST WOMEN AND DOMESTIC VIOLENCE

Declaration no. 19 on Article 8 of the Treaty on the Functioning of the European Union (TFEU) states that '[i]n its general efforts to eliminate inequalities between women and men, the Union will aim in its different policies to combat all kinds of domestic violence'.[20] In 2010, Stockholm Programme indicated that there is a need for special support and legal protection of vulnerable persons, in particular, 'persons subjected to repeated violence in close relationships [and] victims of gender-based violence'.[21]

Various recommendatory conclusions on violence against women have been adopted by the Council of the EU.[22] The objective to combat violence against women and domestic violence was also confirmed in the Gender Equality Strategy (2020–2025).[23] Although these instruments did not create any legally binding norms, they did have an effect of bringing political commitment to start filling the gaps in this area at the EU level.

The most important and legally binding EU efforts came in the form of the so-called Victims' Rights package, at the centre of which is the Victims' Rights Directive.[24] The Directive provides for harmonization of standards on victim protection in the EU Member States. It is secondary EU legislation and needs to be transposed into national law. Furthermore, the Victims' Rights package includes two other legally binding documents that are important to cross-border protection of victims. The European Protection Order (EPO) Directive aims to provide cross-border protection to crime victims who have been granted protection orders;[25] and the Protection Measures' Regulation introduces unified rules on the mutual recognition of protective orders in civil matters.[26] The Regulation is directly applicable and does not need to be

20 Declaration on Article 8 TFEU, annexed to the final act of intergovernmental conference, which adopted the Treaty of Lisbon, signed on 13.12.2007.

21 The Stockholm Programme – An open and secure Europe serving and protecting citizens (section 2.3.4) [2010] OJ C115/1.

22 Council conclusions – 'Preventing and combating all forms of violence against women and girls, including female genital mutilation', Justice and Home affairs, Council of the European Union, Luxembourg, 05.06.2014–06.06.2014.

23 Communication from the European Commission, A Union of Equality: Gender Equality Strategy 2020–2025, COM/2020/152 final.

24 Directive 2012/29/EU of the European Parliament and of the Council of 25.10.2012 establishing minimum standards on the rights, support and protection of victims of crime, and replacing Council Framework Decision 2001/220/JHA, [2012] OJ L315/57. The Directive had to be implemented into national laws of the EU Member States by 16.11.2015.

25 Directive 2011/99/EU of the European Parliament and of the Council of 13.12.2011 on the European protection order, [2011] OJ L338/2. The Directive had to be implemented into national law by January of 2015.

26 Regulation (EU) No 606/2013 of the European Parliament and of the Council of 12.06.2013 on mutual recognition of protection measures in civil matters, [2013] OJ L181/4.

transposed (Article 288 TFEU). Meanwhile, the deadline to implement the Directives passed in 2015.

Besides the Victims' Rights package, the concept of euro-crimes needs to be mentioned. The exhaustive list of euro-crimes is provided in EU primary law.[27] Trafficking in humans, sexual exploitation of women and children, and crimes related to information technologies and digitalization are euro-crimes that relate to violence. The exhaustive list can be extended, and discussions are ongoing whether gender-based violence as such should be seen as euro-crime in the future.

On 8 March 2022, the Proposal for a new Directive was registered by the Commission, focusing precisely on combating violence against women and domestic violence (the 'Proposal for a Directive on Violence' or the 'Proposal').[28] The Proposal builds on the Istanbul Convention and EU law in this area. The Commission stressed:

> This proposal aims to achieve the objectives of the [Istanbul] Convention within the EU's remit by complementing the existing EU acquis and Member States' national legislation in the areas covered by the [Istanbul] Convention.[29]

The first intention of the EU had been to ratify the Istanbul Convention, rather than to create an EU document that tackles the problem. The process was delayed, and the European Parliament requested the European Court of Justice's (ECJ) opinion on the matter. In 2021, the ECJ adopted an Opinion, which approved the idea that the Council may wait for 'a common accord' prior to moving towards ratification.[30] At the same time, this is not a pre-requisite as such for ratification, which could proceed with qualified majority vote. As this book is going to press, the ratification process has been completed. The Istanbul Convention was published in the Official Journal of the EU on 2 June, 2023. According to Article 75(4) of the Convention, it shall enter into force on the first day of the month following the expiration of a period of three months after the date of the deposit of its instrument of ratification, acceptance or approval. The new Proposal for a Directive has been evaluated as a 'bypass' to the ratification of the Istanbul Convention.[31] Nevertheless, the Proposal

---

27 Article 83(1) TFEU. These crimes are considered euro-crimes: terrorism; trafficking in human beings; sexual exploitation of women and children; illicit drug trafficking; illicit arms trafficking; money laundering; corruption; counterfeiting of means of payment; computer crime; and organized crime.

28 Proposal for a Directive of the European Parliament and of the Council on combating violence against women and domestic violence, COM/2022/105 final.

29 ibid., see Objectives of the Proposal.

30 Opinion 1/19 of the European Court of Justice (Grand Chamber), 06.10.2021.

31 S. de Dido, 'A first insight into the EU proposal for a Directive on countering violence against women and domestic violence', 07.04.2022 <https://www.ejiltalk.org/a-first-insight-into-the-eu-proposal-for-a-directive-on-countering-violence-against-women-and-domestic-violence>.

for a Directive on Violence arguably has a different focus from the Istanbul Convention, as analysed next.

After the EU's ratification of the Istanbul Convention, it binds the EU institutions and applies to judicial cooperation between EU Member States in the fields of criminal law, asylum and non-refoulement. The Member States will also need to ratify the Convention, besides the EU (Bulgaria, Czechia, Hungary, Lithuania, Latvia or the Slovak Republic have not ratified it, in May 2023). It remains relevant to discuss what are the problem representations in the Istanbul Convention and EU documents.

3. PROBLEM REPRESENTATIONS IN THE EU AND CoE LEGISLATIVE EFFORTS ON VIOLENCE

3.1. THE PROBLEMS ARE REPRESENTED TO BE: VIOLENCE AGAINST WOMEN AND DOMESTIC VIOLENCE

This section analyses the supranational European legislative efforts while going through six key questions of the WPR approach by Carol Bacchi. The first question is 'What is the problem represented to be?' and the WPR approach requires this to be described in the relevant specific document. Both the EU and the CoE strategies tackle two (partially overlapping) problems in parallel: violence against women and domestic violence. The specific documents analysed are the Istanbul Convention and the Victims' Rights package. In addition, the Proposal for a Directive on Violence is also analysed, but with a reservation, because this document has not been adopted and its future perspectives are unclear.

All analysed documents name the two problems in their titles and in the policy contents: 'violence against women' *and* 'domestic violence'. It is considered reasonable to distinguish the problems as twofold in the titles, because they overlap only partially. For instance, a great extent of violence against women happens at home, but femicides and sexual violence also occur outside of domestic units. Meanwhile, men can also be victims of domestic violence, not just women. At the same time, the naming of two problems rather than one makes the policy documents more complex.

3.2. UNDERLYING ASSUMPTIONS: SUBORDINATION OF WOMEN AND THE NEED TO TACKLE MODERN CRIMES

The second question is 'What assumptions underpin this representation of the problem?' in the analysed legal documents. The underlying assumptions are somewhat overlapping, but there are also some interesting differences that are worth highlighting. The Istanbul Convention is strongly grounded on the underlying knowledge of historic gender inequality that places *women in a subordinate position*. This policy document considers gender-based violence to be a result of structural discrimination against women. It is also assumed in the Istanbul Convention that 'gender roles' (of women and men) are socially constructed and they in fact are the sources of violent behaviours.

EU law has very few references to historical inequality and instead turns its glance towards the present and the future. It underpins the need to fight modern crimes that feature a *cross-border* element[32] and *digitalization*, such as cyber-violence against women.[33] The underlying assumption is that there is a lack of effectiveness at the EU level when dealing with modern crimes such as euro-crimes and cyber-crimes. Victims are suffering secondary victimization because they are underprotected in criminal procedure, especially when they move within the EU.

Under EU law, the assumption is that it is not only women who could be victims of gender-based violence. The Preamble of the Victims' Rights Directive explains:

> Violence that is directed against a person because of that person's gender, gender identity or gender expression or that affects persons of a particular gender disproportionately, is understood as gender-based violence.[34]

This broad formulation reveals the idea that *any person* can potentially be a victim of gender-based violence. Female victims of gender-based violence are considered particularly vulnerable, as well as children.

3.3. HOW HAS THIS REPRESENTATION COME ABOUT?

The third question is 'How has this problem representation come about?' in the analyzed texts. The Istanbul Convention builds on the CEDAW (1979), where violence could only be seen as a form of sex discrimination of women,[35] and on the ECHR (1950), where it is a human rights violation and, possibly yet not always, sex discrimination of women.[36] The Convention is open to non-CoE

---

32 For instance, two out of three Victims' Rights package documents focus on cross-border protection orders, and euro-crimes are tackled precisely due to their cross-border implications.

33 Proposal for a Directive on Violence, objectives of the proposal.

34 Recital 17 of the Preamble of the Victims' Rights Directive.

35 This is due to the scope of the Convention, tackling discrimination as a problem, without the mention of violence. Gradually, violence was found to be a form of discrimination.

36 Case-law of the European Court of Human Rights on violence against women is very varied, with some cases finding a violation of Article 14 (non-discrimination) in combination with another Convention articles, but others focusing only on other Articles of the Convention.

States, so its phrasing is very accommodating and broad, in order to appeal to various actors.

Secondary EU law, such as Directives or Regulations, can be adopted if the EU has legislative competences in the area. Such a competence can be exercised in this field if there is some form of intra-EU element or Union-level interest. Otherwise, it would be difficult to justify why a common EU action is even needed. Due to that, the Union focus on violence is either on the procedural rights of victims, rather than substantive law,[37] and cross-border movement is often underlined.[38]

The Proposal on a Directive on Violence attempts to complement the Victims' Rights Directive (aimed at all victims or all crimes) and to address cyber-violence against women. The legal bases for such a document are Article 83(1) TFEU, which mentions human trafficking, sexual exploitation and cyber-crimes, and Article 82(2) TFEU, which allows for minimum rules on victims' rights to be provided. Rules on victims' rights also need to be justified by 'necessity' in terms of closer cooperation in cross-border matters. Article 82(2) TFEU provides that Directives may be adopted where it is 'necessary to facilitate mutual recognition of judgments and judicial decisions and police and judicial cooperation in criminal matters having a cross-border dimension'. It also demands respect for legal traditions and systems of different Member States.

3.4. WHERE ARE THE SILENCES?

The next question is 'What are the silences or what is left unproblematic?' in the used problem representation. The Istanbul Convention is silent about the feminist critique of essentialism in the current paradigm, where women are seen as victims of discrimination precisely due to their gender.[39] Some feminists suggested tackling domestic violence by detaching it from sex discrimination against women. Some feminists also suggested broadening the focus to gender-based violence rather than violence against women.[40] The Convention policy dismisses this critique but also engages in a dialogue with it, because the paradigm of 'violence against women as sex discrimination' is partially removed. Domestic violence is a broad concept under the Convention, which could encompass male victims.

---

37 The Victims' Rights package was created on the idea that all victims of all crimes shall have certain minimum rights in criminal procedure, and that protection orders (civil, criminal, administrative) will move through EU borders together with the victims.

38 Both in the Victims' Rights package and regarding euro-crimes.

39 D. Rosenblum, above n. 6.

40 See the discussion in J. Goldscheid, above n. 5, p. 623.

The Convention is also silent about the fact that some CoE States are critical of the idea that gender roles are socially constructed. The idea that gender roles are 'natural' rather than socially constructed is very old. For a brief period of the last 50 years, the world seemed to move towards gender equality, as a common value. Currently, certain States within the CoE are experiencing a backlash and are increasingly attempting to regulate the lives of women and those who are LGBTQ+. The Convention is silent about that issue, but it does answer these political sensitivities, in a way. For instance, it limits the genders to only two: female (women) and male (men).

The Convention is also rather silent about providing protection against discrimination against LGBTQ+ persons due to gender identity, sexual orientation or gender expression. *Prevention* of such violence is not covered by the Convention, but an incidental protection is provided when the violence is directed against a woman, or falls within the definition of domestic violence.

Regarding EU law, the Proposal for a Directive and the Victims' Rights Package that the Proposal aims to supplement do not address the problem that violence against women, domestic violence, or a broad definition of gender-based violence are not euro-crimes. It is possible to expand the list of euro-crimes, and the European Parliament has suggested that gender-based violence should be included on the list,[41] but it has not happened yet, and the current legislative reform is restricted to crimes related to trafficking, sex exploitation and cyber-crimes. It might be claimed that the Proposal nevertheless is much more ambitious than these legal bases would allow, *strictu sensu*, but that is a usual observation regarding EU legislation, and is not a critique in itself.

3.5. WHAT EFFECTS ARE PRODUCED BY THIS PROBLEM REPRESENTATION?

The fifth question focuses on effects produced by the problem representation ('What effects are produced by this representation?'). The Istanbul Convention directly addresses, in binding treaty norms rather than recommendations, violence against women and domestic violence. The treaty was ratified by the majority of the EU Member States, with the exception of these Member States that increasingly have an issue with the recognition that gender roles are socially constructed rather than natural.[42] These Member States also have

41 Resolution of the European Parliament of 16.09.2021 with recommendations to the Commission on identifying gender-based violence as a new area of crime listed in Article 83(1) TFEU (2021/2035(INL)).

42 In the EU, the Convention is not ratified by Bulgaria, Czechia, Hungary, Lithuania, Latvia or the Slovak Republic.

an issue with the visibility of LGBTQ+ persons, and the recognition that they can also suffer violence in the family would mean that queer families become more visible.

The Istanbul Convention attempts to reconcile the feminist struggles of the last century. Radical feminist ideas demand that policies tackling violence should remain focused on women due to its disproportionate effect on women, and the historical inequality that remains to this date. Queer theory's[43] ideas challenge the policies designed solely for women, and demand more inclusion of those who are LGBTQ+, who also suffer enormous violence – often precisely because of expectations and assumptions related to gender roles. In wrong hands, these agendas may become distorted and exclusionary (e.g., it could be claimed that only lives of cis-women matter) or diffuse (e.g., it could be claimed that 'all lives matter', or that cis-men are the most vulnerable group).

In the final text of the Convention, the scope of the key obligation towards LGBTQ+ persons is incidental. The only duty of the ratifying States is to make sure that implementation of the Convention should not be discriminatory due to a person's gender, sex, gender identity and other identity markers:

> The implementation of the provisions of this Convention by the Parties, in particular measures to protect the rights of victims, shall be secured without discrimination on any ground such as sex, gender, race, colour, language, religion, political or other opinion, national or social origin, association with a national minority, property, birth, sexual orientation, gender identity, age, state of health, disability, marital status, migrant or refugee status, or other status.[44]

The duty not to discriminate *while implementing* the Convention is much narrower than the independent obligations of the States in the Convention, which relate to protection against violence, preventing violence and specifically addressing violence.[45] This obligation is not independent and does not give any new rights or protections. The narrow promise given by the Istanbul Convention, hence, is merely that those who are LGBTQ+ would not be turned down in situations of violence and refused help *solely* because they are LGBTQ+. For instance, a trans woman could receive help in situations of domestic violence.

This compromise in the Convention, which attempted to accommodate concerns of various actors, has still been considered too radical by some

43 Queer legal theory is a critical theory that emerged in the 1990s in connection to homosexual identity politics and which criticized assimilation and subordination and inter alia was critical of second wave feminism, which was seen as sex negative and essentializing. See, in general M. Fineman, J. Jackson and A. Romero (eds), *Feminist and Queer Legal Theory: Intimate Encounters, Uncomfortable Conversations*, Ashgate, 2009.

44 Article 4(3) of the Istanbul Convention.

45 Explanatory report to the Istanbul Convention, para. 54.

States. Vast misrepresentation regarding key ideas of the Convention has swept through Europe.[46] The Istanbul Convention has been accused of legalizing same-sex marriages, introducing 27 genders and forcing sexual education in schools. The backlash against the Convention culminated with Turkey withdrawing from the Istanbul Convention in 2021. President Erdogan explained that the Convention 'was hijacked by a group of people attempting to normalize homosexuality – which is incompatible with Türkiye's social and family values'.[47]

By problematizing violence descriptively (violence against women and domestic violence), the Convention attempted to avoid the problems arising due to objections to social constructivist theory. The effect is, however, that the Convention gives very little protection to LGBTQ+ persons, and for many States, including some Member States of the EU, that is still considered too much.

EU law, in contrast, was accepted by all the EU Member States. The procedural Victims' Rights package does go much further than vague norms of an international treaty, which seeks to be acceptable by such actors as Russia or the USA. Implementation has not been perfect, but the Victims' Rights package has been tolerated by the EU Member States.

The Victims' Rights package is of rather technical and procedural character, and the Proposal for a Directive appears to be directed towards 'filling the gaps' that the Istanbul Convention leaves. This is arguably the effect of tailor-fitting within the EU legislative competences, and solving the problem that some EU Member States have with the Istanbul Convention. As a result, a descriptive problematization was adopted, similar to the Istanbul Convention. The Victims' Rights package and the Proposal for a Directive cover the problem of 'violence against women and domestic violence'.

It is difficult to evaluate the effects of problematization in the Proposal of 2022, which can still change or be stalled and never mature to adoption. Nevertheless, it is worth stressing that the text of the Proposal for a Directive on Violence envisages not only procedural or technical, but *substantive* legal changes. For instance, it is suggested that reform should take place in re-defining rape, by focusing on consent rather than requirements of force or coercion. As the preamble explains:

> Many Member States still require the use of force, threats or coercion for the crime of rape. Other Member States solely rely on the condition that the victim has not consented to the sexual act. Only the latter approach achieves the full protection of the sexual integrity of victims.[48]

---

46 See, for instance, a paper on the political campaign against the Convention in Bulgaria, M. Ilcheva, above n. 15.

47 Presidency of Turkey, Statement regarding Türkiye's withdrawal from the Istanbul Convention, 20.03.2021.

48 Recital 13 of the Preamble of the Draft Directive on Violence.

The text of the Directive appears to support the 'Yes model' of consent,[49] which requires that it must be shown that an express consent was present. There is also the 'No model' which requires it to be shown that there was no objection, thus allowing *implied* consent.[50] It is also significant that the Directive requires broadening a definition of rape to 'all types of sexual penetration, with any bodily part or object' because in some Member States, 'rape' is defined solely as penetration of a vagina by a penis. Other types of sexual violence are criminalized, but not under the same definition.

As mentioned above, the prospects for the Proposal for a Directive on Violence (2022) are not clear. It is still at a very early stage, and it has happened before that secondary acts related to gender equality have been set aside rather than adopted.[51]

3.6. HOW COULD (OR IS) THE REPRESENTATION OF THE PROBLEM BE QUESTIONED, DISRUPTED AND REPLACED?

Finally, the question 'How has the representation of the problem been questioned, disrupted and replaced?' needs to be addressed. The problem could have been described as *gender-based violence*. Both the Istanbul Convention and the EU Proposal for a Directive on Violence could have focused on 'gender-based violence' rather than on 'violence against women' and 'domestic violence'. The European Parliament suggested the inclusion of gender-based violence in the list of euro-crimes in 2021, and a discussion has been going on for quite some time regarding whether the paradigm needs to be changed and broadened.

In the Istanbul Convention and in EU law, the problem is represented more descriptively: the thing that can be observed is violence against women and domestic violence, and hence it is described as a key problem. In contrast, gender-based violence is not a descriptive definition but an attempt to socially deconstruct deeper reasons for the phenomenon.

49 Article 5(3) of the Directive provides: 'Consent can be withdrawn at any moment during the act. The absence of consent cannot be refuted exclusively by the woman's silence, verbal or physical non-resistance or past sexual conduct'.

50 See 'Feminist Perspectives to Rape' *Stanford Encyclopaedia of Philosophy*, 2009, revised in 2021 <http://plato.stanford.edu/entries/feminism-rape>.

51 For instance, these proposals related to gender equality have not yet been accepted: Proposal for a Directive on implementing the principle of equal treatment between persons irrespective of religion or belief, disability, age or sexual orientation, COM/2008/0426; Proposal for a Directive on improving the gender balance among non-executive directors of companies listed on stock exchanges and related measures, COM/2012/0614.

The relevant documents address gender-based violence as a problem only *incidentally*. For instance, the definition of gender-based violence is included in the Victims' Rights Directive,[52] although that Directive represents its overall aim extremely broadly, that is, the rights of all victims of all crimes.

Descriptions of gender-based violence also differ in analysed policy documents. For instance, the description of gender-based violence in EU Victims' Rights Directive is gender-neutral. In the Proposal for a Directive on Violence, violence against women is briefly described as gender-based violence,[53] but the relevant chapters that contain legal rules and duties focus on violence against women and domestic violence. In the text of the current draft Proposal, there is a combination of strategies, from gender-neutrality to gender-sensitivity.

Gender-based violence may include violence against those who are LGBTQ+ directed against them because of sexual orientation, gender identity or gender expression, or disproportionally affecting this vulnerable group. At the moment, many States in the world do not prohibit violence against LGBTQ+ persons (in contrast to violence against women) and certain States actively engage in violence against LGBTQ+ persons or condone it. For instance, by prohibiting homosexuality and providing criminal sanctions and, exceptionally, even the death penalty for such acts, the States engage in active violence against LGBTQ+ persons. By ignoring hate crimes and leaving the perpetrators unpunished, certain States condone violence against LGBTQ+ persons.

In contrast, all current EU Member States provide some protection for those who are LGBTQ+, hence it should be legally possible to extend protection against gender-based violence to this vulnerable group on EU level. Possibly, in the future gender-based violence could even include violence against men, such as violence directed by men against other men and boys to 'initiate' them into manhood. Currently, however, only violence against women is seen as gender-based violence, and that does not seem to be sufficiently problematized, because the States in fact disagree on the reasons for such violence, as discussed next.

4. VIOLENCE AS NATIONAL HERITAGE?

4.1. GENDER EQUALITY VS COMPLEMENTARINESS OF BIOLOGICAL SEXES

In many States, gender roles are *not* seen as the reason for tension and subordination of women and LGBTQ+ persons, but instead, as a natural, serious

52 Victims' Rights Directive, recital 17.

53 Proposal for a Directive on Violence, Article 4(a).

'order of all things' and also an entertaining game that fills human lives. Gender roles can be unproblematic or entertaining to many people, but the problem is that it is socially risky to deviate from the roles a society considers appropriate for women and men. Violence may also be normalized, latent or ignored in respect of certain people, such as women, girls, and LGBTQ+ persons.

'National heritage' here is understood as broader than national constitutional identity, because national constitutions could be interpreted by constitutional courts as protecting women's rights and LGBTQ+ rights, and there could still be a strong resistance to the idea of gender-based violence. 'National heritage' on gender roles refers to usually unwritten normativity and political emotions related to social phenomena, such as gender roles and sexuality. Law also participates in creating or retaining unwritten social norms by rules on marriage conclusion, partnership and cohabitation, legal effects of the family status, prohibition of forced or non-consensual sex, and sanctioning, preventing or protecting against violence.

Legal categories and concepts which certain States had issues with were related to 'gender', such as the description of gender itself, as well as 'gender roles' as socially constructed, and the idea of 'gender-based violence'. This focus on concepts and categories is not surprising, because concepts and categories are crucial in shaping the political discourse.

Dissenting Judges of the European Court of Human Rights from Czechia and Poland suggested that 'complementariness of the biological sexes of the two spouses is a constitutive element of marriage'.[54] They also referred, in the same place, to the historic definition of marriage by Herennius Modestinus (250 AD), which is understood as the union of the man and the woman in their divine and secular rights. The idea of complementariness of sexes was also recently entrenched as the basis of 'natural family' in Lithuanian law.[55] A new enactment has as its key goal to:

> encourage individuals to create, nurture and preserve a harmonious family as a primary and natural society and the most favourable environment for the growth, development and education of a child, ensuring vitality and historical survival of the state of Lithuania and its nation.[56]

Complementariness of men and women is mentioned in the preamble of the Lithuanian Act on strengthening of the family as the basis for this natural

---

54 *Orlandi and others v. Italy*, 2017, Dissenting Opinion.

55 Act on Strengthening of the Family, entered into force 01.03.2018. In addition, the principle of the complementariness of the father and the mother was included as the fundamental principle of family law. Article 3.3 of the Civil Code of the Republic of Lithuania. The Code entered into force 01.07.2001, but the new principle on complementariness was inserted in 2018.

56 Article 2(4) of the Act on Strengthening of the Family.

family, which is tasked with nothing less than a 'historical survival of the state'. The said complementariness of biological sexes, which as mentioned above Dissenting Judges of the European Court of Human Rights (ECtHR) based on the definition by Modestinus (250 AD), relates to a cascade of hierarchy, in which a woman completes a man and is accountable to him, which allegedly creates a perfect harmony between the sexes, and in the society. This way of thinking is the very problem that international law attempts to address.

Contradictory ideas on 'gender' are common in creating international law.[57] However, in the author's opinion, the idea of equal value of genders (gender equality) is not compatible, on a deeper cultural level, with the idea of complementariness of biological sexes. Gender equality means that human beings are complete by themselves, and potentially women and men can replace each other in work, family, political or social function. Framing the human being's gender or biological sex as an obstacle is not justifiable.

The paradigm of complementariness of sexes is long-lasting and historical, in contrast to a short period of equality. As formulated by Thomas Piketty:

> Historically, women have undoubtedly been subjected to the most massive and systematic discrimination, in the North as in the South, in the East as in the West, in all dimensions and in all latitudes. Nearly all human societies have been patriarchal societies, in the sense that they were constructed on the foundation of a sophisticated set of gendered prejudices that assigned certain roles to each of the two sexes.[58]

The problem of violence is framed differently when gender roles are considered biologically determinative. In the historical 'complementariness of biological sexes' frame,[59] violence is seen as stemming from something else than the lack of gender equality. Instead, women and men can be considered to be *inadequately performing* their assigned (gender) roles, and it could be presumed that the lack of adherence to 'natural' (biologically predetermined) norms results in violence. In other words, greater adherence to gender roles could hence be imagined to be the solution, rather than challenge of gender roles.

The answer then, within the complementariness frame, is not considered to be gender equality, in contrast to the frames employed by the EU and CoE. Instead, the answer to widespread violence in 'complementariness' paradigm is more legal control of family life and stricter adherence to legal and social norms.

---

57 S. Kouvo, *Making Just Rights? Mainstreaming Women's Human Rights and a Gender Perspective*, iUstus, 2004, p. 310.

58 T. Piketty, *Brief History of Equality*, Belknap Press of Harvard University Press, 2022, p. 184.

59 'Frame theory' is connected with the 'problematization' approach and it was first developed by E. Goffman. The theory refers to the bases for interpretation of societal phenomena. See E. Goffman, *Frame analysis: an essay on the organization of experience*, Harvard University Press, 1974.

Instrumentalization of religion and references to national identity become crucial in this paradigm, too.

4.2. KEY ARGUMENTS FOR REJECTION OF FRAMES TACKLING VIOLENCE

It is important to present an overview of certain arguments for rejection of the Istanbul Convention in relation to its ideas on gender, gender roles and gender-based violence, in preparation for the discussion of the Proposal for a Directive on violence. A discussion is possible only if the rationale behind the arguments is understood, rather than dismissed.

First, it needs to be mentioned that some States considered the Convention problematic from the perspective of constitutional law. The problem that some national constitutionalists have is related to the concept of gender. As claimed by the constitutional court of Bulgaria, 'gender' can only mean biological sex, which should result in different treatment of men and women.[60] Such ideas could be evaluated as normative convictions, which pre-date the CEDAW, ECHR and EU Charter.

The international Venice Commission,[61] an advisory CoE body of independent constitutional law experts, has explained that the Convention cannot possibly contradict the national constitutions because of the definition of gender. It must also be mentioned that the definition of 'gender' and 'gender-based violence' is identical to definitions developed under the CEDAW since 1992.[62] All of the CoE States participate in it.

Even the current 'violence against women and domestic violence' frame is still considered to threaten the 'natural' gender order, although it does not *directly* represent the problem to be 'gender-based violence'. The defences are political but they could also relate with deeper layers of culture. The States in Eastern Europe adhere to gender equality in their own constitutional law, and the treaties they signed since 1950, but the period of gender equality in those States is still rather brief. Furthermore, in Eastern Europe and the Balkans, the project of gender equality is associated with the Soviet Union, in which formal gender equality was super-imposed.

---

60 S. Todorov, 'Bulgarian Court's Rejection of "Istanbul Convention" Alarms Activists', *Balkan Insight*, 27.10.2021, <https://balkaninsight.com/2021/10/27/bulgarian-courts-rejection-of-istanbul-convention-alarms-activists>.

61 Opinion on the constitutional implications of the ratification of the Council of Europe Convention on preventing and combating violence against women and domestic violence (Istanbul Convention) adopted by the Venice Commission at its 120th Plenary Session (Venice, 11.10.2019–12.10.2019).

62 General Recommendation No. 19: Violence against women, adopted by the CEDAW Committee in 1992, 11th session.

Another fear relates to extending family law concepts to same-sex relationships. Note that for the purposes of Istanbul Convention, '"domestic violence" ... occurs *within the family* or domestic unit or between former or current spouses or partners'.[63] Under this broad definition, domestic violence may also encompass intimate partner violence in same-sex relationships. Hence, the Convention may open a tiny space for the recognition that same-sex couples are capable of constituting a family. As mentioned above, the States cannot close their eyes on the violence reported in same-sex relationships, because discrimination in providing protection based on sexual orientation is clearly prohibited.[64] Meanwhile, certain States want to keep the legal invisibility of same-sex relationships and restrict the legal protection against domestic violence with the condition of different-sex relationships.

Recognition of an inclusive concept of rape is a significant substantive change. Rape is legally understood in some States as solely traditional cis-gender penetration, often with use of physical force. The Istanbul Convention and the draft Directive describe rape as any penetration without consent. Relevant changes in substantive law could help deconstruct a narrow approach to rape, but resistance is also likely. Nevertheless, the challenge in relation to re-thinking rape and sex seems to be secondary. In contrast, the 'gender' problem has occupied the most time in the debates.

5. PROSPECTS FOR JOINING THE SUPRANATIONAL STRATEGIES

The EU policy line so far is more pragmatic than social constructivist, in contrast to the Istanbul Convention. The justification of rules is related to the necessity of smooth cooperation at EU level. Meanwhile, the Istanbul Convention follows the line of social deconstruction of violence against women as a historical and structural problem. The justification of legal rules is based on inequality of women and men.

In the future, as the Proposal for a Directive on Violence shows, the EU law intends to include the social constructivist approach to a higher degree. That is reasonable, because it is difficult to tackle violence against women and domestic violence without clear understanding what are the reasons for it. It also makes sense, because the EU is more than a pragmatic project; it also relates to values. The Treaty on European Union, which is EU primary law, places the principle of gender equality and non-discrimination at a very high level.[65] The Charter of

63 Istanbul Convention, Article 3.b.
64 Istanbul Convention, Article 4(3).
65 Article 2 of the Treaty of the European Union.

Fundamental Rights also guarantees the right to dignity and equality,[66] which is even broader than gender equality between women and men.

In 2017, the EU signed the Istanbul Convention.[67] The Convention is ratified by the EU very recently (June 2023), and the ECJ has approved the delay.[68] There is no way backwards to impunity. For instance, Russia decriminalized domestic violence in some 'mild' cases.[69] That is not possible in the EU, because legal attempts to de-criminalize 'mild' domestic violence would go against the object and purpose of the signed treaty. Ratification by the EU means that the Istanbul Convention is binding on the EU institutions (including the European Parliament, the European Commission and the ECJ) and in relation to judicial cooperation between Member States in criminal matters, asylum and non-refoulement.

Developing EU law on violence against women, for instance, by integrating the provisions of the Istanbul Convention into an EU Directive, is another possibility of joined strategies. Debating the proposed Directive is no longer possible without taking into account the substantive contents of the Istanbul Convention. For instance, the definition of rape in the future Directive is likely to be focusing on the lack of consent, in the spirit of the Istanbul Convention. EU soft law could be developed that creates a persuasive effect, with consideration of the contents of the Istanbul Convention. Public administration and funding by the EU in this area should also be affected by the newly ratified treaty, which is now binding in relation to EU measures adopted by the Union's institutions.

The Proposal for a Directive on Violence is more than a 'plan B' in response to the delayed or refused ratifications of the Istanbul Convention. It addresses certain problems that the Istanbul Convention does not address in such detail, for instance, cyber-violence against women. A Directives has direct effect, which will make the Member States treat it seriously. However, the prospects for this draft Directive passing are rather unclear.

A question may arise whether the EU and CoE strategies can be combined in substance conceptually and substantively. In the author's opinion, they can be combined,[70] because even where there are some deviations (for instance, a mix

---

66 Title I and III of the EU Charter.

67 'Commissioner Jourová signs the Istanbul Convention on preventing and combating violence against women and domestic violence', 13.06.2017, <https://ec.europa.eu/newsroom/just/items/80397/en>.

68 Opinion 1/19 of the European Court of Justice (Grand Chamber), 06.10.2021. Note that on 10 May 2023, the Istanbul Convention was approved by the European Parliament; the remaining step is approval by the Council.

69 M. Spring, 'Decriminalisation of domestic violence in Russia leads to fall in reported cases', *The Guardian*, 16.08.2018, <https://www.theguardian.com/world/2018/aug/16/decriminalisation-of-domestic-violence-in-russia-leads-to-fall-in-reported-cases>.

70 In contrast, see the Statement by Ms R. Manjoo, Special Rapporteur on Violence against women, its causes and consequences, who warns about the turn to gender neutrality in 2015 <http://www.ohchr.org/Documents/Issues/Women/CSW/StatementCSW2015.pdf>.

of gender-sensitivity and gender-neutrality in EU law), both strategies stress the importance of gender equality and mutually reinforce each other. Both CoE and EU strategies largely represent the problem descriptively, that is, as 'violence against women and domestic violence'. Most importantly, both strategies refuse to keep traditional gender roles as 'natural' cultural heritage, and consider that such roles result in gender hierarchy, in which cis-gender men are given a central role.

Strategies related to gender are in fact often mixed in international law.[71] The Proposal for a Directive on Violence and the Istanbul Convention are both examples of mixed frames. Mixed strategies are also not rare in feminist scholarly analyses, because such scholarship often problematizes the binary way of thinking. In addition, supranational organisations are currently mixing legislative strategies in another way. There is a tendency of adopting instruments in the area of *private international law*, e.g. in the form of the EU Protection Measures Regulation, which was adopted under Article 81 TFEU (judicial cooperation in civil matters). Private international law rules hence complement and reinforce the more classical human rights instruments and measures of cooperation in criminal matters.

6. CONCLUSIONS AND OUTLOOK

This chapter discussed the problematizations of violence against women and domestic violence in European supranational strategies (EU and CoE). Although the strategies have different silences and different ideological character, they both represent the problem descriptively, rather than describing it in a broad 'gender-based violence' frame. Still, the concept of gender, gender roles and gender-based violence is a very significant element in both strategies, although more implied and indirect in (currently existing) EU law. The Victims' Rights Directive, for instance, includes at least partially gender-neutral definition of 'gender-based violence'. The Proposal for a Directive on Violence brings the strategies closer. It could be considered as more than a bypass of the failure to ratify the Convention, on the part of Member States. The Proposal addresses certain crimes which the Istanbul Convention did not address in such detail.

The EU strategy has caused less opposition at the national level so far, while the Istanbul Convention has even been framed as a constitutional problem. It could be claimed that the Istanbul Convention has been seen as problematic

71 For instance, the UN has started from neutral strategies aimed at gender equality; subsequently it moved to women-centred approaches; and finally, it adopted the gender mainstreaming strategy, which is a mixed strategy. See S. Kouvo, above n. 57.

in Eastern Europe and Turkey due to its contradiction with the historical idea of 'complementariness' of biological sexes, currently undergoing a revival. In contrast, the EU Victims' Rights package, which did not challenge such deeper cultural levels, that is, gender roles throughout history, the causes behind violence, and the definitions of gender, sex and rape, was accepted without much ado. The Proposal for a Directive is capable of addressing these deeper cultural levels, but could also trigger a backlash. Its prospects of adoption are not yet clear. Future negotiations offer a possibility to discuss these deeper issues and a chance of bridging the strategies, considering that the EU ratified the Istanbul Convention in 2023.

Despite differences, the representations of the problem at the EU and CoE levels have more similarities than differences. They both represent the problem descriptively, as violence against women and domestic violence. They are in harmony within the greater purpose of striving towards *substantive gender equality*. Both strategies challenge the consideration of traditional gender roles as 'natural' cultural heritage. They both potentially clash with the frame of 'complementariness of biological sexes' which has re-emerged around the world and in Europe, as a backlash against the short history of the broad gender-equality frame.

Within the frame of complementariness of biological sexes, the said sexes, women and men, are considered natural (biologically determinative), rather than 'gender roles', which the gender equality frame considers socially constructed. Violence can be tackled by better adherence to these roles, within the complementariness frame, rather than by frustrating the gender roles, which the equality frame suggests.

At the very least, identification of such issues could open a meaningful discussion on the equal worth of each human being, regardless of their gender or sex, sexual orientation, gender identity or expression. The author considers that problematization of violence against women and domestic violence could also been described as 'gender-based violence', which would have been more direct, but possibly would have caused even more resistance. In the future, it may be possible to develop two frames – on 'gender-based violence' and 'violence against women and domestic violence' – in parallel. Gender-based violence could include not only violence against women but also violence against LGBTQ+ persons, because such type of violence often relates to normative expectations that people must act in accordance to gender roles.

PART V

ADDRESSING DIVERGENCES

A FRAGMENTED PRIVATE INTERNATIONAL FAMILY LAW

Interactions and Intersections of International, European and National Norms

Mónika Csöndes*

1. INTRODUCTION

The legal map of international family law in Europe is a complex one. This is due fundamentally to the current legal framework for resolving and deciding international family law cases. The regulation of international family law has become notably international and European. To a significant extent, however,

* Credit goes to Bereczki Ildikó, PhD, LL.M, Expert Diplomat, Permanent Representation of Hungary to the EU and Nemessányi Zoltán, associate professor at Corvinus University of Budapest, Department of Business Law for their valuable comments and support, which helped to improve the manuscript. I am grateful to Theodore S. Boone, Of Counsel, Dentons Budapest and Master Lecturer at Corvinus University of Budapest, Department of Business Law, for revising my English language text. All errors are mine.

such regulation still falls under the realm of national private international law. No unified or harmonized[1] private international law rules ('PIL rules') entirely regulate any subject of international family law relations. The internationalization and Europeanization of private international law has generally been praised for the benefits to individuals. Based on such rules, individuals can predict what forum will hear their case and what law will be applicable to their dispute.[2] But such unification and harmonization has often been criticized for a fragmentation (to be discussed in detail below) that causes difficulties in the application of PIL rules (especially in cases of overlapping instruments[3]) and creates problems of interpretation especially concerning the scope[4] of different sources of law. These problems of interpretation do not favour anyone seeking to rely on predictable PIL rules.

In view of this, as well as the increased movement of families across borders and the ever-changing realities of personal and family lives (e.g., same-sex couples, transgender parenthood, and new artificial reproductive techniques and surrogacy),[5] the question arises as to how law can react to these changing realities. There is an intense debate in Europe about what to do. Though the EU has no regulatory competence in this area,[6] some argue that there is a need for harmonization of substantive family laws[7] while others would prefer to proceed

---

1 In connection with judicial cooperation in civil matters, the expression 'approximation of the laws and regulations of the Member States' is found in Article 81(1) of the Treaty on the Functioning of the European Union (TFEU) (and the wording was same in ex-Article 65 of the Treaty Establishing the European Community (TEC)). In the literature, the expression of 'harmonization' is generally accepted, also regarding judicial cooperation in civil matters. However, sometimes the notions of 'harmonization' and 'unification' are used in parallel, and sometimes unification is used instead. This chapter does not intend to discuss the theoretical questions behind this terminology.

2 As Martiny argues, this can be viewed as legal certainty and predictability in private international law. See D. Martiny, 'Objectives and values of (private) international law in family law' in J. Meeusen, M. Pertegás, G. Straetmans and F. Swennen (eds), *International Family Law for the European Union*, Intersentia, Antwerpen/Oxford 2007, pp. 69–99, at p. 80.

3 As Czepelak argues, 'one has to properly assess the relations between these various sources often potentially covering the same factual situation'. See M. Czepelak, 'Would We Like to Have a European Code of Private International Law?' (2010) 18 *European Review of Private Law* 705, 715.

4 The material scope of legal sources is usually problematic, as interpretation questions often arise because of the legal content of different notions.

5 As Keller sums up, family structures in Europe today can be characterized by the coexistence of traditional, newer and unfamiliar forms of family life, see H. Keller, 'Article 8 in the System of the Convention' in A. Büchler and H. Keller (eds), *Family Forms and Parenthood. Theory and Practice of Article 8 ECHR in Europe*, Intersentia, Cambridge 2016, pp. 3–28, at p. 3.

6 The EU had no competence under the EC Treaty to unify or harmonize substantive family law, and the Lisbon Treaty has not brought about any changes in this respect.

7 Eg., Boele-Woelki, when referring to the viewpoint of Nina Dethloff, states that in order to guarantee the free movement of persons in Europe, the EU Commission should take appropriate steps to avoid a loss of legal position (which, for instance, can arise with

with the unification of the PIL rules.[8] At the same time, other voices plead for more coherent rules, not just in international family law.[9]

2. A FRAGMENTED PRIVATE INTERNATIONAL FAMILY LAW

2.1. THE MAIN CHARACTERISTICS OF FRAGMENTATION

The unification of private international law on an international level, especially as a result of the work of the Hague Conference on Private International Law (HCCH)[10] and later the Europeanization of private international law,[11] has led to a severe fragmentation of private international law in EU countries. In the area of international family law, this means that separate though connected legal relationships are split up by different sources of law. For example, in a divorce case requiring decisions on parental responsibility and maintenance obligations, a significant number of legal sources will apply. In some instances, every EU regulation concerning family law with cross-border implications will need to be considered. In jurisdiction, recognition and enforcement questions, the Brussels II ter Regulation[12] applies in matters relating to divorce, parental responsibility and access rights. However, questions on the division

a change of residence). On the basis of this broad interpretation, it is argued that the EU could even take measures to harmonize or unify substantive family law in Europe. See K. Boele-Woelki, 'What Family Law for Europe?' (2018) 82 *Rabels Zeitschrift für ausländisches und internationales Privatrecht* 1, 4.

8 As von Hein summarizes, there is an ongoing debate on the question of a future comprehensive codification of EU PIL versus the more modest approach of enacting a 'Rome O' Regulation on general principles of PIL, see J. von Hein, 'EU competence to legislate in the area of Private International Law' in P. Beaumont, M. Danov, K. Trimmings and B.Y. Ripley (eds), *Cross-Border Litigation in Europe*, Hart Publishing, Oxford 2017, pp. 19–34, at pp. 33–34; As Martiny argues, 'more uniformity is necessary and … a European unification will to some extent add some new difficulties, but will bring on the whole more clarity and legal security'. See D. Martiny, above n. 2, pp. 70–71, 98.

9 See also M. Czepelak, above n. 3, pp. 715–24.

10 J. Basedow, 'The Hague Conference and the Future of Private International Law. A Jubilee Speech (Keynote speech at the conference "HCCH 125 – Ways Forward: Challenges and Opportunities in an Increasingly Connected World", Hongkong 18 April 2018)' (2018) 82 *Rabels Zeitschrift für ausländisches und internationales Privatrecht* 922, 922–43.

11 See, e.g., J. Meeusen, 'Instrumentalisation of Private International Law in the European Union: Towards a European Conflicts Revolution?' (2007) 9 *European Journal of Migration and Law* 287, 287–305; J. von Hein, above n. 8, pp. 19–34; A. Fillers, 'Implications of Article 81(1) TFEU's recognition clause for EU conflict of laws rules' (2018) 14(3) *Journal of Private International Law* 476, 476–99.

12 Council Regulation (EU) 2019/1111 of 25 June 2019 on jurisdiction, the recognition and enforcement of decisions in matrimonial matters and the matters of parental responsibility, and on international child abduction (recast) [2019] OJ L178.

of matrimonial property are subject to the Matrimonial Property Regimes Regulation.[13] In matters relating to maintenance obligations (towards children and between spouses) the Maintenance Regulation[14] is applicable. As far as the applicable law is concerned, several sources of law should be considered. The Rome III Regulation[15] determines the applicable law in divorce matters whereas the division of matrimonial property is, again, adjudged according to the Matrimonial Property Regimes Regulation. Besides these, in cases of parental responsibility and access rights the Child Protection Convention[16] and the Child Abduction Convention[17] are applicable. In matters relating to maintenance obligations (towards children and between spouses) the Maintenance Obligations Protocol[18] is the correct legal source.[19] And if in a given case EU Regulations are not applicable, the proper international conventions or national PIL rules are applicable.

In addition, from the end of the 20th century the influence of human rights law on private international law has been growing. This raises complex issues, peculiarly in the family law area,[20] where the substantive law can differ considerably from State to State due to such factors as traditions and religious and cultural values.[21] In my view, since the problem of fragmentation is also present in human rights law, the problem of fragmentation in international family law can be better understood if it, too, is analysed in that context. With the entry into force of the Charter of Fundamental Rights of the European Union as a result of the Lisbon Treaty, the protection of fundamental rights has

---

13 Council Regulation (EU) 2016/1103 of 24 June 2016 implementing enhanced cooperation in the area of jurisdiction, applicable law and the recognition and enforcement of decisions in matters of matrimonial property regimes [2016] OJ L183/1.

14 Council Regulation (EC) No. 4/2009 of 18 December 2008 on jurisdiction, applicable law, recognition and enforcement of decisions and cooperation in matters relating to maintenance obligations [2009] OJ L7/1.

15 Council Regulation (EU) 1259/2010 of 20 December 2010 implementing enhanced cooperation in the area of the law applicable to divorce and legal separation [2010] OJ L343/10.

16 Convention of 19 October 1996 on Jurisdiction, Applicable Law, Recognition, Enforcement and Co-operation in Respect of Parental Responsibility and Measures for the Protection of Children.

17 Convention of 25 October 1980 on the Civil Aspects of International Child Abduction.

18 Protocol of 23 November 2007 on the Law Applicable to Maintenance Obligations [2009] OJ L331/17.

19 If a Member State does not participate in any of the regulations adopted in the context of enhanced cooperation, national private international law is applicable if an international convention is not the adequate legal source.

20 Wærstad argues that 'better communication' is needed between the two legal disciplines: T.L. Wærstad, 'Harmonising Human Rights Law and Private International Law through the Ordre Public Reservation: The example of the Norwegian Regulation of the Recognition of Foreign Divorces' (2016) 1 *Oslo Law Review* 51.

21 However, there are arguments according to which the statement that family law is culturally defined is no longer convincing and more political influence has become the main determinant of the evolution of national family laws, see K. Boele-Woelki, above n. 7, pp. 2, 18.

started to function within a three-fold legal framework. In conjunction with national constitutional laws and international human rights conventions, EU law[22] has formally become a source of fundamental rights. However, as the case law on the Charter of Fundamental Rights and the European Convention on Human Rights (ECHR)[23] demonstrates, the application and interpretation of PIL rules is not always coherent. For example, at times the European Court of Justice (ECJ) and the European Court of Human Rights (ECtHR)[24] have not followed the same path.[25] Nonetheless, the case law of the ECJ and the ECtHR has propelled reforms of substantive family law in Europe,[26] and thus there has been more analysis of the interactions between human rights and family law in recent years.[27] Büchler and Keller have convincingly argued for the importance of shared responsibility between the ECtHR and national courts in protecting the rights guaranteed by the ECHR.[28] According to Büchler and Keller, this interaction explains the continuing evolution of family law at the national level.[29] The same can be said about an interplay between the ECJ and national courts in protecting the rights guaranteed by the Charter of Fundamental Rights in line with its Article 51.[30] The national judge to whom the case is assigned and who moreover is supposed to be in the position to guarantee sufficient protection of human rights in an international family law case[31] can only ensure

---

22 When the ECJ applies the provisions of the Charter of Fundamental Rights, it is bound according to Article 52(3) to guarantee that in so far as this Charter contains rights which correspond to rights guaranteed by the ECHR, the meaning and scope of those rights shall be the same as those laid down thereby.

23 Convention for the Protection of Human Rights and Fundamental Freedoms, Rome, 04.11.1950.

24 There is criticism that the ECtHR's jurisprudence is unpredictable as far as Article 8 is concerned, see A. Büchler and H. Keller, 'Synthesis' in A. Büchler and H. Keller (eds), *Family Forms and Parenthood. Theory and Practice of Article 8 ECHR in Europe*, Intersentia, Cambridge 2016, pp. 501–44, at p. 540.

25 For a critical analysis see: G. de Búrca, 'After the EU Charter of Fundamental Rights: The Court of Justice as a Human Rights Adjudicator?' (2013) 20 *Maastricht Journal of European and Comparative Law* 168, 170; L. Walker and P. Beaumont, 'Shifting the Balance Achieved by the Abduction Convention: The Contrasting Approaches of the European Court of Human Rights and the European Court of Justice' (2011) 7 *Journal of Private International Law* 231, 231–49.

26 K. Boele-Woelki, above n. 7, p. 10.

27 H. Stalford, 'EU family law: A human rights perspective' in J. Meeusen, M. Pertegás, G. Straetmans and F. Swennen (eds), *International Family Law for the European Union*, Intersentia, Antwerpen / Oxford 2007, pp. 101–28; H. Keller, above n. 5, p. 3; above n. 7, p. 19.

28 A. Büchler and H. Keller, above n. 24, p. 522.

29 ibid., p. 522.

30 Article 51 of the Charter declares that the Charter only applies to the institutions of the EU with due regard to the principle of subsidiarity and to the Member States when they are implementing Union law.

31 In case of international family law disputes, the right to respect for family life, the right to marry, and the prohibition of discrimination need to be taken into account while applying and interpreting PIL rules.

such protection if the ECJ and the ECtHR set forth clear requirements, based on correct understandings of the specific PIL provisions, on how to interpret PIL rules on human rights.

This fragmentation makes the application of PIL rules difficult, as it is *per se* a complex task to select the appropriate source of applicable law. Moreover, sometimes the instruments of the HCCH and the EU pursue different objectives even though they cover the same area of legal policy (civil judicial cooperation). This is so because they may serve the needs of different international organizations.[32] A further problem (discussed later) is the incoherence of EU PIL rules.[33] This fragmentation, together with the incoherence of PIL rules, affects individuals' legal positions.

2.2. A SPECIFIC PROBLEM: PERSONAL AND FAMILY STATUS IN CROSS-BORDER CASES

From an individual viewpoint, it is legitimate to ask how the rules of private international law can be of assistance to someone if they would like to retain their personal and family status when they settle in another State.

The establishment of personal and family status (e.g., the existence, validity and recognition of a marriage; the names of the spouses; the establishment of a parent-child relationship; a child's given names and surname; decisions on adoption of a child; the existence, validity or recognition of a registered partnership) presents substantive law questions primarily regulated by national legislators.[34] However, fragmentation is not the real cause of individuals losing their legal status and rights already vested. Rather, the heart of the problem lies in public policy (*ordre public*) which is one of the grounds for refusal of recognition of foreign decisions.[35] If the recognition of a foreign decision is refused, the legal status and the rights determined by that foreign decision are

32 J.-J. Kuipers, 'The European Union and the Hague Conference on Private International Law – Forced Marriage or Fortunate Partnership?' in H. de Waele and J.-J. Kuipers (eds), *The European Union's Emerging International Identity. Views from the Global Arena*, Brill / Nijhoff, Leiden 2013, pp. 159–86, at pp. 166–67.

33 The problems that Czepelak demonstrates in his analysis are 'difficulties arising from the multiplication of the sources of private international law, unsatisfactory technique of legislation, lack of coordination, divergence in terminology, and differences regarding methods applied'. See M. Czepelak, above n. 3, p. 715, and see also S. Szabó, 'Brief summary of the evolution of the EU regulation on private international law' (2011) 7(2) *Iustum Aequum Salutare* 151. It is also argued by Wilke that many structural and topical parallels exist: F.M. Wilke, 'Dimensions of coherence in EU conflict-of-law rules' (2020) 16 *Journal of Private International Law* 163–88 (for this argument, a number of works are cited in footnote 5 by Wilke).

34 See the material scope of the Hague Conventions and the EU Regulations.

35 The rule on public policy is present in several international conventions and in EU regulations.

also refused.[36] If the individual is an EU citizen, this necessarily hinders that individual's right based on Article 20[37] TFEU to move and reside freely within the territory of EU Member States.

A possible solution would be a regulation on mutual recognition of personal and family status.[38] Article 81 TFEU[39] allows the EU to act in that it 'shall adopt measures, particularly when necessary for the functioning of the internal market'. The addition with the Lisbon Treaty of the word 'particularly' demonstrates that the EU can now act in matters of PIL which have more remote links to the functioning of the internal market, such as international family law and legal relationships connected to non-EU States.[40] Furthermore, the Lisbon Treaty has attached another notion to the competence of the EU in this area: the concept of mutual recognition. Pursuant to Article 67(4) TFEU, '[t]he Union shall facilitate access to justice, in particular through the principle of mutual recognition of judicial and extrajudicial decisions in civil matters'. As Fillers argues, mutual recognition can be viewed as the objective and principle of judicial cooperation in civil matters in a manner that does not affect the harmonization of private international law rules.[41] Thus, the principle of mutual recognition does not itself constitute a legal basis for enacting legislation but instead can only inform the policies sought to be achieved through legislation based on Article 81. In this way, Article 81 could constitute an adequate legal basis for establishing a regulation for the recognition of the family and the personal status of EU citizens.

However, Article 81(3) TFEU sets forth a provision concerning a special legislative procedure that requires unanimity regarding family matters. It is a provision that can be viewed as a clear sign that the Member States intended to retain control over the legislative activity of the institutions of the EU in family

---

36 As Szabados explains, see T. Szabados 'A jogi státusz elismerése a magyar nemzetközi magánjogban' (2022) 1 *Hungarian Yearbook of Private International Law* 40.

37 Article 20 (ex Article 17 TEC): '1. Citizenship of the Union is hereby established. Every person holding the nationality of a Member State shall be a citizen of the Union. Citizenship of the Union shall be additional to and not replace national citizenship. 2. Citizens of the Union shall enjoy the rights and be subject to the duties provided for in the Treaties. They shall have, inter alia: (a) the right to move and reside freely within the territory of the Member States'.

38 In an early article Baratta examined the possible treaty basis for establishing a private international law principle of mutual recognition: R. Baratta, 'Problematic Elements of an Implicit Rule Providing for Mutual Recognition of Personal and Family Status in the EC' [2007] 1 *Praxis des Internationalen Privat- und Verfahrensrechts* 4.

39 Article 81(1) TFEU, '[t]he Union shall develop judicial cooperation in civil matters having cross-border implications, based on the principle of mutual recognition of judgments and of decisions in extrajudicial cases'. Article 81(2) TFEU, 'For the purposes of paragraph 1, … in accordance with the ordinary legislative procedure, shall adopt measures, particularly when necessary for the proper functioning of the internal market, aimed at ensuring: …'.

40 J.-J. Kuipers, above n. 32, p. 162.

41 A. Fillers, 'Implications of Article 81(1) TFEU's recognition clause for EU conflict of laws rules' (2018) 14 *Journal of Private International Law* 476, 477, 499.

law matters with cross-border implications. This considerably strengthens the role of the Member States in the legislative procedure.[42] International family law is an area of law in which Member States are more likely to insist on preserving their constitutional, national and cultural identities. Thus, if any regulation on the recognition of personal and family status were to be adopted, the legislation would be adopted through enhanced cooperation under Article 20 TEU. However, regardless of how enhanced cooperation is valued in a particular field of law from the standpoint of integration within the EU,[43] the adoption of such a regulation would in the end lead to the fragmentation of international family law.[44]

3. A POSSIBLE WAY FORWARD: MORE COHERENT RULES AND A MORE HARMONIOUS INTERPRETATION OF THE VARIOUS LEGAL SOURCES

Politically, it is not realistic to expect that Member States will grant competence to the EU in the area of substantive family law in the near future.[45] Thus, the only means for the EU to make more effective law are those which belong to its competence under the TFEU.

3.1. IMPROVE THE FUNCTIONING OF EXISTING PRIVATE INTERNATIONAL LAW INSTRUMENTS

In order to improve existing private international law instruments, what is needed are more coherent EU PIL rules and more cooperation between the HCCH and the EU on the regulation of conflict-of-law rules.[46] Czepelak's argument is convincing: the relationships between these instruments should be coordinated, and the more instruments we have, the more coordination is required.[47]

---

42 J. von Hein, above n. 8, p. 24.

43 See about this question more in: F.M. Wilke, 'Dimensions of coherence in EU conflict-of-law rules' (2020) 16 *Journal of Private International Law* 163, 170.

44 ibid., p. 170.

45 As Antokolskaia argues 'Europe is not ripe for a top-down harmonization of substantive family law by means of biding law', see M. Antokolskaia, 'Objectives and values of substantive family law' in J. Meeusen, M. Pertegás, G. Straetmans and F. Swennen (eds), *International family law for the European Union*, Intersentia, Antwerpen–Oxford 2007, pp. 49–67, at p. 67; see also D. Martiny, above n. 2, p. 81.

46 K. Boele-Woelki, above n. 7, p. 29.

47 M. Czepelak, above n. 3, p. 717.

3.1.1. *The Coherence of the EU Legal Instruments*

As Wilke emphasizes, the preamble of most EU regulations sets forth as goals both certainty and predictability.[48] However, there is a considerable literature on the incoherence of the EU PIL regulations.[49] As Limante explains, the rules providing for party autonomy in EU private international family law lack coherence within and between the instruments. Limante argues that incomplete regulation of party autonomy complicates the planning and smooth completion of proceedings.[50]

For some time now, the EU itself has acknowledged the problem of incoherence and has concluded an interinstitutional agreement for better law-making for the purpose of simplifying the legislation.[51] In addition, the Commission issued guidelines on better regulation and a toolbox that its staff is expected to follow when preparing new initiatives and proposals.[52] In support of the coherence of EU law, Wilke expresses the need for terminological consistency not only within an act but also with regard to related acts.[53] However, the need for improvement applies not just to new legislation but to the existing body of EU law on judicial cooperation in civil matters. Some argue that the already-existing incoherence could be remedied without the need for full-blown codification.[54]

Thus, at the level of law-making in the EU, requirements have been established and changes are underway based thereon. But as the literature[55] shows, there are nevertheless a lot of inconsistencies. What is not known is how the process of eliminating these inconsistencies will unfold. What is the plan? What is the agenda? Although the European Commission has issued a communication which discusses consolidating the progress so far, this communication does not mention the elimination of incoherence and inconsistency. It does however argue in a general way that the codification of existing laws and practices can facilitate 'the enhancement of mutual trust as well as consistency and legal

---

48 F.M. Wilke, 'Dimensions of coherence in EU conflict-of-law rules' (2020) 16 *Journal of Private International Law* 163, 167.

49 For the literature see footnote 8, 33.

50 A. Limante, 'Prorogation of jurisdiction and choice of law in EU family law: navigating through the labyrinth of rules' (2021) 17 *Journal of Private International Law* 334, 352–60.

51 Interinstitutional Agreement between the European Parliament, the Council of the European Union and the European Commission on Better Law-Making [2016] OJ L123/1.

52 Available in the 2021 edition at <https://ec.europa.eu/info/law/law-making-process/planning-and-proposing-law/better-regulation-why-and-how/better-regulation-guidelines-and-toolbox_en> assessed 15.09.2022.

53 F.M. Wilke, above n. 48, pp. 168–69.

54 As to the possibility of achieving more coherence without codification, referred by: ibid., pp. 163, 164–65.

55 For the literature see footnote 8, 33.

certainty'.[56] At the same time, the Brussels II ter Regulation can be mentioned as a positive example, because the requirement for more coherent rules was taken into account during the revision of the Brussels II bis Regulation (see section 3.1.2). However, it would be necessary to screen the whole body of EU law on judicial cooperation in civil matters. This is the only way to truly create better and more coherent rules.

3.1.2. Cooperation between the HCCH and the EU

For a long time, the HCCH occupied a monopoly position in the area of international cooperation on PIL. But in recent decades the EU has emerged as an important institutional player. The function of the HCCH as an intergovernmental organization is to work for the progressive unification of the rules of private international law[57] world-wide. Its mission is 'to promote international judicial and administrative cooperation in the fields of protection of the family and children, civil procedure and commercial law'.[58] The EU on the other hand has its own policy on judicial cooperation in civil matters. This policy was created in order to develop a European area of justice,[59] based on mutual recognition and mutual trust, in order to establish bridges between the different justice systems of the Member States. Thus, while the HCCH and the EU both build on judicial cooperation between States, the aim of enhancing mutual recognition and mutual trust is specific to the EU. It was also envisaged that the principle of mutual recognition should become the cornerstone of judicial cooperation in civil matters within the EU.[60] In this way, judicial cooperation in civil matters necessarily involves special policy considerations which cannot be set aside while applying and interpreting EU PIL. This is clearly apparent in the ECJ's case law on how to interpret a unified EU private international law (see more under section 3.2.). By now, the recognition of the EU in the framework of the Hague Conference[61] has created a basis for a fruitful cooperation[62] between the two international organizations.[63] The cooperation between the HCCH and the EU

56 Communication from the Commission to the European Parliament, the Council, the European Economic and Social Committee and the Committee of the Regions, The EU Justice Agenda for 2020 – Strengthening Trust, Mobility and Growth within the Union, COM(2014) 144 final, p. 9, at no. 4.1 and 4.2.

57 Article 1 of the Statute of the Hague Conference on Private International Law (15-VII-1955).

58 See <https://www.hcch.net/en/about/vision-and-mission> accessed 21.09.2022.

59 It was the Tampere European Council (October 1999) that laid down the foundations for the European Area of Justice. see <https://www.europarl.europa.eu/summits/tam_en.htm> accessed 21.09.2022.

60 As declared under point 33 of the Presidency Conclusions of the Tampere European Council (October 1999).

61 The 2005 Statute of the Hague Conference thus allowed for a synergy between the Union and the HCCH, see J.-J. Kuipers, above n. 32, p. 180.

62 J. Basedow, above n. 10, pp. 923, 931.

63 J.-J. Kuipers, above n. 32, p. 186.

so far, as Kuipers states, has been not a 'forced marriage' but, rather, a 'fortunate partnership',[64] and one can list various findings regarding the achievement of this 'fortunate partnership'.

In matters of parental responsibility, the interplay between the HCCH and the EU has been largely described as well-developed. As Baruffi emphasizes, the protection of children's rights, especially in child abduction cases,[65] has been front and centre in the legislative debates within the HCCH and EU institutions.[66] During the revision of the Brussels II Regulation and the recast of the Brussels II bis Regulation, positive experiences with the Hague Conventions in the area of cooperation between authorities on matters relating to the protection of children were taken into consideration. As a result, in various senses the Brussels II ter Regulation was a step forward for children's rights and for the relationship between the Hague Conventions.[67] One positive change with the Brussels II ter Regulation is that the minimum harmonization of certain aspects of the enforcement procedure has been achieved (Articles 51–63 under the title 'Common provisions on enforcement', Section 3, Chapter IV). The harmonization also affects national procedural laws and was supported by unanimity among the Member States. Critics, however, have pointed out that the exceptions to the return rule (called the 'overriding mechanism'), which were already enacted with the Brussels II bis Regulation and are still present in the Brussels II ter Regulation, can be viewed as a demonstrative display of power by the EU.[68]

Maintenance is another area of the law which has seen a cooperation develop between the HCCH and the EU.[69] Within the framework of the

64 ibid., p.186.

65 The Brussels II bis Regulation, enacted in 2003, did not establish a new regime for child abduction cases within the EU but retained the Hague Child Abduction Convention while amending certain exceptions on the return rule.

66 M.C. Baruffi, 'A child-friendly area of freedom, security and justice: work in progress in international child abduction cases' (2018) 14 *Journal of Private International Law* 385, 419.

67 A. Borrás, 'Institutional framework: Adequate instruments and the external dimension' in J. Meeusen, M. Pertegás, G. Straetmans and F. Swennen (eds), *International family law for the European Union*, Intersentia, Antwerpen / Oxford 2007, pp. 129–48, at p. 137; O. Bobrzyńska, 'Brussels IIter regulation and the 1996 Hague convention on child protection – the interplay of the European and Hague regimes in the maters of parental responsibility' (2021) *Polski Proces Cywilny* 595; T. Kruger and F. Maoli, 'The Hague Conventions and EU Instruments in Private International Law' in W. Schrama, M. Freeman, N. Taylor and M. Bruning (eds), *International handbook on child participation in family law*, Intersentia, Cambridge / Antwerp / Chicago 2021, pp. 69–86, at pp. 78–83.

68 About the critics see I. Bereczki, *Gyermeki jogok a szülői felelősségről szóló nemzetközi magánjogi szabályozás perspektívájából*, Wolters Kluwer, Budapest 2021, p. 171.

69 A critic for more cooperation: T. Kruger and F. Maoli, 'The Hague Conventions and EU Instruments in Private International Law' in W. Schrama, M. Freeman, N. Taylor and M. Bruning (eds), *International handbook on child participation in family law*, Intersentia, Cambridge / Antwerp / Chicago 2021, pp. 69–86, at pp. 83–85.

HCCH, the Community and its Member States held negotiations which led to the adoption, on 23 November 2007, of the Convention on the International Recovery of Child Support and other Forms of Family Maintenance and the Protocol on the Law Applicable to Maintenance Obligations (2007 Hague Protocol).[70] The Maintenance Regulation, adopted later, governs only the issue of which courts have jurisdiction as well as the recognition and enforcement of decisions; as far as the determination of the applicable law is concerned, it refers to the 2007 Hague Protocol. One long-awaited development has been that the Permanent Bureau of the HCCH in 2021 announced on its website that translations were available, in all EU languages, of the Practical Handbook for Competent Authorities on the 2007 Child Support Convention, the 2007 Hague Protocol and the Maintenance Regulation.[71] That is precisely what national judges and lawyers need in order to apprise themselves of the practical aspects of resolving such cases.

Furthermore, within the framework of the HCCH there is an ongoing project on parentage and surrogacy aimed at the establishment or recognition of children's legal parentage. This work has now come to focus on drafting the potential provisions of a general private international law instrument on legal parentage as well as a separate protocol on legal parentage established as a result of international surrogacy arrangements.[72] Within the EU there has also been an initiative to enact a regulation on the recognition of parenthood between Member States.[73] However, it is not known what form any cooperation between the EU and the HCCH will take in this area.

Family agreements involving children are high up on the agenda of the HCCH. The HCCH Experts' Group has put forward a proposal on cross-border recognition and enforcement of agreements in family matters involving children.[74] This proposal aims to facilitate the resolution of family disputes, as the current Hague family conventions lack a 'simple, certain or efficient means for their enforcement'.[75] On this, it useful to compare the new rules under the Brussels II ter Regulation as to the circulation of registered private agreements.[76]

---

70 See Recital 8 in the Maintenance Regulation, which also mentions that 'both those instruments should therefore be taken into account in this Regulation'.

71 See <https://www.hcch.net/en/news-archive/details/?varevent=784> accessed 21.09.2022.

72 See <https://www.hcch.net/en/projects/legislative-projects/parentage-surrogacy> accessed 21.09.2022.

73 See <https://ec.europa.eu/info/law/better-regulation/have-your-say/initiatives/12878-Cross-border-family-situations-recognition-of-parenthood_en> accessed 18.09.2022.

74 See <https://www.hcch.net/en/projects/legislative-projects/recognition-and-enforcement-of-agreements> accessed 15.06.2022.

75 Council on General Affairs and Policy – March 2020 p. 34. See <https://assets.hcch.net/docs/3cd99dea-d087-4999-8016-57f738854e90.pdf> accessed 21.09.2022.

76 See Section 4, Chapter IV of Brussels II ter Regulation and see also M.C. Baruffi, above n. 66, pp. 417–19.

One prevailing view is that party autonomy should be granted an essential role in European private international law because it serves predictability.[77] Private international law facilitates the resolutions of legal disputes, so if consensual solutions are present in family disputes, they can also help serve the legal protection of children.

Cooperation between the HCCH and the EU has thus started to bear fruit and has led to the improvement of some of the existing private international law instruments.[78] However, such cooperation needs to be carried on conscientiously in order to maintain the 'fortunate partnership' relationship.

3.2. THE UNIFORM APPLICATION AND INTERPRETATION OF PIL RULES

Uniform application and interpretation of PIL rules, though essential, is possible only if the regulation of different PIL sources meets the requirement of coherence and consistency. Therefore, it would be useful to have more research on whether EU private international law instruments are being applied correctly and uniformly.[79] In order to become more familiar with how national courts interpret the EU's PIL rules, it would be also helpful to have identified the problems inherent in the provisions of EU regulations.

Furthermore, both the ECJ and the ECtHR within their case law systems should pay more attention to giving clear guidance on the interpretation of PIL rules based on correct understandings of the specific PIL provisions. More cooperation and dialogue between these supranational courts would appear to be necessary in those areas of law in which case law is developed by both. The following portion of this chapter turns to this need for cooperation and dialogue.

Child abduction cases have been in the spotlight due to a case, *Neulinger*,[80] in which the ECtHR found an infringement of Article 8 ECHR based upon the assertion of the child's interests. In their article, Walker and Beaumont[81] stated

---

77 J. Meeusen, M. Pertegás and G. Straetmans, 'General report' in J. Meeusen, M. Pertegás, G. Straetmans and F. Swennen, *International family law for the European Union*, Intersentia, Antwerpen / Oxford 2007, pp. 1–23, at p. 18; also above n. 2, p. 80.

78 See M.C. Baruffi, above n. 66, p. 419.

79 See especially the project on Cross-Border Litigation in Central Europe EU Private International Law Before National Courts (800789 – CEPIL – JUST-AG- 2017/JUST-JCOO-AG-2017) <https://www.unalex.eu/Project/Project.aspx?Project=Cepil> accessed 15.09.2022. See also the result of the research project: C.I. Nagy (ed.), *Cross-Border Litigation in Central Europe: EU Private International Law Before National Courts*, Kluwer Law International, 2022.

80 *Neulinger and Shuruk v. Switzerland*, no. 41615/07, 06.07.2010, ECHR.

81 L. Walker and P. Beaumont, above n. 25.

that national case law concerning the Abduction Convention has long struck the right balance overall as far as ordering the return of children wrongfully removed or retained from their habitual residence. They argue that the ECtHR's and ECJ's case law has disturbed this balance and created major discrepancies. Based on *Neulinger*[82] and subsequently *Raban*,[83] in Walker and Beaumont's view the main problem is that the ECtHR has placed too much emphasis on the best interests of the child as a result of encouraging 'an in depth-examination of the entire family situation'.[84] But this examination is not admissible in abduction proceedings. They also complain that the ECJ has placed too much confidence in the principle of mutual trust and not ensured sufficient protection for the best interests of the child.[85] Walker and Beaumont conclude that these two major European courts should not be operating in complete isolation and that a common understanding and common application of the Abduction Convention are necessary in order to reach a common ground and achieve the correct balance in abduction cases.[86]

Finally, the ECtHR realized that *Neulinger* and subsequently *Raban* had been inappropriately decided because the ECtHR did not give due consideration to the main purpose[87] of the Hague Child Abduction Convention. One year later in *X. v. Latvia*,[88] the ECtHR concluded that Article 8 ECHR is to be interpreted in light the requirements of the Hague Child Abduction Convention and of the Convention on the Rights of the Child (1989). The Court here held that such an interpretation is better suited to the aim of the Hague Child Abduction Convention, and this interpretation was confirmed by the ECtHR in later cases.[89] In interpreting the Brussels II bis Regulation, however, the ECJ has not altered the direction of its interpretation. The legal basis thereof can be explained by the provisions on return proceedings under the Brussels II bis Regulation (Section 4, Chapter III) which did not allow for review of any return decision in the Member State of enforcement. The ECJ thus was committed to not risking a situation that would deprive the Brussels II bis Regulation of its useful

---

82 ibid., pp. 231, 233.

83 *Raban v. Romania*, no. 25437/08, ECHR 26.10.2010.

84 L. Walker and P. Beaumont, above n. 25, p. 231.

85 Case C-195/08, *PPU Inga Rinau*, ECLI:EU:C:2008:406, which was confirmed by e.g., Case C-296/10, *Bianca Purrucker v. Guillermo Vallés Pérez*, ECLI:EU:C:2010:665, Case C-211/10, *PPU Doris Povse v. Mauro Alpago*, ECLI:EU:C:2010:400; Case C-491/10, *Joseba Andoni Aguirre Zarraga v. Simone Pelz*, ECLI:EU:C:2010:828. Referred by I. Bereczki, above n. 68, pp. 297, 307.

86 L. Walker and P. Beaumont, above n. 25, pp. 231, 232–39, 248–49.

87 See the Preamble of the Convention: 'Desiring to protect children internationally from the harmful effects of their wrongful removal or retention and to establish procedures to ensure their prompt return to the State of their habitual residence, as well as to secure protection for rights of access'.

88 *X. v. Latvia*, no. 27853/09.

89 I. Bereczki, above n. 68, pp. 301–2.

effect and to not weakening the principle of mutual trust, which constitutes the basis of recognition and enforcement of judgments under the Brussels II bis Regulation.[90] However, the ECJ will need to rethink its interpretation in response to the new provisions of the Brussels II ter Regulation,[91] which actually overturns the decision delivered in *Povse*.[92] This is because an order on the return of a child, issued by a court of a Member State in which the child was habitually resident immediately before the child's removal or retention, will be automatically enforceable only if the substance of the decision is in regard to parental responsibility.

In the last decade, the problem of surrogacy has also come to the forefront before both the ECtHR and the ECJ. The ECJ has not ruled on surrogacy in the context of the free movement of persons, but in other contexts surrogacy has not previously been recognized.[93] In a situation such as when a child is born to his or her biological father but to a surrogate mother through a lawful surrogacy procedure, however, the ECtHR has already declared that the child's right to have his or her private life respected had been infringed and that the State was thus in breach of Article 8.[94] In another case in which a child had been born in Russia under a gestational surrogacy agreement and there was no genetic link with either of the parents, the ECtHR[95] likewise found a breach of Article 8. However, the Grand Chamber overturned the decision, reasoning that the national interest in preventing illegality and in protecting public order must prevail over the applicants' right to respect of their private life. On the basis of such reasoning, it concluded[96] that there had been no violation of Article 8 ECHR.[97]

---

90 ibid., pp. 297, 306–07. However, as Lenaerts argues, the principle of mutual trust should not lead to a reduction in the level of protection of fundamental rights; '... protecting the best interests of the child and enhancing mutual trust among national courts, are not in competition, but in a mutually depending relationship'. See K. Lenaerts, 'The best interests of the child always come first: the Brussels II bis regulation and the European Court of Justice' (2013) 20 *Jurisprudence* 1302, 1325–26.

91 See Article 29 and Article (1/b).

92 See the citation for the case in footnote 83.

93 See, e.g., Case C-167/12, *C.D. v. S.T.*, ECLI:EU:C:2014:169, Case C-363/12, *Z. v. A Government Department and the Board of Management of a Community School*, ECLI:EU:C:2014:159.

94 *Mennesson v. France*, no. 65192/11, 26.06.2014, *Labassee v. France*, no. 65941/11, 26.06.2014.

95 *Paradiso and Campanelli v. Italy*, no. 25358/12, 27.01.2015.

96 *Paradiso and Campanelli v. Italy*, no. 25358/12, 24.01.2017, see also E. Ignovska, '*Paradiso and Campanelli v. Italy*: Lost in recognition. filiation of an adopted embryo born by a surrogate woman in a foreign country' 04.04.2017 <https://strasbourgobservers.com/2017/04/04/paradiso-and-campanelli-v-italy-lost-in-recognition-filiation-of-an-adopted-embryo-born-by-surrogate-woman-in-a-foreign-country> accessed 15.09.2022.

97 I. Bereczki, 'A gyermek családi jogállása a nemzetközi magánjogról szóló Nmjtvr. revíziója kontextusában' in K. Raffai (ed.), *Határokon átnyúló családi ügyek.Nemzetközi személyes és családjogi kérdések a XXI. században*, Pázmány Press, Budapest 2018, pp. 25–43, at pp. 34–36.

Hence, as long as coherence between these supranational courts' case law has not been achieved, it is hardly likely that national courts will be able to adhere to a uniform interpretation of the PIL rules simultaneously under EU and ECHR law.

4. SUMMARY

International family law disputes are difficult to resolve not only because of the need to determine the proper source of law but also because neither the HCCH conventions nor national PIL rules can be interpreted without giving due consideration to related human rights law. Moreover, the EU regulations cannot be interpreted without the relevant *acquis communautaire*. Unified PIL rules do not operate on their own but interact with national law, especially national procedural law.

Private international law exists because the substantive laws of the different States diverge from one another. However, the goal of private international law is not to bring uniformity to divergent national laws. Fragmentation in private international law is unavoidable as law-making takes place at national, international and EU levels. Therefore, it is not fragmentation which should be eliminated but rather the disadvantages of fragmentation. These disadvantages are what actually adversely affect an individual's legal position. It cannot be expected that there will be a positive effect from more unification and harmonization of PIL rules if the incoherence and inconsistency of different legal sources has not been corrected.

The unification and harmonization of PIL rules is merely one of many elements in the overall coordination of legal systems,[98] and this is true for international family law as well. The convergence of family law across Europe so far has primarily been the result of an ongoing discourse on the subject of human rights.[99] In this context, Article 8 ECHR, which confers a right to have one's private and family life respected, has through decisions of the ECtHR become the most significant building block in the approximation of family laws in Europe. Although for the Contracting States the ECtHR has left a 'margin of appreciation', a minimum standard has also been established.[100] The already-existing common values, reflected in international treaties, will in the

98 J. Basedow, above n. 10, p. 934.

99 A. Büchler, 'The right to respect for private and family life. The case law of the European Court of Human Rights on Parenthood and Family Forms' in A. Büchler and H. Keller (eds), *Family forms and parenthood. Theory and Practice of Article 8 ECHR in Europe*, Intersentia, Cambridge 2016, pp. 29–60, at p. 29.

100 K. Boele-Woelki, above n. 7, p. 11.

long run stimulate further family law reforms and greater convergence. This process fosters respect, on the part of States as well as individuals, for the laws of other States, which may contain different rules but which also share common roots. It contributes to better resolutions of private international law cases and decreases the pressure to rely on public policy. More emphasis and research would be desirable as to how national family law has developed in response to the standards of international and EU law.

Until such a convergence has come about, much remains to be done as far as improving what currently are incoherent rules. More emphasis should be placed on projects and research related to national courts applying unified and harmonized PIL rules and to the education of, and professional support for, those dealing with such cases. Such an emphasis would also have positive effects on the legal position of individuals in the EU.

understand this distinction. *A priori*, the difference between recognition and enforcement lies in the effects they produce.

Recognition enables a judgment, an act or a situation established in one State to produce an effect in another State. For example, recognition in Germany of a Spanish divorce judgment has the effect of preventing the reopening of new divorce proceedings before German court.

As to enforcement, it allows a judgment rendered in one State to become enforceable in another State. For example, the Spanish divorce judgment can be enforced in Germany and thus justify the use of constraint by the German State to enforce it.

Of course, the difference between recognition and enforcement is a difference of degree in the effects they produce: the foreign judgment that is enforceable will *a fortiori* be recognized. Thus, enforcement incidentally includes recognition, whereas recognition does not include enforcement. This difference between recognition and enforcement is important insofar as they are each subject to different legal treatment.

The other important clarification concerns the purpose of recognition and enforcement. A distinction must be made according to whether a family situation has been created abroad by a judgment or in the absence of any judgment. For example, the celebration of a marriage or the establishment of a parent-child relationship does not usually require the intervention of a judge. In such case, the family situation results from an act: generally a civil status act. But it may also result from a notarial act, such as a will or a divorce. Again, this difference between recognition and enforcement of an act and recognition and enforcement of a judgment is essential because it may justify a difference in legal regime.

It is therefore clear from the outset that the circulation of family status in Europe does not reflect a single reality. On the contrary, it raises different issues depending on whether it is a question of recognizing or enforcing a status created abroad, or of recognizing and enforcing a decision or act created abroad. This heterogeneity is reinforced by the diversity of the rules applicable to the recognition and enforcement of acts and judgments in private international family law. There is therefore a fragmentation of systems of recognition and enforcement. But this fragmentation deserves to be questioned: should it be overcome or is it justified, because it adequately addresses specific issued raised in different contexts of recognition and enforcement?

These questions are all the more important at a time when EU law tends to facilitate circulation of family status. While some family situations cross borders easily, others still have to face a number of obstacles without it always being possible to explain the difference in treatment. To address all of these issues, this chapter will first present the different systems of recognition and enforcement (section 1). This will allow us to take stock of the situation. Then, whether the differences in recognition and enforcement systems are justified will be evaluated (section 2).

1. PRESENTATION OF THE RECOGNITION AND ENFORCEMENT SYSTEMS

The recognition and enforcement of acts and judgments in family matters is subject to fragmentation. This fragmentation is due both to the applicable texts (see section 1.1.) and to legal regimes provided for by these texts (see section 1.2.).

1.1. THE FRAGMENTATION OF TEXTS

In Europe, private international family law is not encompassed in one single piece of legislation or code. Its rules, including those on recognition and enforcement, are scattered in different normative instruments. One of the major contributions of EU law is certainly to have standardized the rules of private international law within the Member States, first by means of conventions and then by means of regulations. But these European regulations do not cover all aspects of recognition and enforcement in family matters. European private international law has in fact been developed progressively, in successive waves – area after area, question after question – without ever seeking, until now, to be exhaustive by legislating on all aspects of international private relations.

Thus, in family matters, European regulation only covers the following matters as regards the recognition and enforcement of decisions and documents:

- matrimonial matters, matters of parental responsibility and international child abduction, which were the subject of the Brussels II Regulation in 2000,[1] amended in 2003 to become the Brussels II bis Regulation[2] and again amended in 2019 to become the Brussels II ter Regulation applicable from 1 August 2022;[3]
- maintenance obligations that were the subject of a regulation in 2009;[4]

1 Council Regulation (EC) 1347/2000 of 29 May 2000 on jurisdiction and the recognition and enforcement of judgments in matrimonial matters and in matters of parental responsibility for children of both spouses [2000] OJ L160/19.

2 Council Regulation (EC) 2201/2003 of 27 November 2003 on jurisdiction and the recognition and enforcement of judgments in matrimonial matters and in matters of parental responsibility [2003] OJ L338/1.

3 Council Regulation (EU) 2019/1111 of 25 June 2019 on jurisdiction, the recognition and enforcement of decisions in matrimonial matters and in matters of parental responsibility, and on international child abduction [2019] OJ L178/1.

4 Council Regulation (EC) 4/2009 of 18 December 2008 on jurisdiction, applicable law, recognition and enforcement of decisions and cooperation in matters relating to maintenance obligations [2009] OJ L7/1.

- matters of succession subject to a 2012 regulation;[5]
- matrimonial property regimes and property effects of registered partnerships which were the subject of a regulation in 2016.[6]

Many issues are thus excluded from the European regulation on the recognition and enforcement of decisions and documents. This is the case, for example, of marriage and parentage, which are not subject to any European standardization.

It is also interesting to note that these European texts never have as their sole object recognition and enforcement of decisions and acts in family matters. This issue is resolved in conjunction with that of jurisdiction, as is the case with the Brussels II ter Regulation or the Maintenance Regulation, or with that of the applicable law, as is the case with the Succession Regulation or the Regulation on matrimonial property regimes and the property effects of registered partnerships.

In addition to the European texts, there are international texts drawn up in the framework of the Hague Conference, which contain rules on the recognition and enforcement of foreign decisions and documents. One example is the 1993 Hague Convention on Intercountry Adoption.

Finally, these European and international instruments are supplemented in each Member State by their own rules of private international law concerning recognition and enforcement of judgments and situations in family matters. These national rules then take over in the absence of international and European texts.

This diversity of applicable texts calls for two remarks. First, the question of the recognition and enforcement of judgments and documents in Europe is not treated uniformly as a question that would lead to a homogeneous answer. Depending on the matter, different texts containing different rules will thus apply. Thus, for example, an adoption judgment will not circulate in the same way as a divorce judgment. Second, the regime of recognition and enforcement in Europe varies according to the place where a family situation was created. Family situations created in a Member State will be subject to European rules, whereas those created in a third country will be subject to international rules such as the Hague Conventions or the national rules of each Member State.

---

5 Council Regulation (EU) 650/2012 of 4 July 2012 on jurisdiction, applicable law, recognition and enforcement of decisions and acceptance and enforcement of authentic instruments in matters of succession and on the creation of a European Certificate of Succession [2012] OJ L201/107.

6 Council Regulation (EU) 2016/1104 of 24 June 2016 implementing enhanced cooperation in the area of jurisdiction, applicable law and the recognition and enforcement of decisions in matters of the property consequences of registered partnerships [2016] OJ L183/30.

This fragmentation of the applicable texts therefore leads to a fragmentation of the recognition and enforcement regimes in family matters.

1.2. THE FRAGMENTATION OF REGIMES

It is important to start by pointing out that the European texts on recognition and enforcement are extremely complex texts, which often suffer from an excess of sophistication. It is therefore very difficult to present them in a synthetic and accurate way. This chapter will therefore only outline different systems of recognition and enforcement in family matters, seeking to highlight their main common features and differences.

First, all European texts enshrine the principle of the prohibition of revision on the merits (Article 71 of the Brussels II ter Regulation; Article 42 of the Maintenance Regulation; Article 41 of the Succession Regulation; Article 40 of the Regulation on matrimonial property regimes and property effects of registered partnerships). This principle, which has been firmly anchored in the national law since the middle of the 20th century, means that the court addressed is prohibited from rewriting the decision given by a foreign court. Its role is limited to reviewing the decision against predefined criteria for recognition and enforcement. It may therefore either recognize the decision and make it enforceable, or refuse to recognize it and enforce it, but in no case may it change the content of the decision.

It should also be noted that all European and international texts enshrine automatic recognition of family judgments. This means that a family status established in one Member State may produce effects in another Member State without the need for a specific procedure. However, all the texts reserve the possibility of challenging this automatic recognition on the basis of predefined grounds.

Most of these grounds for non-recognition are common to various Regulations. This is the case, for example, of contravention of public policy, irreconcilability of one judgment with another one rendered between the same parties, or failure to serve the document instituting the proceedings or the equivalent document unless the defendant has unequivocally accepted the judgment (Articles 38 and 39 of the Brussels II ter Regulation; Article 24 of the Maintenance Regulation; Article 40 of the Succession Regulation; Article 37 of the Regulation on matrimonial property regimes and the effects of registered partnerships).

However, there are sometimes some differences or at least some specificities. For example, in matters of parental responsibility, certain specific grounds for non-recognition have been established, such as the impossibility of having been heard by the judge for the person whose responsibility is impeded by the decision (Article 39(1)(c)). Similarly, as in the case of parental responsibility, international public policy, which is a ground of non-recognition, is defined by reference to the best interests of the child (Article 39(1)(a)). In matrimonial matters, it is also provided that the disparity of applicable laws is not a ground for non-recognition (Article 70). This means that recognition of a matrimonial judgment cannot be refused on the grounds that the law of the Member State in which recognition is sought does not allow divorce, legal separation or marriage annulment on the basis of identical facts. This specificity is also reflected in the Regulation on matrimonial property regimes and the effects of registered partnerships, which contains an autonomous clause on respect for the fundamental rights provided for in the Charter of Fundamental Rights of the European Union (Article 38). Finally, it should be noted that certain principles which are a priori common to the various European Regulations do not always appear expressly in the European Regulations. This is the case with the control of the jurisdiction of the court of origin, which is expressly prohibited in the Brussels II ter Regulation (Article 69) and in the Regulation on matrimonial property regimes and the effects of registered partnerships (Article 39), but is not mentioned in the Succession and Maintenance Regulations. Thus, pooling of the grounds for non-recognition of decisions by different Regulations leaves some particularities in their place.

This observation is reflected in the field of enforcement of decisions. Indeed, all the European regulations establish the grounds for non-recognition of decisions as grounds for non-enforcement. More precisely, texts refer, for the grounds of non-enforcement of decisions, to the grounds of non-recognition (Article 41 Brussels II ter Regulation; Article 34 of the Maintenance Regulation; Article 52 of the Succession Regulation; Article 51 of the Regulation on matrimonial property regimes and property effects of registered partnerships). Recognition and enforcement of judgments are here subject to a single, homogeneous treatment by the European law. There is no difference in the substantive grounds for refusing recognition or refusing enforcement of the decision. These grounds are identical. What may be different, however, is the process that may lead to the recognition or enforcement of the decision.

In this respect, one of the major innovations of the European law is the abolition of *exequatur*.[7] This means that a judgment given in one EU Member State will be enforceable in another Member State without recourse to a particular procedure. After automatic recognition of judgments, European texts

[7] Other than in civil and commercial matters (Council Regulation (EU) n° 1215/2012 of 12 December 2012 on jurisdiction and the recognition and enforcement of judgments in civil and commercial matters), the procedure of *exequatur* has been abolished in family matters for certain types of judgments only in the Maintenance Regulation and in the Brussels II bis and ter Regulations (cf. infra).

have established their automatic enforcement. This means that a judgment must be treated as if it had been given in the Member State addressed; consequently, it will be enforced under the same conditions as a judgment given in the Member State addressed.

To ensure the enforceability of a decision, it is sufficient to send a copy of the decision and a certificate that it is enforceable in the country of origin to the competent authority responsible for enforcement. The competent enforcement authority may, if necessary, require a translation of the content of the certificate or decision. The rights of the defence are safeguarded by the effect of prior mandatory notification of the certificate and decision to the sentenced person. For the rest, the enforcement procedure itself is generally governed by the law of the requested Member State in accordance with the principle of procedural autonomy of the Member States. A creditor will therefore be able to rely on the enforcement law of the requested State without having to obtain prior authorization for enforcement in the Member State concerned.

However, the Brussels II ter Regulation has recently brought about a minimum harmonization of national enforcement procedures. This harmonization focuses on the grounds for suspending enforcement proceedings. The aim is to ensure that enforcement can be suspended under largely the same conditions in all Member States. However, as the Regulation does not prejudice application of the grounds for suspension of enforcement provided for by national law (insofar as they are compatible with the Regulation), harmonization is not absolute. Moreover, the abolition of the *exequatur* leaves open the possibility for the convicted party to oppose the enforcement of the decision by operation of law on one of the grounds for non-recognition enshrined in the Regulations.

The fact remains that *exequatur* has not been abolished in all European family law regulations. Thus, the regulations on succession, matrimonial property regimes and the property effects of registered partnerships retain the requirement of *exequatur* for a judgment from one Member State to be enforceable by operation of law in another Member State. But the procedure is simplified along the lines of the Brussels I Regulation. The judgment to be enforced is accompanied by a certificate issued on request in the State of origin and assuring its enforceability. The addressed authority decides, without the party against whom enforcement is sought being able to submit any observations, and declares the decision enforceable as long as certain formalities (e.g., submission of documents) have been complied with, without any examination of the grounds for rejection (Article 47 of the Succession Regulation; Article 47 of the Regulation on matrimonial property regimes and property effects of registered partnerships). While the *exequatur* procedure is thus maintained here, it is greatly simplified.

Some regulations introduce mixed systems: sometimes the *exequatur* procedure is abolished, other times it is simplified under the conditions set out above. For example, in the Maintenance Regulation, a distinction is made depending on whether the judgment was given by a Member State bound by the 2007 Hague Protocol. If this is the case, the *exequatur* procedure is abolished. If not, the *exequatur* procedure is maintained. This mixed system was also observed in the Brussels II bis Regulation; however, it was abandoned by the Brussels II ter Regulation, which generalized the abolition of *exequatur* in matters of parental responsibility.

Whereas in the Brussels II bis Regulation abolition of *exequatur* was only reserved for decisions on rights of access and for certain decisions on return of the child in cases of international abduction, it was extended to all decisions on parental responsibility. The Brussels II ter Regulation, however, has maintained a mixed system regarding the challenge of this automatic enforcement. Indeed, the grounds for non-enforcement differ according to the nature of the decision. For the so-called privileged decisions – i.e., those relating to access rights and some relating to the return of the child in the event of international abduction – automatic enforcement can only be challenged in the event of a subsequent irreconcilable decision. For other decisions, the Brussels II ter Regulation traditionally refers to the grounds for non-recognition. Among these grounds for non-recognition is, of course, that the decision is contrary to the public policy of a Member State. However, enforcement of the decision by operation of law may also be refused if there is a risk of serious danger to the child due to changed circumstances or, subject to exceptions, if a child who is capable of forming his or her own views has not been given the opportunity to express such views. As already mentioned, this is one of the specificities of the Brussels II ter Regulation, which differs in this respect from the other European regulations, by enshrining specific grounds for non-recognition/enforcement.

Finally, one last important remark is needed: the recognition and enforcement of foreign instruments – agreements, authentic instruments or court settlements – have also been facilitated by the European regulations. The question then arose as to how these instruments should circulate in the European area and, more particularly, whether the regime for the circulation of judgments should be transposed to that of agreements and authentic instruments.[8] Should authentic instruments and court settlements be considered equivalent to court decisions?

The question presents important issues in terms of legal reasoning.[9] If one considers that authentic instruments and agreements cannot be equated with a

---

8 P. Lagarde (eds), *La reconnaissance des situations en droit international privé*, Pedone, Paris 2013.

9 P. Mayer, 'Les méthodes de la reconnaissance en droit international privé', in *Le droit international privé: esprit et méthodes. Mélanges en l'honneur de Paul Lagarde*, Dalloz, Paris 2005, pp. 547–569, at p. 547; S. Bollee, 'L'extension du domaine de la méthode de reconnaissance unilatérale', *Rev. crit. DIP* 2007, p. 307; L. D'Avout, 'La reconnaissance dans le champ des conflits de lois', *TCFDIP*, Pedone, Paris 2014–2016, pp. 159–181, at p. 159.

court decision, then their circulation will be subject to the adversarial method. In such case, the validity or effectiveness of the notarial deed or authenticated settlement will be assessed under the law designated by the conflict-of-laws rules – in this case those applicable to the contract. This assessment can be made by any judge with regular jurisdiction. On the other hand, if it is considered that agreements and authentic instruments can be assimilated to a court decision, then they will circulate by virtue of the method of recognition of judgments.

This second alternative was initially favoured by the Commission's 2009 draft Succession Regulation. However, it gave rise to debates within the professional orders concerned (particularly notaries) and among academics, and so the draft was modified. The concept of recognition has been abandoned and replaced by that of acceptance: an authentic instrument drawn up in one Member State may only be recognized as having probative value in the other Member States (Article 59 of the Succession Regulation). There can therefore be no question of recognizing them as having substantial legal value and incontestable character, which is regularly the case with regard to the recognition of judgments. This approach has also been adopted in the Maintenance Regulation (Article 58 of the Maintenance Regulation).

It remains that, as with judgments, the probative value of authentic instruments can be contested. The Succession and Maintenance Regulations distinguish between challenges to the authenticity of the instrument (*instrumentum*) and challenges to its substantive content (*negotium*). If a dispute concerns the authenticity of the instrument, the courts of the Member State of origin have exclusive jurisdiction to rule. If a dispute concerns the substantive content of the instrument, the jurisdiction is determined by the regular rules of Succession and Maintenance Regulation.

As for the enforcement of authentic instruments, its regime essentially follows that of judgments: the procedure is simplified (Article 60 of the Succession Regulation; Article 59 of the Maintenance Regulation). On the other hand, only the manifest conflict of the instrument with public policy can justify revocation of a declaration of enforceability. Despite certain nuances, there is nevertheless a tendency in the Succession and Maintenance Regulations to model the regime for the recognition and enforcement of authentic instruments and court settlements on that of judgments.

This tendency has been clearly reinforced in the Brussels II ter Regulation. Indeed, the Brussels II ter Regulation applies the principles of recognition and enforcement by operation of law, on the basis of a certificate and without *exequatur*, to authentic instruments and agreements. Divorce without a judge will therefore be able to circulate freely in the European area, provided of course that neither party objects to its recognition or enforcement. As with judgments, it is indeed possible to oppose the automatic circulation of the document and the grounds for refusing recognition and enforcement are identical to those for judgments, with the exception of the violation of the defaulting defendant's rights of defence, which, by hypothesis, presupposes judicial proceedings (Article 68 of the Brussels II ter Regulation). The first of these grounds is a clear violation of the public policy of the requested State. Furthermore, although assimilation to judgments does not extend the rules on *lis pendens*, the situation of irreconcilability between authentic instruments, agreements and/or decisions is envisaged and resolved according to the same principles as in the case of judgments. Thus, it will be possible, for example, to refuse in Germany recognition of a French divorce by mutual consent, if a divorce judgment has been issued in Germany, even after the registration of the agreement in France.

The Brussels II ter Regulation thus confirms the current trend towards assimilating the foreign act to a foreign judgment. Further, it shows the extension of the method of recognition of situations, to the detriment of the conflict of laws.

Nevertheless, various recognition and enforcement systems presented above are sometimes perplexing. In addition to their complexity, these systems present a significant number of nuances and even differences. Are these differences appropriate? Are they justified?

2. EVALUATION OF RECOGNITION AND ENFORCEMENT SYSTEMS

This section will inquire into the justifications for this fragmentation (section 2.1) and its possible corrections and remedies (section 2.2).

2.1. JUSTIFICATIONS FOR FRAGMENTATION

The abolition of *exequatur* is a highly symbolic measure for the realization of the European judicial area. The Commission has made it its political priority in the entire field of judicial cooperation in civil matters. However, it is clear that not all European regulations have yet abolished *exequatur*. How can this be explained?

The abolition of obstacles to the recognition and enforcement of decisions and documents in family matters is based in the European Union on the principle of mutual trust. Judicial cooperation in civil matters is indeed justified by the idea that the legal solutions adopted by each Member State are presumed to be compatible with each other. They are presumed to be compatible because the EU postulates a certain equivalence between the Member States' legal systems. There would be a community of values shared by the Member States which would not make it necessary to review decisions and acts issued by another Member State. Respect for fundamental rights, the rule of law and democracy would contribute to the realization of this community of values and, with it, the idea of a certain fungibility of justice and fungibility of decisions.

But beyond this theoretical justification, the abolition of the *exequatur* is based on a number of practical arguments. The slowness of the *exequatur* procedure, its excessive cost due to translations and lawyers' fees, and the scarcity of appeals have been put forward.

The fact remains that all these justifications – theoretical as well as practical ones – hardly justify multiple differences in the regime for the recognition and enforcement of decisions and acts in family matters.

Let us focus on the objective of reducing length and costs of the procedure. If this objective justifies abolition of *exequatur*, why not abolish this procedure in all Regulations? Why, for example, limit automatic enforcement to decisions that have applied the 2007 Hague Protocol in the Maintenance Regulation? Shouldn't all maintenance creditors be able to easily obtain a decision in one Member State that will automatically be enforceable in another Member State?

Let us focus on the principle of mutual trust. There are several degrees of equivalence – several degrees of uniformity in the law and justice of the Member States that can justify the trust that the Member States place in each other. However, uniformity of conflict-of-law rules does not, for example, constitute a criterion for justifying the differences in regime that can be observed. Indeed, the conflict-of-law rules have been standardized in matters of succession, matrimonial property regimes and divorce, and yet only the latter matter benefits from the abolition of *exequatur*. Moreover, many family situations are still excluded from the scope of European family regulation. This is the case, for example, of filiation and marriage. Does this mean that in these areas mutual trust would be breached? In reality, it is not so much the principle of mutual trust as the political will of the Member States to remain sovereign in their decision to recognize and execute decisions or acts in sensitive areas, such as marriage, name or filiation, which may explain the absence of European regulation. On family aspects involving the constitutional identity of the Member States, the review of foreign decisions and acts reappears.

But these differences and the resulting fragmentation can also be explained by the absence of a general theory of the EU private international law. The matter has been built up gradually, in successive waves, so that each new regulation or recast attempts to go further in abolishing obstacles to the circulation of situations. The abolition of *exequatur* in family matters could therefore be only a matter of time. The differences between the regulations that have adopted the measure and those that have not could then simply be explained by a strategic pragmatism: the policy of small steps. The recast of the Brussels II bis Regulation confirms this analysis by having recently taken a further step by generalizing the abolition of *exequatur* in matters of parental responsibility.

The fact remains that the fragmentation of regimes applicable to the recognition and enforcement of foreign decisions and documents is not always unjustified. Uniformity and simplification are laudable objectives only if they nevertheless appropriately address the complexity of the issues raised in different legal contexts. Whether this is the case has to be assessed on a case-by-case basis. In this respect, the difference in treatment between instruments and decisions was originally based on sound arguments. Indeed, an authentic instrument does not have the same guarantees as a court decision. A court decision is given in a fair trial respecting the rights of the defence, by a public authority subject to the principle of impartiality. The authentic instrument is issued or registered by a private authority that is not subject to all the guarantees of Article 6 of the European Convention on Human Rights. Yet, despite these differences, there is a tendency to equate authentic instruments with judgments by subjecting them to a similar if not identical regime in terms of recognition and enforcement. Is such an alignment really necessary? Should not the emphasis here be on the difference between court decisions and authentic instruments, thus encouraging the fragmentation of applicable regimes?

However, this is not the path that EU law seems to be taking. And it is unlikely that this trend will diminish, because the European Courts are also working to assimilate documents and judgments and, more generally, to overcome the obstacles to the circulation of family situations and thus remedy the fragmentation of recognition and enforcement systems.

2.2. OVERCOMING FRAGMENTATION

The development of fundamental rights and freedoms in private international family law has contributed significantly to the removal of obstacles to the circulation of family status and has thus made it possible to homogenize various systems of recognition and enforcement.[10] This is mainly due to the constructive interpretation of the Court of Justice of the European Union and the European Court of Human Rights.

---

10 J. Bomhoff, 'The Reach of Rights: The Foreign and the Private in Conflict of Laws, State Action, and Fundamental Rights Cases with Foreign Elements' (2008) 71(3) *Law and Contemporary Problems* 39; L D'Avout, 'Droits fondamentaux et coordination des ordres juridiques en droit privé' in E. Dubout and S. Touze (eds), *Les droits fondamentaux : charnière entre ordres et systèmes juridiques*, Pedone, Paris 2010, pp. 159–182, at p. 159.

On the basis of freedom of movement and European citizenship, the Court of Justice has in fact helped to remove certain obstacles to the recognition of situations in areas not covered by European regulations. This is the case in the field of names in the *Garcia-Avello*,[11] *Grunkin-Paul*[12] and *Freitag*[13] cases. It is also the case with regard to marriage in the *Coman* judgment.[14] But it is also and more recently the case in matters of filiation. In the *Pancharevo*[15] case, which gave rise to the judgment of 14 December 2021, the Court of Justice required Bulgaria to recognize the parent-child relationship of a child born in Spain as a result of medically assisted reproduction between two women. But this recognition was only imposed to allow the child to move freely within the European area. The right for a European citizen to enjoy the rights attached to this citizenship has thus led to the removal of obstacles to the circulation of personal and family situations. It is interesting to note that these various cases concern the circulation of a civil status record that enshrines a name, a union or a filiation link. Through its case law, the Court of Justice of the European Union thus contributes to reinforcing or strengthening the trend towards assimilation between acts and judgments, which is already at work in the European regulations.

The European Court of Human Rights has not remained aloof from this trend. On the basis of the right to respect for private and family life, it has also forced the States Parties to recognize family situations established abroad. This was the case with regard to adoption in the *Wagner*[16] and *Négrépontis*[17] cases, but also with regard to surrogate motherhood in the famous *Mennesson*[18] case and with regard to partnerships in the *Orlandi*[19] case. If respect for private and family life works for recognition of family situations, decisions of the European Court of Human Rights are not methodological but only substantial. The Court only requires the States Parties to recognize the content of foreign decisions and the situation they establish, but does not require them to adopt a specific method and in particular it does not require them to abandon the conflict method in favour of the recognition method.

The action of the European Courts thus makes it possible to compensate for weaknesses or shortcomings of European regulations in order to facilitate the circulation of family situations. But the European Courts also participate in the implementation of European texts by drawing the contours of public

---

11 Case C-148/02, *Garcia Avello v. Etat belge*, ECLI:EU:C:2003:539.
12 Case C-353/06, *Grunkin-Paul v. Germany*, ECLI:EU:C:2008:559.
13 Case C-541/15, *Freitag v. Germany*, ECLI:EU:C:2017:432.
14 Case C-673/16, *Coman et Hamilton v. Romania*, ECLI:EU:C:2018:385.
15 Case C-490/20, *V.M.A. v. Pancharevo*, ECLI:EU:C:2021:1008.
16 *Wagner and J.M.W.L. v. Luxembourg*, no. 76240/01.
17 *Négrépontis-Giannisis v. Greece*, no. 56759/08.
18 *Mennesson and Labassée v. France*, nos. 65192/11 and 65941/11.
19 *Orlandie v. Italy*, no. 26431/12.

policy. For if there is one constant in the regimes applicable to the recognition and enforcement of family decisions and acts, it is the respect of international public policy. This requirement, which appears in all European and international texts, is at the heart of most international family disputes. However, if each State can unilaterally determine values of public policy that may be opposed to the recognition or enforcement of a foreign decision or act, efforts to harmonize private international law systems risk being in vain. Therefore, by providing an interpretation of fundamental rights which is intended to be binding on European States, the European Courts shape the content of international public policy. The aim is that, thanks to the action of the European Courts, a European public order, the content of which would be common to all European States, would emerge.[20] Such a prospect would contribute to legal certainty by avoiding limping statuses.

However, the prospect of a European public order and its benefits must be put into perspective for two main reasons.

First, the European Courts always reserve a national margin of appreciation in the implementation of fundamental rights.[21] However, this national margin of appreciation is wider in sensitive areas where there is no political consensus and thus, in particular, in family law with the emergence of new methods of procreation. Thus, on the basis of the national margin of appreciation, the European Courts sometimes tend to restrict themselves and not to impose on States recognition of family situations. This is particularly revealing in international cases concerning conversion of the Islamic concept of 'kafala' into adoption. In the *Loudoudi*[22] and *Harroudj*[23] cases, the European Court of Human Rights was very cautious and did not require States to recognize the parent-child relationship between the child taken in by kafala and the child's guardians, partially because the parent-child relationship had not been recognized by the country of origin either.

Second, the existence and supposed benefits of a European public policy must be put into perspective because of the proportionality test.[24] The application

---

20 F. Sudre, 'Existe-t-il un ordre public européen?' in P. Tavernier (eds), *Quelle Europe pour les droits de l'homme?*, Bruylant, Bruxelles 1996, pp. 39–46, at p. 39; P. Kinsch, 'Les contours d'un ordre public européen: l'apport de la Convention européenne des droits de l'homme' in H. Fulchiron and C. Bidaud-Garon (eds), *Vers un statut européen de la famille*, colloque du Centre de droit de la famille (U. Jean-Moulin Lyon 3) et du CREDIP, nov. 2014, Dalloz, Paris 2014, pp. 147–170, at p. 147.

21 C. Picheral, 'L'expression jurisprudentielle de la subsidiarité par la marge nationale d'appréciation' in F. Sudre (eds), *Le principe de subsidiarité au sens du droit de la Convention européenne des droits de l'homme*, Nemesis, Anthémis, Paris 2014, pp. 87–112, at p. 87.

22 *Chibihi Loudoudi and others v. Belgium*, no. 52265/10.

23 *Harroudj v. France*, no. 43631/09.

24 F. Sudre, 'Le contrôle de proportionnalité de la Cour européenne des droits de l'homme. De quoi est-il question?' (2017) 11 *JCP* G 502; D. Simon, 'Le contrôle de proportionnalité exercé par la Cour de justice des Communautés européennes' (2009) 46 *LPA* 17.

and thus the interpretation of fundamental rights generally depend on the concrete circumstances of each case. Their effects may vary according to the specific circumstances of each case. The proportionality requirement reflects this variability and therefore leads to the relativization of the emergence of stable values common to all European States which would oppose, in any legal system, the creation and circulation of family situations. On the other hand, the adoption of proportionality control by the States contributes to the emergence of a common methodology beneficial to the dialogue between judges.

Although values often remain relative, the emergence of common instruments for the implementation of public policy could facilitate the standardization of solutions. Standardization that would not aim at the circulation of family situations at all costs. Standardization that would achieve a rebalancing between the supranational judge and the national judge[25] – between search for continuity in legal situations and protection of the cohesion of the internal order. It is in this constant search for balance that this author believes the systems for recognition and enforcement of family decisions and acts in Europe must be forged.

25 H. Fulchiron, 'Vers un rééquilibrage des pouvoirs en matière de protection des droits et libertés fondamentaux? Libres propos sur le rôle du juge judiciaire en tant qu'acteur du principe de subsidiarité' in *Mélanges en l'honneur de Frédéric Sudre. Les droits de l'homme à la croisée des droits*, LexisNexis, Paris 2018, pp. 245–268, at p. 245.

PARTY AUTONOMY IN INTERNATIONAL FAMILY LAW

Choice of Law and Choice of Court as a Solution to the Challenges of Cross-Border Families

Marlene Brosch*

1. INTRODUCTION

As has been highlighted throughout this volume, multiple developments in the reality of today's families put the default conception of family law more and more into question, calling to acknowledge diversity and individual choices instead.

* This article expresses the personal views of the author only.

Granting more autonomy to couples and families and recognizing individual decisions is a discussion to be held not only at the level of substantive family law, as addressed by several previous contributions, but also in private international law. More specifically, the question arises whether couples and families should be entitled to determine themselves the law applicable to their personal legal relationships and the competent courts for their disputes.

From the standpoint of the EU Regulations on cross-border family matters ('the Regulations'),[1] this question has been, at least to some extent, been answered in the positive: to this date, these Regulations have introduced various possibilities to choose the applicable law and the competent courts in several fields of family law. Party autonomy provided by these Regulations, as well as by related instruments of the Hague Conference, will be outlined in the first part of this chapter.[2] Afterwards, based on selected examples of domestic private international law rules and international conventions, party autonomy will be explored in areas of family law outside of the scope of application of the Regulations, such as the validity of marriage, family names and gender identity. The chapter concludes with overarching remarks on the analysed examples and possible parameters for the future development of party autonomy in international family law.

---

1 In chronological order: Council Regulation (EC) No 2201/2003 of 27 November 2003 concerning jurisdiction and the recognition and enforcement of judgments in matrimonial matters and the matters of parental responsibility, repealing Regulation (EC) No 1347/2000 [2003] OJ L338/1 (Brussels II bis); Council Regulation (EC) No 4/2009 of 18 December 2008 on jurisdiction, applicable law, recognition and enforcement of decisions and cooperation in matters relating to maintenance obligations [2009] OJ L7/1 (Maintenance Regulation); Council Regulation (EU) No 1259/2010 of 20 December 2010 implementing enhanced cooperation in the area of the law applicable to divorce and legal separation [2010] OJ L343/10 (Rome III); Council Regulation (EU) 2016/1103 of 24 June 2016 implementing enhanced cooperation in the area of jurisdiction, applicable law and the recognition and enforcement of decisions in matters of matrimonial property regimes [2016] OJ L183/1 (Matrimonial Property Regimes Regulation); Council Regulation (EU) 2016/1104 of 24 June 2016 implementing enhanced cooperation in the area of jurisdiction, applicable law and the recognition and enforcement of decisions in matters of the property consequences of registered partnerships [2016] OJ L183/30 (Registered Partnerships Regulation); and Council Regulation (EU) 2019/1111 of 25 June 2019 on jurisdiction, the recognition and enforcement of decisions in matrimonial matters and the matters of parental responsibility, and on international child abduction [2019] OJ L178/1 (Brussels II ter).

2 In particular, the Protocol of 23 November 2007 on the Law Applicable to Maintenance Obligations ('2007 Hague Protocol') and the Convention of 19 October 1996 on Jurisdiction, Applicable Law, Recognition, Enforcement and Co-operation in Respect of Parental Responsibility and Measures for the Protection of Children, which entered into force on 1 January 2002 ('1996 Hague Convention').

2. EU REGULATIONS ON CROSS-BORDER FAMILY MATTERS

2.1. SOLUTIONS TO ADDRESS (SOME OF) THE CHALLENGES TO CROSS-BORDER FAMILIES

2.1.1. Legal Certainty, Predictability, Flexibility and Autonomy

According to Recital 15 of Rome III, party autonomy shall lead to 'more flexibility and greater legal certainty' and 'enhance the parties' autonomy'. In a similar fashion, Recital 19 of the Maintenance Regulation, Recital 36 of the Matrimonial Property Regimes Regulation and Recital 37 of the Registered Partnerships Regulation emphasize that the introduction of party autonomy aims to 'increase legal certainty, predictability and the autonomy of the parties'.

Still, according to the Recitals, party autonomy in the areas covered by the Regulations is significantly limited by the principle of proximity, insofar as the choice of a certain law or forum should reflect a close connection to the parties and their relationship.[3] Compared to the freedom of choice in other Regulations on cross-border civil and commercial matters,[4] party autonomy in cross-border family matters is based on predetermined choice options that are concretized by specific elements. These elements mainly correspond to the connecting factors of the parties' nationality and/or habitual residence or combinations thereof.[5]

In this limited system, achieving 'more flexibility' and 'increasing autonomy' consists, in essence, of choosing among objectively connected laws or fora that are potentially applicable via the default rules. One of the solutions offered by choice of law and choice of court agreements in the Regulations is thus to let the parties themselves choose which of the broad categories of objective connecting factors

3 See Recital 19 of the Maintenance Regulation ('… enable the parties to choose the competent court by agreement on the basis of specific connecting factors'), Recital 16 Rome III Regulation ('Spouses should be able to choose the law of a country with which they have a special connection or the law of the forum as the law applicable to divorce and legal separation') and Recital 45 of the Matrimonial Property Regimes Regulation ('… choose … among the laws with which they have close links because of habitual residence or their nationality').

4 See Article 3 of Regulation (EC) No 593/2008 of the European Parliament and of the Council of 17 June 2008 on the law applicable to contractual obligations (Rome I) [2008] OJ L177/6 and Article 25 of Regulation (EU) No 1215/2012 of the European Parliament and of the Council of 12 December 2012 on jurisdiction and the recognition and enforcement of judgments in civil and commercial matters [2012] OJ L351/1.

5 For a detailed overview and comparison of the choice options, see M. Brosch, *Rechtswahl und Gerichtsstandsvereinbarung im internationalen Familien- und Erbrecht der EU*, Mohr Siebeck, Tübingen 2019, pp. 153–62; J. Gray, *Party Autonomy in EU Private International Law. Choice of Court and Choice of Law in Family Matters and Succession*, Intersentia, Cambridge 2021, pp. 156–60.

(mainly habitual residence or nationality) shall apply.[6] However, the range of eligible laws or jurisdictions does not necessarily rely on identical objective connecting factors as the default rules. For instance, Article 5(1)(b) Rome III does not presuppose a temporal limit concerning the choice of the law of the State of the spouses' last habitual residence. In contrast, under the corresponding default rule in Article 8(a) Rome III, the period of the spouses' last residence must not have ended more than one year before the start of divorce proceedings. Another example is Article 22(1) Matrimonial Property Regimes Regulation, according to which the parties may choose the law of the State of nationality of either spouse or of the State in which one of them is habitually resident, whereas the default rule in Article 26 refers to the spouses' common habitual residence or common nationality. In several instances, the specific manifestation of 'close connection' for the purposes of party autonomy is thus looser than in the objective connections defining the default rules. Consequently, party autonomy in the Regulations on cross-border family matters provides a certain flexibility to deviate from the conception of 'close connection' enshrined in the default rules. Moreover, certain choice options particularly support forum shopping, namely the choice of the *lex fori* in combination with generous jurisdiction rules[7] as well as the place where the legal relationship was created.[8]

Flexibility also has a temporal dimension. The rules on party autonomy in the Regulations allow for adaptations where the objective connections in the default rules are immutable, i.e., where they refer to fixed moments in time.[9] This is the case, for instance, in the default applicable law rule for matrimonial property regimes, based on the spouses' first common habitual residence after the conclusion of the marriage (Article 26(1)(a) of the Matrimonial Property Regimes Regulation). To overcome a lack of proximity where they have relocated over the course of their marriage,[10] the spouses can align the applicable law to their new habitual residence via a choice of law agreement under Article 22(1)(a) of the Regulation.

---

6 J. Gray, above n. 5, p. 142; K. Kroll-Ludwigs, *Die Rolle der Parteiautonomie im europäischen Kollisionsrecht*, Mohr Siebeck, Tübingen 2013, pp. 413–14; A. Mills, *Party Autonomy in Private International Law*, Cambridge University Press, Cambridge 2018, p. 445.

7 See Article 7 of the 2007 Hague Protocol in combination with one of the four choice of court options pursuant to Article 4 of the Maintenance Regulation, or the choice of the *lex fori* under Article 5(1)(d) Rome III Regulation in combination with the alternative jurisdiction grounds of Article 3 Brussels II bis/Brussels II ter.

8 See Articles 7(1) and 22(1)(c) of the Registered Partnerships Regulation.

9 K. Kroll-Ludwigs, above n. 6, p. 409.

10 For a more detailed assessment see, among others, A. Bonomi, 'The Proposal for a Regulation on Matrimonial Property' in K. Boele-Woelki, N. Dethloff and W. Gephart (eds), *Family Law and Culture in Europe*, Intersentia, Cambridge 2014, pp. 231–47; B. Heiderhoff, 'Die EU-Güterrechtsverordnungen' [2018] 1 *Praxis des Internationalen Privat- und Verfahresrechts* 5.

Turning to legal certainty and predictability, choice of law and choice of court agreements have an added value, in particular, for couples and families who relocate frequently or whose mobile lifestyle includes complex connections to various countries. In such cases, identifying ex post which law applies and which courts have jurisdiction can be cumbersome and create avenues for litigation. Choice of law and choice of court agreements thus empower parties to determine beforehand which law governs their legal relationship and where they can go to court.[11] For instance, the choice options on applicable law are usually fixed at the time the agreement is concluded,[12] thus avoiding the mutability of the applicable law that could result in certain cases from the default rules.[13] Moreover, choice of law agreements allow to exclude recourse to escape clauses enshrined in the default rules.[14] The admissibility of agreements on the applicable law and jurisdiction under the Regulations is regulated exhaustively and can only exceptionally be reviewed on a discretionary basis.[15]

2.1.2. *Coordination, Uniformity and the Protection of Weaker Parties*

In a typical family law dispute, several intertwined issues are at stake, such as the custody over children, maintenance obligations and the distribution of matrimonial property. Cross-border settings add an additional layer of legal questions to the case. In this context, choice of law and choice of court can be a means to have a single law applicable to related issues and to concentrate disputes in a single forum. This uniformity avoids frictions between different substantive laws and prevents parallel litigation in different countries, which can ultimately save time and money. From this standpoint, coordination on the level of private

---

11 See C. González Beilfuss, 'The Role of Party Autonomy in Pursuing Coordination' in I. Viarengo and F.C. Villata (eds), *Planning the Future of Cross-Border Families. A Path Through Coordination*, Hart, Oxford 2020, pp. 243–57, at p. 247.

12 For a detailed analysis, see J. Gray, above n. 5, pp. 219–22, 243.

13 This is the case, for instance, under the general rule for maintenance obligations in Article 3 of the 2007 Hague Protocol, which refers to the creditor's habitual residence. An example taken from national law is the applicable law rule on the general effects of marriage in Germany (Article 14 Einführungsgesetz zum Bürgerlichen Gesetzbuch, hereinafter 'EGBGB'). In the absence of a choice of law agreement, the applicable law is determined, in the first place, by the spouses' habitual residence.

14 For instance, Article 26(3) of the Matrimonial Property Regimes Regulation allows either spouse to request the competent court, under certain conditions, to decide on the application of a different law than the law of the State of the spouses' first common habitual residence.

15 This is the case for jurisdiction agreements in matters of parental responsibility (Article 12 Brussels II bis and Article 10 Brussels II ter). A further example is Article 8(5) of the 2007 Hague Protocol, pursuant to which the choice of law is invalid in case of 'manifestly unfair or unreasonable consequences'; see A. Bonomi, *Protocol of 23 November 2007 on the law applicable to maintenance obligations – Explanatory Report*, Hague Conference on Private International Law, The Hague 2013, paras 149–50.

international law can be a key issue for the parties concerned.[16] With regard to party autonomy, the Regulations on cross-border family matters consider such interplay through the employment of similar connecting factors, which favour parallel choices.[17]

However, the overarching approach may not seem consistent: only in three out of the five areas of family law concerned – namely for maintenance obligations, for matrimonial property regimes and for property consequences of registered partnerships – both the competent court(s) and the applicable law may be chosen.[18] For divorce and legal separation, Rome III permits spouses to conclude a choice of law agreement whereas Brussels II bis and Brussels II ter do not provide for agreements on jurisdiction in matrimonial matters, which has been widely criticized.[19] In matters relating to parental responsibility, the 1996 Hague Convention (to which all EU Member States are contracting parties[20]), with very few exceptions, does not allow deviation from the jurisdiction centralized in the State of the child's habitual residence.[21] Conversely, Brussels II bis and Brussels II ter endorse greater procedural autonomy, structured upon the best interests of the child.[22]

Is there an explanation for these differences? From a diachronic point of view, there is arguably no consistent development towards more party autonomy in judicial cooperation in family matters. For instance, the Maintenance Regulation adopted in 2008 endorses a wide range of choice of court possibilities, whereas the most recent Regulation, Brussels II ter adopted in 2019, has still not introduced any choice of court possibilities in matrimonial matters. In contrast,

---

16 See C. González Beilfuss, above n. 11, p. 248; K. Kroll-Ludwigs, above n. 6, p. 439.

17 For detailed assessment see C. Kohler, 'La segmentation du statut personnel comme vecteur de l'autonomie de la volonté en matière familiale et successorale' in H. Fulchiron, A. Panet and P. Wautelet (eds), *L'autonomie de la volonté dans les relations familiales internationales*, Bruylant, Brussels 2017, pp. 73–90, at pp. 77, 83–7; L. Walker, 'Party autonomy, inconsistency and the specific characteristics of family law in the EU' (2018) 2 *Journal of Private International Law* 225, 227–40.

18 See Article 4 of the Maintenance Regulation in connection with Articles 7 and 8 of the 2007 Hague Protocol, Articles 7 and 22 of the Matrimonial Property Regimes Regulation and Articles 7 and 22 of the Registered Partnerships Regulation.

19 Among others, J. Antomo, 'Die Neufassung der Brüssel IIa-VO – erfolgte Änderungen und verbleibender Reformbedarf' in T. Pfeiffer, Q.C. Lobach and T. Rapp (eds), *Europäisches Familien- und Erbrecht*, Nomos, Baden-Baden 2020, pp. 13–60, at pp. 20–2; T. Kruger and L. Samyn, 'Brussels II bis: Successes and Suggested Improvements' (2016) 12 *Journal of Private International Law* 143–5.

20 The status table is available at <https://www.hcch.net/en/instruments/conventions/status-table/?cid=70> accessed 12.05.2023.

21 See the Practitioners' Tool: Cross-Border Recognition and Enforcement of Agreements Reached in the Course of Family Matters Involving Children (2022), para 35 <https://assets.hcch.net/docs/c7696f38-9469-4f18-a897-e9b0e1f6505a.pdf> accessed 12.05.2023.

22 For a further analysis of Article 12 Brussels II bis and Article 10 Brussels II ter see J. Antomo, above n. 19, pp. 36–40; T. Kruger and S. Corneloup, 'Le règlement 2019/1111, Bruxelles II: la protection des enfants gagne du ter(rain)' [2020] *Revue critique du droit international privé* 215.

the Property Regimes Regulations, both adopted in 2016, admit choice of court agreements.

A direct relation between, on the one hand, the extent of party autonomy granted and the specific legislative procedure and/or the number of Member States involved in the legislative procedure, on the other hand, does not seem to appear either. For instance, the Maintenance Regulation and the two Property Regimes Regulations grant the widest range of choice options but different legislative procedures (the special legislative procedure and the enhanced cooperation mechanism,[23] respectively) led to their adoption.

A further argument for explaining the sectoral differences seems however to transpire from the foregoing comparison, namely, an articulation between party autonomy and the subject matters of the Regulations. On the one hand, in areas involving primarily economic aspects (maintenance obligations and property regimes), party autonomy is more prominent. Concretely, parties may designate both the applicable law and the jurisdiction and the respective choice options require the loosest degree of 'proximity' (in particular, the habitual residence or the nationality of either spouse).[24] On the other hand, party autonomy is more limited in family matters which are not primarily of economic nature but concern status changes (dissolution of marriage) or the care and protection of children (parental responsibility).From the perspective of substantive law, these different approaches compare to the existence of contracting options or the predominance of mandatory rules in the various areas of family law.[25] In particular, agreements on maintenance obligations and property regimes are not a new phenomenon,[26] as opposed to out of-court divorces or agreements on parenthood.[27] In this context, the protection of weaker parties is a further substantive element raised to justify the limitation or exclusion of party autonomy. For instance, the protection of children and the prevention of conflicts of interests with the person providing their care led to the exclusion of choice of law agreements[28] and choice of court agreements[29] for maintenance obligations

23 On the EU primary law dimension of cross-border family matters, see the contribution of M. Csöndes ('A Fragmented Private International Family Law: Interactions and Intersections of International, European and National Norms').

24 See, for instance, Article 4(1)(a)(b) Maintenance Regulation, Article 22(1)(a)(b) Matrimonial Property Regimes Regulation and Article 22(1)(a)(b) Registered Partnerships Regulation.

25 On the justification of party autonomy in family matters through substantive law see C. Kohler, *L'autonomie de la volonté en droit international privé: un principe universel entre libéralisme et étatisme*, Brill/Nijhoff, Hague Academy of International Law 2013, p. 177; K. Kroll-Ludwigs, above n. 6, p. 450.

26 For a comparative analysis, see the contribution of C. Voithofer ('Emancipatory Potential of Maintenance and Matrimonial Property after Divorce: Reflections Based on the Concept of Relational Autonomy').

27 See the contributions of P. Quinzá Redondo ('The Recognition of Non-Judicial Divorces in Europe') and D. Lima ('Three Models for Regulating Multiple Parenthood: A Comparative Perspective'), respectively.

28 See Article 8(3) of the 2007 Hague Protocol.

29 See Recital 19 and Article 4(3) of the Maintenance Regulation.

towards children.[30] The recent Commission proposal for a Regulation on parenthood confirms this approach by excluding procedural party autonomy precisely because of the mandatory nature of the substantive rights concerned.[31] A more nuanced approach is to grant party autonomy subject to discretionary conditions and with an enhanced focus on the best interests of the child, as it is the case in Article 10 Brussels II ter.[32] While the first approach has the benefit of foreseeability, the latter grants more flexibility in specific cases.[33]

2.2. CHALLENGES WITHIN THE GENERAL FRAMEWORK FOR CROSS-BORDER FAMILY MATTERS

2.2.1. Fragmentation in a Multi-Layered Legal Framework

The general framework of the Regulations encompassing the rules on party autonomy may affect the solutions that can be achieved through the available choice options. An important backdrop is the multiple layers of fragmentation of the current Regulations.[34] First, as the Regulations do not equally apply in all Member States, a choice of law or choice of court agreement could not be recognized under the domestic private international law of those Member States that did not take part in the enhanced cooperation mechanisms.[35] Second, the piece-meal approach[36] of EU legislation in international family

---

30 P. Beaumont, 'International Family Law in Europe – the Maintenance Project, the Hague Conference and the EC: A Triumph of Reverse Subsidiarity' (2009) 73 *RabelsZ*, 509, 533; A. Bonomi, above n. 15, para. 128.

31 See Proposal for a Council Regulation on jurisdiction, applicable law, recognition of decisions and acceptance of authentic instruments in matters of parenthood and on the creation of a European Certificate of Parenthood, COM(2022) 695 final, p. 13: 'Given that, in most Member States, rights concerning parenthood cannot be settled or waived, the proposal does not provide for party autonomy as regards jurisdiction (such as a choice of court or transfer of jurisdiction)'.

32 See J. Antomo, above n. 19, pp. 37–38; A. Schulz, 'Die Neufassung der Brüssel IIa-Verordnung' [2020] *Zeitschrift für das gesamte Familienrecht* 1141, 1142.

33 U. Maunsbach, 'Party Autonomy in European Family and Succession Law' in T. Pfeiffer, Q. Lobach, and T. Rapp (eds), *Facilitating Cross-Border Family Life – Towards a Common European Understanding. EUFams II and Beyond*, Heidelberg University Press, Heidelberg 2021, pp. 21–48, at p. 47 observes in this respect a 'dual development strengthening the position of weaker parties whilst diminishing foreseeability'.

34 See also M. Csöndes ('A Fragmented Private International Family Law: Interactions and Intersections of International, European and National Norms').

35 J. Gray, above n. 5, pp. 281, 285; D. Henrich, 'Zur Parteiautonomie im europäisierten internationalen Familienrecht', in A.L. Verbeke, J.M. Scherpe, C. Declerck, T. Helms and P. Senaeve (eds), *Confronting the Frontiers of Family Law and Succession. Liber Amicorum Walter Pintens*, Intersentia, Cambridge 2012, pp. 701–13, at pp. 710–11.

36 D. Martiny, 'Objectives and Values of (Private) International Law in Family Law' in J. Meeusen, M. Pertegás, G. Straetmans and F. Swennen (eds), *International Family Law for the European Union*, Intersentia, Antwerpen/Oxford 2007, pp. 69–99, at pp. 98.

law comes to the detriment of accessibility and usability of the rules on party autonomy. Practitioners (let alone interested parties without legal education) need to familiarize themselves with a puzzle of EU law rules and domestic law to identify for each area of family law the available options and to verify how these rules interact with domestic law that applies for aspects not covered by the Regulations. More particularly, while the Regulations' uniform rules define the admissibility of choice of law and choice of court agreements, the formal and substantive validity of these agreements is subject to several intersections between EU law and domestic law.[37]

2.2.2. Scope of Application of the Regulations

The open questions on the characterization of 'marriage' and 'divorce' have received much scholarly attention,[38] as they are of overarching relevance for the uniform of application of the Regulations, including the rules on choice of law and choice of court agreements. From the perspective of party autonomy, drawing a narrow line to the scope of application of the Regulations may exclude certain couples and families from enjoying any options for choice at all. Domestic private international law or international conventions that apply instead do not necessarily grant party autonomy in the area of family law. If they do, the enforcement of the respective agreements would likely vary from one Member State to the other.

2.2.3. Public Policy

As highlighted above, the Recitals of the Regulations emphasize choice of law and choice of court agreements as a means to increase the autonomy of the parties. Yet the limitation of party autonomy to predetermined choice options provides only a partial solution to uphold individual choices and to overcome the divergences in substantive family laws highlighted throughout this volume. The Regulations harmonize the admissibility of party autonomy only on an abstract level, i.e., they define a closed list of available choice options. The actual enforcement of an agreement, however, may vary among the Member States from the perspective

---

37 For instance, choice of law agreements may be subject to stricter formal requirements under domestic law pursuant to Article 7(2)–(4) Rome III and Article 23(2)–(4) of the Matrimonial Property Regimes Regulation and of the Registered Partnerships Regulation, whereas no equivalent provisions exist for choice of court agreements; see M. Brosch, above n. 5, pp. 176–80, 185; J. Gray, above n. 5, pp. 222–35, 244–45.

38 See, among others, J. Villaverde ('Same-Sex Couples and EU Private International Law after *Coman*'); I. Viarengo, F. Villata, N. Nisi, L. Valkova, D. Danieli and C. Peraro, 'Defining Marriage and Other Unions of Persons in European Family Law' in T. Pfeiffer, Q. Lobach and T. Rapp (eds), *Facilitating Cross-Border Family Life – Towards a Common European Understanding. EUFams II and Beyond*, Heidelberg University Press, Heidelberg 2021, pp. 151–216, at pp. 166–207.

of public policy by putting to the test the concrete result of a choice. Recent national case law on the application of the Succession Regulation[39] exemplifies the potential impact of public policy on party autonomy.[40]

The interaction between party autonomy and public policy in the Regulations on cross-border family matters is however not necessarily negative. From a conceptual standpoint, the available choice options (as well as the default rules) are mostly subject to similar objective elements for both the applicable law and jurisdiction or are linked to each other. This increases the parallelism between the law and the forum and, consequently, limits the potential application of the public policy exceptions.[41] In addition, the principle of effet utile arguably speaks in favour of restricting public policy, as the available choice options are limited at the outset and would have little practical relevance if domestic courts set the parties' choices aside too easily.

Furthermore, although the content of public policy exceptions in EU legislative acts is in principle defined by the Member States according to their own conceptions, the limits within which national judges have recourse to this exception are not without control by EU law[42] and are reviewed by the Court of Justice of the European Union.[43] It would thus be desirable that domestic

39 Regulation (EU) No 650/2012 of the European Parliament and of the Council of 4 July 2012 on jurisdiction, applicable law, recognition and enforcement of decisions and acceptance and enforcement of authentic instruments in matters of succession and on the creation of a European Certificate of Succession [2012] OJ L201/107.

40 In a succession case in which the deceased had chosen English succession law pursuant to the Succession Regulation, the Austrian Supreme Court ruled that the absence of reserved shares under English law does not violate the Austrian public policy 'in general'. However, it left open whether a different answer would apply in case of a close connection to the forum; see OGH 25.02.2021, 2 Ob 214/20i, *EvBl* 2021/131. Interestingly, the Austrian Supreme Court had been asked by the claimants to file a preliminary reference to the Court of Justice of the European Union (ECJ) but considered the matter an *acte clair*. In a similar case under the Succession Regulation, in which the connection to the forum seemed however stronger, the Upper Regional Court of Cologne held that the absence of reserved shares is 'in general' incompatible with German public policy; see OLG Köln 22.04.2021, *ZEV* 2021, 698.

41 J. Gray, above n. 5, pp. 160–61, 184–85; P. Hammje, 'Ordre public et lois de police. Limites à l'autonomie de la volonté ?' in H. Fulchiron, A. Panet and P. Wautelet (eds), *L'autonomie de la volonté dans les relations familiales internationales*, Bruylant, Brussels 2017, pp. 111–38, at pp. 111–13; L. Rademacher, 'Die Abwehr anstößigen Familien- und Erbrechts: Zwischen Toleranz und Geschlechtergleichstellung' in C.S. Rupp (ed.), IPR zwischen Tradition und Innovation, Mohr Siebeck, Tübingen 2019, pp. 121–40, at p. 128.

42 It is noteworthy that Article 22 of the Proposal for a Council Regulation on jurisdiction, applicable law, recognition of decisions and acceptance of authentic instruments in matters of parenthood and on the creation of a European Certificate of Parenthood (COM(2022) 695 final) states that the public policy exception laid down in this article shall be applied 'in observance of the fundamental rights and principles laid down in the Charter, in particular Article 21 thereof on the right to non-discrimination'.

43 See, most recently, Case C-490/20, *V.M.A. v. Stolichna obshtina, rayon 'Pancharevo'*, ECLI:EU:C:2021:1008, paras 55–56, on the recognition of motherhood (discussed in the contribution of K. Rokas ('Surrogacy and Assisted Reproduction: A Challenge for Family Law and for

courts make use of the preliminary reference procedure to obtain guidance on the handling of public policy exceptions in the field of international family law. Allowing courts to apply the public policy test and to engage with foreign law may actually contribute to developing a narrower conception of what constitutes a fundamental value to the domestic legal order.[44] Examples of nuanced approaches to public policy concern, for instance, foreign divorce law with shorter or no separation periods in contrast to domestic legislation,[45] the validity of child marriages[46] or the recognition of unilateral divorce declarations.[47]

3. DOMESTIC PRIVATE INTERNATIONAL LAW AND INTERNATIONAL CONVENTIONS

The EU Regulations on cross-border family matters cover only a few areas of family law. Subject matters pertaining to the 'core' of personal status, i.e., the establishment of a particular family relationship, such as filiation, adoption or marriage, are expressly excluded from their substantive scope of application.[48] Other sensitive areas that relate more generally to the law of persons are not specifically mentioned, in particular names and gender identity. These areas of

Private International Law Methodology')) and the conclusions of Advocate-General Collins in the case C-646/20, *Senatsverwaltung für Inneres und Sport*, ECLI:EU:C:2022:357, paras 57–59, on the recognition of out-of-court divorces under Brussels II bis (discussed in the contribution of P. Quinzá Redondo ('The Recognition of Non-Judicial Divorces in Europe')).

44 M. Brosch and C.M. Mariottini, 'The European Model of "Couple" within the Dissolution of Marriage' in E. Bernard, M. Cresp and M. Ho-Dac (eds), *La famille dans l'ordre juridique de l'Union européenne*, Bruylant, Bruxelles 2020, pp. 175–94, at p. 187; P. Hammje, above n. 41, p. 137.

45 In Italy, for instance, it is settled case law that foreign law allowing to file directly for divorce without previous separation is not contrary to the Italian public policy. The foreign divorce law must however require the establishment of the irreparable breakdown of the community of life between the spouses; see, among others, Cassazione civile, sez. I, ordinanza 21 maggio 2018 n° 12473, *RDIPP* 2019, 163 on the recognition of a 'direct' divorce pursuant to Romanian law (however, the Court erroneously applied the domestic recognition rules and not Brussels II bis).

46 See the contribution of T.L. Wærstad ('Human Rights Protection in Family Reunification Law and the Recognition of Child Marriages').

47 K. Kaesling, 'The Recognition of Religious Private Divorces in Europe' in K. Boele-Woelki and D. Martiny (eds), *Plurality and Diversity of Family Relations in Europe*, Intersentia, Cambridge 2019, pp. 257–84, at p. 284 (with examples from France, Germany and the United Kingdom).

48 Article 1(3) Brussels II bis and Article 1(4) Brussels II ter exclude, among others, 'the establishment or contesting of a parent-child relationship' and decisions on adoption from its scope of application. Recital 21 Maintenance Regulation states that '[t]he establishment of family relationships continues to be covered by the national law of the Member States, including their rules of private international law'. Article 1(2) Matrimonial Property Regimes Regulation and Article 1(2) Registered Partnerships Regulation exclude, among others, the legal capacity of spouses or partners and the existence, validity or recognition of a marriage or of a registered partnership from their respective scope of application.

law and, consequently, the question of party autonomy thus remain a matter of domestic private international law or international conventions.

Against this background and based on selected examples of domestic legal orders, this chapter will analyse to what extent party autonomy plays a role outside of the scope of the Regulations. For the purposes of this chapter, the term 'party autonomy' refers essentially to the applicable law. Choice of court agreements in these particular areas of family law seemingly play a negligible role, be that because international jurisdiction is exhaustively determined by mandatory rules[49] or because choice of court agreements are limited to particular disputes.[50]

3.1. MARRIAGES AND REGISTERED PARTNERSHIPS

Few examples of direct choice options appear in domestic private international law for the law applicable to the general or personal effects (i.e, non-economic effects) of marriages[51] or of registered partnerships.[52] A noteworthy example is the applicable law rule on the general effects of marriage in Germany:[53] the national legislator amended this provision after the Matrimonial Property Regimes Regulation entered into force and aligned it to the latter. This alignment resulted in a strengthened role of party autonomy.[54] The design of harmonized rules in EU Regulations may thus have a positive impact on party autonomy in connected areas of family law that are still subject to domestic private international law. Entitling spouses and partners to choose the law for the

49 See, for instance, T. Rauscher, 'Artikel 98 FamFG' in T. Rauscher (ed.), *Münchener Kommentar zum FamFG*, vol. 1, 3rd ed., C.H. Beck, Munich 2018, para. 98, for matrimonial matters; ibid., 'Artikel 100', para. 21 for disputes on filiation.

50 In Switzerland, Article 5 of the Bundesgesetz über das Internationale Privatrecht vom 18. Dezember 1987 (IPRG) permits choice of court agreements in matters involving an 'economic interest'. In Belgium, Article 6(1) of the Loi portant le Code de droit international privé, 16 juillet 2004, allows for prorogation and derogation only with regard to 'disposable rights'.

51 For instance, in the Netherlands, Article 10:35 Burgerlijk Wetboek allows the choice of the law of the State of the spouses' common nationality or habitual residence. In Spain, Article 9(2) Código civil provides for the same connecting factors but a connection to only one spouse suffices.

52 Article 10:64 Burgerlijk Wetboek does not limit the choice of law on the basis of certain connecting factors, but requires that the chosen law recognizes registered partnerships.

53 Article 14 EGBGB.

54 D. Looschelders, 'Artikel 14 EGBGB' in J. von Hein (ed.), *Münchener Kommentar zum Bürgerlichen Gesetzbuch*, vol. 12, 8th ed., C.H. Beck, Munich 2020, at para. 3. The amendment added the law of the State of the spouses' common habitual residence or of their last habitual residence (if one of the spouses still resides there at the time of the choice of law agreement) to the previous choice option relating to the law of the State of either spouse's nationality.

personal effects of their legal relationship can actually constitute a complement to party autonomy for economic aspects (property regimes and maintenance obligations).

In contrast, direct choice options seem to be generally excluded for the substantive validity of marriages, the nationality principle being the main connecting factor.[55] Apart from the rather unlikely event of acquiring a certain nationality to have the respective law applied, the connection to the parties' nationality leaves little room to manoeuvre the validity of their relationship, in particular if their home State does not formally recognize their relationship. Party autonomy may however come into play via connecting factors that refer to the place of creation of a certain status to determine its validity. In recent times, national legislators have adopted such connections, for instance, for the registration of a partnership[56] or the place where the marriage was concluded in case of same-sex marriages.[57] By choosing the place of creation of their legal relationship, parties can indirectly influence the applicable law and thus secure the validity of their relationship.[58]

However, keeping the conclusion of a marriage or of a registered partnership largely outside of the scope of party autonomy can actually be an argument in favour of granting choice elsewhere, such as for the effects of these relationships. Once a marriage or registered partnership is validly concluded under the control of the State, in particular concerning the free will of the parties to enter into a legal relationship, it appears more adequate to grant autonomy 'in a second step' for its effects.

---

55 See, for a comparative overview, P. Mankowski, 'Art 13 EGBGB' in J. von Staudingers., *Kommentar zum Bürgerlichen Gesetzbuch mit Einführungsgesetz und Nebengesetzen. Einführungsgesetz zum Bürgerlichen Gesetzbuche/IPR. Art 13-17b EGBGB*, Sellier/de Gruyter, Berlin 2011, at para. 50.

56 For instance, the Austrian provision in §27a of the Bundesgesetz vom 15. Juni 1978 über das internationale Privatrecht (IPRG). The Property Regimes Regulation also refers to the *lex registrationis* as one of the available choice options (Article 22(1)(c)) and as the law applicable by default (Article 26(1)). Similarly, in Germany, Article 17b EGBGB refers, for the establishment and the general effects of registered partnerships, to the law of the State in whose records the partnerships has been registered.

57 In Austria, under Article 17(1a) IPRG, which has been introduced in 2019 after the legalization of same-sex marriages, the validity of a marriage may be assessed in accordance with the law of the State in which the marriage is concluded. This is the case if one of the laws applicable by default (i.e., the law of the State of nationality of each spouse) does not provide for a marriage on the basis of one or both spouses' sex; see S. Nitsch, 'Gleichgeschlechtliche Ehen im IPR – vom Personalstatut zum Begründungsstatut' [2019] *Fachzeitschrift für Familienrecht* 400. In Germany, under Article 17b(4) EGBGB, the law applicable to the validity requirements of same-sex marriages is determined in a similar way to registered partnerships, i.e., by the law of the State in whose records the marriage has been registered.

58 J. Gray, above n. 5, p. 154.

3.2. NAMES AND GENDER IDENTITY

In the European landscape, several examples exist for party autonomy with regard to names of persons.[59] For instance, German law[60] allows the choice of the law applicable to family names for spouses and children, whereas Belgian law[61] and Swiss law[62] both give the possibility to designate unilaterally the law applicable to one's own name. Their common feature is that the options are essentially bound to the law of the State of nationality and/or habitual residence.[63] Nevertheless, these options are noteworthy insofar as they concern an area of law that constitutes a core aspect of a person's individual identity but does not necessarily relate to a family relationship, unlike the options discussed so far.

Could party autonomy for the establishment of names thus act as a gateway for other areas linked to a person's identity and self-determination, for instance with regard to gender identity? In Germany, an expert report of 2017 as well as a ministerial proposal of 2019 discussed the introduction of specific private international law rules for matters of gender, applying nationality as the primary connecting factor and granting limited party autonomy on the basis of habitual residence.[64] Other legal orders already recognize gender as a specific category of a person's identity on the level of private international law. In this respect, Belgian and Swiss law are again an interesting example. Since 2007, Belgian law specifically regulates the law governing the change of gender by referring to the general rule on personal status and capacity, i.e., to the law of the State of the applicant's nationality.[65] In Switzerland, along with substantive provisions for

---

59 With further references C. Kohler, 'Subjektive Anknüpfung: Kommentar' in A. Dutta, T. Helms and W. Pintens (eds), *Ein Name in ganz Europa: Vorschläge für ein internationales Namensrecht der Europäischen Union*, Wolfgang Metzner Verlag, Frankfurt/Main 2016, pp. 63–73, at pp. 63–65.

60 The choice options under Article 10(2)(3) EGBGB refer to the law of the State of either spouse's nationality or German law, if one of the spouses is habitually resident there.

61 Article 37(2) Loi portant le Code de droit international privé permits a choice between multiple nationalities.

62 Under Article 37(2) IPRG, a person may request to have their name governed by the law of the State of their citizenship instead of Swiss law or the law referred to by the private international law rules of their State of domicile.

63 Scholarly proposals for EU private international law rules also advocate for similar parameters; see R. Freitag, 'Subjektive Anknüpfung: Vorstellung des Vorschlags' in A. Dutta, T. Helms and W. Pintens (eds), *Ein Name in ganz Europa: Vorschläge für ein internationales Namensrecht der Europäischen Union*, Wolfgang Metzner Verlag, Frankfurt/Main 2016, pp. 49–62.

64 For comments on these proposals see S.L. Gössl, 'Art. 10a EGBGB-Vorschlag: Kollisionsrechtliche Ergänzung des Vorschlags zum Geschlechtervielfaltsgesetz' [2017] *Praxis des Internationalen Privat- und Verfahresrechts* 339, 341–42, and S. Rossbach, 'Kollisionsrecht und Geschlecht im Wandel' in K. Duden (ed.), *IPR für eine bessere Welt*, Mohr Siebeck, Tübingen 2022, pp. 125–42, at pp. 139–41.

65 Article 35 ter in connection with Article 34(1) Loi portant le Code de droit international privé; see further A. Dutta and W. Pintens, 'Private International Law Aspects of Intersex'

the transcription of gender changes in the civil status records, a new conflict of laws rules entered into force in January 2022 that applies the private international law rules on names by analogy to a person's gender.[66] The reference *en bloc* to the chapter on names includes the option to chose the law of the State of nationality laid down for the change of names. However, according to the preparatory works, if the chosen law permits someone to register a third gender, the entry in the Swiss registers will be made in accordance with the principles applicable in Switzerland (binary gender order) and it is not possible to enter a third gender in the civil status register.[67] However, this situation could change in the future.[68]

3.3. REPRESENTATION OF VULNERABLE ADULTS

As a final example, the representation of vulnerable adults merits special attention in the present discussion from the standpoint of party autonomy and self-determination in cross-border settings. Of particular interest is the possible interaction between different sources of private international law. The Hague Convention of 13 January 2000 on the International Protection of Adults, which applies in 12 Member States,[69] provides for unilateral choice of law options for powers of representation. Specifically, the Convention grants limited choice options based on a closed list of laws, which leaves no room for court discretion.[70] The negotiations viewed this as a more appropriate solution than complete freedom of choice.[71] The underlying rationale thus aligns with the overarching party autonomy approach in the EU Regulations on cross-border family matters. As such, it could set an example for future EU legislation on the protection of adults in Europe. In the context of the public consultation process of the European Commission for an EU initiative, scholarly proposals already seem to point in this direction.[72]

---

in J.M. Scherpe, A. Dutta and T. Helsm (eds), *The Legal Status of Intersex Persons*, Intersentia, Cambridge 2018, pp. 415–26, at pp. 421–22.

66 Article 40a IPRG. The legislative amendment is published at <https://www.fedlex.admin.ch/eli/fga/2020/2689/de> accessed 12.05.2023.

67 See the contribution of S. Duffy ('Gender Identity: A Comparative European Perspective').

68 See the commentary of August 2021 on the legislation amendment, pp. 6, 9–10 <https://www.newsd.admin.ch/newsd/message/attachments/74726.pdf> accessed 12.05.2023.

69 Austria, Belgium, Cyprus, Czech Republic, Estonia, Finland, France, Germany, Greece, Latvia, Malta and Portugal; see the status table at <https://www.hcch.net/en/instruments/conventions/status-table/?cid=71> accessed 12.05.2023.

70 Article 15(2) of the Convention allows the choice of the law of a State of which the adult is a national, the law of a State of a former habitual residence of the adult, or the law of a State in which property of the adult is located, with respect to that property.

71 P. Lagarde, *Explanatory Report on the Hague Convention of 13 January 2000 on the International Protection of Adults*, The Hague Conference on Private International Law, The Hague 2017, paras 100–02.

72 In particular, it is suggested that a unilateral choice of court in an EU instrument could complement the choice of law options in the Convention; see the European Association of

4. OVERARCHING CONCLUSIONS AND A LOOK AHEAD

It results from the above that similar patterns for the construction of party autonomy exist across the EU Regulations, domestic private international law and international sources. First, if party autonomy is granted, it is essentially limited to closed lists of choice options, which are based on predetermined connecting factors. Admittedly, granting unlimited choices to parties at the outset would add flexibility to manoeuvre the applicable law and the jurisdiction in order to secure a certain substantive result (e.g., the conclusion of a same-sex marriage or the establishment of parenthood for children born through surrogacy). However, particularly in areas with significant national diversity as to the legal conception of personal status, this could incite courts to curtail the result of such forum shopping afterwards via public policy,[73] ultimately compromising the benefit of choice of law and choice of court agreements in terms of legal certainty and predictability. Controlling the intensity of the public policy exception and its limits would thus become even more critical.

Second, there is a certain correlation between party autonomy and the areas of substantive family law concerned. At present, party autonomy plays its primary role in those EU Regulations whose subject matters relate to economic aspects of relationships and to the dissolution of a previously established personal status. In this regard, party autonomy seems generally more prominent when the area of substantive law concerned also recognizes contractual or unilateral dispositions of the parties over their legal relationships. Arguably, the effectiveness of party autonomy thus relies on a minimum convergent approach in the substantive laws of the Member States. In contrast, in domestic private international law, party autonomy plays little to no role for the establishment of personal status. The introduction of party autonomy in such sensitive areas (e.g., marriage, filiation or adoption) must however face several reservations. Arguments against the introduction of party autonomy pertain, for instance, to potential conflicts of interest (e.g., concerning the status of minors and parent-child relationships) or to the loss of legal certainty over the validity of personal status (e.g., if party autonomy is granted under discretionary conditions that could lead to invalidating an agreement at a later stage). Hence, party autonomy

---

Private International Law, *Position Paper in response to the European Commission's public consultation on an EU-wide protection for vulnerable adults*, 26 March 2022, pp. 8–11 <https://eapil.org/wp-content/uploads/2022/04/Position-Paper-29.03.22.pdf> accessed 12.05.2023; C. Fountoulakis, G. Mäsch, E. Bargelli, P. Franzina and A. Ward, *Response of the European Law Institute – The European Commission's Public Consultation on the Initiative on the Cross-Border Protection of Vulnerable Adults*, European Law Institute, Vienna 2022, p. 13 <https://www.europeanlawinstitute.eu/fileadmin/user_upload/p_eli/Publications/ELI_Response_Protection_of_Adults.pdf> accessed 12.05.2023.

73 See above, section 2.2.3.

should not be construed as a 'one size fits all' panacea but rather each area of family law requires a specific and tailored assessment as to the adequate extent of agreements or unilateral designation of the applicable law or jurisdiction.[74]

Looking ahead, in order to tackle the issues of fragmentation in EU international family law, a further reflection would be to consider a consolidation and codification of EU international family law in a unified and more consistent framework, which could render the scattered provisions on party autonomy more accessible.[75] In addition, for subject matters that complement the current Regulations, political hurdles to the harmonization of private international law in the EU should not prevent national legislators from becoming active and reviewing their domestic private international law rules.

Finally, the introduction and strengthening of party autonomy should go beyond the pure normative framework. It should go hand in hand with practical efforts to make citizens aware of the impacts of cross-border situations on family law and to inform them of the choice possibilities they have under private international law. With regard to the importance of informed choices in family matters,[76] as stressed in the Recitals of the EU Regulations,[77] specific measures to inform parties and practitioners of the available choice options are to be welcomed.[78]

---

74 On the need to take into account the peculiarities of family law for the construction of party autonomy see C. González Beilfuss, 'Party Autonomy in International Family Law' in *Collected Courses of the Hague Academy of International Law, Vol. 408*, Brill Nijhoff, Leiden 2021, pp. 193–208; L. Walker, 'Party autonomy, inconsistency and the specific characteristics of family law in the EU' (2018) 2 *Journal of Private International Law* 225, 244–50.

75 On coherence and consistency, see also A. Limante, 'Prorogation of jurisdiction and choice of law in EU family law: navigating through the labyrinth of rules' (2021) 2 *Journal of Private International Law* 334, 352; G. Rühl, 'The Protection of Weaker Parties in the Private International Law of the European Union: A Portrait of Inconsistency and Conceptual Truancy' (2014) 3 *Journal of Private International Law* 335, 356–57.

76 C. Kohler, above n. 17, pp. 89–90; for further discussion, see N. Dethloff, 'Denn sie wissen nicht, was sie tun: Parteiautonomie im Internationalen Familienrecht' in N. Witzleb, R. Ellger, P. Mankowski, H. Merkt and O. Remien (eds), *Festschrift für Dieter Martiny zum 70. Geburtstag*, Mohr Siebeck, Tübingen 2014, pp. 41–65; C. González Beilfuss, above n. 11, pp. 256–57; A. Limante, above n. 75, pp. 357–59.

77 See Recital 18 Rome III, Recital 47 of the Matrimonial Property Regimes Regulation and Recital 48 of the Property Regimes Regulation.

78 For model choice of law and choice of court clauses, see F.C. Villata and L. Valkova, 'Choice-of-Court and Choice-of-Law Clauses' in I. Viarengo and F.C. Villata (eds), *Planning the Future of Cross Border Families: A Path Through Coordination*, Hart Publishing, Oxford 2020, pp. 625–798. Within the framework of the research project 'Empowering European Families: Towards More Party Autonomy in European Family and Succession Law', the European Law Institute published practical toolkits for legal advisers and an information sheet for couples on the implications of cross-border relationships <https://www.europeanlawinstitute.eu/projects-publications/completed-projects-old/completed-projects-sync/empowering-european-families> accessed 12.05.2023.

A LOOK INTO THE FUTURE

The Harmonization of Substantive Family Law in Europe

Anna Wysocka-Bar

1. INTRODUCTION

This chapter, as the title suggests, constitutes a look (or rather a glimpse) into the future of harmonization of substantive family law in Europe. These terms require a short explanation. As the notion of 'family' is perceived as a changing concept nowadays, so is the definition of 'family law'. For the purpose of simplicity, it might be perceived as a branch of law which concerns, inter alia, relationships between adults, particularly marriage, divorce and de facto unions, as well as relationships between adults and children, particularly parentage/parenthood, including that resulting from artificial reproductive techniques and surrogacy, parental responsibility and adoption.[1]

'Substantive law is the law which governs rights and obligations of those who are subject to it. It is the body of statutory or written law which creates, defines

[1] J. Scherpe, 'Introduction to European Family Law volume II: The changing concept of "family" and challenges for domestic family law' in J. Scherpe, *European Family Law. Vol. II. The Changing Concept of 'Family' and Challenges to Domestic Family Law*, Edward Elgar Publishing, Cheltenham / Northampton 2016, pp. 1–21, at pp. 1–2.

and regulates these rights'.[2] In contrast to substantive law, private international law does not govern rights and obligations of individuals, but is of 'technical' nature.[3] It addresses three kinds of problems which arise, in connection with legal relationships governed by private law (e.g., family law), where a factual situation is connected with more than one country.[4] These are: jurisdiction; applicable law; and recognition and enforcement of foreign decisions. When it comes to family law, these 'technical' rules are sometimes referred to as international family law.[5] International family law gains its importance at the moment when the families or their members cross State borders.

Harmonization, as compared to unification – which might be understood as 'providing identical rules for different countries so that the same solution applies everywhere'[6] – is more modest as to the result. It means that 'the laws of the legal systems in a specific area are in harmony with each other. The differences are reduced to a minimum and are less pronounced'.[7] Harmonization implies a concern to avoid 'conflicts and clashes' but does not require a uniform solution.[8] If States were separated by Chinese walls with no cross-border movement between them, no conflicts or clashes would appear. No international family law would be needed.

As States are not separated by Chinese walls, especially in the EU, which is built on four freedoms including freedom of movement of persons, and there are differences between family laws in different States, nowadays quite pronounced, 'conflicts and clashes' often appear, and private international law is not able to help to avoid them. The following two cases decided recently by the Court of Justice of the European Union (CJEU) might serve as an illustration of implications of the pronounced differences in substantive family laws, which become evident when families cross borders.

The two cases decided by the CJEU are *Pancharevo*[9] followed shortly after by the order in *Rzecznik Praw Obywatelskich*.[10] In both cases, parentage of

---

2 K. Boele-Woelki, 'Unifying and Harmonizing Substantive Law and the Role of Conflict of Laws' (2009) 340 *Receuil des Cours* 271, 298.

3 M. Bogdan, *Concise Introduction to EU Private International Law*, Europa Law Publishing, Groningen 2016, p. 2.

4 P. Stone, *Private International Law in the European Union*, Edward Elgar Publishing, Cheltenham / Northampton 2018, pp. 3–4.

5 See, e.g., N.A. Baarsma, *The Europeanisation of International Family Law*, T.M.C. Asser Press Springer, The Hague 2011.

6 K. Boele-Woelki, 'Unifying and Harmonizing Substantive Law and the Role of the Conflict of Laws' (2009) 340 *Receuil des Cours* 271, 299.

7 K. Boele-Woelki, above n. 6, p. 300.

8 M.-T. Meulders-Klein, 'Towards a European Civil Code on Family Law? Ends and Means' in K. Boele-Woelki, *Perspectives for the Unification and Harmonisation of Family Law in Europe*, Intersentia, Antwerp / Oxford / New York 2003, pp. 105–17, at p. 106.

9 Case C-490/20, *V.M.A. v. Stolichna obshtina, rayon 'Pancharevo'*, ECLI:EU:C:2021:1008.

10 Case C-2/21, *Rzecznik Praw Obywatelskich*, ECLI:EU:C:2022:502.

same-sex couples was established lawfully under the law of one Member State of the EU, whereas in another Member State recognition of such parentage, for the purpose of transcription into the civil status registry, was refused based on a public policy clause. A concept existing under the family law of one State was perceived as incompatible with fundamental principles of the legal order of the forum in the other. The recognition of a legal status acquired under the law of one State, when analysed from the perspective of another State, was perceived as leading to an outcome that was not only different from what could be expected under substantive law of the forum, but also unacceptable for the legal order of the latter State. The 'conflicts and clashes' resulting from the existing differences in substantive family laws can lead to the outcome where a parent–child relationship legally exists in one State, whereas it does not exist in another. It might be stressed again, that if the family laws of the two States were harmonized, so that any differences would be minimized or less important and therefore no recourse to public policy was justified, recognition would be possible and no 'conflicts and clashes' would appear.

As family law covers numerous legal issues, this chapter will focus on the potential harmonization of the issue used as an example above, namely the establishment of parentage of same-sex couples, where a child is conceived through assisted reproduction techniques and/or surrogacy. This question is inspired by *Pancharevo* and *Rzecznik Praw Obywatelskich*. Additionally, recent works in this field of the Hague Conference on Private International Law and of the EU suggest that this question will be present in the legal debate in coming years.

Harmonization of substantive family laws in Europe is often a result of 'teamwork' as numerous institutions and bodies have direct or indirect impact on the shape of substantive family law. The following can be indicated as examples: the Commission on European Family Law (CEFL),[11] the CJEU,[12] the EU,[13] the European Court of Human Rights (ECtHR) interpreting the European Convention

---

11 See, e.g., K. Boele-Woelki, 'The impact of the Commission on European Family Law (CEFL) on European family law' in J. Scherpe, *European Family Law. Vol. I. The Impact of Institutions and Organisations on European Family Law*, Edward Elgar Publishing, Cheltenham / Northampton 2016, pp. 209–60, at p. 209.

12 See, e.g., G. De Baere and K. Gutman, 'The impact of the European Union and the European Court of Justice on European family law' in J. Scherpe, *European Family Law. Vol. I. The Impact of Institutions and Organisations on European Family Law*, Edward Elgar Publishing, Cheltenham / Northampton 2016, pp. 5–48, at p. 5.

13 See, e.g., D. Martiny, 'The impact of the EU private international law instruments on European family law' in J. Scherpe, *European Family Law. Vol. I. The Impact of Institutions and Organisations on European Family Law*, Edward Elgar Publishing, Cheltenham / Northampton 2016, pp. 261–93, at p. 261.

on Human Rights (ECHR),[14] the Council of Europe,[15] and last but not least the Hague Conference on Private International Law (HCCH).[16]

Here it might be added that the shape of rules on the establishment and recognition of parentage of same-sex couples is quite naturally dependent on the existing rules concerning same-sex couples in a given jurisdiction (e.g., whether the institution of a marriage is available to same-sex couples or not).[17] The important difference between the two sets of rules is that establishment and recognition of parentage must take into account the overarching paradigm of the best interests of the child pronounced, among others, in Article 3(1) of the UN Convention on the Rights of the Child.[18]

2. COMMISSION ON EUROPEAN FAMILY LAW (CEFL)

The work carried out by the Commission on European Family Law (CEFL) might be used as an excellent example of an attempt of a direct harmonization of substantive family law. This institution is quite different than others mentioned above in this chapter, as it is a purely scholarly endeavour

On 1 September 2001 the CEFL was established as an association of experts in family law and comparative law. The inaugural meeting was attended by six law professors: Katharina Boele-Woelki from Utrecht University, Frederique Ferrand from Jean Moulin in Lyon, Nigel Lowe from Cardiff University, Dieter Martiny from Frankfurt (Oder) University, Walter Pintens from University of Leuven, and Dieter Schwab from the University of Regensburg.

---

14 See, e.g., D. Coester-Waltjen, 'The impact of the European Convention on Human Rights and the European Court of Human Rights on European family law' in J. Scherpe, *European Family Law. Vol. I. The Impact of Institutions and Organisations on European Family Law*, Edward Elgar Publishing, Cheltenham / Northampton 2016, pp. 49–94, at p. 49.

15 See, e.g., N. Lowe, 'The impact of the Council of Europe on European family law' in J. Scherpe, *European Family Law. Vol. I. The Impact of Institutions and Organisations on European Family Law*, Edward Elgar Publishing, Cheltenham / Northampton 2016, pp. 95–123, at p. 95.

16 See, e.g., H. Baker and M. Groff, 'The impact of the Hague Conventions on European family law' in J. Scherpe, *European Family Law. Vol. I. The Impact of Institutions and Organisations on European Family Law*, Edward Elgar Publishing, Cheltenham / Northampton 2016, pp. 143–208, at p. 143.

17 On the legal status of same-sex couples in Europe see K. Boele-Woelki and A. Fuchs, *Same-sex Relationships and Beyond*, Intersentia, Antwerpen / Oxford 2017; L. Vaige, *Cross-Border Recognition of Formalized Same-Sex Relationships. The Role of Ordre Public*, Intersentia, Cambridge / Antwerp / Chicago 2022.

18 'In all actions concerning children, whether undertaken by public or private social welfare institutions, courts of law, administrative authorities or legislative bodies, the best interests of the child shall be a primary consideration.'

CEFL functions as a foundation established under Dutch law. Its activities are supported by sponsors. As the goal of its activities, CEFL points to a pioneering undertaking of a theoretical and practical nature, aimed at the harmonization of family law in Europe. This goal is to be achieved by reviewing the current state of work on the harmonization of family law in Europe, seeking common solutions to legal problems based on comparative research involving the legal systems of European countries, and examining the role that European countries can play in the process of harmonizing family law.[19]

In organizational terms, CEFL consists of two bodies: the Organizing Committee and the Expert Group. The Organizing Committee is chaired by Professor Katharina Boele-Woelki, currently associated with Bucerius Law School in Hamburg. The Expert Group is appointed by the Organizing Committee. Its task is to work on issues of interest to CEFL. The experts are mostly representatives of the EU Member States; however Russia, Switzerland and Norway are also represented in CEFL.

CEFL's most important achievement is the development of the so-called Principles of European Family Law, which are intended to provide a starting point for the harmonization of family law in Europe. To date, CEFL has developed four sets of such Principles, namely Principles on Divorce and Maintenance Between Former Spouses;[20] Principles on Parental Responsibilities;[21] Principles on Property Relations between Spouses;[22] and Principles Regarding Property, Maintenance and Succession Rights of Couples in de facto Unions.[23]

Under the auspices of the CEFL's Organizing Committee, Intersentia publishes a series entitled 'European Family Law Series' on family and succession law in Europe. At the time of writing in spring 2023, more than 50 volumes have been published. Volumes containing national reports and general reports are published under the common title 'European Family Law in Action'. The volumes containing the CEFL Principles and Commentaries, unlike the usual 'red' volumes of the European Family Law series, are characterized by yellow

---

19 See, e.g., K. Boele-Woelki, 'The Commission of European Family Law: Taking Stock after Almost Twenty Years' (2019) 6 *Journal of International and Comparative Law* 233.

20 K. Boele-Woelki, F. Ferrand, C. González Beilfuss, M. Jäntera-Jareborg, N. Lowe, D. Martiny and W. Pintens, *Principles of European Family Law Regarding Divorce and Maintenance Between Former Spouses*, Intersentia, Antwerp / Oxford 2004.

21 K. Boele-Woelki, F. Ferrand, C. González Beilfuss, M. Jäntera-Jareborg, N. Lowe, D. Martiny and W. Pintens, *Principles of European Family Law Regarding Parental Responsibilities*, Intersentia, Antwerp / Oxford 2007.

22 K. Boele-Woelki, F. Ferrand, C. González Beilfuss, M. Jäntera-Jareborg, N. Lowe, D. Martiny and W. Pintens, *Principles of European Family Law Regarding Property Relations Between Spouses*, Intersentia, Antwerp / Oxford / Portland 2013.

23 K. Boele-Woelki, F. Ferrand, C. González Beilfuss, M. Jäntera-Jareborg, N. Lowe, D. Martiny and V. Todorova, *Principles of European Family Law Regarding Principles Regarding Property, Maintenance and Succession Rights of Couples in de facto Unions*, Intersentia, Antwerp / Oxford / Portland 2013.

covers. CELF also organizes periodic international conferences on family law devoted to family law issues.

CELF in its name, rules and publications uses the concept of 'European family law'. One may wonder what this term means. It seems that European family law is understood by CEFL as a certain ideal set of model legal norms relating to family law relationships. The set is constructed as a result of comparative law work aimed at looking for a 'common denominator' in the laws of European countries.

As far as the methodology of the work on the Principles of European Family Law is concerned, CEFL points to the application of the so-called 'Six Steps Method'.[24] The work begins with the identification of the part of family law that can be developed ('step one'), followed by the development of a questionnaire that is sent out to experts from various European countries ('step two'). The national reports responding to the questionnaire are prepared by members of the Committee of Experts or other experts from the country concerned ('step three'). These reports are made available to the general public, inter alia on the CEFL website ('step four'). On the basis of the analysis of the national reports and the debates held, the CEFL Organizing Committee produces a draft version of the rules ('step five'). The draft version is then discussed during the Organizing Committee meetings and meetings with national experts. As a result of this work, a final version of Principles is produced and made available to the public ('step six').

CEFL believes that the development of principles of European family law should take as its starting point the substantive law currently in force in European States. Therefore, CEFL decided to use the 'common core method' supplemented by the better law approach. In searching for this 'common denominator', CEFL focuses not so much on the wording of the rules as on the function they perform. In CEFL's opinion, even if it turns out to be possible to find a 'common denominator' in the substantive law of the European States, it is still necessary to make an evaluation as to whether the 'common denominator' is the most appropriate solution. Only as a result of the assessment of this 'common denominator' are the principles of European family law developed, which can be a source of inspiration for national legislators in the future. If, on the other hand, the differences between the legal systems are so great that it is not possible to find a 'common denominator', it will be necessary to evaluate individual solutions in order to identify the most appropriate one. In this case, the better law method is used. According to CEFL, on the one hand, the latter approach leaves CEFL more room for creative work, but on the other hand requires adequate justification of

---

24 K. Boele-Woelki, 'The Principles of European Family Law: Its Aims and Prospects' (2005) 2 *Utrecht Law Review* 160.

the choices made. In some cases CEFL has made such choices and justified them accordingly.

CEFL points out that it may happen that a particular legal system was not adequately represented during the work on the principles, but at the same time no system was treated as a model. The principles developed, according to CEFL, are intended to have a European character and to abstract from individual national systems. CEFL points out (obviously) that the principles are not binding. They also do not constitute a model law, which could be used in extenso by national legislators. The principles may serve as a guideline on the way to harmonization of family law in Europe. The principles should be read not on their own, but together with an accompanying comparative legal analysis and commentaries. This approach is modelled on the American Restatements and, in CEFL's view, will allow legislatures of different countries to draw inspiration when they want to 'modernize' national law.

The language of work of CEFL is English, but the rules are formulated in three languages: English, French and German. None of the language versions are translations, but all were created at the same time. All three language versions are to be considered as authentic versions.

In justifying the existence of CEFL and the activities it undertakes, the emerging trend in Europe to try to harmonize different areas of private law has been pointed out. CEFL notes that family law, because of its cultural colouring, has historically remained outside this trend. Over time, however, there has been an increased interest in comparative family law, and a move towards its harmonization or even, as in the case of international family law, its unification. CEFL believes that the harmonization or unification of family law in Europe is supported by the principles of equality and non-discrimination adopted in the work of the Council of Europe and the case-law of the European Court of Human Rights and the (current) Court of Justice of the European Union.

In the Preamble to CELF Principles on Parental Responsibilities, it is underlined that the free movement of persons in the EU is hindered by the existing diversities of family law systems. The progressing unification of international family law in Europe (e.g., by the Brussels II bis Regulation, recently replaced by the Brussels II ter Regulation[25] or the 1996 Hague Child Protection Convention) is unable to eliminate obstacles experienced by families when moving across borders. Hence, in cross-border situations citizens cannot rely on the continuity of their status when changing residence.[26] Both Brussels II ter Regulation and Hague 1996 Child Protection Convention (similarly to CEFL's

25 Council Regulation (EU) 2019/1111 of 25 June 2019 on jurisdiction, the recognition and enforcement of decisions in matrimonial matters and the matters of parental responsibility, and on international child abduction (recast) [2019] OJ L178/1.

26 K. Boele-Woelki, F. Ferrand, C. González Beilfuss, M. Jantera-Jareborg, N. Lowe, D. Martiny and W. Pintens, above n. 21, pp. 7, 8.

Principles on Parental Responsibility[27]) purposefully exclude the question of the establishment or contesting of the parent–child relationship from their scope.

Given the current situation in Europe revealed by *Pancharevo* and *Rzecznik Praw Obywatelskich*, it seems that a new set of CEFL Principles, namely on Establishment and Recognition of Parentage, which could influence national legislators, would be a challenging, but much appreciated and needed endeavour. It would additionally complement other sets of principles, especially the ones on Parental Responsibility.

3. COURT OF JUSTICE OF THE EUROPEAN UNION

The facts of the *Pancharevo* case mentioned above are as follows. The applicant before Bulgarian authorities, V.M.A., is a woman of Bulgarian nationality. She is married to another woman, K.D.K., a UK national. They have resided in Spain, where in 2019, their daughter, S.D.K.A., was born. In accordance with Spanish law, the child's birth certificate designates both women as mothers.

In 2020 V.M.A. applied in Bulgaria for a birth certificate for her daughter. Together with her application, V.M.A. submitted a legalized and certified translation of the extract from the Spanish register of civil status relating to the child's birth certificate. The birth certificate is needed for a Bulgarian identity document to be issued. Then, V.M.A. was instructed to provide evidence of the child's parentage with respect to her biological mother, arguing that the model birth certificate which forms part of the applicable national law has only one box for the 'mother' and another box for the 'father', and that only one name may be entered in each box. At the same time, it was submitted that Bulgarian law does not provide for same-sex marriages,[28] even though most probably it is not necessary in Bulgaria to be married in order to become a parent. V.M.A. stated that she could not provide such information and additionally that, under Bulgarian law, she was not required to do so. As a result, the application was rejected, because there was no information concerning the child's biological mother and because the registration of two female parents in a birth certificate was considered to be contrary to the public policy of Bulgaria.

A similar matter, this time originating from Poland, was referred to the CJEU in *Rzecznik Praw Obywatelskich*.[29] In this case, again under Spanish substantive law, a child was born and two females, one Polish, the other Irish, were registered on the birth certificate as parents. This case slightly differs from *Pancharevo*, as

---

27 K. Boele-Woelki, F. Ferrand, C. González Beilfuss, M. Jantera-Jareborg, N. Lowe, D. Martiny and W. Pintens, above n. 21, pp. 7, 20.

28 See Case C-490/20, *V.M.A. v. Stolichna obshtina, rayon 'Pancharevo'*, ECLI:EU:C:2021:1008, §23.

29 Case C-2/21, *Rzecznik Praw Obywatelskich*, ECLI:EU:C:2022:502.

the couple revealed which of the two women was the birth mother of the child.[30] The parents wanted the Spanish birth certificate to be transcribed into the Polish civil status register. The transcription was needed to be able to apply for a Polish identity document. Just as in *Pancharevo*, the administrative authorities refused. They explained that such a transcription would be contrary to Polish public policy (*ordre public*), because Polish law does not provide for the possibility that a child has two parents of the same sex.

The above cases are an illustration of differences in substantive family laws as to who can be perceived by law as a parent. Both Bulgarian and Polish law are 'traditional' and, therefore, a mother is a woman which gives birth to the child, whereas paternity results from the scheme of legal presumptions indicating a man as the father.[31] Conversely, Spanish substantive law provides that if a woman in a same-sex marriage conceives a child through assisted reproduction, both women are recognized as legal mothers, without the need of adoption by the non-gestational mother. Only the consent of the non-gestational mother for the treatment is required.[32]

In the decisions the CJEU was asked to clarify whether the parentage established in one Member State of the EU must be recognized in another Member State for the purpose of issuing national identity documents for child in the latter. The CJEU stated that parentage established under the law of one Member State must be recognized in another Member State for the purpose of permitting a child 'to exercise without impediment with each of her two parents, her right to move and reside freely within the territory of the Member States as guaranteed in Article 21(1) [of the Treaty on the Functioning of the European Union (TFEU)]'.

Since in *Pancharevo* the mothers were not willing to reveal which of them gave birth to the child, a doubt arose as to whether the child was a Bulgarian national. Having these doubts in mind, the CJEU confirmed that the above conclusion is valid irrespective the child's nationality, as long as one of the parents, whose parentage was legally established in one of the Member States, was an EU citizen. The CJEU referred on various occasions to the *Coman* case[33] and underlined that an obligation to allow the family to make use of their right

---

30 Case C-2/21, *Rzecznik Praw Obywatelskich*, ECLI:EU:C:2022:502, §16.

31 See K. Trimmings and P. Baumont, 'Parentage and surrogacy in a European perspective' in J. Scherpe, *European Family Law. Vol. III. Family Law in a European Perspective*, Edward Elgar Publishing, Cheltenham / Northampton 2016, pp. 232–83, at pp. 236–237.

32 A. Lamarca Marquès, 'The changing concept of "family" and challenges for family law in Spain and Catalonia' in J. Scherpe, *European Family Law. Vol. II. The Changing Concept of 'Family' and Challenges to Domestic Family Law*, Edward Elgar Publishing, Cheltenham / Northampton 2016, pp. 289–308, at pp. 298–300.

33 Case C-673/16, *Relu Adrian Coman and Others v. Inspectoratul General pentru Imigrări and Ministerul Afacerilor Interne*, ECLI:EU:C:2018:385.

to move and reside freely 'does not require the Member State … to recognise, for purposes other than the exercise of the rights which that child derives from EU law, the parent-child relationship between that child and the persons mentioned on the birth certificate'.

It seems a little bit unclear in exactly what circumstances the recognition of the status acquired in another Member State is required and when it is not. While discussing 'the right to move and reside freely within the territory of the Member States' the CJEU makes references to its previous jurisprudence. By referring to *Grunkin and Paul*[34] the court directly addresses the question of a child's surname stating that 'Article 21 TFEU precludes the authorities of a Member State, in applying their national law, from refusing to recognise a child's surname as determined and registered in a second Member State in which the child was born and has been resident since birth'.

Then, referring again to *Coman*, the CJEU underlines that 'the rights which nationals of Member States enjoy under Article 21(1) TFEU include the right to lead a normal family life, together with their family members, both in their host Member State and in the Member State of which they are nationals when they return to the territory of that Member State'. Later, making reference to the EU Charter of Fundamental Rights,[35] the CJEU underlines that:

> [T]he right to respect for family life, as stated in Article 7 of the Charter, must be read in conjunction with the obligation to take into consideration the child's best interests, recognised in Article 24(2) of the Charter. Since Article 24 of the Charter, as the Explanations relating to the Charter of Fundamental Rights note, represents the integration into EU law of the principal rights of the child referred to in the Convention on the rights of the child, which has been ratified by all the Member States, it is necessary, when interpreting that article, to take due account of the provisions of that convention.

In June 2022 the CJEU handed down a reasoned order in *Rzecznik Praw Obywatelskich*, repeating its findings in *Pancharevo*.

The above suggests that in order for the child to indeed be able to move and reside freely across the EU, the parentage established in one Member State should be recognized for many different purposes (e.g., maintenance claims) in other EU Member States. Implementing the obligations put on EU Member States in this jurisprudence requires more openness to recognition of parentage established in another EU Member State. At the same time, the obligation to recognize the parentage even only for limited purposes literally indicated by the Court of Justice of the EU (e.g., moving to another Member State) means that the public policy clause (which in both of the cases discussed was invoked by

34 Case C-353/06, *Stefan Grunkin and Dorothee Regina Paul*, ECLI:EU:C:2008:559.
35 Charter of Fundamental Rights of the European Union [2012] OJ C326/391.

administrative authorities against the parentage documented in the foreign birth certificate) may not come into play.

One might argue that the obligations put on EU Member States by *Pancharevo* and *Rzecznik Praw Obywatelskich* does not change the fact that the substantive family law of the engaged Member States (Bulgaria and Poland) remains untouched. However, assuming that a change to legislation might be and probably often is impacted by various factors, including legal scholarship, political background, expectations of the society or lobbying of some groups within this society, the two cases might be perceived as a first step towards possible future harmonization of the law on parent–child relationship in Europe, as they undoubtedly put the question of the new trends in family law under the spotlight.

4. EU LAW

As repeated many times, the EU does not have competence to regulate the substantive family law of the Member States, as there is no legal basis to that end.[36] The competence to 'adopt measures' in accordance with Article 81 TFEU encompasses only private international law. Numerous instruments adopted in this field, even though aimed at unifying rules on international jurisdiction, applicable law, as well as recognition and enforcement of foreign decisions, might be perceived as having an indirect impact on harmonizing the substantive law of the Member States of the EU.[37]

On the one hand, when it comes to international family law, the EU legislator acts cautiously and underlines that instruments in this field are not aimed at shaping the substantive family law of the Member States. On the other hand, these instruments are also perceived as a first step towards harmonization of substantive family law in Member States by allowing certain family law concepts created under the law of certain Member States to be recognized in others.[38] This potential for an indirect impact on the harmonization of the substantive family law of the Member States will be explained below.

---

36 J. Scherpe, 'The interaction between family law, succession law and private international law. An Introduction' in J. Scherpe and E. Bergelli (eds), *The Interaction between Family Law, Succession Law and Private International Law*, Intersentia, Cambridge / Antwerp / Chicago 2021, pp. 1–9, at p. 2.

37 D. Martiny, 'The impact of the EU private international law instruments on European family law' in J. Scherpe, *European Family Law. Vol. I. The Impact of Institutions and Organizations on European Family Law*, Edward Elgar Publishing, Cheltenham / Northampton 2016, pp. 261–293, at p. 261.

38 See, e.g., P. Mostowik, 'The Questionable Impact of EU Regulations No 2016/1103 and 2016/1104 on the Identity of Marriage in a Member State' (2018) *Problemy Prawa Prywatnego Międzynarodowego* 29–49.

For example, Article 13 of the Rome III Regulation[39] states that the Regulation does not oblige the courts of a participating Member State whose law does not deem the marriage in question valid to pronounce a divorce. This provision is supposed to guarantee to a Member State which does not provide for same-sex marriage that its courts would not be obliged to pronounce the divorce of such marriages.[40]

Similarly, Article (1)(2)(b) of the Regulation on Matrimonial Property Regimes[41] excludes from its scope the existence, validity or recognition of a marriage. In the Preamble, it explains that the Regulation does not define "marriage", which is defined by the national laws of the Member States (Recital (17)).[42] This Regulation also underlines that it should not apply to preliminary questions such as the existence, validity or recognition of a marriage, which continue to be covered by the national law of the Member States (Recital (21)). Further, it explains that 'the courts of a Member State may hold that ... the marriage in question cannot be recognised for the purposes of matrimonial property regime proceedings' (Recital (38)), and that the 'recognition and enforcement of a decision on matrimonial property regime under this Regulation should not in any way imply the recognition of the marriage' (Recital (64)).

At the same time, however, Article 38 of the Regulation on Matrimonial Property Regimes makes it clear that the public policy clause must be applied by the courts and authorities of Member States in observance of the fundamental rights and principles recognized in the Charter of Fundamental Rights, in particular the principle of non-discrimination. This provision might be understood as obliging a Member State where no same-sex marriages exist (as perceived contrary to, e.g., its constitution) to recognize the effects of such a marriage with respect to matrimonial property regimes.[43]

---

39 Council Regulation (EU) 1259/2010 of 20 December 2010 implementing enhanced cooperation in the area of the law applicable to divorce and legal separation [2010] OJ L343/10.

40 Ch. Chalas, 'Article 13. Differences in National Laws' in S. Corneloup, *The Rome III Regulation. A Commentary*, Edward Elgar Publishing, Cheltenham / Northampton 2020, pp. 261–93, at pp. 164, 169–70.

41 Council Regulation (EU) 2016/1103 of 24 June 2016 implementing enhanced cooperation in the area of jurisdiction, applicable law and the recognition and enforcement of decisions in matters of matrimonial property regimes [2016] OJ L183/1. See also its twin Council Regulation (EU) 2016/1104 of 24 June 2016 implementing enhanced cooperation in the area of jurisdiction, applicable law and the recognition and enforcement of decisions in matters of the property consequences of registered partnerships [2016] OJ L183/30.

42 See also A. Rodriguez Benot, 'Article 3. Definitions' in I. Viarengo and P. Franzina, *The EU Regulations on the Property Regimes of International Couples. A Commentary*, Edward Elgar Publishing, Cheltenham / Northampton 2020, paras 3.02–3.09.

43 Compare M. Gebauer, 'Article 38. Fundamental Rights' in I. Viarengo and P. Franzina, *The EU Regulations on the Property Regimes of International Couples. A Commentary*, Edward Elgar Publishing, Cheltenham / Northampton 2020, paras 38.09–38.12.

Again, one could argue the recognition of same effects of a same-sex marriage (e.g., for the purpose of sharing of the property owned by the spouses) does not change the substantive family law of the State where the property is located, and recognition sought. However, it seems that introduction of a new legislation, for example providing for same-sex marriage, might be easier for the legislator to conceive if certain effects of such marriages already exist and are recognized on the territory of that State. This is where the potential of private international law as a catalyst for harmonization of substantive family law in Europe lies.

Taking the example of Poland, it should be remembered that there is no legislation in place concerning same-sex marriages, or even registered partnerships. Similarly, Poland is a Member State which does not participate in the enhanced cooperation, either when it comes to Rome III Regulation, or to the Regulations on Property Matters. If Poland were a participating Member State (or becomes one in the future), pursuant to Recital 64, it would not be obliged to recognize the marriage, but it would be obliged to recognize certain effects of it, namely the existence or dissolution of a matrimonial property regime. This might already be a small step towards potential future harmonization of substantive family law. Similarly, if Poland were to have in its private international law, a private international law rule indicating the law applicable to property consequences of registered partnerships (even if of EU origin), it would be less easy to justify that the very concept of 'registered partnership' is against public policy of the forum. In that respect one might argue that unification of private international law in the EU might ease harmonization of the substantive law of the Member States.

When it comes to establishment and contestation of parentage, EU instruments on private international law do not cover this legal issue. Pursuant to Article 1(4)(a) of the Brussels II ter Regulation,[44] the establishment or the contesting of a parent–child relationship is purposefully excluded from the scope of application. As Recital (10) of the Preamble explains, the Regulation 'should not apply to the establishment of parenthood, since that is a different matter from the attribution of parental responsibility ...'.[45]

Some time ago the European Commission launched an initiative entitled 'Recognition of parenthood between Member States'. As explained, its aim is to ensure that parenthood, as established in one EU Member State, will be

---

[44] Council Regulation (EU) 2019/1111 of 25 June 2019 on jurisdiction, the recognition and enforcement of decisions in matrimonial matters and the matters of parental responsibility, and on international child abduction (recast) [2019] OJ L178/1. See also its predecessor Council Regulation (EC) 2201/2003 of 27 November 2003 concerning jurisdiction and the recognition and enforcement of judgments in matrimonial matters and the matters of parental responsibility, repealing Regulation (EC) 1347/2000 [2003] OJ L338/1.

[45] See also D. Danieli, 'Parental Responsibility' in I. Viarengo and F. Villata, *Planning the Future of Cross Border Families. A Path Through Coordination*, Hart Publishing, Oxford / New York 2020, pp. 61–70, at pp. 68–9.

recognized across the EU so that children maintain their rights in cross-border situations, in particular when their families travel or move within the EU.[46] A public consultation carried within the initiative indicated, as already clear from the facts of the *Pancharevo* case, that respondents are familiar with instances where parenthood was not recognized between Member States. The aim of the initiative was to prepare a new regulation.

The proposal for the regulation was adopted by the European Commission on 7 December 2022.[47] It contains rules on jurisdiction, applicable law, recognition and enforcement of judgments, as well as acceptance of authentic instruments. It also creates a new instrument called 'European Certificate of Parenthood'. As the Explanatory Memorandum puts it, the future instrument 'covers the recognition of the parenthood of a child irrespective of how the child was conceived or born and irrespective of the type of family of the child. The proposal thus includes the recognition of the parenthood of a child with same-sex parents'. In this proposal, a mechanism like the one in the Property Regimes Regulations exists. Pursuant to Articles 31(1) and 39(1) of the proposal, the recognition of – respectively – a decision or authentic instrument (with binding legal effect) might be refused based on public policy; however, again this could be done only in observance of fundamental rights and principles of the Charter.

The legal basis for the adoption of the regulation is supposed to be Article 81(3) TFEU.[48] It requires unanimity, which is the reason why, so far, certain regulations on international family law have not been adopted under Article 81(3) TFEU. The above-mentioned Rome III Regulation and Regulations on Property Matters were adopted through enhanced cooperation. It provides for an important exception from the rule that regulations are binding on all the Member States. Regulations adopted within enhanced cooperation, on the contrary, pursuant to Article 20(4) of the Treaty Establishing the European Union (TEU), apply only to 'participating Member States'.

Some Member States might oppose the adoption of the regulation on parentage just as some did with respect to other regulations on international family law. In such a case, the regulation will not be adopted under Article 81(3) TFEU but might be adopted under the enhanced cooperation mechanism. As a result, the potential for harmonization of substantive family law by introducing new set of uniform private international law rules will not be spread across the whole territory of the EU.

---

46 Available on the website of the European Commission at <https://ec.europa.eu/info/law/better-regulation/have-your-say/initiatives/12878-Cross-border-family-situations-recognition-of-parenthood_en> accessed 01.06.2022.

47 Proposal for a Council Regulation on jurisdiction, applicable law, recognition of decisions and acceptance of authentic instruments in matters of parenthood and on the creation of a European Certificate of Parenthood (COM(2022) 695 final).

48 Treaty on the Functioning of the European Union [2012] OJ C326/47.

5. EUROPEAN CONVENTION ON HUMAN RIGHTS AND THE EUROPEAN COURT OF HUMAN RIGHTS

Pursuant to Article 8(1) of the European Convention on Human Rights, everyone has the right to respect for his private and family life, his home and his correspondence. The right to family life incorporated in this provision is subject to extensive jurisprudence of the ECtHR.

When it comes to parentage, the ECtHR had the chance to pronounce itself on the creation of parentage, as well as on the recognition of parentage established in another State. In *Gas and Dubois v. France*[49] the ECtHR confirmed that there might be a 'family life' between the child, the biological and legal mother and her same-sex partner, and yet at the same time the State might be permitted to refuse the step-child adoption by the partner of the biological mother if it is similarly unavailable to opposite-sex couples.

In *Wagner v. Luxembourg*,[50] the ECtHR stated that a parent–child relationship should be recognized as established in another State. Later, this view was partly confirmed in a series of cases on surrogacy. In *Labassee v. France*[51] and *Mennesson v. France*[52] the ECtHR underlined the obligation to recognize in France a parent-child relationship that had been legally established abroad between children born as a result of surrogacy as children were genetically related to the fathers (in an opposite-sex marriage scenario).

The above was confirmed also with respect to a single father and a father in a same-sex registered partnership in *Bouvet and Foulon v. France*.[53] In its advisory opinion[54] following the *Labassee* and *Mennesson* cases, the ECtHR held that States are not obliged to register the details of the birth certificate of a child born through surrogacy abroad in order to establish the legal parent-child relationship with the second parent, namely the intended mother, as adoption might be an adequate means of recognizing that relationship. Then, in *Valdís Fjölnisdóttir and Others v. Iceland*,[55] the ECtHR stated that there is no obligation to recognize same-sex partners as parents of a child born through surrogacy abroad, if there is no biological link between the couple and the child and at the same time the child is being brought up by the couple acting as a foster family.

As the jurisprudence of the ECtHR results from particular cases with quite casuistic factual background and closely linked to the legal system of

---

49 *Gas and Dubois v. France*, no. 25951/07, ECHR 2012-II.

50 *Wagner v. Luxembourg*, no. 76240/01, 28.06.2007.

51 *Labassee v. France*, no. 65941/11, 26.06.2014.

52 *Mennesson v. France*, no 65192/11, ECHR 2014-III.

53 *Foulon and Bouvet v. France*, no. 9063/14, no. 10410/14, 21.07.2016.

54 Advisory Opinion concerning the recognition in domestic law of a legal parent-child relationship between a child born through a gestational surrogacy arrangement abroad and the intended mother, requested by the French Court of Cassation, Request no. P16-2018-001.

55 *Valdís Fjölnisdóttir and Others v. Iceland*, no. 71552/17, 18.05.2021.

a particular State, one might expect that other cases concerning 'family life' and parentage of same-sex couples will follow in coming years. Even though, pursuant to Article 46 ECHR, ECtHR judgments are officially only binding on the parties to the case, the purpose of these judgment, which is the creation of a minimum level of protection, requires that legislators and domestic courts take the jurisprudence of the ECtHR into account, even if relating to other States.[56] If there is such willingness among parties to the ECHR, jurisprudence of the ECtHR will inevitably lead to harmonization of substantive family laws.

6. THE COUNCIL OF EUROPE

Apart from the jurisprudence of the ECtHR, the Council of Europe has influence on the shape of substantive family law in Europe through its conventions and recommendations. As underlined by its Committee of Experts on Family Law, the organization had been working for decades 'to harmonise policies and adopt common standards in its member states in the field of family law' and 'has contributed in a decisive manner to the strengthening of the legal protection of the family, in particular the protection of the interests of children'.[57]

One of the achievements of the Council of Europe in the field of parentage is the 1975 Convention on the Legal Status of Children Born out of Wedlock.[58] It has been ratified in 23 States. The aim of the Convention is to assimilate the status of children born out of wedlock with that of children born in a marriage, for example with respect to succession rights.[59] The Convention is complemented by the 1984 Recommendation on Parental Responsibilities, which provides for separate rules on the attribution of parental responsibility depending on marital and non-marital relationship between parents.

A Committee of Experts on Family Law has commenced work on updating the above instruments in order to address new family forms, assisted

56 J. Gerards, 'The European Court of Human Rights and the national courts: giving shape to the notion of 'shared responsibility' in J. Gerards and J. Fleuren (eds), *Implementation of the European Convention on Human Rights and of the judgments of the ECtHR in national case-law. A comparative analysis*, Intersentia, Cambridge / Antwerp / Portland 2014, pp. 13–93, at pp. 21–2.

57 See Council of Europe, 'Council of Europe Achievements in the Field of Law. Family Law and Protection of Children', CJ-FA (2008) 2, p. 11.

58 ETS No. 085.

59 Interestingly, the discrimination of children born outside of a marriage was a consequence of then socially disapproved behaviour of their parents. Nowadays, as illustrated by *Pancharevo* case, there is a somewhat similar instability of status due to similar reasons concerning the children of same-sex parents.

reproduction techniques and surrogacy.[60] The draft of these recommendations contained, inter alia, a separate rule on co-motherhood.[61] The provision was however quickly rejected by Committee of Experts on Family Law. Further, the recommendations were faced with resistance at the Committee of Ministers in 2012. The Committee of Experts on Family Law itself was dissolved a year before.[62]

Hence, it seems that the role of the Council of Europe as a catalyst in shaping the future of substantive family law in Europe by its conventions and recommendation has faded significantly in recent years.

7. HAGUE CONFERENCE ON PRIVATE INTERNATIONAL LAW

As the Hague Conference on Private International Law (HCCH) is a global organization, whose purpose is 'to work for the progressive unification of the rules of private international law' and focusing on family law as one of its main points of interest, the question of establishment and recognition of parentage has been on its agenda for more than 20 years now.[63]

---

60 For details see N. Lowe, 'The Impact of the Council of Europe on European Family Law' in J. Scherpe, *European Family Law. Vol. I. The Impact of Institutions and Organisations on European Family Law*, Edward Elgar Publishing, Cheltenham/Northampton 2016, pp. 95–123, at pp. 117–22.

61 N. Law, *A Study into the Rights and Legal Status of Children Being Brought Up in Various Forms of Marital or Non-marital Partnerships and Cohabitation. A Report for the attention of the Committee of Experts on Family Law* CJ-FA (2008) 5. See Article 13 – The Position of Same-Sex Couples: 'Notwithstanding the absence of genetic connection the woman, who is a. the spouse or registered partner of the mother whose child was conceived by State-approved assisted reproductive treatment shall be considered as a legal parent unless she does not consent to that treatment; b. the partner of the mother shall be considered as a legal parent provided both she and the woman give written consent, before or at the time State-approved assisted reproductive treatment is given, that she should be so treated.'

62 N. Lowe, 'The impact of the Council of Europe on European family law' in J. Scherpe, *European Family Law. Vol. I. The Impact of Institutions and Organisations on European Family Law*, Edward Elgar Publishing, Cheltenham / Northampton 2016, pp. 95–123, at p. 97.

63 For details see the HCCH website under 'Parentage/Surrogacy Project' and R. Schuz, 'Comparative Law and the Work of The Hague Conference on Private International Law in Relation to Family Law' (2022) 2 *Ius Comparatum*, pp. 15–17; M. Mercedes Albornoz, 'Parentage and international surrogacy – common solutions for a contentious issue?' in T. John, R. Gulati and B. Köhler (eds), *The Elgar Companion to the Hague Conference on Private International Law*, Edward Elgar Publishing, Cheltenham/Northampton 2020, pp. 361–372, at p. 361; H. Baker and M. Groff, 'The impact of the Hague Conventions on European family law' in J. Scherpe, *European Family Law. Vol. I. The Impact of Institutions and Organisations on European Family Law*, Edward Elgar Publishing, Cheltenham / Northampton 2016, pp. 143–208, at pp. 195–203.

In 2001, during the informal consultations which took place regarding the future work programme of the HCCH, the topic 'private international law issues surrounding the status of children and, in particular, the recognition of parent–child relationships' was indicated. In 2011 a report 'Private international law issues surrounding the status of children, including issues arising from international surrogacy arrangements' drawn up by the Permanent Bureau of the HCCH was published. In 2012, the Council on General Affairs and Policy of the HCCH requested that the Permanent Bureau prepare and distribute a Questionnaire in order to obtain more detailed information regarding the extent and nature of the private international law issues in relation to international surrogacy arrangements, as well as in relation to legal parentage or 'filiation'. In order to collect data numerous questionnaires addressed to different stakeholders (e.g., HCCH members, legal practitioners, health practitioners and surrogacy agencies) were distributed. On the basis of the answers a document on 'The desirability and feasibility of further work on the Parentage / Surrogacy Project' and an accompanying 'Study of Legal Parentage and the issues arising from International Surrogacy Arrangements' were made available to the public.

In 2015, the Council on General Affairs and Policy of the HCCH decided to establish an Experts' Group, which could explore the feasibility of an international instrument in this field. Meetings of the Experts' Group have taken place between 2016 and 2022. On 1 November 2022, the Experts' Group presented the final report underlining the desirability of, and urgent need for, further work of the HCCH in the form of a general private international law instrument on legal parentage and a separate protocol on legal parentage established as a result of international surrogacy arrangement.

Some of conventions adopted by the HCCH experience numerous ratifications and accessions; others never become law. Nevertheless, even the latter conventions can have an impact on national legislators. Hence, the results of the Parentage / Surrogacy Project of the HCCH will definitely have an influence on the potential harmonization of family law in Europe. This does not depend on how successful in terms of ratifications these instruments are going to be.

8. CONCLUSIONS

The question of establishment of parentage, including parentage of same-sex couples, resulting from assisted reproduction techniques and surrogacy has been present in the works of numerous institutions for decades. It seems that this question will remain on the agenda of some of these institutions for years to come. Any instruments elaborated in this field might impact the harmonization of substantive family law in Europe. The EU proposal on the private international law relating to recognition of parentage and the proposal of the HCCH Convention and accompanying protocol on the same topic will be subject of scholarly and political discussions. However, the most important impact should be expected from the jurisprudence of the ECtHR and CJEU, as currently only some aspects of the recognition of a status acquired in another State were addressed. An academic endeavour consisting of a new set of CEFL principles would also be a very welcome additional input.

PART VI

CHANGING FAMILIES, CHANGING FAMILY LAW

CONCLUDING REMARKS

Changing Families, Changing Family Law

Konrad DUDEN and Denise WIEDEMANN

1. INTRODUCTION

A married, opposite-sex couple that lives with their biological children under the same roof and where the husband is the sole or primary bread-winner – this standard of what a family looks like has for a long time been profoundly eroded. Partnership models other than heterosexual marriage have become more and more common; ways of becoming a parent and raising one's child have multiplied; gender identities outside of the male/female binary are becoming ever more visible. The increased variety of what families in Europe look like does not alter the statistical importance, even dominance, of so-called 'traditional' family models. The pluralization of family models does, however, challenge those family models as normative standards.[1] Many explanations are offered for the de-standardization and pluralization[2] of family models. Prominently, they are associated with growing individual autonomy and a greater tolerance

[1] A.C. KUIJSTEN, 'Changing Family Patterns in Europe: A Case of Divergence?' (1996) 12 *European Journal of Population* 115, 140.

[2] On the pluralization of families recently see N. DETHLOFF and K. KAESLING (eds), *Between Sexuality, Gender and Reproduction*, Intersentia, Cambridge 2023.

in society towards family forms and gender identities outside the traditional model.[3]

The previous contributions have addressed a variety of changes in European family life and have shown how the changing family realities have influenced family law in Europe – often creating frictions between the various jurisdictions. This chapter attempts to bring the different threads together. First, it will take stock of changes in the legal recognition of gender identities (see section 2.1), partnership patterns (see section 2.2) and parenthood patterns (see section 2.3). In doing so it will display a fragmented situation across the European continent. In some areas the developments are marked by a clear divergence between western and eastern European jurisdictions. Nevertheless, it would be an oversimplification and a disservice to describe the fragmented legal landscape merely as an East–West divide (see section 3).

As the differences between national family laws challenge the legal certainty and free movement of European families, it is essential to consider how frictions can be overcome in order to support the lives of families in Europe – in particular if they fall outside of traditional understandings of family and gender identity (see section 4).

2. CHANGING FAMILIES

The proliferation of different family models affects various dimensions of family life. Many of those models remain rather close to the traditional model of an opposite-sex couple living with their biological children. Within this framework changes affect, for instance, the roles of the different members within the family, the perceived importance of marriage as part of creating a family, and the use of various techniques of assisted reproduction. These developments alter the lived realities of families and their recognition significantly affects national family laws (see sections 2.2 and 2.3).

2.1. QUEER IDENTITIES, QUEER FAMILIES

Another development, however, challenges more fundamentally the assumptions of who can form a family and which roles different persons can play in creating a family. It is the growing (legal) recognition of different and changing gender identities and of queer, in particular same-sex, partnerships including their joint parenthood. This change will be addressed first, because it impacts both the

---

3 A.C. Kuijsten, above n. 1, p. 117; F. Willekens, 'Demographic transitions in Europe and the world', *MPIDR Working Paper* WP 2014-004, March 2014, p. 8 <https://www.demogr.mpg.de/papers/working/wp-2014-004.pdf> accessed 04.01.2023.

changing concepts of partnership and of parenthood, which will be addressed subsequently.

The growing societal acceptance and legal protection of same-sex relationships has been a contributing factor to many of the recent changes to national family laws and forms one of the most visible points of contention between legislators in Europe. The first step in protecting – and not only decriminalizing – same-sex relationships was the creation of registered partnerships. The pioneers in this matter were the Scandinavian countries: the Danish 'breakthrough' in 1989[4] created a 'domino effect' in central Scandinavia und gave rise to new laws on registered partnerships for same-sex couples in the region.[5] After registered partnerships came marriage. In 2001, the Netherlands was the first country to open marriage up to same-sex couples.[6] Belgium and Spain were next in line in 2003 and 2005 respectively.[7] Ever since then, civil union and same-sex marriage have continued to spread country by country. Often registered partnerships were introduced first, and same-sex marriage later. In some countries the opening up of marriage came along with the closing of registered partnerships to new couples (e.g., Germany, Sweden).[8] In other countries, civil unions were kept as an alternative to marriage and were opened to opposite-sex couples (e.g., England and Wales).[9]

While this wave of legally recognizing same-sex couples started in the Nordic countries it has swept across much of Western Europe and also reached other parts of the world, in particular North and South America as well as South Africa, Australia and New Zealand.[10] It has, however, not reached eastern and parts of southern Europe, where resistance to recognizing same-sex couples remains and sometimes seems to be increasing.

---

4 Law on registered partnership, law no. 372 of 07.06.1989.

5 Norway in 1993, Sweden in 1994, Iceland in 1996, Finland in 2001: K. DUDEN, 'Art. 17b EGBGB' in M. HERBERGER et al. (eds), juris Praxiskommentar BGB, Vol. 6, juris, Saarbrücken 2020, para. 7; J. RYDSTRÖM, *Odd Couples: A History of Gay Marriage in Scandinavia*, Amsterdam University Press, Amsterdam 2011, pp. 52 et seq.; for a general overview see J.M. SCHERPE, 'Formal recognition of adult relationships and legal gender in a comparative perspective' in C. ASHFORD and A. MAINE (eds), *Research Handbook on Gender, Sexuality and the Law*, Edward Elgar Publishing, Cheltenham 2020, pp. 17–31, at pp. 19–22.

6 Wet van 21 december 2000 tot wijziging van Boek 1 van het Burgerlijk Wetboek in verband met de openstelling van het huwelijk voor personen van hetzelfde geslacht (Wet openstelling huwelijk), Staatsblad 2001, 9.

7 Belgium: Wet tot openstelling van het huwelijk voor personen van hetzelfde geslacht en tot wijziging van een aantal bepalingen van het Burgerlijk Wetboek, Belgisch Staatsblad 2003, 9880; Spain: Ley 13/2005, de 1 de julio, por la que se modifica el Código Civil en materia de derecho a contraer matrimonio, Boletín Oficial del Estado 2005 no. 157, p. 23632.

8 K. DUDEN, 'Vor §1 LPartG' in F.J. SÄCKER et al. (eds), *Münchener Kommentar zum Bürgerlichen Gesetzbuch*, Vol. 9, C.H. Beck, Munich 2022, para. 15; E. GOOSSENS, 'One Trend, a Patchwork of Laws. An Exploration of Why Cohabitation Law is so Different throughout the Western World' (2021) 1 *International Journal of Law, Policy and the Family* 1, 5.

9 E. GOOSSENS, above n. 8, p. 5.

10 K. DUDEN, above n. 5, para. 11; J.M. SCHERPE, above n. 5, pp. 19–22.

Another development in the growing protection of the rights of LGBTQ+ persons relates to the recognition of gender identities outside of the male/female binary as well as changing gender identities. Gender identity affects, first, the individual person themself. As will be underscored subsequently, changing concepts of gender also indirectly affect the concept of family and of the roles of family members to a fundamental degree.

The legal recognition of different gender identities in Europe shows a disparate picture. The right of transgender persons to change their legal gender has been recognized by various States for a significant time.[11] It also has the backing of the jurisprudence of the European Court of Human Rights (ECtHR), who considered in *Goodwin* that it violated Article 8 of the European Convention on Human Rights (ECHR) to refuse a transgender person legal recognition through a change of the gender entry in their birth certificate.[12]

Less common and arguably more controversial among different jurisdictions than the recognition of transgender identities is the recognition of persons who identify outside of the male/female gender binary. Some countries, such as Germany, Denmark or the Netherlands, have introduced measures to recognize gender identities other than male and female.[13] This is, however, a relatively recent and cautious development. As of mid-2022, only Iceland allows for a full non-binary 'neutral recognition of gender' based on self-determination.[14]

The often explorative nature of developments in this area can be seen in the case of Germany. As a first step, in 2013, the German legislator enabled public registrars to leave open the gender entry in birth certificates or to delete a previous entry of male or female later on.[15] This effectively opened a third legal gender category apart from male and female. In 2017, the German Federal Constitutional Court decided that a positive gender entry was necessary and that it was not enough to leave the gender entry blank.[16] This decision led to the introduction of 'diverse' as a new permissible gender entry in 2018.[17]

11 See as an early example the German Transsexuellengesetz (Law of transsexual persons), 10.09.1980, Bundesgesetzblatt 1980 I, 1654.

12 *Goodwin and I. v. United Kingdom*, No. 28957/95, ECHR 2002-VI; cf. S. Duffy, 'Gender Identity: A Comparative European Perspective' (in this volume), pp. 137–155, at p. 142.

13 S. Duffy, above n. 12, p. 151.

14 S. Duffy, above n. 12, p. 150.

15 Art. 1 no. 6 Gesetz zur Änderung personenstandsrechtlicher Vorschriften (Law on the Amendment of Provisions of the Law on the Personal Statute), 07.05.2013, Bundesgesetzblatt 2013 I, 1122.

16 German Federal Constitutional Court 10.10.2017, 1 BvR 2019/16, Entscheidungen des Bundesverfassungsgerichts (BVerfGE) 147, 1 = NJW 2017, 3643.

17 Art. 1 no. 2 Gesetz zur Änderung der in das Geburtenregister einzutragenden Angaben (Law on the Amendment of the Information to be entered into the Birth Register), 18.12.2018, Bundesgesetzblatt 2018 I, 2635.

Now, the current government has announced plans to enact a new law on gender identities which is supposed to be based on self-identification.[18]

Like the recognition of same-sex partnership and parenthood, the liberalization of gender recognition is often met with opposition. Some countries strongly oppose this trend and want to reinforce the immutability of the gender assigned at birth. However, opposition also seems to be increasing in some of the countries which have previously liberalized gender recognition laws.[19]

2.2. MARRIAGE AND PARTNERSHIPS

The married opposite-sex couple was once the only socially and, at least in some jurisdictions, also the only legally permissible framework for relationships.[20] However, in the last decades, the picture of what relationships – and even marriage – look like has diversified. Three changes are at the forefront: the rise of non-marital cohabitation, the increase in divorce, and the ongoing struggle for equal rights of the parties within a marriage.

Over time, the dominance of marriage as the standard form for relationships has declined. It no longer has a monopoly for cohabitation and reproduction. Marriage rates have decreased[21] – even though marriage still remains a widespread and, indeed, the most common form of creating a family in Europe.[22] In relation to the total population, the crude marriage rate in Europe[23]

---

18 See, e.g., J.O. Flindt, *Gewagte Fortschritte im Familien- und Personenstandsrecht? Reformvorhaben im Koalitionsvertrag*, Das Standesamt, 2022, 66, 71.

19 S. Duffy, above n. 12, pp. 153 et seq.

20 For an overview of the criminalization of extramarital sex and cohabitation in Europe see M. Antokolskaia, *Harmonisation of Family Law in Europe: A Historical Perspective*, Intersentia, Cambridge 2006, pp. 177, 200, 367 et seq.; D. Bradley, 'Regulation of unmarried cohabitation in west-European jurisdictions – determinants of legal policy' (2021) 15 *International Journal of Law, Policy and the Family* 22 et seq.

21 J. Miles, 'Financial relief between cohabitants on separation: options for European jurisdictions' in K. Boele-Woelki and T. Sverdrup (eds), *European Challenges in Contemporary Family Law*, Intersentia, Cambridge 2008, pp. 269–87, at p. 270; L.S. Oláh, 'Changing families in the European Union: trends and policy implications', Analytical paper, prepared for the United Nations Expert Group Meeting: *Family policy development: achievements and challenges*, New York, May 14–15, 2015, <https://www.un.org/esa/socdev/family/docs/egm15/Olahpaper.pdf> accessed 22.02.2023.

22 In 2011, almost three quarters (71.2 per cent) of all families were composed of married couples. In contrast, registered partnerships, consensual unions and lone parent families accounted for just over one quarter (28.8 per cent), Eurostat, People in the EU – statistics on household and family structures, <https://ec.europa.eu/eurostat/statistics-explained/index.php?title=%20People_in_the_EU_%E2%80%93_statistics_on_household_and_family_structures&oldid=375234#Marriage> accessed 27.02.2023.

23 The figures refer to the EU Member States plus the United Kingdom.

fell from 7.9 to 4.3 per 1000 inhabitants between 1964 and 2019[24] – a decrease of almost 50 per cent.[25] The decrease of marriage rates, however, does not mean that people refrain from relationships generally. Rather, this trend has been linked to an increasing propensity towards non-marital cohabitation.[26] This is exemplified by the fact that non-marital child-bearing has increased all over Europe.[27]

Non-marital cohabitation, however, is a heterogeneous phenomenon.[28] Couples cohabit for diverse reasons. Many couples live together before they get married. They understand living together as a trial period to see if they are suited for marriage.[29] Other couples cohabit instead of getting married. This cohabitation instead of marriage is often associated with strong socioeconomic development and higher levels of female education as well as labour force participation:[30] Women with higher levels of education in many cases choose to live in de facto unions because their growing individual autonomy and a greater overall tolerance towards family forms outside of the traditional marriage allows them to organize their lives in a self-determined way. Cohabitation instead of marriage can, however, also be connected to poverty and social exclusion.[31]

---

24 Eurostat, 'Crude marriage and divorce rates, 1964–2020' <https://ec.europa.eu/eurostat/statistics-explained/index.php?title=Marriage_and_divorce_statistics#Fewer_marriages.2C_fewer_divordiv> accessed 27.02.2023; Eurostat, 'People in the EU – statistics on household and family structures' <https://ec.europa.eu/eurostat/statistics-explained/index.php?title=%20People_in_the_EU_%E2%80%93_statistics_on_household_and_family_structures&oldid=375234#Marriage> accessed 27.02.2023: 1.4 million marriages were concluded in Europe in 2020, while the corresponding figure back in 1964 had been 3.4 million.

25 A further substantial decrease between 2019 (4.3 per 1000 persons) and 2020 (3.2 per 1000 persons) is interpreted as an effect of the Covid-19 pandemic see Eurostat, 'Crude marriage and divorce rates, 1964–2020' <https://ec.europa.eu/eurostat/statistics-explained/index.php?title=Marriage_and_divorce_statistics#Fewer_marriages.2C_fewer_divordiv> accessed 27.02.2023.

26 M. Covre-Sussai, 'Cohabitation and human development in Latin America and developed countries' (2014) 40 *International Journal of Sociology of the Family* 153, 154; L.S. Oláh, above n. 21, p. 4.

27 L.S. Oláh, above n. 21, p. 3; N. Dethloff and K. Kaesling, 'From Marriage to Family' in N. Dethloff and K. Kaesling (eds), *Between Sexuality, Gender and Reproduction*, Intersentia, Cambridge 2023, pp. 1–22, at p. 2. In 2020, the proportion of births outside of marriage was estimated at 41.9 per cent, see Eurostat, 'Live birth outside marriage, 1964–2020' <https://ec.europa.eu/eurostat/statistics-explained/index.php?title=Marriage_and_divorce_statistics#Fewer_marriages.2C_fewer_divordiv> accessed 27.02.2023.

28 E. Goossens, above n. 8, pp. 3–9; L.S. Oláh, above n. 21, p. 5; for an overview of European systems see K. Boele-Woelki, C. Mol and E. van Gelder (eds), *European Family Law in Action, Vol. V: Informal Relationships*, Intersentia, Cambridge 2015, pp. 13 et seq.

29 E. Goossens, above n. 8, p. 14; A.C. Kuijsten, above n. 1, p. 119.

30 M. Covre-Sussai, above n. 26, p. 154; T. Sobotka and C. Berghammer, 'Demography of family change in Europe' in N.F. Schneider and M. Kreyenfeld (eds), *Research Handbook on the Sociology of the Family*, Edward Elgar, Cheltenham, 2021, pp. 162–86, at p. 163.

31 M. Covre-Sussai, above n. 26, p. 154; B. Perelli-Harris, W. Sigle-Rushton, M. Kreyenfeld, T. Lappegård, R. Keizer and C. Berghammer, 'The Educational Gradient

Sociologists interpret this correlation as a 'pattern of disadvantage', which means that poorer segments of the population would not be able to afford a wedding or are unable to produce the necessary documents.[32]

This variety of reasons why couples and which couples do not get married makes it difficult to attach legal consequences to cohabitation. Different jurisdictions have therefore taken different approaches in addressing such couples. A first group of countries has no specific and comprehensive statutory regulation for cohabitation. Conversely, some European jurisdictions have introduced default regimes for cohabitation. If partners live together for a certain period of time or have children together legal consequences are attributed to their relationship. A registration or partnership contract is not necessary. Legal consequences automatically take effect by law if certain criteria are fulfilled. Other States have introduced opt-in regimes. Legal consequences will only be attributed to those couples who register their relationship. Where countries attach consequences to cohabitation – be it through default or through opt-in regimes – the rules applied to those couples often mirror the consequences attached to marriage.[33] However, alternative models that move away from marriage centrism might better reflect the realities of non-marital cohabitation.[34]

Besides the declining importance of marriage, also the stability of marriages has decreased. Divorce rates have been increasing in the EU for a long time.[35] Between 1965 and 2020, they have essentially doubled. In 1964, the divorce rate stood at 0.8 divorces per 1000 inhabitants, compared to a rate of 1.6 divorces per 1000 inhabitants in 2020.[36] Many European legal systems have addressed the growing demand for divorce, first, by relaxing the substantive divorce requirements and, second, by making divorce more accessible by way of decreasing or even eliminating judicial supervision of divorce.[37] Instead of

---

of Childbearing within Cohabitation in Europe' (2010) 36 *Population and Development Review* 775, 797; T. Sobotka and C. Berghammer, above n. 30, p. 163.

32 B. Perelli-Harris, W. Sigle-Rushton, M. Kreyenfeld, T. Lappegård, R. Keizer and C. Berghammer, above n. 31, p. 777.

33 E. Goossens, 'New Models for Family Solidarity between Unmarried Partners' (in this volume), pp. 59–72, at p. 60.

34 For the presentation of two alternative models see E. Goossens, above n. 33, pp. 61 et seq.

35 A.C. Kuijsten, above n. 1, p. 120; L.S. Oláh, above n. 21, p. 5; T. Sobotka and C. Berghammer, above n. 30, p. 170.

36 Eurostat, Crude divorce rate, 1964–2020, <https://ec.europa.eu/eurostat/statistics-explained/index.php?title=Marriage_and_divorce_statistics#Fewer_marriages.2C_fewer_divordiv> accessed 27.02.2023; Eurostat, People in the EU – statistics on household and family structures, <https://ec.europa.eu/eurostat/statistics-explained/index.php?title=%20People_in_the_EU_%E2%80%93_statistics_on_household_and_family_structures&oldid=375234#Marriage> accessed 27.02.2023.

37 N. Dethloff and K. Kaesling, above n. 27, p. 3; B. Verschraegen, 'Moving to the same destination? Recent trends in the law of divorce' in M. Antokolskaia (ed.), *Convergence and Divergence of Family Law in Europe*, Intersentia, Cambridge 2007, pp. 159–67, at

courts, increasingly the dissolution of marriages is administered by notaries, civil registries or public prosecutors.[38] Such non-judicial divorces are not completely private but are less cumbersome and less invasive than a court intervention. The level of intervention, however, varies considerably among different States.

The decreasing stability of marriage and also the above-mentioned increase of non-marital child-bearing leads to an increase of children living with only one of their parents or in reconstituted families or stepfamilies.[39] Custody disputes, which may often ensue, are difficult to solve, in particular where the parents do not intend to live in the same state. In this context, the growing ease of cross-border movement has added to increasing cases of child abduction.[40] The 1980 Hague Convention on International Child Abduction attempts to draw the difficult balance between a prompt return of the child to his or her country of habitual residence and exceptions to the return, especially in cases involving domestic and family violence.[41]

A third societal change not only affects the importance of marriage as an institution but also the concept of what a marriage constitutes and who can enter into a marriage. The growing number of European countries which have permitted same-sex marriages has already been mentioned.[42] Another instance of these changes is the growing consensus that marriage is an institution that only adults can and should enter into. The mean age at first marriage has increased in European societies; most Europeans nowadays delay marriage until after the age of 30.[43] On the legislative side, many legislators have increased the legal marriage age during the last decades.[44] Child marriages contracted under non-European law are often not recognized. While the reasons behind combatting early marriages are important, the non-recognition of these marriages in

p. 160; for a comparative overview see A. Dutta, D. Schwab, D. Henrich, P. Gottwald and M. Löhnig, *Scheidung ohne Gericht? – Neue Entwicklungen im europäischen Scheidungsrecht*, Verlag Ernst und Werner Gieseking, Bielefeld 2017.

38 P. Quinzá Redondo, 'The Recognition of Non-Judicial Divorces in Europe: Where there is a Will, there is a Way' (in this volume), pp. 23–38, at p. 28.

39 N. Dethloff and K. Kaesling, above n. 27, p. 3; L.S. Oláh, above n. 21, p. 5.

40 O. Momoh, 'The Challenges of the Hague Convention on International Child Abduction: Cases involving Domestic and Family Violence' (in this volume), pp. 217–39, at pp. 218 et seq.

41 O. Momoh, above n. 40, pp. 219 et seq.

42 Above, 2.1., cf. J.M. Lorenzo Villaverde, 'Same-sex Couples and EU Private International Law after the *Coman* Case' (in this volume), pp. 157–76, at p. 160.

43 T. Sobotka and C. Berghammer, above n. 30, p. 166; L.S. Oláh, above n. 21, p. 4; for the statistical figures see Eurostat, People in the EU – statistics on household and family structures, <https://ec.europa.eu/eurostat/statistics-explained/index.php?title=%20People_in_the_EU_%E2%80%93_statistics_on_household_and_family_structures&oldid=375234#Marriage> accessed 27.02.2023.

44 N. Yassari and R. Michaels, 'Die Frühehe im Rechtsvergleich: Praxis, Sachrecht, Kollisionsrecht' in N. Yassari and R. Michaels, *Die Frühehe im Recht*, Mohr Siebeck, Tübingen 2021, pp. 17–98, at p. 47.

migration settings can create situations which cause harm to the girls and women that it is meant to protect.[45]

Within marriages, traditional roles for married men and women have become less pervasive. An instance of this can be seen in the female presence in the labour market. This development has influenced legal regulations on post-divorce maintenance and pension splitting as well as the dissolution of the marital home. An analysis of the emancipatory potential of different family laws reveals that in particular post-divorce maintenance might have a negative effect on both spouses' autonomy.[46] Moreover, post-divorce support can be perceived as internalizing societal problems, namely a still remaining gendered division of labour and a gendered division and devaluation of care work.[47]

Lastly, alongside the departure from patriarchal family concepts and the empowerment of women, the legal protection of vulnerable persons subject to domestic violence has gained importance. Various instruments have been adopted at European and international level.[48] European and international instruments often distinguish domestic violence from violence against women because domestic violence and violence against women overlap only partially.[49] However, a strict separation could conceal the fact that domestic violence is also related to the structural issues of violence against women, i.e., remaining inequalities and traditional perceptions of men and women.[50]

2.3. CHILDBEARING AND PARENTHOOD

Changes in family realities have also affected childbearing and parenthood. These changes result on the one hand from changing relationship patterns, family models and gender identities. On the other hand, evolving techniques of assisted reproduction have fundamentally changed how families can be created. These changes have affected the law of parenthood and discussions about its reform.

One suggestion that has arisen is to open up parenthood to more than two persons.[51] Such a change could address the needs of patchwork families,

---

45 T.L. Wærstad, 'Human Rights Protection in Family Reunification Law and the Recognition of Child Marriages' (in this volume), pp. 3–22, at pp. 5 et seq.

46 C. Voithofer, 'Emancipatory Potential of Maintenance and Matrimonial Property after Divorce: Reflections Based on the Concept of Relational Autonomy' (in this volume), pp. 39–57, at p. 57.

47 C. Voithofer, above n. 46, p. 57.

48 L. Vaigė, 'Violence as National Heritage? The EU and COE Strategies on Violence against Women and Domestic Violence' (in this volume), pp. 241–262, at pp. 243 et seq.

49 L. Vaigė, above n. 48, pp. 244, 248.

50 L. Vaigė, above n. 48, p. 244.

51 D. Lima, 'Three Models for Regulating Multiple Parenthood: A Comparative Perspective' (in this volume), pp. 95–111, at pp. 97 et seq.

but also of persons who co-parent independent of a romantic relationship. For instance, a same-sex couple of two women could have a child with a male friend and co-parent afterwards. While the idea of multiple parenthood is still a theoretical debate within Europe, some jurisdictions in the United States and Canada recognize the parenthood of more than two persons.[52]

A second challenge to the concept of parenthood is the parenthood of trans persons, most prominently the pregnancy of trans men, i.e., child-bearing by persons who were assigned female at birth but later changed the gender entry to male.[53] The traditional laws of filiation do not offer flexibility for such cases of 'seahorse fatherhood'. According to the Roman law principle of *mater semper certa est*, the person who gives birth to the child is identified as the mother and not as the father.[54] In most cases, trans men are therefore entered into the birth certificate as mothers – sometimes even with their female birth name. They are legally men, but in the law of filiation they remain women. This approach is often criticized – not least because it forces trans parents to continually declare themselves as trans since the birth certificate does not match their current legal gender and gender presentation. To address this criticism, a small but growing number of European jurisdictions have adjusted their legal regulations and recognize trans parents in their current gender.[55]

A development which has had a broad effect on very different family models are the advances in technologies of medically assisted reproduction.[56] In opposite-sex couples the use of such techniques correlates with the rise in the mean age of women at birth of their first child.[57] For same-sex couples, however, the need for technologies of assisted reproduction is self-evident. Lesbian couples need recourse to a sperm donor – be it privately or through an official sperm bank. In some European countries this option is legally available, thus making it relatively easy for a woman in a lesbian partnership to bear a child there.[58] Even if the two women have jointly agreed to have a child through assisted reproduction, it is more difficult, however, for the women to become the legal parents of the child. Some countries grant motherhood to both women, at least if they are married.[59] However, many countries demand that the woman

52 D. Lima, above n. 51, pp. 101 et seq.

53 A. Margaria, 'Trans(forming) Fatherhood? European Approaches to Regulating "Seahorse Fatherhood"' (in this volume), pp. 177–91, at pp. 177 et seq.

54 A. Margaria, above n. 53, pp. 178 et seq.

55 A. Margaria, above n. 53, pp. 186 et seq.

56 K.A. Rokas, 'Surrogacy and Assisted Reproduction as a Challenge for Family and for Private International Law Methodology' (in this volume), pp. 75–94.

57 For this development see A.C. Kuijsten, above n. 1, p. 122; T. Sobotka and C. Berghammer, above n. 30, p. 172.

58 Cf. K.A. Rokas, above n. 56, p. 81.

59 UK: Sec. 42 et seq. Human Fertilisation and Embryology Act 2008; France: Art. 342-11 French Civil Code; Belgium: Art. 325/2 old Belgian Civil Code; Austria: §144 para. 2 Austrian

who is not the birth mother adopts the child, even if she is married to the birth mother.[60]

For a male same-sex couple to have a child who is genetically related to one of the fathers, a surrogate mother is necessary – unless the couple plans to co-parent with the birth mother. The same can be true for opposite-sex couples if the female partner is not able to bear a child herself. In such a case, surrogacy can be a way to create a family where the child might be related at least to one of the intended parents. While surrogacy is prohibited in many countries across Europe, many couples – same-sex, but also opposite-sex – go abroad to commission a surrogate there. Afterwards, their home jurisdiction will be faced with the question whether to grant legal parenthood to the intended parents, even if surrogacy is prohibited in that country. In many cases, the parenthood of the intended parents will eventually be recognized by the home jurisdiction. In some cases filiation can be established through recognition of a foreign court decision or through applying a foreign parenthood law. If no court decision exists or if the applicable law sees the surrogate mother and her husband (if she is married) as the legal parents it will be necessary for one or both of the intended parents to adopt the child in order to establish a parent-child relationship.[61] An adoption can also be necessary – both in the case of the parenthood of intended parents after surrogacy and of co-motherhood of two women – if their respective parenthood is considered as an infringement of the public policy of the state where the family lives.[62]

The prospective parents in such family models are therefore often forced to undergo adoption proceedings in order to create a legal parent-child relationship with a child who is already living in their household and whom they might already be caring for. In such cases adoption serves a twofold purpose. On the one hand, it creates a legal family that is not envisaged by the normal workings of family law. On the other hand, the formalized adoption procedure includes the examination of the fitness of the potential parents and serves as a safety net which is meant to control in every individual case that the best interest of the child is not harmed by the creation of a family outside of the legal norm.

This use of adoption can also, however, be seen as a discrimination against certain families and children. The detour through adoption can be time consuming, costly and can contain administrative supervision which is very

---

Civil Code; cf. also Austrian Constitutional Court 30.06.2022, G 230/2021-20, *Zeitschrift für das gesamte Familienrecht (FamRZ)* 2002, 1486; for an overview see J. Ferrer-Riba, 'Multiparentality and New Structures of Family Relationship' in E.-S. Zehelein, A. Carosso and A. Rosende-Pérez, *Family in Crisis*, transcript Verlag, 2020, pp. 59–77, at p. 70.

60 E.g., Germany: see the gendered reference to 'woman' and 'man' in the regulation of parenthood in Sec. 1591 et seq. German Civil Code.

61 K.A. Rokas, above n. 56, pp. 78 et seq.

62 K.A. Rokas, above n. 56, pp. 78 et seq.

invasive upon the privacy of the family affected (e.g., waiting or trial periods, age requirements, marriage).[63] This can be particularly frustrating and humiliating for the potential parents, because in these cases, the adoption is often a formality, with the result predetermined. It is hard to imagine that an adoption would be denied – and in consequence the child would be taken from the family – in a case where the child already lives with the perspective adoptive parents as a social family and where often one of the parents is even already the legal parent.[64] In these cases, adoption serves more as an obstacle which complicates, but does not stop the creation of families that the law does not approve of.

In addition to this potentially discriminatory nature, the detour through adoption can be counter-productive and might hurt rather than help the person who it is meant to be protected: the child. The duration of adoption proceedings puts the welfare of the child in danger. If the intended parents separate and discontinue the adoption proceeding the child can be left without a second legal parent or sometimes without any[65] legal parent within reach.[66] A reform of parenthood might therefore be a more convincing way to address the needs and realities of diverse families.[67]

3. AN EAST-WEST DIVIDE?

All European countries share the general trend of de-standardization and pluralization of identities and families.[68] While non-marital cohabitation, cohabitation without children, and lone parenthood are increasing and households become smaller, the percentage of traditional families – i.e., a married opposite-sex couple with children – declining.[69] However, the extent of and the pace at which the family patterns are changing differs significantly across Europe.[70]

---

63 C. von Bary, 'When Filiation Fails: Adoption as a Fallback Mechanism for Modern Family Forms?' (in this volume), pp. 113–33, at pp. 123 et seq.

64 See however the unusual facts underlying *Paradiso and Campanelli v. Italy*, 24 January 2017, No. 25358/12.

65 The home jurisdiction of the intended parents might consider other persons to be the legal parents – e.g., the surrogate mother and her husband. However, these persons might not be within reach and might not be considered as parents in their respective home jurisdiction.

66 C. von Bary, above n. 63, p. 123.

67 C. von Bary, above n. 63, p. 132.

68 T. Fokkema and A.C. Liefbroer, 'Trends in living arrangements in Europe: Convergence or divergence?' (2008) 19 *Demographic Research* 1351, 1408 et seq.; A.C. Kuijsten, above n. 1, p. 123; T. Sobotka and C. Berghammer, above n. 30, p. 168 (on cohabitation).

69 For household studies see T. Fokkema and A.C. Liefbroer, above n. 68, p. 1409.

70 A. Nussberger and C. Van de Graaf, 'Pluralisation of family forms in the jurisprudence of the European Court of Human Rights' in N. Dethloff and K. Kaesling (eds), *Between Sexuality, Gender and Reproduction*, Intersentia, Cambridge 2023, pp. 111–32, at p. 112.

First, even in respect of general trends, States move at a different pace.[71] Already in the 1990s, those differences brought Kuijsten to the conclusion that 'the Swedish variant of pluralization of family-life forms, the most extreme of all in terms of emergence of "new household types" and decline of the traditional family sector, does not necessarily predict the future situation in other countries'.[72] Moreover, trends might look the same in different countries but they are sometimes connected to different underlying reasons. For example, the decline of the importance of marriage is not everywhere the result of growing individual autonomy and overall tolerance of non-traditional family concepts. As already explained, the propensity towards cohabitation may also be explained as a 'pattern of disadvantage'. This is true in particular in Central Eastern Europe, where the diminishing marriage rates can be connected to growing economic uncertainty.[73]

Second, some trends have been more pronounced or even remained limited to specific parts of Europe.[74] Most prominently, a rift has opened up between western and eastern Europe on matters relating to queer families and identities.[75] Tolerance and acceptance towards LGBTQ+ persons has increased considerably in Western Europe whereas politics, society and culture in most Eastern European countries continue to have negative perceptions.[76] The legal regulation reflects those differences. Progress for the protection of gender identities has been made in many European States but in Eastern European States, in particular, a considerable backlash against the rights of LGBTQ+ persons can be witnessed.[77] The *Coman* and *Pancharevo* cases by the Court of Justice of the European Union (CJEU) can be read as emblematic of the divide in the EU between countries with policies that are favourable to LGBTQ+ persons and countries with policies that are ignorant or even hostile towards them.[78]

---

71 For the slower spread of cohabitation in Eastern Europe see, e.g., T. Sobotka and C. Berghammer, above n. 30, p. 165.

72 A.C. Kuijsten, above n. 1, p. 139.

73 L.S. Oláh, above n. 21, p. 4.

74 See Fokkema and Liefbroer who concluded that 'differences in living arrangements across Europe might have grown larger in the last fifteen to twenty years. Large differences in living arrangements remain along geographical divides'. T. Fokkema and A.C. Liefbroer, above n. 68, p. 1409.

75 A. Nussberger and C. Van de Graaf, above n. 70, pp. 112 et seq., 129; K. Stojanovski, B, Kotevska, N. Milevska, A.P. Mancheva and J. Bauermeister, 'It Is One, Big Loneliness for Me: the Influences of Politics and Society on Men Who Have Sex with Men and Transwomen in Macedonia' (2015) 12 *Sexuality Research and Social Policy* 115 et seq.

76 For Poland see M. Bucholc, 'Conditions for LGBTIQ* Families in Poland' in N. Dethloff and K. Kaesling (eds), *Between Sexuality, Gender and Reproduction*, Intersentia, Cambridge 2023, pp. 155–72; for Hungary see K. Kaesling, 'Rainbow Families on Social Media' Poland' in N. Dethloff and K. Kaesling (eds), *Between Sexuality, Gender and Reproduction*, Intersentia, Cambridge 2023, pp. 227–52, at p. 246.

77 S. Duffy, above n. 12, pp. 153 et seq.

78 J.M. Lorenzo Villaverde, above n. 42, p. 160.

Furthermore, an East–West divide has been asserted in this volume for cases of child protection. An analysis of cross-border child protection cases between Finland and Central-Eastern European states, including Russia, reveals that concepts and practices of child protection vary considerably between those states.[79] One reason might be that state intervention is distrusted because of the legacies of the Soviet ideology of collective childcare and upbringing in line with public interests. Therefore, care orders issued against parents of Eastern European or Russian background or the out-of-home placements of their children are viewed as contrary to the best interests of the child.[80]

A final example of geographic divisions – this time relating in large part to countries outside of the EU – affects the Convention on preventing and combating violence against women and domestic violence (the Istanbul Convention). Certain countries, most prominently Turkey, but also certain EU Member States are very critical of the Convention.[81] They argue, in particular, that – unlike the Convention suggests – gender roles are not socially constructed but result from natural characteristics of men and women.[82]

As will be discussed subsequently, these differences between Eastern and Western European perceptions of gender identity and family have a tremendous symbolic and political importance and undermine efforts to harmonize (international) family law within Europe. Nevertheless, these differences should not be exaggerated, so as not to deepen the existing rifts even further.[83] Whereas this volume is mindful of differences in certain areas of family law it does not focus on an East–West dichotomy. Rather than overemphasizing differences between European States, several chapters of this volume have analysed different ways of bridging gaps between the different family laws.

4. ADDRESSING DIVERGENCES

The divergences between family laws in Europe, which were highlighted above, can have far reaching effects on those living in Europe. If families or individuals move across borders the recognition of their family ties and gender identity can be called into question. The differences between family laws can lead to the

79 S. Mustasaari, 'Challenges of Cross-Border Child Protection between Eastern and Western Europe' (in this volume), pp. 195–216, at p. 206.

80 S. Mustasaari, above n. 79, p. 208.

81 L. Vaigė, above n. 48, pp. 245, 251.

82 L. Vaigė, above n. 48, p. 245.

83 P. Ayoub and D. Paternotte, 'Europe and LGBT Rights: A Conflicted Relationship' in M.J. Bosia, S.M. McEvoy and M. Rahman (eds), *The Oxford Handbook of Global LGBT and Sexual Diversity Politics*, OUP, Oxford 2019, pp. 153–67, at p. 160.

outcome that a status relationship exists in one State, but not in another.[84] The threat of losing a legal status by crossing a border can keep the persons affected from crossing the border in the first place. If the intended move is between different EU Member States such a deterrence can undermine a core promise of the Union: the free movement of EU citizens as guaranteed under Article 21 of the Treaty on the Functioning of the European Union (TFEU). It is therefore imperative to consider how families and individuals can move across borders without changes to their legal status.

Various ways are conceivable in which the parties could be protected from the negative effects of regulatory divergences. A first, rather theoretical approach would be to harmonize or unify substantive family law. A prominent effort in this regard are the Principles of European Family Law that have been developed by the Commission on European Family Law (CEFL). These cover a wide range of topics reaching from divorce and maintenance between former spouses, parental responsibilities, and property relations between spouses, to property, maintenance and succession rights of couples in de facto unions.[85] While this effort is only an academic one, it might, nevertheless, be a source of inspiration for European legislators in the future.[86]

More politically feasible than a harmonization of substantive family law are measures aimed at avoiding limping relationships through a harmonization or unification of private international law and the law of international civil procedure. After all, these are the areas of law that are classically concerned with the avoidance of limping legal relationships. While there are now a number of EU Regulations on private international law and the law of international civil procedure, efforts to harmonize or unify international family law have been much less successful than unification efforts in other areas of private international law and international civil procedure.

In contrast to other forms of cooperation, measures in family law require unanimity in the Council.[87] However, such unanimity among Member States has been very hard to achieve. With the exception of the Brussels II bis and II ter Regulations, EU measures in international family law have all been enacted

---

84 A. Wysocka-Bar, 'A Look into the Future: The Harmonization of Substantive Family Law in Europe' (in this volume), pp. 317–335, at pp. 318 et seq.

85 K. Boele-Woelki et al., *Principles of European Family Law Regarding Property, Maintenance And Succession Rights of Couples in De Facto Unions*, Intersentia, Cambridge 2019; K. Boele-Woelki and D. Martiny, *Principles of European Family Law Regarding Property Relations Between Spouses*, Intersentia, Cambridge 2013; K. Boele-Woelki et al., *Principles of European Family Law Regarding Parental Responsibilities*, Intersentia, Cambridge 2007; K. Boele-Woelki et al., *Principles of European Family Law Regarding Divorce and Maintenance Between Former Spouses*, Intersentia, Cambridge 2004.

86 A. Wysocka-Bar, above n. 84, p. 323.

87 Art. 81(3) TFEU.

through enhanced cooperation – the EU Regulation on the law applicable to divorce and legal separation ('Rome III Regulation') was even the first legislative act ever to be enacted through enhanced cooperation.[88] This role as a historical precedent again shows the particular political salience of family law and the divergences between national laws in this area.

Apart from Ireland and Denmark, which have a special status regarding the EU judicial cooperation in civil matters, the following States are outside the EU Regulations on property consequences of marriage and registered partnerships: Estonia, Hungary, Latvia, Lithuania, Poland, Slovakia and Romania.[89] Poland and Slovakia are also outside the Rome III Regulation.[90] However, the need for enhanced cooperation was not exclusively the result of the reservations of these more conservative Member States. Conversely, Sweden, which also did not take part in the Rome III Regulation, was apprehensive of that Regulation's impact on the applicability of Sweden's liberal divorce laws.[91] Unfortunately, but unsurprisingly, the Member States that tend to be at the political ends of the regulatory spectrum in family law did not participate in the unification efforts. Thus, it is precisely in relation to those States where the risk of a limping legal relationship is particularly great that the existing EU international family law is least likely to help.

The participation of only some EU Member States in the unification of international family law is one of the reasons for a fragmentation of private international law[92] and the law of international civil procedure[93] in family matters which further exacerbates the problems for cross-border families. Overcoming negative consequences of fragmentation and incoherencies within international family law is therefore viewed as an important task – for legislators, but also for courts.[94]

---

88 For the historical background of the Rome III Regulation see A. Fiorini, 'Harmonizing the Law Applicable to Divorce and Legal Separation – Enhanced Cooperation as the Way Forward?' (2010) 59 *The International and Comparative Law Quarterly* 1143, 1144; for the enhanced cooperation in the Regulations on matrimonial property regimes and property consequences of registered partnerships see A. Wysocka-Bar, 'Enhanced cooperation in property matters in the EU and non-participating Member States' (2019) 20 *ERA Forum* 187.

89 Recital 11; A. Wysocka-Bar, above n. 84, p. 329.

90 Participating countries are: Austria, Belgium, Bulgaria, Estonia, France, Germany, Greece, Hungary, Italy, Latvia, Lithuania, Luxembourg, Malta, Portugal, Romania, Slovenia and Spain.

91 A. Fiorini, above n. 88, p. 1144.

92 M. Csöndes, 'A Fragmented Private International Family Law: Interactions and Intersections of International, European and National Norms' (in this volume), pp. 265–281, at p. 272.

93 R. Legendre, 'Recognition and Enforcement in International Family Law: A Legal Patchwork or Systems Made to Measure?' (in this volume), pp. 283–97, at pp. 285 et seq.

94 R. Legendre, above n. 93, pp. 294 et seq; M. Csöndes, above n. 92, p. 266.

Another remedy against limping legal relationships could be to give greater consideration to party autonomy in international family law.[95] Currently, party autonomy is granted mainly in EU Regulations on whose subject matters there is a certain minimum agreement of the EU Member States in substantive law.[96] In contrast, party autonomy does not seem to be a way forward in areas with significant national diversity in substantive law. Additional obstacles to party autonomy in international family law include the fear that party autonomy can be harmful to the protection of vulnerable family members, who might agree to a choice of law, because they are not aware of the disadvantages it can cause them or because they are in a dependent position where they cannot oppose the choice. Even if party autonomy was given more room, judges could undermine the parties' choice by refusing to recognize choice-of-law-clauses because the chosen foreign law conflicts with their domestic understanding of public policy[97] – a threat which is, however, not specific to the application of a foreign law based on a choice of law. Quite the contrary, different perceptions of public policy generally pose a particularly pervasive obstacle to the elimination of limping relationships in family law, which persists even where private international law measures have been adopted between Member States. Here again, the salience of and weight given to different perceptions of family life becomes apparent.

A final avenue that can protect families from limping relationships is the intervention of courts, in particular the ECtHR and the CJEU. Their jurisprudence has already established certain guidelines for families in Europe.

Protection by the ECtHR could affect almost all of Europe and is not limited to the EU. The court has already issued a variety of decisions addressing the loss of a status or status relationship because of a border crossing as a potential violation of Article 8(1) ('right to respect for private and family life') and Article 12 ECHR ('right to marry and to found a family'). The case-law has addressed, inter alia, the recognition of same-sex marriages[98] and of parent-child relationships where the children were born by a surrogate mother.[99] However, the harmonization potential of the ECtHR's case-law is rather restrained. This is because the danger of limping legal relationships affects precisely those types of families and gender identities in relation to which the laws and the underlying socio-political values of the different Contracting States are particularly different. This discord between

95 M. Brosch, 'Party Autonomy in International Family Law: Choice of Law and Choice of Court as a Solution to the Challenges of Cross-Border Families' (in this volume), pp. 299–315, at p. 299 et seq.

96 Cf. M. Brosch, above n. 95, pp. 314 et seq.

97 M. Brosch, above n. 95, p. 314.

98 See A. Nussberger and C. Van de Graaf, above n. 70, pp. 114 et seq.

99 K.A. Rokas, above n. 56, pp. 78 et seq.; A. Wysocka-Bar, above n. 84, p. 331; also see A. Nussberger and C. Van de Graaf, above n. 70, pp. 120 et seq.

the legal systems leads the ECtHR to grant the Contracting States a wide margin of appreciation in applying the ECHR. The demands of the Court are therefore rather restrained. Nevertheless, as the examples mentioned above show, the ECtHR has an important role to play. Even if the Court does not take the role of a pioneer for the protection of rare family forms and gender identities, it helps by ensuring a uniform minimum standard.[100]

The CJEU's case-law could reach further. First, the institutional framework within the EU gives the CJEU more influence than the ECtHR. Second, limping relationships can infringe one of the EU's fundamental freedoms: the free movement of persons.[101] As this freedom relates to cross-border situations, the CJEU can directly address the specific infringement that exists because of limping legal relationships created by border crossings.

In its case-law, the CJEU has a long line of jurisprudence on the infringement of fundamental freedoms because of limping legal relationships, which started in the area of company law.[102] When first addressing family law, the CJEU held that it was an infringement of the free movement of Union citizens if they lose their name when they cross the border.[103] In the ground breaking *Coman* and *Pancharevo* cases,[104] the CJEU applied this jurisprudence to the areas of partnership and parenthood. Thus, Member States are obliged – for the purposes of free movement – to recognize same-sex partnerships and parenthood legally established in another Member State.

The reach of this case-law is not yet clear. It can be argued that, albeit the Court's ruling concerned the inclusion of same-sex marriages within the term 'spouse' only for free movement purposes, it has to be transferred to other uses of that term. In particular, this could mean that the existing Regulations on international family law now have to be applied to same-sex couples as well – at least if the respective regulation does not expressly refer to national marriage laws.[105] Same-sex couples would thus profit from the unification achieved for the protection of opposite-sex couples.

---

100 A. Wysocka-Bar, above n. 84, pp. 331 et seq.; sceptical in view of the ideological East–West divide and the different views on where the minimum lies A. Nussberger and C. Van de Graaf, above n. 70, pp. 129, 132.

101 A. Wysocka-Bar, above n. 84, pp. 324 et seq.

102 Case C-212/97, *Centros Ltd v. Erhvervs- og Selskabsstyrelsen*, ECLI:EU:C:1999:126; Case C-208/00, *Überseering BV v. Nordic Construction Company Baumanagement GmbH (NCC)*, ECLI:EU:C:2002:632; Case C-167/01, *Kamer van Koophandel en Fabrieken voor Amsterdam v. Inspire Art Ltd*, ECLI:EU:C:2003:512.

103 Case C-353/06, *Stefan Grunkin and Dorothee Regina Paul*, ECLI:EU:C:2008:559.

104 Case C-673/16, *Relu Adrian Coman and Others v Inspectoratul General pentru Imigrări and Ministerul Afacerilor Interne*, ECLI:EU:C:2018:385; see J.M. Lorenzo Villaverde, above n. 42, p. 159; Case C-490/20, *V.M.A. v. Stolichna obshtina, rayon 'Pancharevo'*, ECLI:EU:C:2021:1008, §23, see A. Wysocka-Bar, above n. 84, pp. 324 et seq.

105 J.M. Lorenzo Villaverde, above n. 42, pp. 170 et seq.

Even if one does not attribute such a broad scope to the *Coman* and *Pancharevo* cases, the potential of the CJEU's case-law in protecting European families should not be underestimated. The case-law addresses directly only cases of international mobility – the normative basis is after all the free movement of EU citizens. However, the CJEU's case-law might have a further reaching indirect effect. The case-law can carry legal situations in family law from one Member State into the entire EU and pierce the borders between national family laws. If the mobility of families within the EU continues to increase, the number of such cases will also increase. Over time, foreign family law institutions may appear less unusual. This familiarization could contribute to a slow change in public debate and opinion and could prepare subsequent changes in substantive family law. Until then, it is of paramount importance to be mindful of the different perceptions of how family and gender are understood across Europe while at the same time working to secure the protection of the individuals affected. Apart from legislation and court intervention a more humble approach to achieve this is through academic dialogue that includes all parts of Europe. This volume attempts to engage a younger group of European scholars in such dialogue.

European Family Law Series

1. *Legal Recognition of Same-Sex Couples in Europe*, K. Boele-Woelki and A. Fuchs (eds.)
2. *European Family Law in Action Volume I: Grounds for Divorce*, K. Boele-Woelki, B. Braat and I. Sumner (eds.)
3. *European Family Law in Action Volume II: Maintenance Between Former Spouses*, K. Boele-Woelki, B. Braat and I. Sumner (eds.)
4. *Perspectives for the Unification and Harmonisation of Family Law in Europe*, K. Boele-Woelki (ed.)
5. *Family Law Legislation of the Netherlands*, I. Sumner and H. Warendorf
6. *Indépendance et interdépendance patrimoniales des époux dans le régime matrimonial légal des droits néerlandais, français et suisse*, B. Braat
7. *Principles of European Family Law Regarding Divorce and Maintenance Between Former Spouses*, K. Boele-Woelki, F. Ferrand, C. González Beilfuss, M. Jänterä-Jareborg, N. Lowe, D. Martiny and W. Pintens
8. *Inheritance Law Legislation of the Netherlands*, I. Sumner and H. Warendorf
9. *European Family Law in Action Volume III: Parental Responsibilities*, K. Boele-Woelki, B. Braat and I. Curry-Sumner (eds.)
10. *Common Core and Better Law in European Family Law*, K. Boele-Woelki (ed.)
11. *All's well that ends registered?*, I. Curry-Sumner
12. *Model Family Code – From a global perspective*, I. Schwenzer and M. Dimsey
13. *Harmonisation of Family Law in Europe. A Historical Perspective*, M. Antokolskaia
14. *Brussels II bis: Its Impact and Application in the Member States*, K. Boele-Woelki and C. González Beilfuss (eds.)
15. *Tensions between Legal, Biological and Social Conceptions of Parentage*, I. Schwenzer (ed.)
16. *Principles of European Family Law Regarding Parental Responsibilities*, K. Boele-Woelki, F. Ferrand, C. González Beilfuss, M. Jänterä-Jareborg, N. Lowe, D. Martiny and W. Pintens
17. *Juxtaposing Legal Systems and the Principles of European Family Law on Divorce and Maintenance*, E. Örücü and J. Mair (eds.)
18. *Convergence and Divergence of Family Law in Europe*, M. Antokolskaia (ed.)
19. *European Challenges in Contemporary Family Law*, K. Boele-Woelki and T. Sverdrup (eds.)
20. *Children and their parents*, M. Vonk
21. *La capacité de l'enfant dans les droits français, anglais et écossais*, L. Francoz Terminal
22. *Joint Parental Authority*, C.G. Jeppesen de Boer
23. *Debates in Family Law around the Globe at the Dawn of the 21st Century*, K. Boele-Woelki (ed.)
24. *European Family Law in Action Volume IV: Property Relations between Spouses*, K. Boele-Woelki, B. Braat and I. Curry-Sumner (eds.)

25. *Foundational Facts, Relative Truths. A Comparative Law Study on Children's Right to Know Their Genetic Origins*, R. Blauwhoff
26. *Imperative Inheritance Law in a Late-Modern Society. Five Perspectives*, C. Castelein, R. Foqué and A. Verbeke (eds.)
27. *Juxtaposing Legal Systems and the Principles of European Family Law on Parental Responsibilities*, E. Örücü and J. Mair (eds.)
28. *La justice des mineurs en Europe*, Y. Favier and F. Ferrand (eds.)
29. *The Future of Family Property in Europe*, K. Boele-Woelki, J. Miles and J. M. Scherpe (eds.)
30. *The Place of Religion in Family Law: A Comparative Search*, J. Mair and E. Örücü (eds.)
31. *Reconstructing Marriage. The Legal Status of Relationships in a Changing Society*, C. Sörgjerd
32. *Legal Recognition of Same-Sex Relationships in Europe*, K. Boele-Woelki and A. Fuchs (eds.)
33. *Principles of European Family Law Regarding Property Relations Between Spouses*, K. Boele-Woelki, F. Ferrand, C. González Beilfuss, M. Jänterä-Jareborg, N. Lowe, D. Martiny and W. Pintens
34. *Der nacheheliche Unterhalt: Grundlagen und Ausgestaltung im deutschen Unterhaltsrecht und in den Prinzipien der Commission on European Family Law*, P. Beuermann
35. *Family Law and Culture in Europe: Developments, Challenges and Opportunities*, K. Boele-Woelki, N. Dethloff and W. Gephart
36. *Children's Rights in Intercountry Adoption. A European Perspective*, C. Fenton-Glynn
37. *Nordic Cohabitation Law*, J. Asland, M. Brattström, G. Lind, I. Lund-Andersen, A. Singer and T. Sverdrup
38. *European Family Law in Action Volume V: Informal Relationships*, K. Boele-Woelki, C. Mol and E. van Gelder (eds.)
39. *Divided Parents, Shared Children. Legal Aspects of Residential Co-Parenting in England, the Netherlands and Belgium*, N. Nikolina
40. *Family Forms and Parenthood. Theory and Practice of Article 8 ECHR in Europe*, A. Büchler and H. Keller (eds.)
41. *The Child's Interests in Conflict. The Intersections between Society, Family, Faith and Culture*, M. Jänterä-Jareborg (ed.)
42. *Same-Sex Relationships and Beyond. Gender Matters in the EU*, K. Boele-Woelki and A. Fuchs (eds.)
43. *Nacheheliche Verantwortung in Frankreich und Deutschland*, K. Kaesling
44. *The Future of Registered Partnerships: Family Recognition Beyond Marriage?*, J.M. Scherpe and A. Hayward
45. *Plurality and Diversity of Family Relations in Europe*, K. Boele-Woelki and D. Martiny (eds.)
46. *Principles of European Family Law Regarding Property, Maintenance and Succession Rights of Couples in* de facto *Unions*, K. Boele-Woelki, F. Ferrand, C. González Beilfuss, M. Jänterä-Jareborg, N. Lowe, D. Martiny and V. Todorova
47. *Die Familienschiedsgerichtsbarkeit in Recht und Praxis: Eine Rechtsvergleichende Untersuchung des Deutschen und Englischen Rechts*, S.C. Zellerhoff
48. *Elderly Care and Upwards Solidarity: Historical, Sociological and Legal Perspectives*, E. Alofs and W. Schrama (eds.)

49. *Party Autonomy in EU Private International Law: Choice of Court and Choice of Law in Family Matters and Succession*, J. Gray
50. *The Interaction between Family Law, Succession Law and Private International Law: Adapting to Change*, J.M. Scherpe and E. Bargelli (eds.)
51. *International Handbook on Child Participation in Family Law*, W. Schrama, M. Freeman, N. Taylor and M. Bruning (eds.)
52. *The Child's Right to Participate in Family Law Proceedings: Represented, Heard or Silenced?*, C. Mol
53. *Cross-Border Recognition of Formalized Same-Sex Relationships: The Role of* Ordre Public, L. Vaigė
54. *Between Sexuality, Gender and Reproduction: On the Pluralisation of Family Forms*, N. Dethloff and K. Kaesling (eds.)

www.ingramcontent.com/pod-product-compliance
Ingram Content Group UK Ltd.
Pitfield, Milton Keynes, MK11 3LW, UK
UKHW051925100926
8556IPUK00022B/1383

9 781839 703805